The Lord's Prayer

Web site: www.thelordsprayercode.com
e-mail: abba@thelordsprayercode.com

The Lord's Prayer

A Secret Code Revealed

Code of the Past

Present and Future

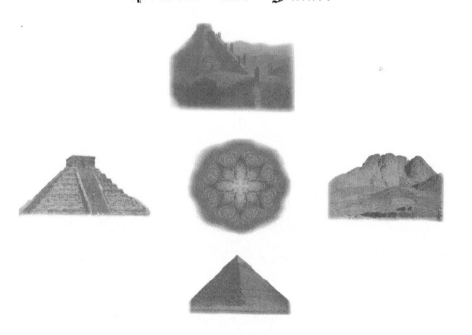

Miguel C. Suarez Jr

To order additional copies of this book, contact:
Xlibris Corporation
1-888-795-4274
www.Xlibris.com
Orders@Xlibris.com
45149

Made in the USA
Lexington, KY
30 July 2016

CONTENTS

INTRODUCTION

The Jews are very prayerful people and believe in miracles that they attribute to the prayers and holy names of God uttered by the miracle workers. With a tradition going back to Adam, Noah, Moses, and Solomon, the apostles knew that by the right rituals or prayers, one could perform miracles. Thus, when they saw Jesus performed miracles that they could not perform, they were very impressed. They could not suppress their curiosity that they asked Jesus to teach them how. But Jesus surprised them by teaching them a simple prayer instead of a complicated ritual or prayer. The prayer that Jesus taught is now known as the Lord's Prayer or the Our Father.

Since then, the Apostles were able to perform the same miracles as Jesus did. Was the Lord's Prayer the key to the miracles performed by the apostles? If so, then this must be a very powerful prayer and would answer the question why Jesus taught only one prayer. The Lord's Prayer may not be as simple as it seems. This book will reveal to the readers the secret code that has been hidden from the masses but revealed to his beloved disciples John, James, and Mary Magdalene. This book will also show the past civilizations of Sumer, Egypt, Israel, China, and the Meso-Americans and their relations to the Lord's Prayer. Probable and possible events will also be revealed. We will be apprised of how to harness the power of the Lord's Prayer and how the miracles performed by Jesus and the Apostles could be experienced.

The Kabalists maintain that the Old Testament is a code and can only be the subject of a fairly accurate interpretation if one is equipped with the knowledge of the Hebrew language and the esoteric teachings of the Jews called the Kabalah, an oral tradition handed down from generation to generation originating from Adam to Seth, Abraham, Moses, David to Solomon, and to the high priest. In the Kabalah, various methods of decoding were used to show how illogical and unintelligible passages in the Old Testament could be interpreted. As the Old Testament was written in Hebrew, it was easy to use the Kabalistic method in decoding the Old Testament. However, there was a problem with the New Testament.

Intriguingly, the New Testament, whose main characters were Jews, came out written in Greek and not in Hebrew, when supposed to be Jesus spoke ancient Hebrew or Aramaic. This peculiarity placed an obstacle using Kabalistic

interpretation of the New Testament for reasons that the Kabalah is based on Hebrew alphabets. A Hebrew interpretation of the New Testament now will be subject to debates just like the Hebrew version of the Lord's Prayer used in this book, which can be said to be not an original version of the Lord's Prayer. However, there is a saying that nothing happens in this world without a reason. There are several Hebrew versions of the Lord's Prayer based on the original Greek version; however, the actual use of the Hebrew version mentioned in this book was meant to be. Some would criticize the version of the Lord's Prayer used in this book; however, this will be a challenge for them to provide a better version and come out with the same astonishing revelations contained in this study. The contents of this book will only confirm that the Hebrew version used is truly accurate of Jesus's prayer.

The different books about the Bible Code have inspired me to look more closely at the Lord's Prayer. An unseen hand has helped me come across with the materials needed to complete this book. This book will show that the Lord's Prayer is not only a prayer but is a code that reveals untold doctrines and settles issues like the following:

- Is Jesus a myth?
- Who was the author of the Lord's Prayer?
- Where is the Hebrew version of the Lord's Prayer?
- Why did the Apostles ask Jesus to teach them how to pray?
- Did Jesus teach secret doctrines to the Apostles?
- Can we perform the miracles the Apostles did?
- What is the speech of "Babies"?
- Why are ancient civilizations like Sumer, Egypt, Israel, Meso-America, and China in the Code?
- Why are the Pyramids and the Sphinx mentioned in the Code and who built them?
- Why is President Bush in the Code?
- Was the September 11, 2001, tragedy in the Code?
- Why is Senator Barack H. Obama in the Grid?
- Is there really an "End Time"?

Another interesting aspect of this book is the question about Jesus being a myth. If Jesus is mythical, who wrote the Lord's Prayer? And if there are many forgeries in the New Testament, what is the truth? There are many challenging questions poised for the seekers of the truth.

To say I was inspired to write this book is a lie. I was not inspired. I was told to write this book. I felt I was just being guided and directed as to what should be written as the contents of this book require vast knowledge of the Bible, the

Kabalah, and history. Thus, the question as to my qualification to write this book as I am not a Bible scholar, a Jew, or an expert Kabalist is not tenable. I myself cannot pinpoint the author of this book. As I was mechanically writing this book, I also asked myself why was I chosen to write it, why an Asian and not a Jew, why an ordinary person and not a Bible scholar. The answer was shown to me in the chapter "Why Me?"

I have used two methods of decoding the Lord's Prayer called the Kabalah and Equidistant Letter Sequence also known as ELS. As ELS is a very scientific and precise method and eliminates luck and coincidences, I made the ELS the primary method of decoding the code.

This book will provide new insights for both the Christians and non-Christians alike and the seekers of Truth.

THE LORD'S PRAYER: A SECRET CODE REVEALED

A BOOK FOR OUR TIME

BY NANJU FRANCISCO

If you think that the worldwide bestseller book *The Da Vinci Code* by American author Dan Brown and the documentary "The Lost Tomb of Jesus" by award-winning *Titanic* director James Cameron—which was shelved by Discovery Channel for the meantime because it reportedly offended the Christian communities throughout the world as well as a group of archeologists and scientists—are the two biggest controversies in the century, then you are in for a big surprise! Just off the press is another controversial and intriguing book entitled *The Lord's Prayer: A Secret Code Revealed, Code of the Past, Present, and Future* by Filipino author Atty. Miguel C. Suarez Jr. This book will surely create another great controversy, which would certainly raise the eyebrows of not only the church leaders in the country but also the entire Christian world and in the process may change the way one looks at Christianity.

An Amazing Book

The 443-page book by Atty. Suarez is provocative, controversial, and relevant to the present time as well as "apocalyptic" in nature as it describes certain events—good and bad—which would happen in the Philippines as well as around the globe in the near future. The new book is centered on the Lord's Prayer, which Jesus taught the Apostles based on the Gospels of Matthew (6:9-13) and Luke (11:2-4) and Atty. Suarez's desire to prove that there was a "code" behind the prayer, which would reveal secrets concerning mankind and the future of the world. However, during the course of his search for answers, one question led to another—and another, and before Atty. Suarez knew it, he had unlocked something more intriguing and mysterious than the code itself.

"When I started writing this book, my purpose was to reveal the existence of a code and not *who* the author of the Lord's Prayer was as it was the general consensus that Jesus is the author of the prayer," Atty. Suarez explained. "Are

there other sources besides the Gospels of Matthew and Luke to prove that Jesus indeed taught this prayer? What can the code prove? Is there a secret in the Lord's Prayer that will guide humanity in its existence?"

At the beginning of the book, Atty. Suarez narrated his long and arduous search for the "original Hebrew version" of the Lord's Prayer to prove his point because it was the main language used during the time of Jesus aside from Aramaic and that there was a "code" behind the prayer, which, if discovered, could reveal amazing facts and secrets of the past, present, and future.

After a long search, he finally found a Hebrew version of the Lord's Prayer which is believed to be the nearest replica or copy of the ancient version of the prayer in the book entitled *Words of Power: Sacred Sound of East and West* by Brian and Easter Crowley. Atty. Suarez used the book *Words of Power* as the model for decoding the secrets contained in the Lord's Prayer as there is no record of any surviving original Hebrew version at present.

Methods Used in Decoding the Lord's Prayer

In his book, Atty. Suarez carefully used two methods to unlock the secret code of the Lord's Prayer namely the Kabalah and the Equidistant Letter Sequence (ELS). The Kabalah is the "esoteric tradition" handed down from generation to generation which used by the Jews in decoding the Old Testament and other Biblical texts.

"According to Kabalists, if one knows the Kabalah it would be easier to understand a number of passages in the Bible that seemed to be illogical and unintelligible," Atty. Suarez pointed out in his book. "Thus, for anyone to interpret the Bible based only in the English translation and without knowledge of the Kabalah will be questionable."

The ELS, on the other hand, is a popular decoding system. In this method, there is "an interval of letters between the encoded or desired letters." It is made easy because of computers and modern technology. As this method is very scientific, it is normally used to decipher any language. However, Atty. Suarez stressed that the ELS does not explain the esoteric teachings in the decoding made, more particularly in the ancient manuscripts or texts. Hence, this would explain why he combined these two methods in unlocking the secret code of the Lord's Prayer.

Discovering the Code

After obtaining a copy of the Hebrew version of the Lord's Prayer and selecting which methods he would use in decoding the secrets embedded or hidden in the prayer, Atty. Suarez was faced with another great challenge, and that was to come up with the possible "grid or rows of letters that could possibly contain the code that would ultimately reveal the secrets of the Lord's Prayer." After so many difficulties

and years of searching and meditating, Atty. Suarez finally succeeded in finding the "right grid" that confirmed the existence of a code in the said prayer, which we have always considered a "simple prayer." This discovery has proven that the Lord's Prayer is not as simple as it seemed to be as it contained a code, which reveals the secrets of the past, present, and amazingly, the future.

Controversial Issues Discussed in the Book

The code discovered by Atty. Suarez in the Lord's Prayer raised several controversial issues, which will most likely have a deep impact and repercussion on everyone concerned particularly the Christian faith. Among the questions discussed and examined in the book were: Is Jesus the real author of the Lord's Prayer? Is Jesus a myth? What is the connection of Jesus to ancient saviors? What is the relationship of Jesus to Mary Magdalene? Who is the Holy Spirit in the Blessed Trinity? Was it Jesus or someone else? What events will take place prior to the End times or the Apocalypse? What is the destiny of man? Did God create man, or are there any other beings involved in the creation? Surely these questions would shock Christian believers everywhere, for they would shake the very foundation of their faith.

Events That Already Took Place as Revealed by the Code

What is mind-boggling about the code used in the Lord's Prayer is that it revealed so many secrets of the past that already took place, and all these were "revealed" to Atty. Suarez in advance. While examining the messages embedded in the Lord's Prayer through the use of this code, Atty. Suarez was able to predict some of the major events, which already took place with amazing accuracy. He predicted the result of the 2000 U.S. presidential election, details of the 9-11 tragedy, wars and famines and the reelection of U.S. president George Bush, and the weather changes simply by "reading" the messages or secrets revealed by the code in the Lord's Prayer. Atty. Suarez was also able to predict the result of the last presidential election in the Philippines, the foiled coup d'état and certain events affecting Pres. Gloria Macapagal-Arroyo's administration. He said he even sent a copy of the article pertaining to the president to warn her of the impending events, but he wasn't sure if the president got the article or not.

Why the book *The Lord's Prayer: A Secret Code Revealed* Is Written?

In this exclusive interview, Atty. Suarez explained to *The New Vanity Magazine* the real reason why he wrote the book *The Lord's Prayer: A Secret Code Revealed, Code of the Past, Present, and Future*.

"To tell you that I was inspired to write it would be a lie," he told this writer. "I was 'told' to write it, for the millennium. This contains so many things about the past, present, and the future, that is why the title of the book is *The Lord's Prayer: A Secret Code Revealed, Code of the Past, Present, and Future.*"

When asked who instructed or "told" him to write the book, Atty. Suarez replied matter-of-factly, "Who else? The God of all. Not the God of the Christians, not the God of the Muslims, but the God of all."

So when did he get the message to write the book?

"Before 2000," he answered. "Actually, I don't want to talk about messages because people might not believe me. So I just tell them I was 'inspired,' but actually it's a lie. It is not really the truth. It's just to cover it up. People might say that the lawyer is a cuckoo. I should be the last one to believe this because I am a lawyer. But what if you experienced the presence of these beings? What if you can see them? What if you can feel and talk to them? I was told to write this book.

"You know it is very hard to say things or to tell you things that are unbelievable. If you are one with the Above, then you can connect at anytime. What seems to be a miracle to others is just an ordinary thing to anybody who is at one," he said. "If you are talking or you're speaking to the God of Love, what must you do? We must also be loving to have the same frequency and vibration. How can you connect to the God of love if you have so much hate, disappointments, and hurts in your heart? No way."

So what then is his real purpose in writing the book?

"There are so many things that will happen in this world," he answered. "Some things have to be corrected—some things have to be revealed especially in the coming years, especially what we call the End Times. I am not a prophet of doom, but something will happen, and in this book I enumerated the things that will happen, the events leading to the Apocalypse."

Atty. Suarez added that he does not mind if his book would "raise" certain eyebrows from different groups in the society particularly in the church.

"I wrote like a lawyer," he said. "I will welcome criticism—it is easy to criticize, but to write a book is difficult. They can criticize. I won't mind but refute the book the way a lawyer does, for I wrote the book like a lawyer. Don't argue 'Oh, it is against the faith.' Why? If you can answer that question logically, then good. But don't give me, you know, out-of-this-world reasoning. Make it a logical presentation."

Atty. Suarez also stressed that he is a Catholic, but "the way I was brought up is this: If Jesus Christ did not exist, will I still believe in the teaching? Yes, because the teaching is very good. If Jesus Christ is married to Mary Magdalene,

will I still believe? Yes! Because it does not matter whether he's married or not, whether he existed or not. What matters is the teaching because if you'll go to personality, then something is wrong—what if it was Buddha who said, 'Love one another,' do you mean to say I will not follow? What if it was Krishna who said, 'Love one another,' do you mean I will disregard it because he was not Jesus Christ? That's wrong. That is religiosity and not spirituality."

Isn't he afraid of being excommunicated by the church for his bold and astounding revelations in his book?

"I don't mind because there must be and should be a change," Atty. Suarez emphasized. "God gave us a brain, a mind to discern. If God wanted only robots, He would have created robots who would just say 'yes, yes, yes.' But our God is a loving and caring God and will answer all our questions. He does not want us to be robots. That is why He gave us a free will so that we can question. I am sure that some might say that it is against the teachings of the church, but it does not mean it is against the teachings of Christ. Being against some teachings of the church does not make one an Antichrist. There is a difference. The teaching about 'loving one another is always true forever.' Not just for a moment."

The Philippines, being a strict Catholic country, might not be ready to accept the revelations he made in his book like what happened to the movie, *The Da Vinci Code*, which was not warmly welcomed and accepted by the Filipinos when shown in the country last year. Isn't he afraid his book *The Lord's Prayer: A Secret Code Revealed* might suffer the same fate or consequences?

"This will test the maturity of the Filipino people," he quipped. "When you believe because of personality, then you are still way off the spiritual ladder. I'm a Catholic, but if my God will ask me if I am a Catholic to be saved, then I don't think he is my God because my God is the God of all—the God of the Catholics, the God of the Muslims, the God of everybody—not just the Catholics. Again, I don't mind being criticized. What I only wish is that the Filipinos will learn how to love one another. It is sad that we keep on complaining and fighting one another. There is even a collective consciousness that this country will fall or will fail. That is not good. If everybody is thinking that we're going to fail, then for sure we will fail. But if for example, one is thinking ten times that this country will fail, make it only eight times so that 20 percent of the negativity will be lessened, don't make it ten. See the change that will follow. Let us have more positive thoughts. Let us change ourselves first before changing others."

What Is in Store for Us in the Future?

"The reason why this book is being revealed now is because of the coming times," Atty. Suarez stressed. "There will be more difficult times even in the United States and also in the Philippines and all over the world. People are afraid to talk

about the violent earth changes to come. But one can sense this because of the weather changes and global warming around the world. They do not want to talk about the earth changes as predicted by the Incas, the Mayans, the Egyptians, and other sacred groups about the year 2012. Scientists said that in the last one million years, there have been fifteen polar shifts wherein the North Pole became the South Pole and the South Pole became the North Pole. There was an exchange of positions. Fifty thousand years ago, the North Pole was in the Hudson River, USA. I am not a prophet of doom, but you can see the weather changes, so it's beginning to happen, and people would just like to deny that thing."

Atty. Suarez also mentioned other tragic and catastrophic events in his book and the future of the United States as well as the Philippines and their leaders particularly the fates of Pres. George Bush and President GMA. He also made remarkable revelations as to who will win the 2008 U.S. presidential election. In the end, Atty. Suarez reminded us the main theme of his book.

"What is important is the message of the Lord's Prayer, which is to love one another," he said. "It is only now that the code is revealed, for there is still time for man to save himself from extinction as man has done to other species in the world. The Lord's Prayer is a way to save humanity," he concluded.

The book *The Lord's Prayer: A Secret Code Revealed, Code of the Past, Present and Future* by Atty. Miguel C. Suarez Jr. is published by MSA Publishing House with offices located at #315 Katipunan Avenue, Loyola Heights, Quezon City, Philippines, and tel. no.: (+632) 646-8245.

PART I

THE SEARCH

The inquisitive nature of man has made his existence exciting. The saying that curiosity kills the cat does not stop man from his pursuit of the unknown. Great discoveries have been made due to his daring determination. Since the spread of the Old Testament, man has tried to unlock the secret of the Holy Scripture. Few have tried to decode the New Testament, but none has tried to decipher the Lord's Prayer, hence this book. Is there a secret in the Lord's Prayer that will guide humanity in its existence?

CHAPTER I

THE PRAYER

The Bible, the sacred book of the Christians, contains a number of stories about the miracles performed by holy people. Fascinating stories like the parting of the Red Sea by Moses, the destruction of the walls of Jericho by Joshua, and the many miraculous healings by Jesus have kept people wondering how the miracles were accomplished. Was it magic? Or were they just tall tales? According to one of the great Kabalists Aleister Crowley, magic "is the Science and Art of causing change in conformity with Will."[1] If this was so, how was the change done in conformity to the will achieved? Being involved in occult studies, I wanted to know how Jesus enabled the apostles to perform the miracles He had promised—to bring the dead back to life, to make the lame walk and the blind see. Ancient esoteric teachings like Gnosticism, Kabalism, Sufism, Hinduism, and Buddhism have talked about relationship with God, mantras, names of God and rituals for the performance of supernatural powers. Did Jesus teach secret doctrines to the apostles that made them miracle workers? What was the secret?

a) Strange Request by the Apostles

According to Gnostic teachings, Jesus taught the apostles secret doctrines unmentioned in the New Testament. However, in the New Testament, he was said to have taught often in parables that reminded us of what Matthew said about the apostles asking Jesus:

> "Why dost thou speak to them in parables?" and Jesus answered, "To you it is given to know the mysteries of the kingdom of heaven but to them it is not given."[2]

That was a shocking answer for was not the purpose of Jesus to save and enlighten people and not to condemn? To clarify his statement, Jesus said,

---

1

"This is why I speak to them in parable, because seeing, they do not see, and hearing they do not hear neither do they understand."[3]

This verse showed the disappointment of Jesus with the masses who seemed not to learn from their past experiences. This forced Jesus to teach the secrets about the kingdom of God only to the apostles. It is obvious, therefore, that Jesus taught secret doctrines to the apostles that were not taught to the masses. What secret doctrines did Jesus reveal? The New Testament narrated that the apostles requested Jesus to teach them how to pray. Such request was strange, for the Jews were very prayerful people with knowledge about the different names of God or Semiphoras. They were much aware about talismans, amulets, chants, spells, and the use of the different names of God to cause miracles. What moved the apostles to make such strange request? Were they impressed and overwhelmed by the miracles performed by Jesus? Did Jesus use secret rituals or prayers? Unable to suppress their curiosities to know how the miracles were performed, the apostles asked Jesus to teach them how to perform the rituals or prayers.

In response to their request, Jesus taught the apostles just one prayer, which is now called the Lord's Prayer. For sure the apostles were very much surprised as they were expecting a complicated ritual as commensurate to the miracles performed like exorcism, yet they were taught only one short and simple prayer. However, since then, they were able to perform many miracles. What was that prayer? What were its secrets? Was the Lord's Prayer the key to the miracles performed by the apostles? If so, then this must be a very powerful prayer and will answer the question as to the secrets about the kingdom of God. Thus, The Lord's Prayer may not be as simple as it seems.

b) Versions of the Lord's Prayer

Although the Lord's Prayer is a very important part of Christian doctrine, however it is enveloped with much controversy. In all the New Testament writings and documents, only the Gospels of Matthew and Luke have references about the Lord's Prayer. Even St. Paul in all his epistles never mentioned the Lord's Prayer. He even said that the Christians did not know how to pray. All the supposed writings of the apostles like Peter, James, John, Thomas, Philip neither mentioned anything about the prayer nor did the Gnostics with all their writings said anything about the Lord's Prayer. What happened? Did Jesus really teach the Lord's Prayer? Why did not the apostles, St. Paul, Mary Magdalene, and the Gnostics mention the prayer considering the importance of the prayer? Was this prayer only taught to Matthew who in turned revealed it to Luke? The only reason why this prayer exists today is because of the Gospels of Luke and Matthew. Without these Gospels, the Lord's Prayer would have remained unknown. However, the appearance of the Lord's

Prayer in the said Gospels instead of dispelling the controversy added more fuel to it. More questions as to its authenticity were raised as the two versions appearing in the Gospels are in conflict with one another. Matthew's version was longer than Luke's version with different style of writing although both were written in Greek instead of Aramaic or ancient Hebrew that was the language of Jesus and the Jews. As to which one was the correct version and the closest to the renditions of the words actually spoken by Jesus, we might never know. There is even a possibility that neither one is the exact rendition of the words actually spoken by Jesus as the Gospels were written a century or more after the death of Jesus. John Dominic Crossan[4] does not believe that the Lord's Prayer originated with Jesus but was composed by later Christians.

Without these Gospels, the Lord's Prayer does not exist and its author unknown. When I started writing this book, my purpose was to reveal the existence of a code and not who the author of the Lord's Prayer was as it is the general consensus that Jesus is the author of the prayer. If, however, there will be a question as to who is the author of the Lord's Prayer, then there would be more messy consequences. Even Jesus's historical existence would be put in doubt. Are there other sources besides the Gospels of Matthew and Luke to prove that Jesus indeed taught this prayer or is the Lord's Prayer more ancient than we assume? What can the code prove?

Matthew and Luke Versions

Going back to Matthew, it was said that when the apostles asked Jesus to teach them how to pray, Jesus responded by saying, "When you pray, say,

> Our Father who art in heaven
> Hallowed be thy name
> Thy Kingdom come
> Thy will be done on earth as it is in heaven
> Give us this day our daily bread
> And forgive us our debts
> As we forgive our debtors
> Lead us not into temptation
> But deliver us from evil, Amen."[5]

Luke on the other hand said,

> Father
> Hallowed be your name,
> Your kingdom come.

Give us each day our daily bread.
Forgive us our sins
For we too forgive all
Who do us wrong;
And subject us not to the trial.[6]

A look at the two versions would show glaring differences between them. Luke's version is shorter and direct to the point, deleting some petitions while Matthew's version is longer with additional petitions. Why were the versions different? Could the reasons be that the versions came from different sources, and that the prayer was corrupted for the Bible was only collated around four hundred years after Jesus death? The Christian churches have not given a satisfactory answer to the question, but there are now well-researched books that could give credible answers why. There are two books worthy of mention that could answer some of the questions, namely, *The Jesus Mysteries* by Timothy Freke and Peter Gandy and the *The Christ Conspiracy* by Acharya S.

Unmentioned by Mark, John, and Paul

According to Bible scholars, the Gospel of Mark is the oldest Gospel among the four Gospels of the New Testament, yet Mark never mentioned the Lord's Prayer. For sure, Mark in writing the Gospel must have asked the apostles and the close followers about the teachings of Jesus. Biblical researchers have placed the Gospel of Mark between the second and third century AD instead of the first century AD. This new date would actually put the Gospel of Mark in question as this would put in doubt as to whether Mark really wrote the Gospel or somebody used his name in writing it. Also by that time Mark and the apostles were already dead. According to Randel Mccraw Helms[7], Mark was an associate of Peter who wrote down oral traditions, stories, and sayings about Jesus and not necessarily the memoirs of Peter. His knowledge of Jesus was based on materials handed to him from earlier generations.

Again it is said that the basis of Luke's Gospel was the Gospel of Mark; if this was so, where did Luke get the Lord's Prayer version? Who told him about the prayer? Was Luke the author of the prayer? And where did Matthew get his long version of the Lord's Prayer? Who taught him? Supposedly, Jesus taught the prayer to the apostles, but why is it that John, the closest of the apostles to Jesus, did not mention the Lord's Prayer neither did St. Paul in all his writings nor the Gnostics who had other kinds of prayers? What is really the truth? Did he or did he not teach the Lord's Prayer? This is a question that is difficult to answer. This also put in doubt as to whether Jesus really taught the prayer.

Possible Origin of the Prayer

Some Biblical scholars say that the Lord's Prayer is a composite of ancient sayings taken from the Old Testament, the Talmud, and the ancient Egyptian prayers to Osiris. It has similarities with some of the verses in the Maxims of Ani, an ancient Egyptian record written around fourteenth century BC to eighteenth century BC and cited by Ralph Ellis.[8] Of the ancient prophets only Isaiah (700 BC) addressed God as the Father, and his verses have similarities with the Lord's Prayer as shown in Isaiah 63:16-17:[9]

> Thou. O Lord, is our Father, our Redeemer, from everlasting is thy Name. Why hast thou made us to err, O Lord from thy ways: why hast thou hardened our hearts, that we should not fear thee? Return for the sake of thy servants, the tribes of thy inheritance.

Also in Isaiah 64:8-9[10], Isaiah said,

> O Lord thou art our Father . . . Be not very angry, O Lord and remember no longer our iniquity; behold, see we are all thy people.

Based on the quoted verses, it is apparent that the theme of Isaiah's prayers is similar to that of the Lord's Prayer. As to the ancient civilizations, it was in Sumer where the highest god was always addressed as Father who dispensed everything. As the Sumerian gods were said to have come from Niburu and the Sirius constellation, then the prayer could have galactic origin. Thus, this tradition of calling God Our Father could have a very ancient origin. As Abraham came from Ur, a part of Sumer, this tradition of calling God as Father could have been carried over by his descendants. However, during the time of Moses, the concept of God became different. He became the powerful and very strict God. Only during the supposed time of Jesus that he brought back this tradition. As I continue writing this book, many questions began to bother me, questions that are very troubling, for they affect my very personal beliefs as a Christian. However, I have to continue what I have started.

There are many secrets in the Lord's Prayer. With proper understanding, one can harness its power and perform the miracles the apostles did as we also experienced in the spiritual healings we performed for others.

Our group called the One-Tenth was able to get the secret of the Lord's Prayer discussed in the appendix on "Harnessing the Power of the Lord's Prayer" that has helped in the spiritual transformation of people and has produced many miraculous cures in spiritual healings. We were contented with what we had learned and experienced from the Lord's Prayer until the publication of the different books on

the Bible code. This aroused my curiosity about the Lord's Prayer. Could there be a code in the Lord's Prayer? Is there something in the Lord's Prayer that remains unrevealed, a mystery that could help people to have a better understanding of the New Testament and their relationship with one another? With that in mind, I began the quest to secure a copy of the Lord's Prayer in Hebrew.

c) Missing Hebrew Version

With the proliferation of the many books on the Bible code, I began to wonder why nobody attempted to decode the only prayer that Jesus taught us. What could be the reason? Is the Lord's Prayers so simple and short that it cannot possibly contain hidden information and will not be ideal for Equidistant Letter Sequence (ELS) decoding? Could it be possible that someone has already tried to decode the Lord's Prayer but found nothing? Or could it be that there was no version of the Lord's Prayer in Hebrew that could be the subject of Kabalistic study?

The Kabalists invented different methods of decoding the Old Testament centuries before the use of the ELS. As the old Kabalists were rabbinic scholars and their Kabalistic writings and literatures were in Hebrew, it would be necessary therefore that the document or writing to be decoded should be in the Hebrew language. Most of the books and documents to be used for decoding are based in the Hebrew alphabet. The Kabalists have proven by the use of the different methods of Kabalistic decoding that the Old Testament was a code. Thus, if the Old Testament is coded, there is a great possibility that the New Testament if in Hebrew is also coded. Another reason why the New Testament must be in the Hebrew language more particularly the Lord's Prayer is that only the Hebrew alphabet besides the Greek alphabet that has numeral correspondence that is used in the decoding. Also, the use of the original Hebrew version and not the transliterated version will minimize mistakes in decoding. The acquisition of a Hebrew version of the Lord's Prayer is therefore a necessity. Although the Equidistant Letter Sequence is very logical and scientific and can be used to decipher any language, it does not explain the esoteric teachings hidden in the decoding made, more particularly in the ancient Hebrew scripts. Only the Kabalah can be used for such purpose. In the present case, I will be using these two methods, namely, the Kabalah and the ELS in decoding the Lord's Prayer.

With the many bookstores and through the Internet, I thought it was very easy to get the original Hebrew version of the Lord's Prayer. I was mistaken. My search for a Hebrew version has left me confounded. There was no original Hebrew version. There were several Hebrew versions available but based on the transliterations of the original Greek version. The Aramaic and Greek versions were easily obtainable, but the problem was that even if the Greek alphabet had number correspondences, materials about the Greek Kabalah were limited, hence the necessity to find the

Hebrew version. Another problem was that although the Greek transliterations were based on the Greek original, the writers/translators were using the Latin form of the Greek alphabet without regards to its numeral correspondences. An example is the letter *O* in Greek. There are two Os in the Greek alphabet, namely, omicron with a numeral value of *seventy* and omega with a numeral value of *eight hundred*. Most often the translators just wrote the Latin form of the letter *O* without distinction as to whether it was the letter omicron or the letter omega that was the intended letter. For those knowledgeable about the Hebrew gematria or the Greek Isopsephy or the modern numerology, this omission would result in decoding error. The word *omicron* has a different number correspondence than omega.

It was puzzling that Jesus and the apostles, who were Jews in the Jewish town of Galilee with old Hebrew or Aramaic language being spoken, could not possibly have a Hebrew version of the Lord's Prayer. Could it be that there was a Hebrew version but was shelved for a Greek version and was edited by Hellenized Jews like Paul, or there was a Hebrew version, which had been lost like the Dead Sea scrolls awaiting discovery?

d) Why only a Greek Version?

I made a research about the missing Hebrew version and found the same answer from several books. The *Reader's Digest Book*[11] said the New Testament was written in Greek and not in the Hebrew language because the literary language between the years AD 50 and 100 in Galilee was Greek, thus:

1. The Christians for convenience wrote in the language of their literary contemporaries who spoke and wrote in Greek.
2. The Bibles used by the early Christians was the Greek translation of the Old Testament known as the Septuagint; thus, quotations from the Old Testament were in Greek, and thus, for convenience the New Testament was written in Greek. Early Christians accepted the Septuagint as official translation of the Bibles, but due to the many errors, Aquila, Symmachus, and Theodation[12] made three new and different translations.
3. Christian writers wanted to reach a wider audience both in Palestine—and Greek-speaking Jews. Paul, a Jew, supposedly wrote all his letters in Greek and not in Aramaic.

The Greek version of the Lord's Prayer is as follows:

Pater Hmoon O EN
Toiw Ouranoiw
Agiasth H Too

7

To Onoma Sou El The Too
H Basileia Sou
Genhth H Too To
Thelhma Sou Oow En
Ouranoo kai Epi Ghw
Ton Arton Hmoon Ton
Epiousion Dow Hmin
Shmeron Kai A Few
Hmin
Ta Ofeilhmata Hmoon Oow
Kai Hmeiw
Afhkamen Toiw
Ofeiletaiw Hmoon Kai
MH Eisenegkhw
Hmaw Eiw Peirasmon
Allla Rusai Hmaw
Apo Tou Ponhrou[13]

Another book[14] said that the first language of Galilee was Greek, and that in Alexandria, the Jews had abandoned their language and adopted Greek by the middle of the third century BC. These findings answered the question about the missing Hebrew version. Presently, Bible scholars placed the Gospel of Mark that was considered the oldest of the Gospels between the second and third century AD and not the first century dating advocated before.

The first Latin translation was made about the fourth century called Vetus Latina. St. Jerome found many inaccuracies in the translation that he made his own translation that became known as the Vulgate. John Wycliffe in the fourteenth century made the first English translation of the Vulgate.

Thus, we have the Greek, the Latin, and the English translations except the original Hebrew version. Despite the difficulty in finding an original Hebrew version, still I continued the search for the Hebrew version. I could not believe that the Jews who are a proud people would just abandon their language. There must be a Hebrew version somewhere that has been lost and just awaiting to be discovered.

I asked my cousin Lina to help me find in the Internet a version of the Lord's Prayer in Hebrew. She did not only furnish me several Hebrew versions of the Lord's Prayer in Hebrew but also she gave me an article from the Internet[15] that claimed that the Gospel of Matthew was written in Hebrew based on the statements of the early fathers of the church, namely, Papias (AD 150-170), Ireneus (AD—170) and Origen (AD—210) who said that the Gospel of Matthew was written in the Hebrew language. Other Christian fathers like,

1. Eusebius (AD—315) said that Matthew was originally published in Hebrew and was found in different parts of the world like India.
2. Gregory of Nazianzus (AD 329) said that Matthew was originally written in Hebrew.
3. Epiphanius (AD—370) said that the Nazarene believers have the Gospel of Matthew in complete Hebrew as it was first written in the Hebrew letters.
4. Jerome (AD—382) claimed that Matthew was written in Hebrew and later translated into Greek. He said that a copy of the original Hebrew version was available in Caesarea in his day. He claimed he had a copy of the Hebrew version from the believers in Syria and used it as a basis for his Latin translation.
5. Ishodad (AD—850) claimed that an original copy of Matthew in Hebrew was preserved in a library in his days.

In this article it was also said that in 1553, Pope Julius III, through a decree, banned the Talmud in Rome resulting in the confiscation not only of the Talmud but anything resembling the Talmud. As the Gospel of Matthew was in Hebrew, many copies of the Hebrew version of Matthew were burned along with the Talmud. It is claimed that three copies of the original Hebrew version still survive today. Although this article if true, confirmed my belief about the existence of a Hebrew version of the Lord's Prayer but it created more questions in my mind. If there are many credible people claiming that there are original Hebrew versions of the Gospel of Matthew, why is there not even one copy in existence? If there is an existing copy of the Gospel of Matthew in the original Hebrew language, who has in possession of it? Why is it not being revealed despite the importance and impact that it will bring to the world? Is that version very different from the Gospel of Matthew that we know of today? Whose interest is being served by hiding the Gospel if it exists? One writer said that the Gospel of Matthew could not have been written in the Hebrew language as claimed by Papias, for it used Greek sources like Mark, Q, and the Septuagint Bible.[16]

In the book Secret Book of James the apostle James said,

> Since you have asked me to send you a secret book revealed to me and Peter by the Lord, I could not turn you down or refuse you. So I have written it in HEBREW and sent it to you and only you.[17]

If James, the apostle could send a secret book that he personally wrote in Hebrew (capitalization mine), could he or the other apostles not written also the Lord's Prayer in Hebrew? I was surprised that I could not find a Hebrew version of the Lord's Prayer in religious or occult books. Aramaic versions of the Lord's Prayer

were available, but there were no dictionary and Kabalistic books in Aramaic that could support the research, and also most of the books of the Kabalah were based on the Hebrew language. Further, the Aramaic version was also based on the Greek version of the Lord's Prayer. Hence, if there is any error in the Greek version, it will be carried over to the Aramaic version. The problem with the Aramaic version is similar to that of the Greek version. Although the Greek alphabet has numeral correspondences, however, there are very few Greek Kabalistic books. Hence, I continued and concentrated in searching for the Hebrew version of the Lord's Prayer.

e) Available Hebrew Version

After a long search, I finally found a Hebrew version of the Lord's Prayer in the book entitled *Words of Power: Sacred Sound of East and West* by Brian and Easter Crowley that was printed not in the traditional Hebrew way of reading from right to left but in the modern way as shown below:

> Avenu Sh'ba Sh'maiyim
> Yitkadash Shemeycha
> Tavo Malkutecha
> Y'asseh Retzoncha
> K'mo Ba-Sh'maiyim Kain B'Aretz
> Et Lechem Hukeynu Ten-Lonu Ha-yom
> U'slach Lonu Et Hovetheynu
> K'Asher Solachnu Gam Anachnu L'Ha Yaveynu
> Vi-al Tivi-Aynu Li-y 'Dey Nisa Yon
> Ki Im Hal-Tzeynu Min Hara[18]

Together with this version are the three versions from the Internet[19] that my cousin Lina furnished me, namely:

1) Version taken from the Targum Franz Delitsch, a classical Hebrew New Testament version.

> Avinu sheba Shamayim
> yitqaDash shemekha
> Tavo malkhutekha
> ye aseh retsonkha
> kemo vaShamayim
> Ken ba'arets
> et—lehem huQenu Ten—lanu ha Yom
> uclah—lanu et—hovotenu

ka'asher calahnu Gam—anahnu leha Yavenu
ve'al—Tevi'enu lide niCayon
ki'im haLtsenu min—hara.

2) Version given by the Convent of Pater Noster. The convent itself is located in the alleged site where Jesus supposedly gave the prayer to the apostle.

Avinu sebasamajim, jitqades simka
Tavo malkuteka,
je ase reconka kevasamajim ken ba arec.
Et lehem huqenu ten lanu hajjom,
uslah lanu al hata enu, kemo sesolhim
gam anahnu lahot im lanu.
We' al tevi enu lide nisayon,
Ki im halcenu min hara.

3) Versions from the database called the Scriptures of the World.

Avinu shebashamayim
yitkadesh shimcha, tavo malchutecha,
yease retsoncha kebashamayim ken ba'arets.
Et lechem chukenu ten lanu hayom,
uslach lanu al chataeinu,
Kefi shesolchim gam anachnu
Lachot'im lanu.
Veal tevienu lijdei nisajon
Ki im chaltzenu min hara.

All the three Hebrew versions from the Internet contain the expanded ending "For thine is the Kingdom, the Power and the Glory forever and ever, Amen." However, since the original Greek version did not contain the said expanded ending, I did not include it anymore in the prayer.

As there was no original Hebrew version of the Lord's Prayer, all the four Hebrew versions quoted in this book could be considered as new and based on the personal interpretations of the persons or institutions concerned. Although, all the versions are about the Lord's Prayer based on the Matthew Gospel, it would be noticed that the spelling of the words with the same English meaning like Kadesh (Holy) could be written in several ways like Kadesh or Qadash or Qades. Sometimes, the words are written in its defective form or without vowels; thus, the result of the research would depend on the version used with its unique form or style. This would also show the intricacy of the Hebrew language.

f) Reason for the Version Used

Some people might question the Hebrew version used in this book as a new translation, but as I have said since there was no original Hebrew version available, so any version would be considered a new version. I do not know how old the version of the Lord's Prayer used as a model in this book is; however, the accuracy of this version will be tested by its contents.

Why did I choose the version from the book *Words of Power* as the model for this book? Ancient prayers like the mantras usually have a rhyme scheme and intonation, which when recited seemed like a poem with a beautiful cadence and rhythm. This version had those qualities. As I was able to read the whole book containing the version, I had a feel of the said book and its credibility that I did not have in the versions obtained from the Internet as I have not read the sources of the quotations. Further, the version used was the only one I found in a Kabalistic book after a long search. Also, I felt it was the better version, and the contents of this book would justify my choice of the version used. It could be almost like the original version if there was any. I tested the other versions with sample words and found the version from the book with more astonishing results. Even if we combine the results of the other versions, they cannot compare with the results from the version used in this book. This only made me more confident that the model I used could be the closest to the missing original Hebrew version. I made this conclusion even before I wrote the section on gematria/isopsephy that further showed the uniqueness of this version of the Lord's Prayer. The contents of this book would justify my choice of the version used and validate my assumptions that the Lord's Prayer is a code.

There would always be questions about this book as it was not based on the original Hebrew version of the Lord's Prayer, but I was inspired to write this book to show that even a semblance of the original Hebrew version if it existed could create a book that would be mind-boggling and fantastic. How much more if the original Hebrew version was used! Maybe, we do not deserve the original version; hence, it was lost to us and we were given instead the edited versions of the Lord's Prayer like the Ten Commandments, the original version of which was destroyed by Moses.

There is a saying that nothing happens in this world without a reason. The Hebrew version that was placed in my possession after a long search was meant to be the model for this book. What matters is that a step has been made to decipher the Lord's Prayer, and this would serve as a catalyst for others who might not agree to improve on this book. Other writers could use the other versions of the Lord's Prayer to add, subtract, or refute this book.

PART II

THE DISCOVERY OF THE CODE

The Lord's Prayer is a short and simple prayer, yet it has an encompassing code that reveals the past, the present, and the future. It contains secret doctrines, information about ancient civilizations, religion, and the future of the world.

CHAPTER II

THE GRID

After finding several Hebrew versions of the Lord's Prayer, the next step was to construct the possible grid or rows of letters that could possibly contain the code that would ultimately reveal the secrets of the Lord's Prayer. For reasons stated previously, I used the Hebrew version from the book *Words of Power* as my model. With God's guidance, I was able to find the right grid that confirms the existence of a code or a *fantasy* as others might say.

There is a legend that when Moses in a vision received the Torah from God, the letters appeared in a continuous sequence without any cuts or spacing that the Kabalists called it the Torah of God. Only Moses knew where the commas and the periods would be. He was also the only one who knew what and where the vowels would be, for the Hebrew language used to be written without the vowels. When Moses introduced the cuts, spacing, or intervals between the letters or the words, it became the Torah of Moses. In the present case, in order to produce the grid, I introduced cuts in the verses of the Lord's Prayer without changing the order or sequence of the letters. Hence, it is up to the decoder to arrange the Lord's Prayer in several grids or rows to find out what the correct grid is, what the author of the Lord's Prayer has hidden, and what he would like to reveal to the determined seeker. In looking for the grid, the original order of letter is never changed.

a) Number of Letters and Rows

According to Michael Drosnin[1] the computer in order to find the words "End of Days" divided the 304,805 letters of the Bible into 40 rows of 7551 letters. In our case, I arranged the letters of the Hebrew version of the Lord's Prayer composed of 198 letters in twelve columns and seventeen rows as shown in figure 1 without changing the order of the letters and reading from right to left direction. The letters are side by side without periods or commas following the

---

Moses legend. With the Hebrew letters, I made several grids or rows of letters composed of seven, eight, nine, ten, eleven, twelve, and thirteen letters per row. Intuitively, I started with the grid consisting of twelve columns and seventeen rows as shown in figure 1 in deference to the twelve apostles. And it proved right. The discovery awed and astonished me. Although the different grids provided some startling discoveries, however, the grid with the twelve columns (the "Grid") produced the most astounding and unbelievable revelations that only reinforced my belief that the Lord's Prayer was not as simple as it seemed to be. The Lord's Prayer was like a Bible and the Ten Commandments put together. The Grid unfolded more secrets beyond expectations and confirmed doctrines contained in the New Testament and revealed new ones and several unknown facts.

Several letter-row combinations also contained revelations, but none could equate or compare with the twelve letters column combination. The use of the number 12 only confirmed that the author of this code knew what he was doing, and it was a way to help the decoder easily find the letter-row combination to be used to reveal hidden meanings. This also showed that the author of this code knew Kabalah and, like a painter, would surely leave his name in the code as will be shown later.

	A	B	C	D	E	F	G	H	I	J	K	L
1	A	V	E	N	U	Sh	B	A	Sh	M	A	I
2	Y	I	M	Y	I	T	K	A	D	A	Sh	Sh
3	E	M	E	Y	Ch	A	T	A	V	O	M	A
4	L	K	U	T	E	Ch	A	Y	A	S	S	E
5	H	R	E	Tz	O	N	Ch	A	K	M	O	B
6	A	Sh	M	A	I	Y	I	M	K	A	I	N
7	B	A	R	E	Tz	E	T	L	E	Ch	E	M
8	H	U	K	E	Y	N	U	T	E	N	L	O
9	N	U	H	A	Y	O	M	U	S	L	A	Ch
10	L	O	N	U	E	T	H	O	V	E	Th	E
11	Y	N	U	K	A	Sh	E	R	S	O	L	A
12	Ch	N	U	G	A	M	A	N	A	Ch	N	U
13	L	H	A	Y	A	V	E	Y	N	U	V	I
14	A	L	T	I	V	I	A	Y	N	U	L	I
15	Y	D	E	Y	N	I	S	A	Y	O	N	K
16	I	I	M	H	A	L	Tz	E	Y	N	U	M
17	I	N	H	A	R	A						

Fig. 1 The Grid.

If the Lord's Prayer is not a code, no matter how many grids one makes, there will be no revelations like the ones shown in this book. We cannot stop people from commenting that the version used in this book is not the original version of the Hebrew Lord's Prayer, but the mere fact that even a semblance of the said original Hebrew version could create a book like this should fill us with awe and wonderment. How much more if the original was used? Maybe we do not deserve the original version like the case of the Ten Commandments which were originally written by the fingers of God but, due to the transgressions of the Jews, were destroyed by Moses, and a new set with some portions written by Moses were given to the people. There was a legend that the first set of commandments was different from the second set, and that the first set was withheld from the people, for they were not yet ready to receive the said commandments. Maybe, we are faced with the same problem; thus, the original version of the Lord's Prayer had been withheld from us and the edited version was given to us instead. This could also be the reason why Jesus taught the esoteric interpretation of the Lord's Prayer to the apostles while the apostles taught the exoteric interpretation to the masses. Jesus has emphasized the meaning of the Lord's Prayer to the apostles while the succeeding disciples just taught us to memorize the prayer without knowing its importance. Had we understood the meaning of the Lord's Prayer, this could have been a different world. The Lord's Prayer is so short that the Hebrew version used in this book is composed of only 198 letters, and its contents are comparable to the Bible that is composed of 304,805 letters. The Lord's Prayer could be said to be the other form of the Ten Commandments. The table below will show the letters of the Hebrew alphabet and the number of times the letters were used in the Lord's Prayer code.

Letters	No. of Times Used	Letters	No. of Times Used
A	30	K	7
E	19	Ch	7
N	17	Sh	6
Y	15	V	6
I	14	S	5
U	13	R	4
M	12	Tz	3
L	10	B	3
O	9	D	2
T	7	Th	1
H	7	G	1

Table 1

b) The Hebrew Alphabet

The Kabalah is divided into four classes, one of which is the literal Kabalah that deals with the different methods of deciphering the Bible and other ancient scriptures in accordance to the corresponding number, shape and mystical attributes of each letter of the Hebrew alphabet. Each letter has a corresponding number to convey mathematical and esoteric information. The names of God are not mere words but contain numerical values that are significant in their esoteric meanings like the holy name IHVH.

As we are dealing with the Hebrew language in our search for the code, a table of the Hebrew alphabet with corresponding numeral values is shown for reference.

Numerical Value of Each Letter					
V = 6	H = 5	D = 4	G = 3	B = 2	A = 1
L = 30	K = 20	J = 10	T = 9	Ch = 8	Z = 7
Th = 90	P = 80	O = 70	S = 60	N = 50	M = 40
		T = 400	Sh = 300	R = 200	Q = 100

Table 2

Due to these numeral correspondences, letters, words, phrases, or even entire verse of the Torah can be explained in the context of allusion rather than in the realm of the literal meaning of the letters, words, or verse written.

Kabalists believe that God is hidden, and words are just veils that cover up what is something hidden and mysterious; it is an enticement for determined seekers to unveil. Thus it is said,

> It is the glory of God to conceal a matter, but the glory of Kings, is to search out a matter.[2]

It behooves, therefore, on the seeker of knowledge to seek the hidden as its revelation is a glorification of God. According to the Gnostic book the Gospel of Truth

> the knowledge of the living book was revealed to the aeons by letters which are neither vowels or consonants but letters of truths which only those who know speak. Each letter is a complete thought like a complete book, written by the Father for the aeons to know the Father.[3]

If this statement will be taken in a modern context, the letter that is a complete thought or a book can be likened to a computer disk that contains complete and vast reservoir of information. What is then a letter that is neither a vowel nor a consonant but contains a complete thought? This is a matter for the seeker of truth to resolve.

c) Gematria/Isopsephy/Numerology

There are two ancient languages that are unique for they have numeral correspondences. They are the Hebrew and the Greek languages. They are said to be the language of the gods, for they can be understood not only in this world but also through out the universe. As all creations are based in numbers, then these languages can be understood mathematically by any beings who have numbers/mathematics in their systems.

Actually there is a debate as to which of the two languages was the source of the method of decoding known as gematria in Hebrew and Isopsephy in Greek and now known as numerology. It is argued by some writers like Kieren Barry[4] that it was the Greeks who invented the alphabetic numerals as early as the eight century BC that became the basis of the Hebrew gematria. According to some writers, Babylonian inscriptions showed that the art of interpreting letters or numbers by gematria was known at the time of Sargon 11 (723-705 BCE).[5]

However, based on a Sumerian writing called the Cylinders of Gudea[6] dated around the time of Gudea of Lagash 2125 BC, it was said,

> Laid out the plan of the house,
> (As) a very Nidaba knowing the innermost
> (secrets) of numbers,

This verse could only mean that the Sumerians already knew the secrets of numbers during that time. This knowledge could then have been later handed down to the Akkadians to the Mesopotamians or Babylonians and then to the Egyptians and later to the Jews and the Greeks. If the secret of numbers started from Sumer, it would have been impossible that the Greeks learned it first from the Sumerians for the people who had interactions with the Sumerians were the later Akkadians, Mesopotamians, Babylonians, and the Egyptians. There is a great possibility that the Jews learned the secret of numbers first than the Greeks because of their geographical position and interactions with these Middle Eastern civilizations.

CHAPTER III

METHODS OF DECODING

After discovering the grid, it is now a question of what methods to use in decoding the Lord's Prayer—the Kabalah or the Equidistant Letters Sequence (ELS). I will be using both methods with the ELS as the primary method as it is very precise and scientific in showing logical patterns to prove the existence of a code; however, in proving the esoteric teachings contained in the Bible and ancient Hebrew scriptures, the different Kabalistic methods have to be used. The Hebrew alphabet and words have numerical values that can only be subject to decoding by the different Kabalistic methods and not by the ELS method. Although there are several Kabalistic methods of decoding, I will focus on the gematria method and sparingly the temurah methods.

a) The Kabalah

What is then the Kabalah? By its spelling alone, it is very confusing as the word can be spelled in various ways, Kabala, Kabalah, Kabbala, Kabbalah, Cabala, Cabbalah, Qabala, or Qabbala. Whatever the spelling is, the most important thing is to understand why there is a need to know about it. Most people are contented with just being told what the English interpretation of the Bible is and to believe it without question. Do we belong to that group? What if the interpretation is wrong, half-truth, or a lie? Can one really interpret the Old Testament without the Kabalah? God gave us brains to think, to discern, and to ask questions. If God wanted a yes person, He would have created robots. So let us read this book and ponder.

According to the Kabalists, if one knows the Kabalah, it would be easier to understand a number of passages in the Bible that seemed to be illogical and unintelligible. Thus, for anyone to interpret the Bible based only in the English translation and without the knowledge of the Kabalah will be questionable.

Kabalah is the esoteric tradition of the Jews supposed to be handed down from generation to generation starting from Adam, whom the angels out of pity taught the Kabalah for his survival in the outside world. Adam in turn handed

down this knowledge to Seth who later on gave it to Noah, then to Abraham, down to David, to Solomon, and then to the high priests.

There are some Jewish scholars who believe that the Jewish mysticism called the Kabalah just started in the thirteenth century due to the important Kabalistic books that appeared during that time like the famous book *Bahir*. On the other hand, it could also be said that the thirteenth-century Kabalah was just a rediscovery of an ancient Jewish tradition for how could the Kabalah be applied to the decoding of the Old Testament unless the source of the Old Testament was a Kabalist and wrote it in a Kabalistic way.

It is the literal Kabalah that deals with the different methods of decoding the Bible and other ancient scriptures. The Hebrew alphabet is interpreted based on its corresponding number, shape, and sound. Each letter is like a computer diskette that contains mathematical and esoteric information.

b) The Kabalistic Method of Decoding

In their search for the hidden code in the Old Testament, the Kabalists had invented various methods to decipher the ancient writings. As I would be using mainly the methods of gematria known as the Aiq Becker and sometimes the temurah method that is similar to the anagram, then an explanation of the methods has to be given.

Gematria—the method of discovering the true and hidden meaning of words by replacing or substituting letters or words with the same numerical values (numerology) that shows the interconnections between letters or words. An example would be the words *Achad* and *Ahebah*, which both have the numeral value of *thirteen* as shown in the following computation.

$$Achad = A (1) + Ch (8) + D (4) = 13$$
$$Ahebah = A (1) + H (5) + B (2) + H (5) = 13$$

As both words have the numeral sum of thirteen, thus the word *Achad* (unity) is considered to be connected and related to the word *Ahebah* (love). There seems to be truth in this as love creates unity.

King Sargon, who ruled Babylon in the eight century BC used the numerical value of his name to determine that the wall of Khorsabad should be built to the same equivalent of sixteen thousand two hundred eighty three cubits.[1]

Simple Gematria is the straight translation of words into figures and numbers on the basis of the numbers corresponding to the letters. Each Hebrew letter has a corresponding number.

Aiq Beker—one of the examples of gematria is the method Aiq Beker known as the Table of Nine Numbers wherein letters of the Hebrew alphabet are grouped

together according to the similarity of number or values, and the zeroes are taken out reducing the numbers to single digit. The letters with the same numerical values are grouped together like in table 3. Based on the table, the letters in the same group can be interchanged with one another, for they have the same numerical values. Thus, the letters *A*, *J*, and *Q* with the numerical values of one, ten, and one hundred respectively are grouped together. Taking the zeroes out of the numbers 10 and 100 will result in number-1; thus *A*, *J*, and *Q* are equal to 1 and therefore can be interchanged like the other letters. It is just a case of more essence, substance, or intensity one would like to portray in using a letter or number.

Aiq Beker								
Tet	Ch	Z	V	H	D	G	B	A
9	8	7	6	5	4	3	2	1
Tz	P	Ayin	S	N	M	L	K	J
90	80	70	60	50	40	30	20	10
Tz	P	N	M	K	T	Sh	R	Q
900	800	700	600	500	400	300	200	100

Table 3

It is said that the simple number like one to ten or numbers of ten are *divine numbers. Celestial numbers* are numbers of hundreds or more but less than a thousand while *terrestrial numbers* are those by the thousands that refer to future age.

I prefer this method of decoding because it is based on the numeral correspondences of the Hebrew alphabet and also due to the grouping of the letters with the same numeral equivalents.

The best example of Christian gematria is the name of Jesus itself where the Greek name of Jesus—Iesous—expresses the number of 888 as shown in table 4.

In Greek, the number 888 is regarded as sacred and magical as it is the sum total of the numeral correspondences of the twenty-four letters of the Greek alphabet. There was even a Gnostic myth about the young Jesus teaching the rabbis at the Jerusalem temple about the mystical meaning of the Greek alphabet that would be further discussed in the chapter on gematria and Isopsephy.

Letter	Value
I	10
E	8
S	200
O	70
U	400
S	200
Total	888

Table 4

Temurah—is the rearranging of the letters of a word to spell another word like BHN that is rearranged to become BNH that are both equal numerically. Letters in a quadrant or a cluster can also be rearranged to form a word like in the example given in table 5 and the subtables. This is similar to anagram where there is a transposition of letters to arrive at the hidden message or code.

		A	B	C	D	E	F	G	H	I	J	K	L
8													
9								M	U	S			
10								H	O	V			
11								E	R	S			
12													

Table 5 Example of Temurah.

From this cluster of letters, the names of Jesus in Pilipino Hesus, the Jewish prophet Moses, Roman god of love Eros, and the Egyptian god Horus can be permutated or formed as shown in the subquadrants of table 5. Also the names of some countries and cities mentioned like USSR, US, UE, Sumer, UR, and Rome. From the example given, it is apparent that the ELS method of decoding cannot be used.

Hesus		
M	U	S
H	O	V
E	R	S

Moses		
M	U	S
H	O	V
E	R	S

Horus		
M	U	S
H	O	V
E	R	S

Although this method of decoding like the anagram is accepted; however, to avoid any criticism being made about easily getting results from this kind of method, I have minimized the use of said method unless extremely necessary.

Criticism against the Kabalistic methods

Some people might question the use of the Aiq Becker method as it can cover many possibilities due to the replacement or substitution of letters with equal numeral values. Critics would argue that it would be easy to find the desired letters or words as they can be interchanged or replaced by letters with the same numeral values like the word *MAN*. Since the letter *M* can be replaced by the letters *D* and *T* while the letter *N* can be substituted by the letters *H* and *E* and the letter *A* by the letter *I*, then the word *MAN* can easily be decoded as DAN, TAN, DIN, TIN, HAT, HAM, or HIM. To avoid this criticism, there will be minimum use of substitution of letters. As much as possible, I will not combine the different Kabalistic methods in looking for results, for it would really be easy to manipulate the findings.

Also with temurah or anagram, I will only use a cube or a square as a quadrant, for the bigger the quadrant, the easier it is to find the desired letters. Unless there is a pattern, I will not use more than a four-by-four square.

c) ELS (Equidistant Letter Sequence)

There is another method of decoding the Bible, which has become very popular due to the extensive publicity given to the different books about the biblical code. This is called the Equidistant Letter Sequence or known as ELS wherein there is an interval of letters between the encoded or desired letters. The ELS has become very accessible because of the use of computers. In a long document composed of thousand of letters to decode like the Bible with 304,805 letters according to Michael Drosnin,[2] the computer is very helpful in

discovering the ELS. Will ELS be applicable to a short writing like the Lord's Prayer composed of only 198 letters? Unbelievably, yes!

It is amazing that there are so many examples with different ELS in the grid. Based on mathematical probabilities, the only conclusion is that these examples were placed there deliberately and not due to coincidence.

Is the method ELS in the Bible? According to Yacov Rambsel,[3] the full phrase "equidistant letter sequence" is found in Hebrew at equal intervals in Genesis through Deuteronomy. He said that in every fifth letter of Genesis 20:2, the Hebrew phrase "hacharak oht shalav," which means "the latticework of the equidistant letter sequence" can be found. "Shalov Aot"[4] also means "equidistant letter sequence." With that as a basis, let us look for the examples of ELS in the code.

As this book is about the prayer to the Father, are we going to find evidences or proofs in the grid that the Lord's Prayer is truly about the Father? Will the name of the Father or matters related to the Father be found in the grid? For this purpose, we will look at the holy name of God that was given to Moses in Mt. Sinai. According to the Old Testament, God in the symbol of a burning bush appeared to Moses and gave His name as "I Am that I Am," which in Hebrew is "AHIH AShR AHIH" or in short "AAA" as stated in occult books. For sure many readers will doubt the presence of the holy name in the Lord's Prayer. But since the Lord's Prayer is a code, one really cannot just see the name for it is hidden. The presence of the Holy Name AAA in the Lord's Prayer will surely astonish many people as it is not expected that the holy name of God given to Moses can be found in the Lord's Prayer. Further, if one is not aware of the code, the name will be nonexistent.

Examples of ELS in the Grid

Figure 2 will illustrate several examples showing the different skip intervals between the desired letters using the letters AAA. The minimal skip interval illustrated is one letter between the desired letters as shown in the grid. The lesser the skip intervals are the better. The examples shown here are one of the best with respect to ELS because of the minimal intervals involved. There are even examples without ELS as the letters are side by side horizontally, vertically, or diagonally.

For convenience in locating the desired letters, the twelve columns are given the first twelve letters of the alphabet as their designations while the seventeen rows are designated in numbers. These designations serve as the coordinates for the letters. In addition, I mention the ELS or the number of letters/spaces separating the encoded letters. Thus, to find the letter *A* of the word *Avenu*, we have to go to A-1 meaning the first column and the first row.

The number of examples illustrated is a confirmation that the Lord's Prayer is truly a prayer to the Father, and that if one discovers the right grid, one can uncover the hidden code in the Lord's Prayer. The seventeen examples can be read in the reverse order and have the same ELS whether going in the right or the left direction or diagonally upward or downward. To find seventeen examples in a small grid consisting of 198 letters is overwhelming.

Number of Examples	Coordinates			ELS
1st example	A = A-1	A = B-7	A = C-13.	72 letters

This first example has many esoteric connotations. It shows its importance by starting with the first letter *A* on A-1. This emphasizes that this holy name is supreme, the first among the first. The ELS of seventy-two letters also refers to the seventy-two holy names of God or Semiphoras.

2nd example	A = H-1	A = H-2	A = H-13.	11 letters

		A	B	C	D	E	F	G	H	I	J	K	L
1		A							A				
2									A				
3									A				
4													
5													
6													
7			A										
8													
9													
10													
11													
12													
13				A									
14													

Fig. 2 The first and second examples of AAA.

3rd example	A = H-1	A = H-2	A = H-3.	None
4th example	A = H-1	A = J-2	A = L-3.	13 letters.

	A	B	C	D	E	F	G	H	I	J	K	L
1								A				
2										A		
3								A				A
4												
5								A				
6												

Fig. 2-a The third and fourth examples.

5th example

5th example   A = H-1   A = J-6   A = L-11   61 letters

	A	B	C	D	E	F	G	H	I	J	K	L
1								A				
2												
3												
4												
5												
6										A		
7												
8												
9												
10												
11												A
12												

Fig. 2-b The fifth example.

6th example   A = H-2   A = I-4   A = J-6.   24 letters

	A	B	C	D	E	F	G	H	I	J	K	L
1												
2								A				
3												
4									A			
5												
6										A		
7												

Fig. 2-c The sixth example.

7th example   A = J-2   A = G-4   A = D-6.   20 letters
8th example   A = F-3   A = G-1   A = H-5   12 letters

	A	B	C	D	E	F	G	H	I	J	K	L
1												
2										A		
3						A						
4							A					
5								A				
6				A								
7												

Fig. 2-d The seventh and eighth example.

9th example   A = A-6   A = D-9   A = G-12.   38 letters

		A	B	C	D	E	F	G	H	I	J	K	L
4													
5													
6		A											
7													
8													
9					A								
10													
11													
12								A					
13													

Fig. 2-e The ninth example.

		A	B	C	D	E	F	G	H	I	J	K	L
7			A										
8													
9													
10													
11						A							
12													
13													
14													
15									A				
16													
17													

Fig. 2-f The tenth example.

10th example	A = B-7	A = E-11	A = H-15	52 letters
11th example	A = D-9	A = E-13	A = F-17	48 letters

	A	B	C	D	E	F	G	H	I	J	K	L
9				A								
10												
11					A							
12					A							
13					A							
14												
15												
16												
17						A						

Fig. 2-g The eleventh and twelfth examples.

12th example   A = E-11   A = E-12 A = E-13   13 letters
13th example   A = E-11   A = L-11 A = G-12   6 letters

	A	B	C	D	E	F	G	H	I	J	K	L
11					A							A
12							A					
13												

Fig. 2-h The thirteenth example.

14th example   A = E-12   A = G-12 A = I-12   1 letter
15th example   A = E-12   A = C-13 A = A-14   9 letters.

	A	B	C	D	E	F	G	H	I	J	K	L
12					A		A		A			
13			A									
14	A											
15												
16												
17												

Fig. 2-i The fourteenth and fifteenth examples.

16th example   A = I-12   A = E-13 A = A-14   7 letters.
17th example   A = I-9   A = G-11 A = E-16   21 letters

	A	B	C	D	E	F	G	H	I	J	K	L
12									A			
13					A							
14	A						A					
15												
16					A							
17												

Fig. 2-j The sixteenth and seventeenth examples.

The seventeen examples given show the names of God with skip intervals or equidistant letter sequence of one, two, seven, nine, eleven, twelve, thirteen, twenty, twenty-one, twenty-four, thirty-eight, forty-eight, fifty, sixty-one, and seventy two letters. The number of examples and the variety of ELS illustrated can more than satisfy the rigid requirements of the Israeli researchers about the proximity of equidistant letters or ELS and the mathematical probability of finding the examples given. What is shown in the grid have the minimum skip intervals possible, and sometimes there are no intervals as the letters are side by side. Considering the number of times the names appeared and the different ELS involved in this very short grid composed of 198 letters, can this still be a coincidence? With examples shown in the grid, there can only be one conclusion—this grid is a well-thought-of grid.

Criticisms about the ELS

The publication of the Bible code by M. Drosnin has awakened the interest of many to decipher the Bible, and as a result many books about hidden codes in the Bible have come out since then. There have been legitimate criticisms put up by noted mathematicians against the ELS more particularly about the big skip intervals between the encoded letters, thus the convenience of finding an ELS. As the Old Testament is composed of thousands of letters it is really possible and convenient to find the desired words with the relevant ELS. According to Michael Drosnin,[5] there are 304,805 letters in the Bible and sometimes the ELS is by the thousands of letters. But it is also true that even if the ELS is by the thousands of letters, if the desired word is not there, one cannot do anything about it. However, in the Lord's Prayer, which is a short prayer composed of 198 letters that criticism about the long interval cannot stand especially if short ELS interval occurs, the encoded letters are in a cluster and sometimes the words are sharing common letters. The skip intervals in the Lord's Prayer code are the shortest that can be found ranging from one, two, three, or four-letter intervals; and sometimes the letters are side by side without ELS.

Considering that this is a prayer to the Father, the encoding of the Father's name a number of times just shows the deliberateness of the act. Despite the criticism about the ELS, there are many well-known mathematicians and computer experts who have written exhaustive articles about the validity of the ELS.

As the ELS has been extensively explained in all books about the Bible codes, we will show the other methods of decoding the Bible more particularly the different Kabalistic method. We will also look at patterns and symbols like the crop circle phenomenon in Europe that cannot just have appeared as coincidences but apparently were placed in the Lord's Prayer code deliberately. Thus, this in-depth study will be based not only on the ELS but also on other methods. Although the ELS will be a great help in the further study of the Bible; however, the Kabalah still remains the main pillar for the esoteric interpretation of the Bible and the Lord's Prayer code as will be shown by the illustrations.

Due to the extensive media promotion of the Bible code by M. Drosnin, it has captured the imagination of the world. The book has been subject to much criticism, but whether the contentions of Drosnin in his book are valid or not, the book has created a positive effect worldwide by returning the interest of many people to the Bible whether for intellectual or spiritual transformation. The ELS has given additional evidence to the theory that the Old Testament is coded as has always been contended by the Kabalists. In proving this allegation, I would always like to start with the book of Genesis, for if one could not find any code in the first book of the Torah, then for sure there is no code in the Torah.

Why do we have to prove that the Old Testament is coded? If it can be shown that the Old Testament is coded then there is the big possibility that the New Testament including the Lord's Prayer is also coded. The Kabalistic method of decoding shall be used to show that the Old Testament is a code. Later on, the very precise method of ELS will demonstrate that without doubt the Old Testament as alleged by the Kabalists is truly coded.

d) The Old Testament Is a Code

It has been the belief ever since that the Old Testament written in Hebrew is coded and therefore could not just be translated and be the subject of interpretation without the knowledge of the Hebrew language and the secret esoteric traditions of the Jews called the Kabalah. The publication of several books more particularly *The Bible Code* by Drosnin provided additional proofs through ELS about the Old Testament being coded.

The Jews are very meticulous in their writings. They don't use a word without a reason. An example is the saying of Isaiah in 43:37 when he said that God created man for His glory and formed man and made man. To an ordinary man,

the words *created, formed,* and *made* have the same meaning; but for a Kabalist, they have different meanings, namely:

a) Create = to materialize something out of nothing
b) Form = to change something from another thing
c) Make = to complete an action or to form something out of something

Thus, God created man in His image, formed man from the dust, and made a woman from the rib of Adam. With the above definitions of the different words, one will get a new perspective about the creation of man. God needed dust or clay to form man while God took a rib from Adam to make Eve. Thus, God did not create the physical Adam and Eve from nothing. This matter is further explained in the section about the "Interplay of Words." There are many examples that can be given to show the intricacy and profoundness of the Old Testament.

With evidences about the Old Testament being coded, there is therefore a big possibility that the New Testament, including the Lord's Prayer is also coded. Based on such premise, we will unlock the succeeding quoted sayings in the New Testament.

In the Gospel of St. John, there have been serious allegations made about the divinity of Jesus that have fueled debates and animosities for centuries, more particularly when John said,

> In the beginning was the Word, and the Word was with God and the Word was God.[1]

It was interpreted as Jesus Christ being the Word and therefore God. Why did St. John write this controversial assertion? Did he have evidences to support this claim? Where could we find the evidences? Could these be found in the Old Testament? If not, to find them only in the New Testament would only be self-serving. Again this controversial allegation came up when Jesus supposedly said,

> Do you not believe that I am in the Father and the Father is in Me?[2]

Where do you find the answers to this allegation? How do you find it? Can ELS resolve this question? No! How about the Kabalah? Yes! But what has the Kabalah to do with the Lord's Prayer, which is part of the New Testament? Can it answer the questions as to whether Jesus was really the author of the Lord's Prayer like the question about his divinity? Is it not enough to decipher the ancient writings with ELS as explained in various books about the Bible code?

The allegation that Jesus is the Word and is therefore God must be proven with evidences or cross-references besides the said statements. The evidences must be found in other ancient scriptures to give credence to the allegations. Since John was talking about the beginning of time, I felt that the best evidence would be found in Genesis, the story of creation.

Jesus Name in Genesis

In Hebrew, Jesus is called Yehoshuah, Yeshuah, or sometimes Joshua. His Kabalistic name is YHShVH, which is based in the holy name of God YHVH. Is it possible to find Jesus's name in the Old Testament more particularly in Genesis?

In Genesis, the first verse starts with the Hebrew phrase "Berashit Bara Alhim Ath Ha-Shmym Vath Ha-Aretz,"[3] which was translated "In the beginning God created the heavens and the earth." The phrase can be subject to very different interpretations depending on one's knowledge of the Kabalah. It has a hidden meaning, which by the method of Notarikon can be revealed. Notarikon is the method by which the initial or final letter of every word is used for coding purposes or every letter of a word is given a meaning. Thus from the said Hebrew verse, the following letters can be taken: *B*, *B*, *A*, *A*, *H*, *Sh*, *V*, *H*, and *A*. Among the letters, the most important to us would be the following A H Sh V H. As explained previously by gematria, an *A* can be interchanged with a *Y*, thus the word A H Sh V H can become Y H Sh V H, which according to the Kabalah is the name of Jesus in Hebrew—Yehoshuah. Since Jesus is the "Shin" or fire of the Father, the letter *Sh* is inserted in the unpronounceable name of YHVH. Usually the *Sh* is inserted after the YH and becomes Y H Sh V H. Thus, from this decipherment, it could be said that Jesus was indeed present in creation, for He was in the Father and the Father was in Him. Hence, there was a basis to what Jesus said:

> The Father and I are one[4]

It is obvious that the ELS method cannot be used in this kind of decoding, hence my reliance to the Kabalistic method of decoding more particularly in revealing the esoteric meaning of the phrase or verse.

Mr. Grant Jeffreys[5] cited Mr. Yacob Rambsel as the one who discovered the hidden name of Jesus in Isaiah 53:8-10. He has found the name by counting forward in every twentieth letter from right to left beginning from the second Hebrew letter yod in the phrase "He shall prolong 'Ya'rik'" which produces the phrase "Yeshua Shmi" that means "Yeshua is my Name."

Many Christian scholars have quoted the Old Testament regarding the prophesies of Jesus's coming and His being the Messiah. Such studies are just supplementary to our search for the code and the possible answer to the question as to who is its author.

PART III

THE FINDINGS

A code was found, and the findings were incredible. The personalities, doctrines, and symbols narrated and expounded in the Bible were in the code, even the genealogy of Adam.

CHAPTER IV

THE NEW TESTAMENT

As the source of the Lord's Prayer is the New Testament, it is but natural that the New Testament be scrutinized as to its genuineness and authenticity. What is the New Testament?

The New Testament is the story about the Christian Savior of the world named Jesus who descended into this world and became man. He performed many miracles like raising the dead, making the blind see, and the lame to walk. Although he came from Israel, he taught a different doctrine from the Jews—"Love your enemies"[1] instead of "An eye for an eye."[2] Because of his revolutionary doctrines, he was crucified and killed, yet he cried out in the cross, "Forgive them for they know not what they do."[3] Jesus's death instead of discouraging his followers became very zealous missionaries that resulted into what is now the Christian religion.

The New Testament is composed primarily of the four Gospels supposedly written by the four evangelists, namely, SS. Matthew, John, Luke, and Mark. Many Christians believe that the evangelists apostles Matthew and John were the apostles of Jesus. However, present studies and researches show that these were different persons who assumed the names of the apostles to give credence to their writings. The early Christian fathers, the most prominent of whom was Justin Martyr, did not know the existence of the Gospels even during the middle of the second century. Thus Justin defended the divinity of Jesus from writings based on the Old Testament and the prevailing apocryphal books. The Gospels were unheard of until AD 150. As to whether the apostles Matthew and John were the writers or not of the Gospels, are we still going to find evidences or references about Jesus and the other personalities mentioned in the New Testament in the grid if only to show that there is truly a code in the Lord's Prayer? As this is about the Lord's Prayer, for sure we will find references about it in the Gospels, and the name of Jesus and the other personalities mentioned in the New Testament will be found in the grid if only to show that there is truly a code in the Lord's Prayer.

The four Gospels were all written in Greek, and the earliest translation into another language was done around the third century. All writings about the Gospels up to AD 325 were lost or destroyed. The Gospels were again rewritten upon the order of Emperor Anastasius with so much revisions and editions to suit the interest of the church.

Biblical scholars say that the Gospel of Mark is the oldest among the four Gospels although Mark was not an eyewitness to Jesus, but a follower of Peter. He depended so much on the oral traditions, written stories and sayings handed down to him without verifying the authenticities of the stories/sources; thus, his Gospel was full of errors particularly in his citations from the Septuagint and descriptions of places in Palestine. Due to his ignorance of the Palestinian geography, he was not considered a Palestinian. There are evidences to show that the Gospel of Mark is based on the Latin version of the Gospel of the Lord written by Marcion decades before the Gospel of Mark. Yet Marcion was excommunicated by the church for supposedly plagiarizing the Gospel of Mark. Matthew and Luke were forced to write their own gospels due to the compelling necessity to correct the mistakes and wrong assumptions made by Mark in his Gospel. According to Rondel Maccraw Helms, author of the book *Who Wrote the Gospels?*, Matthew used six hundred verses out of the 666 verses in the Gospel of Mark while Luke used 50 percent of Mark's Gospel. These findings by the biblical scholars should awaken those who fanatically believe that the words in the Bible all came from God.

With respect to the Gospel of Luke, there is an opinion that the Gospel was written by a woman because of its contents that gave much importance to women and even discussed the subject of giving birth. There are also evidences that the Gospel of Luke is based on the Greek version of the Gospel of the Lord by Marcion whose Gospel was based on the story of Lord Krishna hence the title Gospel of the Lord. Marcion did not mention the name of Jesus in his Gospel but talked about a person addressed as the Lord. It is said that Marcion based his Gospel on the story of the Hindu savior Krishna, which he learned from the writings of Apollonius who had travelled to India.

As to the Gospel of John, the author also committed mistakes in the geographical descriptions of places in Judea that placed the nationality of John in question and as to whether he really came from the place. Further, many doubt that a mere fisherman could write such beautiful and elitist Greek language.

Even the writings of Paul are now in question. The supposedly genuine writings of Paul mentioned only a person addressed as Christ but not Jesus. The word *Christ* is a title meaning the "Anointed" or "Messiah" and does not refer to a name of a person. Thus, Paul did not mention any sermons of Jesus, his genealogy, the miracles Jesus performed, and even the Lord's Prayer. The name of Jesus was said to be just a later insertion to show that Paul was speaking about Jesus. It is

even alleged that Paul was actually a Gnostic, but his writings were revised to delete the Gnostic elements. Biblical scholars of different faiths have concluded that thirteen writings of Paul were all forgeries and even the seven supposed genuine writings of Paul were questionable. Thus, presently the authenticity and the genuiness of the New Testament are now in question.

The section on the "Authenticity of the Gospels" further explains the question about the authenticity and genuiness of the Gospels.

a) The Name

One of the most loved and revered name in the world is the name Jesus. This name has given hope and inspiration to millions of people, yet it has also brought sufferings and death to many. Though the name connotes "salvation," it has also brought "destruction." There is nothing wrong about the "name" but the misinterpretation and fanaticism that went with the "name."

Jesus was known in Israel as Yehoshuah, Yeshuah, Yeshua, or Joshua. In Greek, he was known as Iesous while in the modern world he is now known as Jesus. According to the Gospels of Matthew and Luke, Jesus was the source of the Lord's Prayer. If this is so, then the name of Jesus must be in the grid.

The holy name IHVH in relation to Jesus

The holiest name of God in Hebrew is IHVH or YHVH. As this most revered name is supposed to be the name of the Father, it only follows that the name of Jesus has connection to this holy name as Jesus has said, "The Father and I are One." How do we prove the truth of Jesus allegation? Kabalistically, the name of Jesus is written as YHShVH. It is obvious that the name of the Father is in the name of Jesus. It is only the insertion of the letter *Sh* that differentiates the name of the Father, YHVH from the Son, YHShVH. As the letter *Sh* means "fire," then Jesus is the "fire" of the Father. In the holy name IHVH the letters *I*, *H*, and the final *H* refer to the father, mother, and daughter respectively while the letter *V* in the holy name represents Jesus or the Son, which is the result of the union of *I* and *H*, the father and mother, the masculine and feminine energies respectively. It alludes to the power to convert and interrelate to all of creations. Thus, the V form or the alignment of letters or words in a V formation refers to the Son who is known as Zauir Anpin, the Microproposos or the Less Countenance, the Son of God. The form of V in Hebrew is like an upright stature of a man standing on the ground looking up to heaven.

Numerically, the letter *V* is equivalent to six, which refers to the six days of creation and to the Sephera Tiphereth, which is located at the center of the Tree of Life and which the Christian Kabalists call the Christ Center. The letter

V also alludes to Zauir Anpin, which according to the Kabalah covers the six Sephera beginning from Tiphereth to Malkuth. In other words, the Son rules the six worlds or heavens.

		A	B	C	D	E	F	G	H	I	J	K	L
1			V				Sh			Sh			
2												Sh	Sh
3										V			
4													
5													
6			Sh										
7													
8													
9													
10										V			
11							Sh						
12													
13							V					V	
14						V							
15													
16													
17													

Fig. 3 The letters Sh and V.

The letter *V* can be written as a *V*, *O*, or as *U*. Out of the 198 letters of the Lord's Prayer, there are nineteen *V* letters with six *V* letters in *V* form and thirteen letters in *U* form as shown in figure 3. To write the letter *U* six times in the form of the letter *V* could not have been a coincidence, but a deliberate act. As the *V* form and the number six refer esoterically to the Son; thus the choice of the *V* formation is an acknowledgment of the Kabalistic knowledge of the author of the code.

As stated before, the letter *Sh*, which means "fire" has been inserted between the letters *IH* and *VH* to form the name YHShVH, which means YEHOShUAH. The reason why it is the letter *Sh* that is inserted is because the Son is considered the "fire of the Father." It will be noted that the letter *Sh* has also been written six times as if to emphasize the importance of the number 6, which again alludes to the Son. It is obvious therefore that the use of the letters *V* and *Sh* six times each is to emphasize the references to the son. If this is so, where is the name of Jesus in the grid?

Jesus's Name in the Grid

How do we look for the name? How will it appear or be spelled in the grid? Will it be the English version—Jesus or the Hebrew name Yehoshuah or the shortened name Yeshu or Yeshua? Mr. Grant Jeffreys explained how the name Yeshua, which he believed as the true name of Jesus, became transformed to the shortened form Yeshu. According to him, due to the expansion of the church in the first century, the Jews became resentful of Jesus and the shortened name of Jesus—Yeshu—began to appear in the rabbinic literature known as Toledot Yeshu, which was anti-Jesus. This literature revealed that some Jews shortened the name of Jesus to show their rejection of Jesus claim to be the Messiah and the Son of God. In ancient time, shortening of a name was a derogatory way of rejecting or cursing a person. Thus,

> The ancient enemies of Jesus used the expression as a curse "Yiach Shemo Uzikhro" which means, "May his name and memory be blotted out." The First letter of each word of the curse formed the three acronyms—the same spelling as Yeshu.[4]

However, today most modern Jews who commonly use the name Yeshu do not have the knowledge of this possible reason why the Jews have historically chosen to call Jesus by that name.

Search for the Name?

With 198 letters in the grid, there will certainly be many names that can be formed or found. However, one of the best proofs to prove who is the real author of the Lord's Prayer is to find his name in the grid, like a painter placing his signature in his work otherwise, the code will be questionable. As this is a Hebrew code, the name of Jesus must be in the Hebrew language. To find the name of Jesus in another language will be amazing. To find it in different languages will be incredible.

b) YESHUA: Hebrew Name of Jesus

From the Bible code, ancient writings, and the Dead Sea scrolls, the name of Jesus in Hebrew appears to be YEShUA that means "He shall save." Can this name be found in the grid? Yes! And there are other variants and other names of Jesus in other languages.

	A	B	C	D	E	F	G	H	I	J	K	L
1	A				U				Sh			
2	Y											
3												

Fig. 4 Yshua, the Hebrew name of Jesus.

Figure 4 shows the holy name YEShUA. The name YShUA is pronounced YEShUA, the holy name of Jesus. The example would seem to confirm that Jesus was indeed called YEShUA. The position of the name in the top of the grid implies the importance of the name. Coordinates = "Y" = A-2 "Sh" = I-1 "U"= E-1 "A" = A-1. ELS = 3 letters

Variants of Yeshua

The first variant of the holy name is YShU and pronounced as YEShU.

Coordinates: "Y"=A-2   Sh = I-1   U = E-1   ELS = 3 letters

	A	B	C	D	E	F	G	H	I	J	K	L
1					U				Sh			
2	Y											
3												

Fig. 5 Yshu.

The second example of the holy name shown in figure 5 is YShV and pronounced also as YEShU.

Coordinates: Y = D-2   Sh = I-1   V = B-2   ELS = 6 letters

	A	B	C	D	E	F	G	H	I	J	K	L
1		V							Sh			
2				Y								
3												

Fig. 6 The name Yshv.

The third example is YShA. The name is pronounced as IShA or EEShA and is also known in Arabia and India as ISSA/ISA. There are four other examples of the name YShA with different ELS namely:

Number of Examples	Coordinates			ELS
1st example	Y = D-2	Sh = K-2	A = F-3	6 letters
2nd example	Y = D-2	Sh = L-2	A = H-3	7 letters
3rd example	Y = D-3	Sh = L-2	A = H-2	3 letters
4th example	Y = E-8	Sh = F-11	A = G-14	36 letters.
5th example	Y = H-13	Sh = F-11	A = D-9	25 letters.

	A	B	C	D	E	F	G	H	I	J	K	L
1												
2				Y				A			Sh	Sh
3				Y		A		A				
4												
5												
6												
7												
8					Y							
9					A							
10												
11						Sh						
12												
13								Y				
14							A					
15												

Fig. 7 The name Ysha with different ELS.

Jesus's Name in Other Languages

As we go over the grid, it is surprising to find the name of Jesus in other languages.

The first example is the name of Jesus in Celtic and Gaellic—HESUS. The letters are found in the spaces composed of G-10-11, I-11, H-9 and I-9. By permutation, the name is formed. Although this is a name of Jesus,

what is surprising is that this name has been in used by the Celts around 834 BC, hundreds of years before the birth of the Christian Jesus.

	A	B	C	D	E	F	G	H	I	J	K	L
8												
9								U	S			
10							H					
11							E		S			
12												

Fig. 8 Hesus, Celtic and Gaellic ancient name of Jesus.

The second name of Jesus is in Hindu—ISSA/ISA/ISHA in different ELS. In India, Jesus was known as a holy man, a teacher, and a prophet who supposedly left India at the age of thirty and died in his country three years later. According to legends, the eighteen lost years of Jesus were spent in Egypt, Tibet, and India. In those countries, He studied and learned the Egyptian religion, Buddhism, and Hinduism.

	A	B	C	D	E	F	G	H	I	J	K	L
1												I
2												Sh
3												A
4												
5												
6							I			A		
7												
8												
9												
10												
11					Sh							
12												
13												
14												
15												
16		I			A							
17												

Fig. 9 Isha, Hindu name of Jesus.

Thus, many are saying that the teachings of Jesus have traces of Buddhism, especially the doctrines about love and compassion. In the book *The Lost Years of Jesus* by Elizabeth C. Prophet,[5] she said that there were documents in the monastery of Himis, Tibet, that confirmed about the stay of Jesus in Tibet she quoted some beautiful sayings about women that were supposedly made by St. Issa (Jesus) namely:

Chapter XII

9. Then Issa held forth: xxx Whosoever respecteth not his mother the most sacred being after his God, is not worthy of the name of son . . . .

12. She gives birth to you in the midst of suffering. By the sweat of her brow she rears you, and until her death you cause her the gravest anxieties. Bless her and worship her, for she is your new friend, your one support on earth.

14. In the same way, love your wives and respect them, for they will be mothers tomorrow, . . .

21. All that you do for your wife, your mother, for a widow or another woman in distress, you will have done unto your God.

	A	B	C	D	E	F	G	H	I	J	K	L
2												
3												
4				T								
5												
6			M	A	I							
7			R									
8												
9							M					
10						T	H					
11								R				
12							A					
13												
14			T	I								
15												
16			M	H	A							
17					R							

Fig. 10 Isa, Arabic and Hindu name of Jesus.

The third example is again the name of a holy man called ISSA/ISA who around 400 BCE lived in the western region of Hajaz, Arabia,[6] where places like Galilee, Bethsaida, and Nazareth existed unlike the town of Nazareth in Palestine that was nonexistent during the supposed time of Jesus. There were many similarities between Jesus and Issa/Isa. He was also born of a virgin and worshipped as the Divine Word by the ancient Arabian Nazara or Nazarenes of Arabia.[7] It could also be possible that the Isa of India was the same Isa of Arabia whose story became that of Jesus. Figure 10 shows the many names of Isa in the grid with different ELS excluding its variants Ysha and Isha, which are shown in figures 7 and 9 respectively. Why are there so many names of this holy man in the grid? What does it imply?

Number of Examples	Coordinates			ELS
1st example	I = L-1	S = I-9	A = F-17	96 letters
2nd example	I = K-6	S = I-9	A = G-12	33 letters
3rd example	I = F-15	S = G-15	A = H-15	none
4th example	I = A-17	S = G-15	A = A-14	17 letters

	A	B	C	D	E	F	G	H	I	J	K	L
6												
7									E			
8									E			
9									S			
10									U			
11									S			
12												

Fig. 11 Eesus, variant of Jesus.

Figure 11 shows the fourth example that is written as EESUS without ELS. This name is similar to the Celtic and Gaelic word HESUS. As previously explained in gematria, the letter *E* and the letter *H* can be interchanged for they both have the same numerical value of five hence EESVS can become HESVS, also the Philippine word for the name JESUS. It is uncanny how the Filipino name for Jesus is the same as that of the Celts and the Gaellic.

The appearance of Jesus name in different forms in Hebrew and other languages seem to attest to the truth about the existence of a person named Jesus and who could possibly be the author of the Lord's Prayer.

c) The Mysterious Names

The succeeding illustrations are intriguing because of the mysterious messages and names being conveyed by them. The first illustration is figure 12 in the middle of which is a cluster of letters that are in ELS in sequence and close to one another. The letters are:

	A	B	C	D	E	F	G	H	I	J	K	L
9							M					
10						T	H					
11						Sh						
12				G		M						
13			A		A							
14		L										
15				Y								
16												
17				H								

Fig. 12 What is the hidden name of the Messiah?

MShAYH = *"Messiah"* with ELS of twenty-two letters
Coordinates = M = G-9   Sh = F-11   A = E-13 Y = D-15 H = C-17

GAL = *"Redeemer"* has ELS of ten letters.
Coordinates = G = D-12   A = C-13   L = B-14.

The words MH meaning "what" is found at G-9-10, while TSh meaning "hidden" is at F-10-11. The word ShM meaning "name" is found at F-11-12 with the letters side by side without ELS.

The words can be formed into the following sentence: "MH TSh ShM MShAYH GAL." This Hebrew phrase can be translated "What is the hidden name of the Messiah, the Redeemer?" Why is this question being asked? Is not the Messiah Jesus? Does Jesus have a hidden name that only the apostles knew? Or are we talking about the name that Jesus gave to the apostles:

"And I have made known to them thy Name?"[1]

This name has never been explained by the New Testament and has remained a secret. Many occultists have searched for this name. As if to confirm this story about a secret name, the grid mentions SOD ShM which means "secret name."

	A	B	C	D	E	F	G	H	I	J	K	L
1									Sh	M		
2									D		Sh	Sh
3										O	M	
4											S	
5												

Fig. 13 Secret Name.

Whose Name Is in the Grid?

In figure 14, the following Hebrew words appear with different ELS, namely, *ShM*, *ShMI*, and *ShMO* which mean "name," "my name," and "his name" in English respectively. As can be gleaned from the grid, these words are mentioned many times as if emphasizing the importance of the name. Whose name is the grid referring to? Are we talking about the name of the author of the code or the Messiah? Is this a hint that we are not talking about Jesus, but another personality? There are many names that can be formed in the grid, but which is the right name and to whom does it refer? This kind of writing and formation is not a coincidence, but a deliberate act. This could only be a code, and this unbelievable writer is conveying a message here.

	A	B	C	D	E	F	G	H	I	J	K	L
1						Sh			Sh	M		
2		I									Sh	Sh
3										M		
4												
5												
6		Sh	M					M				
7												
8												
9												
10												
11						Sh				O		
12						M						
13												

Fig. 14 The words name, my name, and his name.

As we look over figure 15, there appears the word *ShMI*, which means "my name" with ELS of three letters between the desired letters *Sh* at F-1, *M* J-1, and *I* at B-2. Besides the letter *I* at B-2 is the letter *Y*, which is the initial letter of the name *YShUA*, the Hebrew name of Jesus and, going in the reverse direction, has also an ELS of three letters between the encoded letters *Sh* at I-1, *U* at E-1, and *A* at A-1. The two words *ShMI YShUA* mean "My Name is Jesus." It is unbelievable that in the first and second horizontal rows, we will find this message. Who is this YShUA? Is he JESUS of the Christians, the HESUS of the Druids and the Gaelic, the IUSA of the Egyptians, the JESEUS of India, the IASEUS of Crete, or the ISA of India and Arabia? Placing his name at the start of the grid is like naming the author of a book. How will we know?

	A	B	C	D	E		G	H	I	J	K	L
1	A				U	Sh			Sh	M		
2	Y	I										
3												

Fig. 15 Shmi Yshua.

ANI (I AM)

The word *ANI*, which means "I or I AM" has been mentioned in the grid fifteen times with different ELS. Who is this I or I AM? Is this the I AM THAT I AM, the AHIH ASHR AHIH, the God of Israel that the name should be written down fifteen times? Or is this the name of the mother INNA or INA whose number as AMA is 15?

Number of Examples	Coordinates			ELS
1st example	A = A-1	N = A-9	I = A-17	7 letters
2nd example	A = H-2	N = F-8	I = D-14	69 letters

	A	B	C	D	E	F	G	H	I	J	K	L
1	A											
2								A				
3												
4					A							
5						N						
6					I							
7												
8						N			N			
9	N											
10												
11					A							
12												
13								N				
14				I								I
15												
16	I											
17	I											

Fig. 16 ANI, I Am, first to fifth examples.

3rd example	A = H-2	N = J-8	I = L-14	73 letters
4th example	A = G-4	N = F-6	I = E-6	10 letters.
5th example	A = E-11	N = I-13	I = A-16	27 letters.

	A	B	C	D	E	F	G	H	I	J	K	L
1												I
2					I							
3												
4												
5												
6					I							N
7												
8						N			N			
9												
10			N									
11					A							A
12												
13					A				N			
14	A						A		N			
15						I		A				
16	I											
17												

Fig. 16-a I Am, sixth to eleventh examples.

6th example	A = L-11	N = L-6	I = L-1	14 letters
7th example	A = L-11	N = I-13	I = F-15	20 letters
8th example	A = E-13	N = I-14	I = A-16	15 letters
9th example	A = A-14	N = C-10	I = E-6	45 letters.
10th example	A = G-14	N = F-8	I = E-2	72 letters.
11th example	A = H-15	N = J-8	I = L-1	81 letters

		A	B	C	D	E	F	G	H	I	J	K	L
12													
13													
14					I-		.I						
15									,A			.N-	
16			,I.								N.		
17					A.		.A-						

Fig. 16-b I Am, twelfth to fifteenth examples.

12ᵗʰ example	A = H-15	N = K-15	I = B-16	2 letters
13ᵗʰ example	A = D-17	N = K-15	I = F-14	16 letters
14ᵗʰ example	A = F-17	N = K-15	I = D-14	18 letters
15ᵗʰ example	A = F-17	N = J-16	I = B-16	7 letters

To find fifteen examples with different ELS in a small grid is overwhelming. What kind of person has made this code? With many examples in different ELS, the possibility of this matter just being coincidences is already remote. For sure there was deliberateness and purpose. This could not just be coincidence, and we are just in the first part of the book.

Who Is ANI?

There are many examples of ANI that the question now is, who is ANI? The word *ANI* can be associated to several names mentioned in the grid. Foremost of the name is the holy name given to Moses—"Ahih Asher Ahih" (AAA). There are many examples in the grid, but I am only showing those examples sharing common letters with the word *ANI*.

		A	B	C	D	E	F	G	H	I	J	K	L
1		A											
2													
3													
4													
5													
6													
7			A										
8													
9		N											
10													
11													
12													
13				A									
14													
15													
16													
17		I											

Fig. 17 Ani AAA.

Number of Examples	Coordinates			ELS
1st example	A = A-1	N = A-9	I = A-17	7 letters
	A = A-1	A = B-7	A = C-13	13 letters
2nd example	A = H-2	N = F-8	I = D-14	69 letters
	A = H-1	A = H-2	A = H-3	13 letters

		A	B	C	D	E	F	G	H	I	J	K	L
1									A				
2									A				
3									A				
4													
5													
6													
7													
8						N					N		
9													
10													
11													
12													
13													
14				I									I
15													

Fig. 17-a Ani AAA (second and third examples).

3rd example	A = H-2	N = J-8	I = L-14	73 letters
	A = H-1	A = H-2	A = H-3	11 letters
4th example	A = G-4	N = F-5	I = E-6	10 letters
	A = J-2	A = G-4	A = D-6	20 letters

	A	B	C	D	E	F	G	H	I	J	K	L
1												
2										A		
3												
4							A					
5						N						
6				A	I							
7		A										
8												
9												
10												
11					A							
12												
13									N			
14												
15								A				
16	I											
17												

Fig. 17-b Ani AAA (fourth and fifth examples).

5th example	A = E-11	N = I-13	I = A-16	27 letters
	A = B-7	A = E-11	A = H-15	52 letters
6th example	A = E-11	N = I-13	I = A-16	27 letters
	A = E-11	A = E-12	A = E-13	13 letters

	A	B	C	D	E	F	G	H	I	J	K	L
11					A							A
12					A		A					
13					A				N			
14												
15							A					
16	I											
17												

Fig. 17-c Ani AAA (sixth and seventh examples).

7th example	A = E-11	N = I-13	I = A-16	27 letters
	A = E-7	A = L-11	A = G-12	6 letters
8th example	A = L-11	N = L-6	I = L-1	14 letters
	A = E-11	A = L-11	A = G-12	6 letters

	A	B	C	D	E	F	G	H	I	J	K	L
1												I
2												
3												
4												
5												
6												N
7												
8												
9												
10												
11					A							A
12							A					
13									N			
14												
15						I						
16												
17												

Fig. 17-d Ani AAA (eight and ninth examples).

9 example	A = L-11	N = I-13	I = F-15	20 letters
	A = E-11	A = L-11	A = G-12	6 letters
10 example	A = E-13	N = I-14	I = A-16	15 letters
	A = D-9	A = E-13	A = F-17	48 letters

	A	B	C	D	E	F	G	H	I	J	K	L
9				A								
10												
11					A							
12					A							
13					A							
14									N			
15												
16	I											
17						A						

Fig. 17-e Ani AAA (tenth and eleventh examples).

11th example   A = E-13   N = I-14   I = A-16   15 letters

                       A = E-11   A = E-12   A = E-13   13 letters

	A	B	C	D	E	F	G	H	I	J	K	L
6					I							
7												
8												
9												
10				N								
11												
12	A								A			
13			A		A							
14	A											
15												
16												
17												

Fig. 17-f Ani AAA (twelfth and thirteenth examples).

12th example	A = L-14	N = C-10	I = E-6	45 letters
	A = E-12	A = C-13	A = A-14	9 letters
13th example	A = A-14	N = C-10	I = E-6	45 letters
	A = I-12	A = E-13	A = A-14	7 letters
14th example	A = H-15	N = J-8	I = L-1	81 letters
	A = B-7	A = E-11	A = H-15	52 letters
15th example	A = H-15	N = K-15	I = B-16	81 letters
	A = B-7	A = E-11	A = H-15	52 letters

	A	B	C	D	E	F	G	H	I	J	K	L
1												I
2												
3												
4												
5												
6												
7		A										
8										N		
9												
10												
11					A							
12												
13												
14												
15								A			N	
16		I										
17												

Fig. 17-g Ani AAA (fourteenth and fifteenth examples).

16th example	A = F-17	N = K-15	I = D-14		18 letters
	A = D-9	A = E-13	A = F-17		48 letters
17th example	A = F-17	N = J-16	I = B-16		18 letters
	A = D-9	A = E-13	A = F-17		7 letters

	A	B	C	D	E	F	G	H	I	J	K	L
9				A								
10												
11												
12												
13				A								
14				I								
15											N	
16		I								N		
17						A						

Fig. 17-h Ani AAA (sixteenth and seventeenth examples).

I am ISA

A further examination of the grid shows very fascinating phrases in figure 18. In A-1 is the letter *A*, which is the initial letter of the word *ANI* which means "I or I AM."

		A	B	C	D	E	F	G	H	I	J	K	L
1		A											
2													
3													
4													
5													
6						I							
7													
8													
9		N											
10				N									
11													
12													
13													
14		A											
15								S					
16													
17		I											

Fig. 18 Ani Isa.

It reads vertically downward with ELS of seven letters between the encoded letters. Its final letter *I* on A-17 is the initial letter of the name ISA, which goes to G-15 and then to A-14 with ELS of seventeen letters between the desired letters. The verse ANI ISA means "I AM ISA." To start at the first slot of the grid and the first vertical row shows the importance of the name, and it is a continuing verse with the final *I* of ANI becoming the initial letter of ISA.

The next verse shown in figure 19 starts with the letter *A* of the word *ANI* at L-11 and going vertically upward has ELS of four letters between the encoded letters. The final letter of ANI, the letter *I* becomes the initial letter of the word *ISA* and going diagonally downward has ELS of ninety-two letters between the desired letters *I* at L-1, *S* at I-9, and *A* at F-17.

The next example has an ELS of seventeen letters between the letters *I* at A-17, *S* at G-15, and the final *A* at A-14, which is the initial letter of the word *ANI* with ELS of forty-five letters between the letters *N* at C-10 and *I* at E-6. The phrase formed is "ISA ANI" or "ISA, I AM, or I AM ISA."

	A	B	C	D	E	F	G	H	I	J	K	L
1												I
2												
3												
4												
5												
6					I							N
7												
8												
9									S			
10			N									
11												A
12												
13									N			
14	A											
15						I	S	A			N	
16		I										
17	I					A						

Fig. 19 I am Isa.

The other example has ELS of twenty letters between the encoded letters *A* at L-11, *N* at 1-13, and *I* at F-15. The final letter *I* of ANI becomes again the initial letter *I* of the name ISA whose letters are side by side without ELS at F-15, G-15 and H-15.

The last example starts with the letter *I* of the word *ISA* at F-15 and going in the right direction, the letters *I*, *S*, and *A* are side by side without ELS. Again the final letter *A* of ISA becomes the initial letter *A* of ANI and going in the right direction has an ELS of two letters between the encoded letters forming the verse "ISA ANI," "I AM ISA."

Who is ISA?

Who is this entity whose name has been mentioned five times in the grid? ISA in Sanskrit means "Lord" or "Master." In Filipino, ISA means "One." According to a legend narrated by Elizabeth C. Prophet,[2] Jesus stayed in India and was known as St. ISA. Acharya S[3] said that there was a holy man in Arabia who was similar to Jesus, worshipped by the Nazarenes as the Divine Word and lived in the town of Nazareth when Jesus was not yet born and the town of Nazareth in Philistine has not yet existed. His name was ISA. The name ISA is a variant of ISHA or YSHA, which is a variant of YSHUA. Horus was also known as IUSA. According to Murry Hope,[4] there is a planet called by the psychics as ISHNA in the Siriun system where an advanced race of hominids known as the Crystal People or Ishnaans lived. Is ISA from ISHNA like IUSA and AS/ISIS who were supposed to be from the Siriun system? Who is ISA?

The unbelievable examples given show the importance of this entity. It also presents one of the most compelling evidences to show that the Lord's Prayer is not just a prayer but a code with a message. What could be the mathematical ratio/odds of finding five verses with the same words and letters with different ELS and yet giving the same message in a grid composed of only 198 letters? In all my research and study, I have never found anything like this.

According to Michael Drosnin[5] quoting Dr. Eli Rips, the words *code key* crossing twice the words *mouth of the obelisks* have odds of one million to one. In the words of Dr. Rips, "in the history of code research no other has had such high statistics." I wonder what could be the odds of this discovery.

I am IEVE

Another intriguing example is the verse "ANI IEVE," which means "I AM IHVH." In Greek, the holy name IHVH is written as IEVE, which is said to be the right pronunciation of the unpronounceable name based on the Greek alphabet. The verse was mentioned thrice in the grid.

The first example has ELS of twenty-seven letters between the encoded letters *A* at E-11, *N* at I-13, and *I* at A-16. The final letter *I* of ANI, which is the first letter of IEVE is at A-16 and going upward in a diagonal direction, has an ELS of nine letters between the encoded letters *I*, *E*, *V*, and *E*. It is noticeable that the ELS of ANI, twenty-seven is a multiple of the ELS of IEVE—nine.

	A	B	C	D	E	F	G	H	I	J	K	L
1												
2					I-							
3	E								V			
4					E							
5												
6												
7												
8						N-						
9												
10												
11					.A							
12					A							
13					A.		E		.N			
14					V	A-			N.			
15			E									
16	.I.											
17												

Fig. 20 Ani IEVE.

The second example of ANI has ELS of fifteen letters between the desired letters *A* at E-13, *N* at I-14, and *I* at A-16. The last letter *I* of ANI, which is the initial letter of IEVE is at A-16 and going diagonally upward, has ELS of nine letters between the encoded letters.

The third example has ELS of seventy-two letters between the encoded letters *A* at G-14, *N* at F-8, and *I* at E-2. Again the final letter *I* of ANI in E-2 is the initial letter of the name IEVE, which has ELS of seven letters between the desired letters going in the right direction.

The examples show the word *ANI* sharing the letter *I* with IEVE. Also the letter *A* of ANI in the first and second examples comprises the two letter As of the name AAA in E-11-12-13, which means "AHIH ASHR AHIH" or "I AM THAT I AM," the holy name given to Moses at Mt. Sinai. What could be the odds of these words being connected in a verse and in different ELS?

	A	B	C	D	E	F	G	H	I	J	K	L
1	A				U				Sh			
2	Y											
3												
4												
5												
6												
7												
8												
9	N											
10												
11												
12												
13												
14												
15												
16												
17	I											

Fig. 21 Yeshua Ani.

One more beautiful example shown in figure 21 is the verse "YSHUA ANI," which means "I AM YSHUA" or "JESUS." The name YShUA has an ELS of three letters between the desired letters *Y* at A-2, *Sh* at I-1, *U* at E-1, and *A* at A-1. The final letter *A* of YShUA is the initial letter *A* of the word *ANI* that has ELS of seven letters between the desired letters. Again, what could be the odds of these words being interconnected?

Who is Aeshhu?

Another interesting discovery is a mysterious name in the center of the grid in a letter V formation as shown in figure 22. It starts with the letter *A* on D-9 and going down diagonally to the letter *Sh* and then diagonally upward, forms the name AEShHU.

	A	B	C	D	E	F	G	H	I	J	K	L
9				A				U				
10					E		H					
11						Sh						
12												

Fig. 22 Who is Aeshhu?.

I placed this name in a separate illustration to show the beauty of its formation and the hidden names contained within this name. But whose name is this? Why should it be in the center of the grid? Is this the name of Jesus? If so, why is it spelled differently, and why are the letters in V formation? Or is this the new name promised in the Bible to be given to the worthy.

Reasons for the V formation

What is the significance if the name is in a V formation as shown in figure 22? The V formation in the Kabalah as previously explained has a very profound implication, which only a Kabalist can understand. The presence of such formation itself is a confirmation that the placing of the letters was carefully designed and thought of and not just plain coincidence.

	A	B	C	D	E	F	G	H	I	J	K	L
1						Sh				M		
2		I										
3												
4												
5												
6								M				
7												
8												
9				A				U				
10					E		H					
11						Sh			O			
12												

Fig. 23 Shmo Aeshhu.

The mere choice of a V formation hinted to the Kabalistic knowledge of the author of this code for the letter *V* is part of the *unpronounceable* name of God IHVH or YHVH and refers to the Son. This in itself is already a clue as to who is the owner of that name, thus, interest to look at this new name. It is even located at the center of the grid. My curiosity was aroused because I did not know this name, and why would such a name be located in the center? Furthermore, it was at this point when I began to encounter surprises in making this book. When I started this book, I only knew how to input the words but not underlining or accentuating the words, thus my surprise when suddenly I found the word *unpronounceable* underlined. I left the style as is as it might be a reminder for me to be respectful of the holy name.

The words *ShMI AEShHU* or *ShMO AEShHU* can be translated as "My Name is Aeshhu" or "His Name is Aeshhu" respectively.

Is AeShhu Yeshhu?

As written, the name AEShHU cannot be the name of Jesus, for there is no Kabalistic book whether old or new that discusses it. How then do we prove that it is connected to the name of Jesus? In this case, I have relied on the Kabalah particularly in gematria rather than ELS to analyze such.

As previously explained, letters with the same numerical values like the following letters *A, I, Y, J,* and *Q* could be interchanged as they all have the same numerical values of one as shown below.

A-1   I-10   Y-10   J-10   Q-100

Taking out the zeroes from the number correspondences of the letters *I, Y, J,* and *Q*, we will have all the letters with the numerical value of 1; hence, such letters are equal and can therefore be interchanged.

Based on the above explanation, if the letter *A* will be replaced by the letter *Y*, the name AEShHU can become YEShHU, the Hebrew name of Jesus. If we did not know gematria, this word would have remained hidden and taken only as a cluster of letters without meaning. Hence, we can see the importance of the Kabalah in the interpretation of Jewish esoteric teachings. The name YASHU is read as YESHU.

	A	B	C	D	E	F	G	H	I	J	K	L
8												
9				A				U				
10					E		H					
11						Sh						
12				A								
13				Y								
14												

Fig. 24 Yashhu, a variant of Yeshuh.

As I looked for other possible hidden name in the new name AEShHU, I found one. It is a name with much mystery and implications. If we will add the letter *E* to YEShHU as seen in the pattern, it will become YEShHUE. Using gematria, the letters *E* and *H* have the same numerical values of five; hence, they can be interchangeable. YEShHUE can therefore become YEShHUH, which in Hebrew can also be written down as YShHVH without the vowel *E*.

According to the Kabalah, the Son is the fire of the Father thus the letter word *Shin* meaning "fire" is inserted in the unpronounceable name YHVH to refer to the Son. There are two versions as to where the letter *Sh* will be inserted, one is YHShVH and the other is YHVShH. Most of the old and well-known Kabalistic writers say that the name of Jesus in Hebrew should be written down as YHShVH. Some modern writers suggest that it should be YHVShH. However, the writers never explained why the *Sh* should be placed in a particular position. As to who is right, nobody is sure. The place where the letter *Sh* is inserted is very important in ritualistic rites as one is used for invoking and the other is used for vanishing.

Personally, I tried to rationalize why the letter *Sh* is placed in a certain position. There must be a very good reason for it for Kabalists just do not place or write a letter or word without a purpose. If the word *Shin* means "fire" or "energy"; then placing it between the letters *H* and *V* as in YHShVH can mean that the fire or energy is coming from *H* the Mother to *V* the Son that made the Son tender and loving. While the Shin between the letters *V* and the final *H* can mean the fire or energy between the Son and the Daughter that created the doctrine of brotherly love in the Christian teachings. Thus, the third and newest version, the missing one, the letter "Shin" is placed between the letters *Y* and *H* as in YShHVH, which means that the energy coming from *Y* the Father unites with *H* the Mother resulting in *V* the Son. Thus, if one can unite the positive and the negative, the yin and the yang then there will be unity, balance and harmony or energy.

70

The New Name

The new and third version YShHVH, which is different from the names espoused by the old and modern Kabalists can only be found in the code, which is based on the Lord's Prayer. Only meditations, ritualistic use of the name, and future experiences will show the power and effectivity of this new name, which brings to mind Revelations 3:12[6] that states:

> And I write upon him . . . my new Name.

Can this be the possible hidden name of Jesus or the secret name of the Father, whom Jesus said was given to the apostles? Some people advised me not to print this new name as this is supposed to be a secret and only for those who are worthy. But who am I to decide who is worthy? I felt also that this might be the right time after several centuries to reveal this name.

I was determined to print the name until I was invited to a Taoist temple where mediumship was being practiced. There I was told by automatic writing not to print the name, as it was not yet time and to let each man receive the name individually according to his worth.

Considering that I am a Catholic, and to me, the temple was a neutral ground, I reconsidered my desire to print the name. Many months have passed since I again took up writing this book.

Another name which seems to point to Jesus is shown in figure 25 and starts with the letter *Y* on the D-13 and going diagonally upward, forms the word *YAShHU*, which if combined with the name AEShHU forms the letter *Y*. *Y* is the first letter of Jesus's name in Hebrew—YHShUH—pronounced Yehoshuah and the symbol of the crucified Christ.

The word *YAShHU* can be read as "YEShHU." By gematria, if we add the letter *E* at the end of the name, it would become YShHUE, which can be converted into YEShHUH then to YShHUH. Through such Kabalistic method of decoding, it can be inferred that it can be the name of Jesus; however, it can be the secret name of another divine entity or the Messiah that the Jews are still awaiting to come.

	A	B	C	D	E	F	G	H	I	J	K	L
7												
8									E			
9								U				
10							H					
11						Sh						
12					A		A					
13				Y				Y				

Fig. 25 Another variant of Yeshuh.

Although, we are able to show some connections with the name of Jesus, still there persisted this feeling that these newly discovered names maybe the names of ancient personalities that became the basis of Jesus name and story. As we are supposed to look for the author of the Lord's Prayer, then let us continue with our search.

d) Symbols

Jesus is known by many affiliations and symbols like Lamb of God, Fish, The Way, The Truth and the Life. Although these symbols have been known and used before Jesus's time, it was the New Testament that made them famous and popular in the present time. Is it possible to find all these symbols in the grid? To find them all will further affirm that this code is not just a coincidence but a well-thought-of code. The succeeding figures will show the symbols, Hebrew affiliations ands words related to Jesus. In the illustrations, you will notice that the words are very close to one another and sometimes even crisscrossing each other. Figure 26 shows the following words with the letters side by side without ELS except "KBSh" and forming the desired words.

The Lamb

EL = "God" which is written many times in the grid.
KR = "Lamb" Coordinates = B-4-5 and C-8-7
TL = "Lamb" Coordinates = G-7 and H-7; H-8-7; C-14 and B-2.
KBSh = "Lamb" Coordinates = G-2-1 and F-1.
CHI = "Life" Coordinates = E-3-2; G-5-6; J-7 and K-6

	A	B	C	D	E	F	G	H	I	J	K	L
1						Sh	B					
2					I		K					
3	E				Ch							
4	L	K										
5		R					Ch					
6							I				I	
7			R				T	L	E	Ch		
8			K					T				
9						O						
10						T	H	O				
11												
12												
13												
14		L	T									
15			E									
16												
17												

Fig. 26 The different words meaning the "Lamb."

One of the most famous titles addressed to Jesus is being the Lamb of God. It is unbelievable that the words *KR*, *TL*, and *KBSh*, which all mean "Lamb" are written seven times in Hebrew for the number 7 connotes spirituality or holiness, which aptly describes Jesus.

Figure 27 shows the following words:

BAR = "Son" Coordinates = A-7, B-7 and C-7 without ELS.

		A	B	C	D	E	F	G	H	I	J	K	L
1													
2													
3		E											
4		L	K										
5		H	R										
6		A	Sh	M	A								
7		B	A	R									
8													
9							O						
10								H	O				

Fig. 27 Words related to the Lamb.

AB = "Father" Coordinates = A-6-7; B-7 and A-7 without ELS.
HO = "Search" Coordinates = G-10, H-10 and F-9 without ELS.
HSh = "Salvation" Coordinates = H = A-5 and Sh = B-6;

The words *AB BAR* can mean the "Son of the Father." And "KR AB" can be translated as "Lamb of the Father."

Other phrases that can be formed out of figures 26 and 27 are the following:

"ShMA KR EL BAR AB MR" can be interpreted as "Listen to the Lamb of God, Son of the Father, speak."

"ShMa HSh KR EL BAR AB" can be interpreted as "Search for Salvation in the Lamb of God, Son of the Father."

The above translation conjoins with what St. John said,

The next day, John saw Jesus coming to him, and he said, "Behold, the Lamb of God who takes away the sins of the world."[1]

The Fish

Another famous symbol of Jesus is the Fish, which is here represented by the Hebrew word *NUN* shown in figure 28. It will be noted that the word *NUN* was printed many times and sometimes crisscrossing one another. This reminds us of what Matthew said:

> As he was walking by the Sea of Galilee, he saw two brothers, Simon who is called as Peter, and his brother Andrew, casting a net into the sea (for they were fishermen). And He said to them "Come, follow Me and I will make you fishers of men."[2]

The Greek word *ICHTUS* means "Fish" shown in the quadrant composed of K-6, J-6, H-8-9 and I-9. By permutation, the word is formed. By notarikon, IChThUS was interpreted "Iesous Christos Theou Uios Soter or Jesus Christ, the Son of God, the Saviour."[3]

The Egyptian word *RM* means "FISH" and when reversed forms the word *MR*, which means to "LOVE." This again is an apt description of Jesus, the God of Love. The fish has been a favorite symbol of ancient deities and saviors. The god Oannes of Sumer was in the form of a merman while the god Vishnu of India reincarnated as a fishman called Matsya.[4] The ancient gods of China like Emperor Yu and Nu Gun were supposed to be mermen from another planet.

	A	B	C	D	E	F	G	H	I	J	K	L
4												
5		R										
6			M						I			
7			R							Ch		
8								T				
9	N	U						U	S			
10			N		T							
11		N	U									
12		N	U	G							N	
13			Y						N	U		
14									N	U		
15											N	
16												
17												

Fig. 28 Words related to fish.

The Cross

The cross is another symbol of Jesus, which is represented here by the Hebrew word *TAU* and the Greek word *CHI*; both words also symbolize the ANKH, the Egyptian cross. Figure 29 shows the words.

	A	B	C	D	E	F	G	H	I	J	K	L
1												
2					I							
3					Ch		T	A	V			
4							A					
5						N	Ch	A				
6							I				I	
7							T			Ch		
8		U	K									
9			H	A								
10			N			T						
11												
12			U									
13			A								U	
14		A	T									
15												

Fig. 29 Words related to the Cross.

TAU/TAV = the symbol of the "Cross." There are other examples in the grid.

CHI = the Greek word symbolizing the "Cross" and the Hebrew word for "Life."

ANKH/ANCH = the Egyptian "Cross" symbolizing also "Life."

This symbol of the cross is one of the most misunderstood teachings of Jesus. When Jesus said to carry one's cross, it was interpreted to mean that everyone has to carry the cross of sufferings and poverty, but what is actually meant was for everybody to carry the cross of love, for without love there would be much sufferings and poverty.

Even the simple making of the sign of the cross was handed down to us erroneously all because of the chauvinistic attitude of the early Christian fathers.

The Gnostic Sign of the Cross

The Gnostics, who believed in the God the Mother were expelled by the church and were considered heretics for this belief. The irony, however, is that the church is only short of proclaiming Mary a goddess. She is called the Immaculate Conception, the Queen of Archangels, the Queen of Heavens. The early Christians believed in God the Mother; thus, their sign of the cross included the Mother. The church banned this form of the sign of the cross although it is very logical than the present sign of the cross by Christians. The cross is supposed to symbolize four points, four directions, and four corners of the world. Thus the sign of the cross that I used is as follows:

> In the Name of the Father, (fingers at the forehead) and of the Mother, (fingers at the navel) and of the Son (fingers at the right shoulder) and of the Holy Spirit. (fingers at the left shoulder) Amen.

These four entities are mentioned to truly reflect the four points in the cross. I placed the "Son" at the right shoulder because according to the Nicene Creed "The Son is seated at the right hand of the Father." Hence symbolically the Son is at the right side of the Father. The Christian's sign of the cross represents the "Trinity." The Christians just accepted what the church imposed without any question even if it was illogical since a Trinity could not possibly represent a cross that is symbolic of four points. In its desire to justify the representation, the church cut up into two, the words *Holy Spirit* with the word *holy* referring to the left shoulder and the word *spirit* referring to the right shoulder. This was made in order that the Trinity could represent the four points of the Cross. Another seeming mistake is the referral of the Son to the abdomen when making the sign of the cross since it is stated in the Nicene Creed that Jesus is seated at the right hand of God. Thus, the Son should be referred to the right shoulder as the Gnostics did with the Mother being referred to the abdomen and the Holy Spirit to the left shoulder. This matter was just discussed to show our tendency just to follow without question the teachings of our religious leaders no matter how illogical.

JHS

Another well-known symbol of Jesus are the letters IHS or JHS, which means "Jesus Homo Salvador" or in English "Jesus Savior of Men." This symbol is shown in figure 30 in a beautiful circular design composed of seven letters. As stated previously, by gematria the letters *A, Y, I,* and *J* are interchangeable because they have the same numerical value of 1; hence, A=Y=I=J. Thus, YHS becomes JHS or IHS while AHS becomes JHS or IHS. And also the letter *U* is

interchangeable with the letter *S* as both letters have the same numerical values of 6. Thus, AHU becomes JHS or IHS.

In this kind of decoding, we cannot use the ELS, hence the reliance on the Kabalistic method of decoding.

A famous Filipino occultist, M. Sabino[5] explained the initials JHS as follows:

JOC HOC SANGUINIS   JAC HOC SARSOMO
JESUS HOC SALVATOR   JESUS HOMINU SALVATOR
JAH HOCLUM SARSOMOM   JER HUH SALEM
JUMEN HITRES SUVIT   JUPJAUM HOLJUM SABTISJIS

	A	B	C	D	E	F	G	H	I	J	K	L
6												
7												
8							U					
9					Y				S			
10							H					
11					A				S			
12							A					
13												
14												
15							S					
16				H								
17		I										

Fig. 30 A beautiful pattern representing JHS.

It will be noticed that the words are a mixture of Latin, Hebrew, and another language that unfortunately is unknown to me. Maybe a reader will be able to translate the words.

JHS and Dionysus

It is said that the first one to use the symbol IHS was DIONYSUS a prototype of Jesus who was worshiped by the Jews in 1 BCE before Jesus was supposed to be born. If one will take out the letters *D*, *I*, *O*, and *N* from the name, what will be left will be the letters *Y*, *S*, *U*, and *S*, which can be read as YSUS or JESUS.

Actually he was also called IASIUS. The letters IHS or IES have the etymological meaning of "One" for "I" and "Fire" or "Light" for "ES."

What is so important about Dionysus? What is his relation to Jesus? What were astonishing about Dionysus were his similarities with Jesus. According to Acharya S,[6]

1. Dionysus was born of a virgin on December 25 and rose from the dead on March 25.
2. A miracle worker who was called King of Kings, God of Gods, Only Begotten Son, Saviour, Redeemer, Sin Bearer, Anointed One, and the Alpha and Omega.

If this will be the first time that one will know about the correspondences between Jesus and Dionysus, one will be amazed and some questions might begin to wander in one's mind. But the story of Dionysus is just one of those stories that are similar with Jesus, which shall be discussed later.

Greek Symbol 888

Another symbol of Jesus is represented by the numbers 888. These are very sacred numbers for the Greeks, for they represent the sum total of the numeral correspondences of the Greek alphabet and the name of Jesus in Greek—IESOUS—shown in table 4.

The numbers are represented by the letters *Ch* in the grid as the numeral correspondence of the letter *Ch* is 8. Thus if the three letters *Ch* in the grid will be replaced by the number 8, the letters will appear as 888.

	A	B	C	D	E	F	G	H	I	J	K	L
1												
2												
3					8							
4						8						
5							8					
6												
7												

Fig. 31 Greek symbol for Jesus.

e) Christian Doctrines

Some of the most beautiful sayings of Jesus are about love and forgiveness that became fundamental teachings of Christianity. As the basis of this code is the Lord's Prayer, can we find these Christian doctrines in the grid? Figure 32 shows a cluster of Hebrew words and their meanings that are very familiar to us, known as basic doctrines of Christianity. They are,

Bread of Life

ANI = *I*   LECHEM = *Bread*   ChI = *Life*

The phrase "ANI LECHEM ChI" means "I am the Bread of Life" that St. John said,

> I am the Bread of Life. He who comes to Me shall not hunger and he who believes in Me shall never thist.[1]

	A	B	C	D	E	F	G	H	I	J	K	L
1												
2												
3												
4							A					
5						N	Ch					
6					I		I					
7								L	E	Ch	E	M
8												

Fig. 32 Bread of Life.

Light of the World

ANI = *I, I am*   AR= *Light*   MA = *nation, world*
B'ARETz = *Earth, World*

Another phrase is "ANI AR B'ARETz" that can be translated as "I am the Light of the World," which reminds us of John's saying,

I am the Light of the World. He who follows Me does not walk in darkness but will have the light of life.[2]

	A	B	C	D	E	F	G	H	I	J	K	L
4							A					
5						N						
6			M	A	I							
7		B	A	R	E	Tz						
8												
13												
14						I						
15											N	
16			M									
17				A	R							

Fig. 33 Light of the World.

The verse "ANI AR MA" also means "I am the light of the world." The word *ANI* has ELS of sixteen letters between the desired letters *A* at D-17, *N* at K-15, and *I* at F-14. The word *AR* starts with the letter *A* also on D-17 and is side by side with the letter *R*. The word *MA* starts with the letter *M* on C-16 and going to the right direction has an ELS of twelve letters before reaching the letter *A* on D-17.

The Way, the Truth, and the Life

ANI = *I, I am*   VIA = *Way*   AMET= *Truth*   CHI = *Life*

The verse "AMET ANI" means "I am the Truth." The word *AMET* is in a perfect square in the middle of the grid while the word *ANI* starts with the letter *A* of AMET on E-11 and going in the right direction has an ELS of twenty-seven letters between the encoded letters *N* at I-13 and *I* at "A-16.

	A	B	C	D	E	F	G	H	I	J	K	L
1												
2					I-							
3					Ch							
4												
5												
6												
7												
8						N-						
9												
10						T						
11					A.		E					
12						M						
13									N.			
14					V	I	A-					
15												
16	I.											
17												

Fig. 34 I am the Way, the Truth, and the Life.

The verse "ANI CHI" means "I am the Life." The word *ANI* has ELS of seventy-two letters between the encoded letters *A* at G-14, *N* at F-8, and *I* at E-2. The last letter *I* of ANI is also the final letter of the word *CHI*.

The words *VIA ANI* mean, "I am the Way." The word *VIA* is found at E-14, F-14 and G-14 without ELS. The final letter *A* of VIA is the initial letter of the word *ANI* on G-14, *N* at F-8, and *I* at E-2 with an ELS of seventy-two letters between the encoded letters.

The preceding verses became the famous saying of Jesus "ANI VIA AMET CHI" that means, "I am the Way, the Truth and the Life" that John wrote,

> Thomas said to him, "Lord we do not know where thou art going. How can we know the way?" Jesus told him: "I am the Way, The Truth and the Life. No one comes to the Father but Through Me.[3]

This is one saying that has been misinterpreted by many to mean that if one is not a Christian or does not believe in Jesus, one cannot come to the Father or be saved. Can it not be said that Jesus is Love and without Love (Jesus), no one can come to the Father of Love? Thus any Christian or pagan who knows how to love can be with the Father. This reminds us of what John said,

God is Love, and he who abides in love, abides in God and God in him.[4]

Here there is no mention of a person being a Christian or a Jewish or a Muslim, but a person who knows how to love.

	A	B	C	D	E	F	G	H	I	J	K	L
5												
6									K	A		
7								L	E	Ch		
8												

Fig. 35 Word meaning doctrine.

The word *LEKACh* which means "doctrine" again reminds us of what St. John said in chapter 7:16:

My doctrine is not mine but his that sent me.[5]

The Son of God

The Hebrew words *BN EL* mean "the Son of God" that Luke said,

But Mary said to the angel, "How shall this happen since I do not know Man?" And the angel answered and said to her, "The Holy Spirit shall come upon thee and the Power of the Most High shall overshadow thee; and therefore the Holy One to be born shall be called the Son of God."[6]

	A	B	C	D	E	F	G	H	I	J	K	L
5												B
6												N
7											E	
8											L	

Fig. 36 Son of God.

As I was writing the book, the phrase "How can this be since I do not know man?" became in italic form without my intervention, it just appeared in such

format. It would seem that a message is being given emphasizing the purity and chastity of Mary. If the Quran, the holy book of the Muslims accepts the virgin birth of Jesus, how come many Christian sects cannot accept the same?

The Word Became Flesh

Figure 37 shows a cluster of words without ELS but conveying a famous doctrine of the church.

A = from   MO = womb   CHN = immaculate   EL = God
BN = son   M = mother   AIN = Infinite   AS = conceive

From the cluster of words, one can form the following verse "A MO CHN AM BN AIN EL AS," which can loosely be interpreted as "From the womb of the Immaculate Mother the Son of the Infinite God was conceived," which reminds us of St. John's saying,

And the Word became flesh and dwelt among us.[7]

The Christians accept the doctrine as a matter of fact without questions. Nobody bothered to ask what the saying that the "Word" became "Flesh" means. Does it mean that the "Word" being a "Spirit" had to change into "Flesh" or the "Word" was in a different form and had to assume the form of man to be acceptable?

	A	B	C	D	E	F	G	H	I	J	K	L
2												
3												A
4											S	
5										M	O	B
6										A	I	N
7										Ch	E	
8										N	L	
9												

Fig. 37 From the womb of the Immaculate Mother.

I posed this question because of the myths and legends of ancient civilizations like Sumer, Mesopotemia, Egypt, China, and India about our ancestors having reptilian features. There are terra-cottas dating 3,000 BC that showed humans with reptilian features.

Another group of Hebrew words in figure 37 are shown, namely:

HSh = *Salvation*   ShM = *Name*   EL = *God*
ShMA = *Listen*   EMET = *Truth*   KR = *Lamb*
BAR = Son   ABA = Father   B-ARETz =Earth, world

From the cited words, one can form several phrases, namely:

a) "HSh ShM ABA," which means "Salvation is in the Name of the Father"

	A	B	C	D	E	F	G	H	I	J	K	L
1												
2												
3	E	M	E									
4	L	K		T								
5	H	R	E									
6	A	S	M	A								
7	B	A	R	E								
8												
9												

Fig. 38 Salvation is in the name of the Father.

b) "ShMA EMET HSh B-ARETz ShM KR BAR EL AB," which can be translated to "Listen to the truth: Salvation of the world is in the name of the Lamb, the Son of God the Father."

c) The words "BN EL AIN" can mean "the Son of God Infinite."

	A	B	C	D	E	F	G	H	I	J	K	L
4												
5												B
6										A	I	N
7											E	
8											L	
9												

Fig. 39 Son of God Infinite.

In figure 40 is another cluster of Hebrew words that has a connection to biblical teachings. They are:

AIN = *Infinite*   AAA = *God*   EL = *God*
DV = *Love*   DSh = *Door*

The preceding Hebrew words can be formed into the following sentence:

"DV DSh AAA" meaning "Love is the door to God."

	A	B	C	D	E	F	G	H	I	J	K	L
1								A	Sh			
2								A	D			
3								A	V			
4												

Fig. 40 Love is the door to God.

This is a wonderful teaching that can only come from the God of Love that reminds us of John 5:16, which states:

God is love, and he who abides in love, abides in God and God in him.[8]

The Anointed, Messiah

Figure 41 shows the words that refer to Jesus as the God of Love and Peace, the Anointed, the Redeemer, or the Messiah. To find these words in this grid is truly astonishing. This will further affirm the validity of the grid.

The word *Messiah*, which can be spelled in the Hebrew language in several ways like MShH, MShayh or MeShiach or Messiach can be found in the other quadrants of the grid by permutation. The repetition of the word is just an emphasis on the doctrine about the Messiah. As to whether this Messiah is Jesus is a matter still to be resolved. Only the Christians believe that the Messiah had already come in the person of Jesus. The discussion in this book on the different saviors in the ancient world will surely fascinate and surprise the readers.

The word *MShAYH* has ELS of twenty-two letters between the letters *M* at G-9, *Sh* at F-11, *A* at E-13, *Y* at D-15, and *H* at C-17.

The word *BLL* which means "Anointed" has ELS of two letters between the encoded letters *B* at A-7, *L* at A-10, and *L* at A-13.

The word *GAL*, which means "Redeemer" has ELS of ten letters between the desired letters *G* at D-12, *A* at C-13, and *L* at B-14.

The word *ShALM* means "Peace" and has an ELS of sixty letters between the encoded letters *Sh* at I-1, *A* at J-6, *L* at K-11, and *M* at L-16

The sentence "MShAYH GAL" can be loosely interpreted as "The Messiah is the Redeemer."

"MShAYH GAL AM" can be interpreted as "The Messiah is the Redeemer of the World."

	A	B	C	D	E	F	G	H	I	J	K	L
1									Sh			
2												
3												
4												
5												
6									A			
7	B											
8												
9							M					
10	L											
11						Sh					L	
12				G		M	A					
13	L		A		A							
14		L										
15				Y								
16												M
17			H									

Fig. 41 The Messiah of Peace.

By permutation, additional words relevant to the matter about the Messiah could be found.

The word *ABA* means "Father" and is found in A-6-7 and B-7.

The Hebrew word *ShLH* when it is written ShILOH means the "Messiah." It is found in the quadrant composed of B-6, A-4, and A-5.

The Hebrew word *YOTzAI*, which means the "Begotten" can be found in the quadrant composed of D-5-6, E-5-6, and F-6.

	A	B	C	D	E	F	G	H	I	J	K	L
1												
2												
3	E											
4	L											
5	H				Tz	O						
6	A	Sh	M	A	I	Y						
7	B	A	R	E								
8												
9												

Fig. 42 Words related to the Messiah.

The cited words can be placed together to form the following phrases.

"ShLH YOTZAI BAR ABA," which can be translated as "The Messiah is the Begotten Son of the Father."

"YOTZAI BAR EL ABA ShLH," which can mean "The Begotten Son of God the Father is the Meshiah."

The word *SOTER*, which means the "Messiah" is found in the quadrant composed of J-9-6, H-10-11, G-10-11, and F-10.

Another Hebrew word referring to Jesus is *MOREH*, which means "Teacher of Righteousness." It is found in the quadrant composed of B-9-10-11 and H-10-11.

	A	B	C	D	E	F	G	H	I	J	K	L
8												
9							M	U	S			
10						T	H	O				
11							E	R	S			
12												
13												

Fig. 43 Teacher of Righteousness.

Relevant to the preceding are the following Egyptian words, which by permutation could be found in the quadrant composed of horizontal rows 9 to 12 and columns F, G, H, and I.

Only Son

MUT = *Mother*   MS = *Give Birth*
UA = *Only*   SA = *Son*
AS/AS(h)T = ancient name of *Isis*

The letters are side by side without ELS. By permutation, the following words can be formed:

HERU = ancient name of HORUS   MESSU = Messiah

The said Egyptian words can be formed into the following sentences:

"HERU MESSU," which means "Horus is the Messiah"
"MUT AS MS UA SA HORUS," which means "The Mother Isis gave birth to an only Son, Horus."

	A	B	C	D	E	F	G	H	I	J	K	L
6												
7							T					
8							U					
9							M	U	S			
10							H	O				
11							E	R	S			
12								A				
13										U		
14												
15												

Fig. 44 Horus the Messiah.

This is similar to the Christian belief that Mary conceived an only Son, Jesus, God of Love.

In figure 45 are two Filipino words near each other and sharing the letters *A, N,* and *A* to form the words *INA* meaning "MOTHER" and the word *ANAK* meaning "SON," again implying the Madonna and Child. Actually there are fifteen examples of the word *INA* in the grid.

In this grid there are two Hebrew words *BAR* and *BN*, one Egyptian word *SA* and English word *SON* and a Filipino word *ANAK* all mean "SON" or "OFFSPRING." These repetitions of words in different languages with the same meaning are not coincidences but an emphatic message about the Begotten Son of God, the Messiah, the Redeemer of the World.

	A	B	C	D	E	F	G	H	I	J	K	L
1												
2												
3												
4							A			S		
5						N	Ch				O	B
6					I							N
7		B	A	R								
8												
9												

Fig. 45 The word *Son* in different languages.

f) Mary, the Mother of Jesus

After the discussion about Jesus and His teachings, we now come to one of the most beloved person in Jesus's life, his earthly mother, Mary. If in ancient times Isis was the most popular and beloved feminine entity, now it is Mary, the mother of Jesus. There is much devotion of the Catholics to Mary that it has become the subject of controversy with other Christian sects. In some countries, particularly the Philippines, the devotion to Mary surpasses that of Jesus. As this grid is about Christianity, we should find the name of Mary in this grid. For if not, then there will be doubts as to the validity of the grid and would confirm the allegation that Mary was taken for granted by Jesus as alleged by some Christian preachers.

Name of Mary in the Grid

The name MARY is based on the root word *MRA* or *MARA* that means "SEA." An ancient name of ISIS was MERI because she was the "Queen of the Sea." This is also the reason why Mary is called the "Patroness of Sailors" and

the "Queen of the Sea." In figure 46 is a cluster of Hebrew letters that shows the name of Mary, the Mother of Jesus in different ELS. As the letters *A* and *Y* have the same numerical value of 1 the letter *A* can be exchanged with the letter *Y*; thus MARA can become MARY. "MA-RA" can also be interpreted as the "Mother of Ra." The Egyptian sun god as MARY can be said to be the "Mother of Jesus, the Son of God."

	A	B	C	D	E	F	G	H	I	J	K	L
1												
2												
3		M										
4												
5		R										
6								M				
7		A										
8												
9												
10										E		
11								R				
12						M						
13												
14												
15												
16								E				
17												

Fig. 46 Name of Mary, first to third examples.

Number of Examples	Coordinates			ELS
1st example "MRA"	M = B-3	R = B-5	A =B-7	1 letter

As stated previously, the letters *A* and *Y* can be interchanged; hence, MRA can become MRY.

| 2nd example "MRE" | M = H-6 | R = H-11 | E = H-16 | 4 letters. |
| 3rd example "MRE" | M = F-12 | R = H-13 | E = J-10 | 9 letters |

	A	B	C	D	E	F	G	H	I	J	K	L
5												
6						Y						
7			R									M
8												
9												
10												
11								R				
12												
13												
14												
15				Y								
16												
17												

Fig. 46-a Name of Mary, fourth and fifth examples.

4th example "MRY"   M = L-7   R = C-7   Y = F-6   8 letters
5th example "MRY"   M = L-7   R = H-11   Y = D-15   43 letters

	A	B	C	D	E	F	G	H	I	J	K	L
4												
5										M		
6				A								
7												
8												
9												
10									E			
11								R				
12						M						
13												
14												
15												
16												M
17						A						

Fig. 46-b Name of Mary, sixth to eight examples.

6th example "MRE"   M = F-12   R = I-11   E = J-10.   9 letters

The word *MRE* also means the "Sea." Sometimes the letter *A* is written as an *E* for pronunciation purpose.

7th example "MRA"   M = J-5   R = H-11   A = F-17   69 letters
8th example "MRA"   M = L-16   R = H-11   A = D-6   63 letters

By permutation, one will find the succeeding examples in the designated quadrants.

The first example is the name MARIA, which can be found in the quadrant composed of B-7, C-6-7, D-6, and E-1.

The second example is the name MARA at B-7, C-6-7, and D-6.

	A	B	C	D	E	F	G	H	I	J	K	L
4												
5		R										
6	A		M	A	I							
7		A	R									
8												
9												
10												
11												
12												
13												
14												
15				Y		I						
16			M		A							
17				A	R							

Fig. 47 The name Maria.

The third example is the word *MARA* at C-6, B-7-5, and A-6.

The fourth example is the word *MARIA*, which is found in the quadrant composed of C, D-17, E-16-17, and F-15.

The fifth example is the word *MARA* in the cluster of letters at the bottom of the grid. Again by gematria, the letter *A* can be interchanged with the letter *Y*, thus MARA can become MARY.

The sixth example is the word *MARY* in C-16, D-17, E-17, and D-15.

93

The number of times that the name of Mary appeared in the grid will leave no doubt as to the emphasis made by the author of this code about Mary, the mother of Jesus or even Mary Magdala.

Mary is addressed in many ways one of which is VM, which means "Rose of Heaven." Figure 48 shows a quadrant composed of E-12, F-11-12-13, G-12, H-11, and I-12, which letters can be formed into the following sentence "SHM AMA MARA VM," which can be translated as the "The Name of the Mother is Mary, the Rose of Heaven." Except for the word *MARA*, all the letters of the words are side by side without ELS.

	A	B	C	D	E	F	G	H	I	J	K	L
10												
11						Sh		R				
12					A	M	A		A			
13						V						
14												

Fig. 48 The name of the Mother is Mary, the Rose of Heaven.

Blessed Are You among Women

In figure 49 are shown the words "ASHER AT GU Ash," which can be translated as "Blessed art thou among women."[1] Again, the letters of the words are side by side without ELS. To find these words together in the said quadrant is titillating."

	A	B	C	D	E	F	G	H	I	J	K	L
9												
10						T						
11					A	Sh	E	R				
12			U	G	A							
13												
14												

Fig. 49 "Blessed art thou among women."

Is this not mind-boggling to find all these words in the grid? And the letters are in clusters and side by side? According to the Gnostics, Jesus supposedly said,

Even so did my mother, the Holy Spirit.[2]

This saying about the Holy Spirit being the mother of Jesus has never been accepted by Orthodox Christians, but was accepted by the early Christians, the Gnostics. If the Holy Spirit is the spiritual mother of Jesus, is not Mary, his earthly mother, the most blessed among women?

In the quadrant composed of horizontal rows 6, 7, 8, 9 and columns A, B, and C are the letters that by permutation can be formed into the following words.

Behold Thy Mother

BAR = *Son*   HN = *Behold*   AMK = Thy *Mother*

The words "HN AMK" can be translated as "Behold, Thy Mother"[3] that reminds us of the crucifixion when Jesus entrusted His beloved mother to His faithful apostle, John.

	A	B	C	D	E	F	G	H	I	J	K	L
5												
6			M									
7	B	A	R									
8	H		K									
9	N											
10												
11												

Fig. 50 Behold thy Mother.

Behold thy Son

The words "AM HN BAR" can be translated "Mother, behold thy Son,"[4] which seems to be the right saying instead of the impersonal words "Woman, behold thy Son" and which is more in consonance with the saying "Behold, thy Mother."

The Hebrew words "O MARIE" can mean "Hail Mary" while the words "ALMAH MARA" can mean the "Virgin Mary."

	A	B	C	D	E	F	G	H	I	J	K	L
4												
5					O							
6			M	A	I							
7			R	E								
8												
15												
16			M	H	A	L						
17				A	R	A						

Fig. 51 Hail Mare.

Words Related to Mary

There are other words related to Mary, which are descriptive of her and can be found in figure 52.

> VM = means "Rose of Heaven," which is a title given to Mary, mother of Jesus. Mary is the representation of the feminine entity in the Catholic religion. In *Karunungan* Mary is called the Gumamela Celis (the Heavenly Flower) or the Rosa Mundi (the Flower of the World). The word is found in C-1 and D-2. VM can also mean the "Virgin Mary."
>
> MRA/MARA = The Sea, root word of the name Mary and another title of Mary, the Lady of the Sea, Patroness of Sailors.
>
> BNH = *Binah* which means "understanding" is the Supernal Mother in the third Sephera, the highest feminine entity in the Tree of Life.

	A	B	C	D	E	F	G	H	I	J	K	L
1			V									
2				M								
3												
4												
5												
6			M	A								
7		B	A	R								
8		H										
9		N										
10												

Fig. 52 Mara, Rose of Heaven.

ChN = means "Immaculate." Another title given to Mary, which refers to the Catholic dogma that the Virgin Mary is conceived without original sin thus, the title Immaculate Conception. The word is written several times.

Asher/AshAR = means "Blessed"

ETzChI/Otz = means the "Tree of Life," which is also a title given to Mary who gave us the best fruit, Jesus.

	A	B	C	D	E	F	G	H	I	J	K	L
3												
4												
5				Tz	O		Ch					
6							I					
7					Tz	E				Ch		
8										N		
9												
10												
11		N		A	Sh	E	R					
12	Ch	N								Ch	N	
13									N			

Fig. 53 Immaculate.

The Paraclete

In the New Testament, the role of the Paraclete is very important. But who is the Paraclete? The Paraclete known also as the Advocate or the Comforter is the Holy Spirit or the Holy Ghost known in Hebrew as Ruach or Ruah, which means "wind" or "spirit." In the Hebrew language, the word *Ruach* is feminine in gender, thus supposed to be the Spirit is a "She," but because of mistranslation has become an "It." Her symbol is the dove Yonah. Figure 54 shows the words "Ruach or Ruah" and "Yonah or Yona."

Mary and the Holy Spirit or the Paraclete share a special connection. Besides being overshadowed by the Holy Spirit during the conception of Jesus, Mary and the Holy Spirit as explained in the chapter on the Mother, both represent the feminine aspect of the world. There is a subtle connection between them, which was revealed by Jesus when Jesus said in the Bible:

> I have to go to the Father so that the Paraclete can come down and guide you.[5]

	A	B	C	D	E	F	G	H	I	J	K	L
6												
7		A	R									
8	H	U										
9			H	A								
10		O	N									
11	Y											
12												
13												
14									N			
15								A		O		
16									Y			
17												

Fig. 54 The Dove.

Has this promise by Jesus been fulfilled? Yes! But most of us are not aware of it.

During the time of Moses, God manifested. During the time of the apostles, Jesus appeared. After Jesus, who kept manifesting but Mary the "Mother," why? This is in fulfillment of Jesus's promise. Since the nineteenth century, there had been reported almost four hundred appearances of Mary around the world. And she had been the guiding light of the church ever since. If we believe in the Trinity and that the second person of the Trinity can manifest as Jesus in this world, cannot the Paraclete, the third person, appear in Her feminine form, which we address in different names like the Lady of Lourdes, Fatima, Medjugorie or Manaog, Isis, Kuan Yin or Tara? If the Paraclete does not have the same power as that of the Son, then there is no Trinity. The Trinity is supposed to have the same powers.

g) Mara Magdala/Mary Magdalene

There are two very important women in the life of Jesus, and both are named Mary. One of them is very controversial and is called Mara Magdala known as Mary Magdalene. She was supposed to be a harlot who transformed when she met Jesus. She was the one who washed the feet of Jesus with oil and was the first to see Jesus after the resurrection. Because of her closeness to Jesus, she became the envy of some apostles and in some Gnostics writings questions were raised about this closeness.

In the Gospel of Mary,[6] it was said that Peter questioned the private talks between Jesus and Mary:

And he speak privately with a woman and not openly to us?
Are we to turn about and all look to her? Did he prefer her to us?

Mary wept when Peter confronted her, and she told Peter why would she lie. Levi, a disciple, intervened and said to Peter:

If the Savior made her worthy, who are you indeed to reject her? Surely the Savior knows her very well. That is why he loved her more than us.[7]

Due to this closeness, there was even a story about Jesus kissing Mary Magdalene in the lips. She was said to be the Beloved Disciple and not St. John as averred by others.

According to the Gospel of Philip,[8]

Magdalene, the one who was called his (Jesus) companion
And the companion of the [Savior is] Mary Magdalene. [But Christ loved] her more than [all] the disciples [and used to] kiss her [often] on her [mouth]. The rest of [the disciples were offended] by it and [expressed disapproval]. They said to him" Why do you love her more than all of us?

Some writers say that she was the mistress or wife of Jesus, and that they had children. We do not know the veracity of these stories, but whether they are true or not should not take us away from the beautiful teachings of Jesus.

	A	B	C	D	E	F	G	H	I	J	K	L
11												
12				G	A	M						
13			A		A							
14		L										
15			D	E	Y	N						
16			M		A							
17					A	R						

Fig. 55 The name Mara Magdala or Mary Magdalene.

Spirituality is not dependent on the teacher but on the student. Thus, the story of Mary Magdalene should serve as an inspiration and not a source of hatred and bigotry. It shows the capability of a person to change and the love that God has

for everyone whether one is a sinner or saint. Everyone falls. What is important is one does not stay fallen but rises from his fall and starts again.

Even by permutation, Mary Magdala's name would have been difficult to find considering that there are only two Ds and one letter *G* in the grid, but because of her importance, her name could be found in the Hebrew and English forms. Figure 55 shows the name whether as Mara Magdala or Mary Magdalene.

h) Names of the Twelve Apostles

As this is about Jesus and the Lord's, Prayer for sure the apostles will be mentioned in the grid. In gematria as previously explained, letters can be interchanged or substituted if they have the same numerical values. As an example, the letter *P* or *Ph* with a numeral value of 8 can be substituted by the letter *Ch*, which has also a numeral value of 8 to hide the meaning of the word or name like Chilich can mean Philip. With that in mind, let us look for the names of the apostles in the grid. Are we going to find the names of the twelve apostles in the grid—Peter or Simon, James, John, Matthew, Andrew, Judas, Bartholomew, Thadeus, Thomas, Philip, James, and Simon?

1) The name KEPhA means "rock," which refers to Peter. By gematria, the letter *Ch* can be interchanged with the letter *P* or *Ph* as both have the same numerical value of 8. Thus, KEChA can become KEPhA.

   Coordinates: K = L-15   Ch/Ph = L-9 A = L-3   ELS = 5 letters.

2) The name MATThEW can be written several ways in Hebrew, but in this grid, it is written MTI.

   Coordinates: M = C-6   T = D-4   I = E-2. ELS = 22 letters

	A	B	C	D	E	F	G	H	I	J	K	L
1												
2					I							
3												A
4				T						S		
5										M	O	
6			M					M			I	N
7												
8						N						
9												Ch
10												
11												
12												
13												
14			T									
15		D										K
16	I											
17												

Fig. 56 Names of the Apostles.

3) The name ThADEUS can be written in Hebrew as TDI.

Coordinates: T = C-14   D = B-15 I = A-16   ELS = 10 letters

4) The name SIMON is written in its defective form as SMN. There were two apostles named Simon, one of them was Peter.

Coordinates: S = J-4 M = H-6 N = F-8   ELS = 21 letters

The name can also be permutated from the cluster of letters found on J-4-5, K-5-6, and L-6.

5) The name JOHN, the Beloved Apostle of Jesus is written as YOHANN or YOChNN.

Coordinates: The name can be permutated from the cluster of letters found at A-11-12, B-10-11, C-9-10, and D-9.

	A	B	C	D	E	F	G	H	I	J	K	L
8												
9			H	A								
10			O	N		T	H	O				
11	Y	N							S			
12	Ch				M	A						
13												
14												

Fig. 57 John and Thomas.

6) The name THOMAS is found in the cluster of letters on E-10-12, F-10-12, G-10, and H-11.

	A	B	C	D	E	F	G	H	I	J	K	L
1												
2												
3									V	O		
4								Y	A		S	E
5									K	M		
6										A	I	
7												

Fig. 58 Names of James and Yakov.

7) The name JAMES or IAMES can be found in the cluster of Hebrew letters located on H-4, I-4, J-5, K-4, and L-4 and can be permutated to form the name JAMES.

8) The name JAMES is also written in Hebrew as YAKOV, which can be found on I-5-4-3 and on J-3.

		A	B	C	D	E	F	G	H	I	J	K	L
1													
2										D			
3										V			
4									Y	A	S		
5													

Fig. 59 Name of Judas.

9) The name JUDAS, which is written in the grid as YUDAS, the betrayer of Jesus, is found in the cluster of letters found on H-4, I-2-3-4, and on J-4.

   It is uncanny that the name of Judas is in the form of an inverted TAU or Cross. What does it mean?

It is not amazing to find the names of the apostles in a very small grid? Can we truly say that this is only a coincidence? This is just a little portion of the secrets still to be revealed in this code.

i) The Four Evangelists Plus One

After getting the names of the apostles, it appears that it would be an easy task to find the names of the four evangelists who supposedly wrote the New Testament. Although there is the question about the authenticities of the Gospels, let us search for the names of the four evangelists in the grid who are supposed to be Matthew, John, Luke, and Mark. It is said that the oldest Gospel was that of Mark, which became the basis of Matthew's and Luke's Gospels. Their names in Hebrew are sometimes written differently. Matthew can be written as MTI while John can be written as YOCHANAN or YOHANN. It is unbelievable that the names of Mark and Luke are in the English forms when this is supposed to be a Hebrew grid. Figure 60 shows the names of the four evangelists. However, there is another name in the grid together with the four evangelists, MARCION. Who was this person and why was his name with the evangelists?

Marcion was the Christian-Gnostic who wrote the Gospel of the Lord in Latin and Greek that became the basis of Mark's, Luke's, and Matthew's Gospels. Although Marcion's Gospel was ahead by decades to the Christian Gospels, he was accused of plagiarizing and copying the Christian Gospels. He was charged of expurgating the Gospel of Luke and making it appear that Jesus was not a

Jew. In the Marcion Gospel, he just said that Jesus went to Nazareth, but in Luke's Gospel, there was added after the word *Nazareth*, the phrase "where he had been brought up" to show the Jewish heritage of Jesus. Who was copying whom? According to literary scholars like Waite and Acharya S,[9] Marcion wrote and published in Greek the Apostolicon, which became later on ten of Paul's Epistles, namely: Galatians, First and Second Corinthians, Romans (except the fifteenth and sixteenth chapters), First and Second Thessalonians, Ephesians, Collosians Philemon and Phillipians. The writings of Marcion were based on the story of Krishna. Thus, the Christ that the Gnostic Marcion was talking about was not a Jew but a Hindu. He was expelled from the church in AD144 for plagiarizing the Gospels and the Epistles. Be that as it may, let us continue with our search for the code.

Figure 60 shows the names of the four evangelists and the fifth evangelists, namely:

1) The name MARK starts with the letter M on C-6-7-8 and going vertically downward, the letters are side by side without ELS.
2) The name LUKE starts with the letter L on A-10, U on B-9, K on C-8, and E on D-7; and going diagonally upward, the letters are side by side without ELS. Even, the names MARK and LUKE share the common letter K.
3) The name MATTHEW is written in Hebrew as MTI, which starts with the letter M on C-6, D-4, and E-2 and reading from right to let has an ELS of twenty-two letters between the letters M, T, and I.
4) The name JOHN or YOChNN, the Beloved Apostle of Jesus can be found in the cluster of Hebrew words from A-11-12, B-10-11, C-9-10, and D-9.
5) The name MARCION whose Gospel was the basis of the Gospels of Matthew, Luke, and Mark can be found in the quadrant composed of C-6-7, D-6, E-5-6, and F-4-5.

	A	B	C	D	E	F	G	H	I	J	K	L
1												
2					I							
3												
4				T								
5				Tz	O	N						
6			M	A	I							
7			R	E								
8			K									
9		U	H	A								
10	L	O	N									
11	Y	N										
12	Ch											
13												
14												

Fig. 60 The Evangelists and Marcion.

It is intriguing to find the names of the four evangelists and the fifth person in a cluster. Figure 60 shows the names of Marcion, Mark, Matthew, and Luke intertwined, lumped together, and even sharing common letters as if to imply the closed relations of the persons or their works.

j) Authenticity of the Gospels

Lately the Gospels have been under literary criticisms as to their authenticities and genuineness that placed the story of Jesus and the Lord's Prayer questionable. Thus there are some questions to be resolved like:

1. Who wrote the Gospels?
2. When were the Gospels written?
3. Was the story of Jesus a myth?
4. If Jesus was a myth, who was the author of the Lord's Prayer?

The traditional belief is that the Gospels were written fifty to one hundred years after the death of Jesus. By this reckoning, it would be safe to assume that most of the apostles were already dead.

According to Acharya S,[1] the Gospels were unheard of until AD150 when Jesus had been dead for nearly 120 hundred years. No writer mentioned Jesus before AD150. She further said that even Justin Martyr,[2] one of the most eminent of the early fathers who wrote in the middle of the second century AD did not know the existence of the Gospels; thus, in his defense of the divinity of Christ, he used "more than 300 quotations from the books of the Old Testament, and nearly one hundred from the Apocryphal books of the New Testament; but none from the Four Gospels. Rev. Giles says "The very names of the Evangelists, Matthew, Mark, Luke and John, are never mentioned by him (Justin)—do not occur once in all his writings."

Even St. Augustine was quoted to have said,

> I should not believe in the truth of the Gospels unless the authority of the Catholic Church forced me to do so.[3]

Barbara Walker[4] commented,

> The discovery that the Gospels were forged, centuries later than the events they described, is still not widely known even though the Catholic Encyclopedia admits. The idea of a complete and clear-cut canon of the New Testament existing from the beginning ... has no foundation in history. No extant manuscript can be dated earlier than the 4th century A.D.; most were written even later. The oldest manuscripts contradict one another, as also do even the present canon of synoptic Gospels.

Existence of the Gospels

It would appear that all the four Gospels did not exist before AD 200; thus, nobody knew about them. This would also mean that the apostles were already dead when the Gospels were written. Thus, Matthew, John, Luke, and Mark could not have been the authors of the Gospels and were written at the end of the second century AD purposely to protect the doctrines and interest of the church and were collated in the fourth century AD to be part of the New Testament. Although there could have been misrepresentations as to the authors of the Gospels, however, it does not mean that the Gospels are false. However, these misrepresentations could cast doubt in the credibility of the Gospels that is further damaged by the conflicting stories in the Gospels.

Even the Catholic encyclopedia admitted that the Gospel of Luke was written nearly two hundred years after the death of Jesus. It was a compilation of dozen of older manuscripts by a writer or writers who put the name of Luke

as the writer for credibility. It can be proven that passage after passage has been added to the original Gospel to suit the interest of the church. An example is in the Gospel of the Lord by the Gnostic Marcion written decades before the Gospel of Luke and which was the basis of the Gospel of Luke, Marcion wrote,

> Saying, the Son of Man must suffer many things, and be put to death, and after three days rise again.[1]

In Luke 9:22, the phrase was revised to read as follows:

> Saying, the Son of Man must suffer many things, and be rejected by the elders and the chief priests and scribes, and be put to death, and on the third day rise again.[2]

The phrase in bold letters was inserted to show the Jewish heritage of Jesus. It must be remembered that the Marcion Gospel was based on the Krishna story hence the omission of the italicized phrase. The Lukan writer interpolated and removed and revised many passages of Marcion's Gospel, but the irony of it, Marcion was the one accused of plagiarizing the Gospel.

It is said that Marcion got a copy of the story of Krishna that Apollonius secured when he went to India. It was this story that became the basis of Marcion's Gospel of the Lord.

	A	B	C	D	E	F	G	H	I	J	K	L
1												
2												
3												
4												
5				Tz	O	N						
6			M	A	I							
7			R	E								
8			K									
9		U										
10	L											
11												
12												

Fig. 61 Mark, Luke, and Marzion.

107

Again according to Acharya S.:

> The style of language used in Mark shows that it was written in Rome)
> by a Roman convert to Christianity whose first language was Latin
> and not Greek, Hebrew or Aramaic.

> It would seem, then, the compiler of Mark used the Latin version of
> Marcion's Gospel, while Luke and Matthew used the Greek version,
> accounting for the variances between them. Indeed, the author of Mark
> was clearly not a Palistinian Jew, as Wells points out that Mark "betrays
> in 7:31 an ignorance of Palistinian geography."[3]

With respect to the Gospel of John, Acharya S also cited:

> There are also many errors in reference to geography of the country.
> The author speaks of Aenon, near to Salim, in Judea; also of Bethany,
> beyond Jordan, and of a city of Samaria, called "Sychar." If there were
> any such places, they were strangely unknown to other writers. The
> learned Dr. Bretschneider points out such mistakes and errors of
> geography; chronology, history and statistics of Judea, as no person
> who had ever resided in that country, or had been by birth a Jew, could
> possibly have committed." In addition as Keeler states: "The Gospel of
> John says that Bethsaida was in Galilee. There is no such town in that
> district, and there never was. Bethsaida was on the East of the sea of
> Tiberias, whereas Galilee was on the West side. St. John was born at
> Bethsaida, and the probability is that he would know the geographical
> location of his own birthplace."[4]

It can be said that the most beautifully written Gospel was that of John.
Some people have questioned the ability of a mere fisherman to really write such
a cultured and cultivated Greek with quotations and references from the Greek
Septuagint. Though these critics may be possibly right yet people just really
believe blindly on anything said in the Bible.

Is Jesus a Myth?

The story of Jesus is told in the Gospels without which there is no story of
Jesus. Presently, however, the authenticity of the Gospels is being questioned
due to its many inconsistencies and conflicting verses. As a result, even the
historical appearance of Jesus is placed in doubt. Some of the inconsistencies and

mistakes in the New Testament are cited here besides those that have already been discussed.

One serious mistake in the New Testament was calling Jesus a Nazarene because he was supposed to have come from the town of Nazareth. The truth is there was no town of Nazareth during the supposed time of Jesus. Thus, he did not grow up in Nazareth. If ever Jesus was called a Nazarene, maybe it was because Jesus belonged to the sect of the Nazarenes. These were the ascetics who never cut their hairs because these were the symbols of their holiness and strength like Samson. This would explain why the portraits of Jesus had him having long hairs. Also, if one would look for the town of Nazareth during the supposed time of Jesus, it was in the western Arabian region of Hijaz where another savior very similar to Jesus was worshipped around 400 BC named Isa (see figure 10). It was also where the places called Galilee and Bethsaida were located.

This savior Isa was born from a virgin and came from the town of Nazareth, Hijaz, in western Arabia. He was also called the Word or the Logos. Could this Isa be the Isa that according to Hindu legend was a holy man, a teacher, and a prophet who studied in India and at the age of thirty years returned to his native land where he was killed? The Hindus considered Isa as Jesus of the Christians. Could the story of Isa who stayed in Nazareth, Galilee, and Bethsaida be the story of Jesus of Nazareth? Were the Arabian towns the forerunners of the towns in Palestine?

It is said that there are approximately 150,000 variant readings found in the New Testament and probably 149,500 were additions and interpolations. There were many contradicting and conflicting histories and genealogies like Jesus being born two years before Herod's death according to Matthew but more than nine years according to Luke. The genealogies in both Matthew and Luke contained fictitious names. It even contained the name of Rabah who was a prostitute according to the book of Joshua. Somebody has really messed up the genealogies of Jesus. Actually, there was no need for the genealogies as Jesus was supposed to be conceived by the Holy Spirit. But in the desire of the church to associate with the lineage of King David, it had to conceive a genealogy. Jesus was supposed to be born in 1 CE when Herod ordered the slaughter of the innocents, but Herod died before April 12 BCE; thus, making some Christians to redate Jesus birth to 6-4 BCE. Jesus was also supposed to have been born during the census of Quirinus, but this census took place ten years after Herod's death. Jesus was supposed to be born in Bethlehem, but John said he was from Galilee. Furthermore, the birth date of the Persian sun god Mithra on December 25 was given to Jesus as a concession to Emperor Constantine who worshipped Mithra. Shepherds would not have been tending their sheep in a cold winter night. Thus, we should not be surprised about the authenticities of the Gospels

now being questioned. As a consequence, even the historical or actual presence of Jesus is now being doubted.

Without the Gospels, there is no story of Jesus. Considering the supposed greatness and popularity of Jesus, no known historians in his time wrote about Jesus. There were forty known historians in Jesus's time—Greek, Roman, Jews and others, but no one wrote about Jesus. Josephus Flavius, the great Jewish historian (35 BC to 95 BC) who wrote detailed history of his times in many volumes never mentioned Jesus in his writings. The supposed references to Jesus were later found out as forgeries. Also, it is intriguing that in all his Epistles, Paul never quoted any of Jesus's sermons, parables nor did he mention the miracles and wonders performed by Jesus. He did not even know the Lord's Prayer and even said the followers did not know how to pray.

With the preceding as a premise, do we still continue with our search for the code? Yes, for whether the Gospels are fakes or Jesus is a myth, there is a beautiful Prayer before us that has helped millions in their problems and spiritual transformations, the study of which can still lead us to more fulfillment and enlightenment. Whatever we will find, for sure it will add something beneficial to this smoldering question about the Gospels and Jesus. For blessed is he who did not see yet believe. So let us continue with our journey of enlightenment.

CHAPTER V

THE OLD TESTAMENT

Although it is expected to find some information in the Lord's Prayer about the New Testament, however, to discover so much data in a 198 letter code is overwhelming. It was beyond my expectation. This encouraged me to look for information about the Old Testament in the Lord's Prayer. The evolution, formation, and foundation of the state of Israel are based on the sacrifices and heroism of its holy prophets, patriarchs, kings, judges, and heroes. If we will find these personalities in the grid, then this will be mind-boggling and will attest to the intellectual superiority of the author of the code.

The Old Testament contains many personalities that we know of today like Adam, Eve, Noah, Abraham, Moses, David, and Solomon. To find them more particularly the first family Adam and Eve and their children Seth, Kain, and Abel will be very fascinating. Their presence in the grid will show the connection between the Old Testament and the New Testament and some teachings that are not being taught by the church but advocated by the Gnostics. Furthermore, this will also reveal the depth of this code.

a) Genesis, Creation Story

I have always been fascinated by the book of Genesis in the Old Testament and have made an in-depth study of its verses that revealed many intriguing information that fortunately could be found in the grid. The grid would seem to confirm my findings. It has been my belief that there are actually three stories in Genesis, which were made into one story by the church, namely, Genesis 1:26-27, 2:7, and 2:21-22. In Genesis, God supposedly said,

> Let us make man in our own image and likeness. God created man
> in His Image; the divine image He created him; male and female, He
> created them.[1]

This verse in the Bible postulated the first creation story about man being created simultaneously, male and female without the use of dust or a rib to create man. This is truly pure creation, creating something out of nothing. This is a very different story from the other creation story wherein God supposedly

> formed man of the dust of the ground, and breathed into his nostrils the breath of life; and man became a living being.[2]

In this story, God needed a material to form man, in this case, the dust of the ground. Like a potter, God formed man from the dust or clay of the earth, and a clay statue emerged, which however was lifeless or incomplete and needed another element. God gave or injected the breath of life or his spirit or DNA to make man alive. When man had evolved and beasts and fowls were created to give him company, God realized it was not enough, so Adam was put to sleep and

> "took one of his ribs . . . and the rib, which the Lord God took from the man, he made into a woman."[3]

This is the third story that is about the making of a female. But again God needed a substance to make a woman. This time God took the rib or bone or DNA of man.

b) Interplay of Words: Creation, Formation, and Making

Traditional Christian teaching has instilled in us that there was only one creation story. Unless we are told about these seemingly different creation stories, we assumed that there was only one creation story. We overlooked the play or manipulation of words in the verses cited. The prophet Isaiah showed us the interplay of words and what they implied. In describing God as a Creator, he used the words *creation, formation,* and *making.* Why did Isaiah use these words? What was he trying to tell us? The creation story will tell us why. A careful reading of the verses will explain the very reasons why Isaiah used the words.

1. The first creation story was about the simultaneous creation of man and woman from nothing. The man and woman were created in the image and likeness of God and were told that they would have dominion over the fish, the birds, the cattle, the wild animals, and all the creatures that crawled over the ground. This story never talked about man being created from the dust and given the breath of life or about the woman being taken

from the rib of man; thus, the assumption was that man and woman were created from nothing. If this was so, then the use of the word *creation* was correct for creation implied making something out of nothing.

2. While the other creation story was about the formation of man from the dust and the giving of the breath of life that gave man a living soul. It also talked about God realizing that it was not wise to have man without a partner. This second story never talked about man being created in the image and likeness of God and his dominion about the creatures on the earth, but to cultivate and care for the Garden of Eden. What was created was a laborer or a gardener or a slave. This revealed the nature of the being supposedly creating man, a being with limitation who could not create something out of nothing but needed material to form or make man. Thus, the use of the word *creation* in this story was not correct. The right words should be *formation* or *molding*, for these words imply the making of a thing from something, not from nothing. In this case, God as a potter formed a clay statue of Adam, and to animate, it was given the breath of life or a soul.

In the case of Eve, God took the rib of Adam and made it a woman. There was no mention of the breath of life or soul being given for she came from Adam who had already a soul. The woman was made because God realized that Adam needed a helpmate. The words used in the Bible about the creation of man, the formation of the male and the making of the female would conform to what Isaiah said:

> And every one that calleth upon my name, I have created him for my glory, I have formed him and I made him.[4]

The use of these words would have remained unnoticed except that in the Kabalistic world, words are used meticulously and with a reason. Why did God use the words *created*, *formed*, and *made*? Was God just being emphatic or was there a purpose to it? Aryeh Kaplan[5] commented about these words, *created*, *formed*, and *made*.

1. Bara/Bra = means "to create" out of nothing. The letters are found at L-6, H-13, and D-17 with ELS of sixty-seven letters.
2. Yatzar/Ytzr = meaning "to form" out of something. The letters are at I-15, G-16, and E-17 with an ELS of nine letters.
3. Asah/Ash = which means "to make" or complete an action. The letters are written several times in the grid without ELS.

Although they have almost similar meanings, yet they are not the same. It is unbelievable that these words with different ELS could be found in the grid as shown in figure 62. This matter is already sacred knowledge that is taught only to the initiates. For the grid to confirm these secret interpretations is an acknowledgment of the Kabalistic superiority of the author of this code.

	A	B	C	D	E	F	G	H	I	J	K	L
1											A	
2											Sh	Sh
3			E									A
4												
5	H.	R										- B
6	A	Sh		A								
7	B	A	R									
8												
9												
10												
11					A	Sh		-R				
12					A		A					
13												
14												
15									Y			
16						Tz						
17				- A	R							

Fig. 62 Words about BRA, YTZR, and ASH.

These words were used in the Bible to differentiate the actions taken by God in creation. As the translators of the Bible were not Kabalists, they thought that the three words meant the same, creating something out of nothing. Had they known the differences, there would not have been a misleading story. There could have been a different belief system that is more conducive to the present conditions.

From the words, it would seem that a spiritual being was created from nothing and another physical being was formed from the elements of earth and was animated by giving or injecting the breath of life or a part of God to make him live. And because man had already a part of God in him, God took a rib or his DNA to make a woman. Thus, Adam was created, a male was formed, and a female was made. To whom do we belong, the created, the formed, or the made?

Zecharia Sitchin[6] commented also about the possible meddling of aliens in the creation of man. The three words would explain why Charles Darwin could not find the missing link, for there was none; there was no evolution from the apes.

The Kabalists have reconciled the stories by saying that the first creation story was about the creation of the spiritual man Adam Kadmon, whose image was made in the likeness of the Creator while the other story was about the making of the physical man from the dust and the woman from the rib. It is the spiritual man Adam Kadmon, who was made in the image and likeness of God. It is the soul or spirit that is like God and not the physical man. The church has not commented on these two conflicting versions of the creation. It could be said that the taking of the rib is actually the taking of the DNA of man from the bone that was used in cloning the woman. This is also the verse being quoted by psychics in saying that psychic surgery or medical operation without the use of instrument is possible.

It would seem that there is a silent conspiracy to shelve the first creation story as it carries a very serious implication about the equality of man and woman, for they were created simultaneously unlike the second creation story, which is given the utmost importance, for it tends to show the superiority of man over woman, as woman was just taken from the rib of the man. This chauvinistic story does not fit in the twenty-first century. As to when the Christian churches will make a comment, we will never know. There are other conflicting versions of the creation story.

The verse also about God's realization of His shortcoming for creating man without a helpmate is also very controversial, for it describes a God who is not omniscient and makes a mistake that is very ungodly. If this story is true, then the only explanation is that the term Elohim, used in Genesis thirty-two times as the Creator, refers not to a God but to a hierarchy of angels who were present in the creation of man. As the Elohim is not a god, then it is susceptible to commit a mistake or they could be the aliens Sitchin was talking about.

Man is a funny creature. He cannot accept the possibility that he was cloned as suggested by Sumerian texts, but would rather accept the possibility of evolving from the apes. Which is better, being cloned or originating from the ape? Man is like the orthodox Egyptologist who insists that Egypt developed on its own without outside help. Maybe there is truth to the theory that man really came from the apes.

As stated previously, the English version of the Bible only translated the Holy Name IHVH ELOHIM as simply God, without realizing that in Hebrew, a holy name not only implies the power and function it carries but also the gender of the entity being mentioned. In this case, the holy name IHVH ELOHIM, which is the divine name of the feminine entity in the third Sephera, has been mentioned thirty-two (32) times in chapter 1 of Genesis as the Creator. For one ignorant

of the Kabalah, the mention of the name is nothing but for one versed in the Kabalah, it is very important. It would show that the use of the holy name was not a coincidence, but a deliberate act. This would further support and strengthen the theory that God the Father was not the Creator, but the planner of creation while the Mother was the implementer of the plan, thus the Creatress. She was the spirit of God who hovered over the water like the creation story of the Hindus about the goddess Nari hovering over the water. The book on wisdom of the Bible has supported this story. It would seem that the companion of God during creation was a feminine entity who had to be represented in this physical world by the creation of EVE. Why create a woman if there is no feminine entity above? The Bible said:

Let us make man in our own image and likeness.[7]

This is a very important verse for it connects with the Sumerian creation story that narrates the gods who were discussing the creation of workers who would perform the mining operations of the gods. Bible scholars believe that the Genesis creation story is based on the Sumerian/Mesopotamian creation story with certain revisions to fit the monotheistic belief of the Jews. This verse does not only relate to the Sumerian creation story, but to some verses in the Bible more particularly Wisdom, Proverbs, and Sirach. From these sources, I will explain the verse "Let us." This verse has become very controversial for the Christian churches maintain that God was alone in creation despite the phrase "Let us." In their desire to instill the doctrine about monotheism, some translators of the Bible tried to delete words that would allude to the plurality of gods. However, they forgot this verse and other verses that say "Let us" in the Bible.

c) Companion of God in Creation

In the creation story of Genesis, God supposedly said,

Let us make man in our own image and likeness. God created man in his image. In the image of God He created him male and female, He created them.[8]

It is obvious from the above that God was not alone during creation. He was addressing somebody, His companion. Yet despite this obvious statement, the Christian churches insist that God was alone in creation. If, however, God was with somebody, who was that companion of the Creator? Was it Jesus or the Trinity? Unfortunately not! This question was answered by King Solomon when he declared,

Now with you is Wisdom, who knows your work and was present when you made the world.[9]

Wisdom confirmed her presence in creation when she said,

When He prepared the heavens, I was there; when He set a compass, upon the face of the depth; when He established the clouds, above; when He strengthened the foundations of the deep; when he gave to the sea, His decree that the water should not pass His Commandment, when He appointed the foundation of the earth. Then I was by Him, and I was daily His delight rejoicing always before Him.[10]

The Lord by Wisdom hath founded the earth.[11]

Again, the new American Bible in its footnote said,

She was present at the creation of the world . . . . and concurred with God when He planned and executed the creation of the universe adorned it with beauty and variety and established its wonderful order.[12]

King Solomon said, "Give me Wisdom, the attendant in your throne."[13]

From the preceding, it is obvious that wisdom was the companion of God during creation. Wisdom was the one addressed to by the Creator to "let us make man in our image, after our likeness." The beautiful verses in the book on wisdom need no fancy interpretation, yet why do we take them for granted? Is it because of our chauvinistic attitude? Despite the obvious meaning of the verse, the Christian churches still insist that God was alone in creation. Maybe to have a better appreciation of the biblical creation story, there is a need to discuss the Sumerian/Mesopotamian creation story that provides the answer why the words "let us" were used in Genesis.

d) Sumerian Creation Story

The Sumerian creation story is the oldest in the world that was retold and retold until there were the Mesopotamian, the Assyrian, Akkadian, Babylonian, and the Genesis versions. In the Sumerian/Mesopotamian version, the gods Anu, Ea (Enki), Enlil, and Ninmah (Ninveh in the Mesopotamian version) were discussing the creation of workers who would do the difficult work of mining

117

and digging canals and rivers. The lesser gods were performing the dirty jobs for forty sars or 144,000 years. This difficult situation led the lesser gods to mutiny and conveyed their disgusting problems to Nin.Mah the spouse of En.Ki (in another version it was Mami, the mother of En.Ki to whom the problem was conveyed). The lesser gods pleaded their problems to Nim.Mah who told En.Ki about the problems. En.Ki, the god of wisdom of the Sumerians, remarked that the creatures that could take the dirty works of the lesser gods already existed.

The Sumerian text "Myths of Cattle and Grain"[14] describes the creatures En.Ki was referring to.

> The men of those days of yore,
> Knew not the eating of bread,
> Knew not the wearing of clothes,
> Ate herbs with their mouths, like sheep;
> Drank water from the furrows.

These were the creatures that Enki said existed and where their image could be imprinted to raise the level of the creatures' intelligence. Sitchin quoted the Sumerian text as:

> When mankind was first created,
> They knew not the eating of bread,
> Knew not the wearing of garments,
> They ate plant with their mouths, like sheep;
> They drank water from the ditch.[15]

	A	B	C	D	E	F	G	H	I	J	K	L
11												A
12											N	
13	L								N	U		
14		L		I	V				N			I
15			E		N			A				K
16		I	M	H				E				
17		N		A								

Fig. 63 Words about ANUNNAKI, ANU, ENLIL, E.A., and NINMAH.

Another ancient Sumerian text "Atra Hasis"[16] dated 1750 BC also described the mutiny and the decision of the gods to fashion workers who would perform

the manual labors of digging and refining gold from the mines instead of the lesser gods. The task of fashioning the workers from the apelike primitives called the LU.LU was given to Ninveh/ Ninmah. After much trial and error, the goddess Ninmah was able to perfect the method of forming a worker by taking the "essence" and not the "rib" from one of the lesser gods and mixing this essence with the essence from the LU.LU. This combination or extract was placed in the womb of one of the lesser female gods, and after ten months a creature called NUMUN[17] the mixed breed was born with similarities to the gods. This was the return of the *Homo Sapiens* for they had degenerated due to cataclysms and technology mishaps. The gods formed more creatures and placed them in a place called E.DIN, which means "HOME OF THE RIGHTEOUS" to separate them from the hominids roaming the surroundings

	A	B	C	D	E	F	G	H	I	J	K	L
11											L	
12												U
13							E				V	
14	A				V							L
15		D	E							U		
16		I	M								N	
17		N								N	U	M

Fig. 64 Words about Numun Lu.Lu, E.Din, Adm, and Eve.

This creation story would seem to have a scientific connotation. It looks like a test breeding or cloning was made. The capability of these highly advanced beings to perform such complex medical operation could not be discounted. If they were able to come to earth, then for sure they were capable of other scientific feats. When the *Homo Sapiens* multiplied, they intermingled and had sexual relations with the hominids. These were the sons of the gods now procreating with the daughters of the hominids. This hastened the evolution of the hominids into *Homo Sapiens*. Those who did not have any union with the sons of gods had a slow evolution. However, the descendants of this mixed union later on intermingled with the slow-developing hominids that resulted in the disappearance of the hominid types.

In 3,000 BC, the Egyptians were considered nomadic and were using flint stones, yet only after three hundred years, they were able to build the pyramids, the Sphinx, the obelisks, etc. They became astronomers, mathematicians, doctors, and scientists. This could not have been due to evolution. Even the scientists who espouse the theory of evolution would not be able to explain this puzzling event. Based on the period of evolution of the species, man could not have evolved so

radically and dramatically in so short a period of time. According to the *Chicago Tribune* magazine dated January 8, 2006, page 12-13, the first single-cell organism called the bacteria appeared on earth 3.9 billion years ago. Supposedly all living organisms, including man evolved from this single-cell organism. It was only eighty million years ago that the first apes appeared, who are supposed to be the ancestors of the evolutionist believers. It was only one hundred thousand years ago that *Homo Sapiens* appeared. Like the Egyptians, could man suddenly become so sophisticated and intelligent in a very short period of time? Even the wolves could not have produced a Doberman even given million of years of evolution for it requires special breeding. Somebody meddled with our evolution whether we call the meddler, god, alien, or man. Someone intelligent did it. The scientists argue as if the Darwinian theory of evolution is a fact, yet they have never proved that man evolved from the apes, hence the "missing link." The physical can never give birth to a spirit. However, if the scientists insist that they come from the apes, then let it be. Maybe that is why Einstein, who believes in an intelligent being, is way above most scientists. The Sumerian creation story could be the compromise between evolution and intelligent design. This could be the missing link to the Darwinian theory.

Sitchin in his books has extensively discussed this Sumerian creation story. Actually in the story the gods deprived man, the Lu.Lu, the ability to procreate. This inability to procreate became the romanticized story in the Bible about man eating the fruit of the Tree of Knowledge that was actually about learning the ability to procreate and with the serpent being blamed for the knowledge.

According to the Sumerian version of the story, the gods became angry when the Lu.Lu. learned to procreate and began to multiply. They knew one of the gods tampered with the genetic makeup of the Lu.Lu. They found out that E.A. who saved mankind from the deluge was the culprit. E.A. became the serpent of the Bible. He was able to evade the anger of the gods by reasoning out that procreation of human was more convenient than the difficult method of fashioning them out in the laboratories. This reason appeased the other gods. From the different Sumerian texts, it is obvious that the Sumerians are not really gods, but are highly advanced beings that came from another planet. They were called AN. NUN.A.KI, which means "Those who from heaven to earth come."[18] They are not our concept of a God, for they also do manual works, susceptible to jealousy and anger. They also have sex and procreate. The difference, however, in procreation between man and the gods is that the female gods give birth only after nine days while humans give birth after nine months. They also fight each other and die. Thus, when men began to multiply, they became afraid when they saw man united with one language.

And the whole earth was of one language.[19]

Sumerian texts also said that man had only one language.

> The whole universe, the people in unison
> To Enlil in one tongue gave praise.[20]

When did earth only have one language? This is possible if only Noah and his children survived the flood, for sure there would only be one language. The Bible is silent as to how long man has only one language. However, there is a puzzling statement in the Bible that said that after the birth of the great grandson of Noah Peleg, the earth was divided.[21] From the occurrence of the flood to the birth of Peleg, there was a period of two hundred years. Does it mean that there was only one language for two hundred years? And what is meant by the phrase "the earth was divided"? The Bible is silent on this point. If what is meant is that people began to go to different parts of the world, and then only a calamity of great proportion could have forced the people to leave their homes. The destruction of a tower would not be enough to make a mass evacuation of people. The Bible said,

> The Lord scattered them abroad from thence upon the face of the earth.[22]

What did the gods do for the people to flee Sumer? According to Sitchin, there was a war between the gods, and several cities in Sumer were destroyed. Could this be the reason and not just the destruction of one tower?

A 2,500 BC Sumerian text called "Lamentation Over the Destruction of Ur" excavated from Nippur[23] narrated the destruction not only of Ur but the cities and towns in Sumer like Nippur, Kish, Isin, Erech, Eninkug, Eridu, Larak, Unma, Lagash, Urukug, Sirara, and Kinirshag including their temples and shrines. Why did the gods allow the destructions of these cities? According to the text, Anu and Enlil ordered the destruction of the cities, its temples and shrines and the inhabitants. Fires razed the homes killing many inhabitants. Flood swift the children away. Parents abandoned their children to save themselves. In the streets were scattered dead bodies. Stephanie Dally in her book *Myths from Mesopotamia* quoted the ancient text "Atra-Hasis" that actually gave the reasons for the genocide and atrocities committed by the gods. It narrated that the gods actually tried to eliminate the human race three times already because of overpopulation and the noise and unruliness that ensued from it. The gods first introduced sickness, diseases, and plagues. Then after six hundred years when there was again overpopulation and unruliness and noise, the gods cut the food and water supplies to the people, causing draught and the death of vegetation and trees. Starvation ensued, and the people sold their relatives in exchange for food. On the sixth year of the draught,

They served up a daughter for a meal.
Served up a son for food.

Cannibalism started. Humans began to eat humans for food. Again after six hundred years, there was the overpopulation problem and its accompanying unruliness and noise, and this time the gods initiated the flood. These were the actions of the gods that forced the people to flee in different parts of the world. Men went to far-flung places to avoid the wraths of the gods. Thousands of years have passed, and because of this separation, new words evolved based on their surroundings; thus, new dialects developed, and men began to have different languages. It is not instant confusion of languages as others believed. The Sumerian gods were not capable of confusing the language of man by just decreeing. They were just a bit higher or evolved than humans, thus their capability to perform supernatural things. These are the ancient gods that evolved as the personal gods of man. There were also the Sumerian gods who were good to men like EA /ENKI or NINMAH or the Egyptian gods OSIRIS and ISIS.

Sumerian texts said that there was only one language on earth when there were yet no snakes, scorpions, hyenas, lions, wild dogs and wolves in the world. Thus, man had no rivals.[24] To settle therefore the time when the present modern man had one language, one has to know when these animals came to exist on earth. All dogs including wolves, coyotes. and jackals come from the specie *Canis Familiaris*.[25] They might have originated from Eurasia around twelve thousand to fourteen thousand years ago. They were domesticated around ten thousand years ago although there are fossils in China dating fourteen thousand years. Fossils of dogs found in Europe date around six thousand to eight thousand years old. It could be said that during the time of the mythical continents of Lemuria/Mu and Atlantis, there was only one language for it was said that Lemuria and Atlantis were destroyed by a global calamity between the years 8,000 BC to 10,000 BC. It was after this calamity that new languages evolved. The Sumerians also said that it was En.Ki who caused the confusion of language. En.Ki was the deity who, together with his spouse Nin.Mah, fashioned man from the clay. He also disobeyed the decisions of the gods to destroy the world by saving mankind from the flood. He was also the one responsible for the fertility and cultivation of earth. Maybe the reason why En.Ki was responsible for the confusion of language was because he was the god of wisdom and was told by the assembly of gods to confuse[26] man:

Changed the speech in their mouths, put contention into it
Into the speech of man that (until then) had been one.

The gods were afraid of the increasing population of man who had the blood of the gods, hence their strength and size and their capability to invent things. Man

also started acknowledging their fellow humans as heroes and treating them like gods. Thus, the gods scattered men all over the earth. With their new surroundings and distant separations, new words were formed and different languages evolved. With the introduction of different languages and regionalism, man has become divided ever since. They cannot fight as one race. Hence it would be very easy for any alien invasion of earth.

According to Sitchin,[27] fossils found in Israel showed that sixty thousand years ago the Neanderthals had already a language. The University of California, Berkeley, revealed that there was a single mother tongue one hundred thousand years ago. Based on this scientific research, maybe there should be a reconciliation of biblical time and scientific time with respect to man's evolution.

My own story about creation is that when there was still no beginning, for time has not yet existed, there was only the Infinite One. Everything is in unity. In this vast expanse of unity, a stirring occurred that expanded and expanded that caused a big bang. Separation of the Spiritual (the One) and the spiritual matter (Essence of God and Matter) occurred. Duality came into existence. With the separation, space and time were created and became known as Mother Space and Father Time. They became the constraints of all things created, formed, or made. With time, there is now a beginning and an end. Thus angels or heavens having been created have a beginning and now also have an end. With space and time, numbers and measures ensued, symbolized by sons and daughters; and from them, distance, length, width, height, volume, weight and area came about. Evolution began.

From the essence of the Holy One came the different spirits from the dwarfs to the angels. From the combination of the essence and matter came the terrestrial elements like air, fire, water, earth (matter), ether, and nonterrestrial elements. From them came the planets, the stars, the constellations, the galaxies, and the universes. Then came the living creatures, including man as narrated in Genesis

e) Time and Numbers

Time has been a ticklish question between religion and science. In the eighteenth century AD, it was the popular belief that earth was only six thousand years old based on what Psalm 90:4[28] said about a day of God being equivalent to one thousand earthly years. Thus, six days of creation means six thousand earthly years of existence. However scientific evidence shows that earth is approximately between 4 to 4.5 billion years old. This estimate almost tallies with the Hindu day of Brahma that is 4.32 billion years. New estimate of the age of the universe is around fourteen billion years.

It would seem that there is an irreconcilable difference between science and religion when it comes to "time." According to the Bible, a period of 1,656 years

has passed from the birth of Adam to the flood. Archaeological and geological findings, however, showed that a hominid similar to modern man has already existed 1.7 million years ago.

		A	B	C	D	E	F	G	H	I	J	K	L
7													
8			6										
9				5									
10					6								
11						1							
12													

Fig. 65 Period from the birth of Adam to the flood.

Scientists also say that a massive flood happened between six thousand to eleven thousand years ago during the Ice Age. How can the Bible time and the scientific time be reconciled?

Following the natural course of evolution, it would seem impossible that man in just a short period of 1,656 years plus the succeeding years after the flood could have evolved into *Homo Sapiens* capable of building the Pyramids and other wonders of the world without genetic manipulation by the gods. Just the evolution of language takes much time, how much more the evolution of man as he is now.

Sitchin said that the count of the Sumerians either start with the number 1 or the number 60; however, even if the years 1656 will be multiplied by 60, the result will only be 99,360 years, which would not be enough for man to evolve as he is now, a *Homo Sapiens*. However, this time period will tally with the findings of the University of Berkeley about man having a common language around one thousand years ago. When God talked to man, it meant that Adam had already a language. He even named all the animals. All these confusions can only come from wrong appreciation of time. The following archaeological findings also contradict biblical time, namely:

1.   There are terra cottas of female deities dating from 22,000 BC to 5,000 BC excavated in Africa and Europe. It means that there was a mother cult in predeluvian times. Sitchin said that thirty thousand years ago the Sumerian worshipped Nin.Mah who was called Mami, the origin of the word *mama/mommy*.
2.   Pottery making in Japan dates back to 10,500 years BC. This shows a civilization already existing at that time.

	A	B	C	D	E	F	G	H	I	J	K	L
1					6	3						
2												
3												
4												
5											7	2
6												
7								3				
8							6					
9		6							6	3		
10	3								6			
11			6									
12			6	3								
13										6	6	
14										6	3	
15							6					
16						3						
17												

Fig. 66 The number 36 representing the numbers 360 and 3600.

3. Catal Huyuk in the Kenya Plain of Turkey showed a settlement dating around 7,200 BC that was well organized, with a labor force and a population of around six thousand. Female statuettes dating around 23,000 BC were found in the area. The Kenya Plain was a lake that dried up 16,000 BC.[29]

4. The Sumerian kings' lists enumerated a list of kings reigning for 23,000 years BC after the flood.

Sumerian text states that 3,600 earthly years are equivalent to just one Annunaki year, which is called Saroi, Sari, or Sar. Due to this long span of life, the gods can be considered as "immortals," for they can live for thousands of years; but they are, however, not "eternals," for they can not exist for more than millions of years like the Egyptians gods.

The Jews say that a day of God is equivalent to one thousand earthly years.

The Hindus on the other hand teach that one day of Brahma is equivalent to 4,320,000,000 earthly years. This is almost the age of planet earth that according to scientists and geologists is approximately 4 to 4.5 billion years. There have been Hindu legends about man reaching the age of thirty thousand, sixty thousand to one hundred thousand years. Methuselah only reached almost one thousand years. This happened because man had committed already many transgressions. Presently, man already has reached the lowest level of existence. Thus the age

of man has hardly reached one hundred years. This period will go up, and man will be able to live for more than a hundred years gradually going up as man becomes more spiritual. Our concept of God presently is one who is Infinite without beginning or end.

	A	B	C	D	E	F	G	H	I	J	K	L
3												
4					E							
5					O	N						
6												N
7				E								
8												O
9												
10												E
11												
12			U	G	A							
13				Y								
14												
15												
16												
17				A								

Fig. 67 Time.

Like the Egyptians and the Mayans, the Hindus are very obsessed with numbers and time. Sometimes people wonder about the need of computations reaching up to billions and trillions. Only these ancient people seemed to know why.

The Hindus[30] have divided the existence of man into four yugas or ages namely, Krita Yuga (4800 years), Treta Yuga (3,600 years), Dapra Yuga (2,400 years), and lastly Kali Yuga (1,200 years).

Some people may ask, why the need for these numbers? Are these numbers important to us? Well, maybe that is the purpose, for us to ponder why the ancients like the Sumerians, Egyptians, Hindus, and the Mayans delved in these things. There must be some secrets in the knowledge of these matters.

In ancient times as well as in the present, we use certain numbers to compute time like:

60 seconds = 1 minute
60 minutes = 1 hour
60 seconds x 60 minutes = 3,600 seconds = 1 hour

3,600 seconds x 12 hours = 43, 200 seconds in 12 hours
43,200 x 2 = 86,400 seconds in 24 hours
3,600 x 24 hours = 86,400 seconds in 1 day
3,600 seconds x 72 hours = 259, 200 seconds in 3 days

In the computation of time, we use watches or clocks that are usually in circular forms. This is also true with the computation of zodiacal time where we use the circle and its degrees as units. There are 360 degrees in a circle that we divided into twelve sections that became the twelve zodiac signs. Each section has thirty degrees in it; thus 30 degrees x 12 equal to 360 degrees. It takes 864 years to pass through 12 degrees of the zodiac. Hence 864 x 30 degrees equal to 25,920 years—the complete cycle for the earth to travel across the zodiac.

	A	B	C	D	E	F	G	H	I	J	K	L
1					6	3						
2												
3												
4												
5												
6												
7							3					
8							6					
9		6			0		6	6	3			
10	3							6				
11			6							3		
12			6	3								6
13										6	6	
14										6	3	
15							6					
16						3						
17												

Fig. 68 Examples of numbers 36 and 360.

All the preceding numbers are actually lined to the Sar of the Annunakis. The following computations will show us why.

3,600   earthly years = 1 sar 3,600 earthly years x 60 Sars = 216,000 earthly years
3,600   earthly years x 120 Sars = 432,00 earthly years
3,600   earthly years x 240 Sars = 864,000 earthly years

One will notice that the numbers used in the computation of time, degrees, and sars are similar and therefore have relationships and kinships. Except for the zeroes or decimal points, they all show the same numbers.

In gematria, the zeroes and the decimal points can be deleted without affecting the results as what is important is to show the relationship and kinship of the resulting numbers. An example would be 2,592; 25,920; 259,200 or 2.592; 25.92; and 259.2. In the examples 2,592; 25,920; and 259,200, if we take out the zeroes the numbers become 2,592, 2592, and 2592. If we reduce the numbers to single digit, the results will be 9, 9, and 9. Since the numbers are equal, then they are related. This is also true with the examples with the decimal points. If we take out the decimal point and reduce the numbers to single digit, the results will be the same. Thus, the number .36 can represent the numbers: 3.6, 36, 360, or 3600, etc. We will notice that in the computation of time, the earth time, zodiacal time, and the cycle of precession, there are similarities and kinships in the numbers.

Even Berossus's writing in the third century BC said that the ante deluvian kings ruled for 432,000 years (i.e. 86,400 x 5), five years being sixty months.[31]

The Calendar

In very ancient times, the calendar had only 360 days a year composed of twelve months of thirty days each. Records, documents, artifacts, and monuments discovered attested to this fact. All over the ancient world, the year consisted of 360 days. Sumer and Egypt have identical systems of dividing the calendar into twleve months composed of three weeks that lasted for ten days each. Thirty-six of these weeks would add up to 360 days.[32] The Babylonians also counted the years as twelve months of 360 days like their predecessors, the Sumerians.

The Hindu ancient text "Aryabhatiya" stated that the year consisted of twelve months of 360 days. The circle of Avebury consisting of monuments in Britain, represent the 360 days calendar. Ancient Rome during the time of Romulus had also the 360 days calendar. The Mayas also had their 360 days calendar called Tun. The Incas had also their 360 days calendar like the Chinese who had also theirs. Why did the ancients have a 360 days calendar? Were they ignorant that the earth orbited the sun in 365 days? It is difficult to accuse the ancients of ignorance considering their great astronomical knowledge and records that reached hundreds of thousands of years. The Egyptian and Mayan astronomers are more knowledgeable than the present day scientists. They knew about the polar field of the sun that only the satellites in orbit can see.

The Dogon tribes of Mali, Africa, knew about the Sirius constellation centuries before modern men discovered it. The Dogons talked about the three stars in the Sirius constellation now known as Sirius A, B, and C. Sirius B is totally invisible to the naked eyes and was only seen thru the telescope in the

last century. It was only last 1970 that the U.S. Naval Observatory[33] was able to photograph it. It was also only in 1995 that the scientists confirmed the existence of Sirius C. Yet for centuries, the Dogons knew about the three stars and their orbits. With their astronomical knowledge, the ancients for sure knew the orbit of the earth around the sun unlike in the sixteenth and the seventeenth centuries when people thought the sun orbited the Earth, and the church forced Galileo to recant his theory about the Earth orbiting the sun. What made the ancients changed the calculation of the orbit of the earth from 360 days to 365 days? How could the ancients all over the world synchronize their calendars considering the vast distances separating them? What happened?

It was only during the Age of Cancer that the five days period called the Epagomenal Days[34] was added. Something happened in the orbit of the earth that made the ancients changed the calendar. What was the cause? Could it have been the precessional reversal that Patrick Geryl and Gino Ratinckx discussed in their book *The Orion Prophecy*? The Epagomenal Days that the Egyptians added at the end of the 360-days period were attributed to the birth dates of the gods:

Day 1 = Osisis   Day 2 = Horus   Day 3 = Seth
Day 4 = Isis   Day 5 = Nepthys

According to the book *Manetho*,[35] the epagomenal days were only added around 4236 BC.

	A	B	C	D	E	F	G	H	I	J	K	L
1				5	6	3						
2												
3												
4	3		6		5							
5												
6		3										
7												
8												
9		6										
10	3			6			5					5
11			6			3	5		6		3	
12		5	6	3							5	6
13	3										6	
14											3	
15											5	
16												
17												

Fig. 69 Examples of number 365.

There is another verse in Genesis that tells about "time" or a "period of time." It says that Adam was around 130 years when he begot Seth. Then, Genesis 4:26 said,

> And to Seth, to him also there was born a son; and he called his name
> Enos; then began men to call upon the name of the Lord.

Based on this Christian translation of the Old Testament, it would seem that only after the birth of Enos did man began to call on God or pray. This statement can be interpreted in two ways: (a) after the birth of Enos or (b) during the time of Enos or after his death, and then man began to call on God. Based on the time period given, if the basis is after the birth of Enos, then 235 years have passed before man began to worship God. This is a puzzling statement for supposed to be the gods appeared to men and communicated with them. If man considers them as gods, why did it take 235 years before man began to call on them when the gods were just around and mingling with man? Maybe it was only during the time of Enos that the whole humankind became a *Homo Sapien*, or could there be a wrong interpretation of the Hebrew verse?

I looked for verse 4:26 of Genesis in the Hebrew Bible, and I was very surprised by the different interpretation in the Hebrew Bible[36] that said that man began to profane God. This was also the interpretation in the book *The Mysteries of the Creation.*[37] How could there be so much difference in the interpretation of the verse? It would seem that the right interpretation is that man began to practice idolatry by worshipping heroes like Nimrod and Gilgamesh instead of God.

	A	B	C	D	E	F	G	H	I	J	K	L
1										4		1
2			4		1	4			4			
3		4					4	1			4	
4				4				1				
5										4		
6												
7												4
8												
9							4					
10						4						
11					1							
12												
13												
14	1											
15		4				1						
16			4									4
17				1								

Fig. 70 The year 144.

Patrick Geryl and Gino Ratinckx[38] discussed the numbers that were holy to the Egyptians and the Mayans like the numbers 144. They presented mathematical proof about the coming destruction of the world as prophesied by the Egyptians and the Mayans on December 21, 2012. They said that the proof of the existence of Atlantis and its destruction is contained in the Book of the Dead of the Egyptians based on the new translation by Albert Slosman. This new translation espoused new theories about the End Times.

Dating Methods

Even the process of dating and creating chronologies has become a controversial subject that Mr. Will Hart has discussed in his book *The Genesis Race*. Usually carbon method dating is used in dating human origins and artifacts. However, new researches show that carbon dating is not very accurate compared to the more accurate method of uranium dating. Carbon dating is off by thousands of years when compared to the results of uranium dating. There have been some controversial findings that have been shelved because they do not conform to the accepted theories like man crossed the Bering Strait to the Americas only around 25,000 BC. One of these controversial findings narrated by Mr. Hart[39] was that of Virginia Stern McIntyre, a geologist of the United States Geological Survey in the 1970s who performed tests on artifacts found at Hueyatlaco near Pueblo and cross-checked her results by using four different methods like uranium series, tephra hydration, fission track, and stratigraphy. When she submitted her findings to the anthropologist, showing the artifacts to be more than two hundred years old, she was told to change her finding to less than twenty-five thousand years old as it is ten times older than the accepted theory. When she refused to change the findings, she was ridiculed and was even removed out of her professorial position in an American university. In 1981, McIntyre wrote the "Quarterly Research":

> The problem I see is much bigger than Hueyatlaco. It concerns the manipulation of scientific thought through the suppression of "Enigmatic Data," data that challenges the prevailing mode of thinking.

There are other cases like this one, the most famous of which is that of Galileo who was suppressed from revealing his theory about earth revolving around the sun. Another controversy is about the age of the Pyramids and the Sphinx. Why are orthodox scientists and archeologists sticking to their established beliefs despite mounting evidences to the contrary? Before, the belief was that earth was only six thousand years old. When somebody suggested it was 2.2 billion years old, the suggestion was dismissed. Now it is agreed that earth is around 4 to 4.5

billion years old. What is wrong if we discover that there was already a civilization on earth five hundred years ago as told in the legends of the Egyptians, Sumerians, the Mayans, the Hindus, and the Chinese? The fragment of a nonplayable flute dated forty-five years old was unearthed in Slovenia. Could noncivilized people been playing the flutes? Are not flutes a sign of civilization?

The primitive Dogon tribe of Africa knew for centuries about the Siriun constellation consisting of the three Siriun stars that modern man learned only recently. Our astronomers learned about Sirius C only last 1995. Ancient people knew the polar and equatorial fields of the sun that became known only to man by the use of the satellites. The Mayans calculated the solar year as 365.24 days. The modern calculation is 365.242 days. The Mayans were off only by .08 seconds or an error of .000000003 percent. Where did they get this knowledge?

f) Origin of Man

According to science, the oldest known fossils that referred to Homo (man) date around 2.5 million BC. The fossils of a twelve-year-old boy dug up in Narrokotome, Kenya, are dated 1.7 million years old.[1] There is only a slight difference between the fossils and the skeletal structures of a modern boy. This would seem to imply that modern man has almost the same skeletal structures as the primitive boy during that period of time, 1.7 million years ago. Remains from the Klasies River Mouth in Southern Africa and Omo in Ethiopia dating at least one hundred thousand years showed anatomically modern people.

These findings will conflict with the time period given in the Bible. According to the Bible, the existence of Adam to the time of the deluge was only around 1656 years. This will be impossible to correlate with the scientific and archaeological findings of at least 1.7 million years from Kenya or even the one hundred thousand years fossils from Ethiopia. How can this be resolved? Could Sitchin be correct in suggesting that we should multiply the 1,656 years stated in the Bible by sixty?

According to Genesis 6:3:

Yet his days shall be a hundred and twenty years.[2]

Due to this verse, people believe that man can only live up to 120 years that seem to be factually confirmed by the life span of man presently. Although as noted by Sitchin,[3] the descendants of Noah lived more than 120 years old like Shem (660 years), Arphakhshad (438 years), Shelach (433 years), and so was Abraham (175 years.). Still man believes that the 120 years is the limit of man's existence. Even Psalms 90:10 states,

The days of our years are threescore years and ten, and if by reason of strength they be fourscore years, yet is their strength labour and sorrow for it is soon cut off, and we fly.[4]

Based on the lives of Noah's descendants, it would seem that there was another meaning to the verse. Let us remember that Adam and Eve were immortals and only experienced death after their transgression. Their lives were only shortened because of the manipulations of their genes and the introduction of diseases by the Sumerian gods and interbreeding with other species but their descendants still live more than 120 years. Further, the Anunnaki year, a Sar, is equivalent to 3,600 earthly years. If the 120 years will be converted to Sars, then it will total 432,000 years, which is equivalent to an age or yuga of the Hindus. It would seem that what is meant here is period of time at the end of which change occurs like what the Hindus believe.

According to the Sumerian king's list, the Anunnakis arrived on earth 120 Sars ago meaning 432,000 years ago. This arrival date became the basis of their count of the number of years of their stay on earth. It also became the basis of their standard count.

Even Egypt has a word for 120 years—henti. What is so important with the period 120 that the Egyptians set aside a word for it? Why not 100? Could it be that they knew the Sumerian tradition of counting or a sar? There are ancient documents that show that Egypt was once part of Sumer.

	A	B	C	D	E	F	G	H	I	J	K	L
1										M		I
2								D		Sh	Sh	
3							A					
4												
5												
6								M		A		N
7									E			
8									N			
9												
10			N									
11							E					
12						M	A	N				
13			A				E					
14	A											
15		D										
16			M									
17												

Fig. 71 Words referring to Adam, Ish, and Man.

As we are discussing about the creation of man, then the book of Genesis will be a good reference as it deals with creation. It narrates the first human family consisting of Adam, Eve, Kain or Seth, and Abel. If this grid is truly remarkable, then it must contain this story about the first family.

First Family

Figure 72 shows the names of the first family and according to the Gnostics, the other supposed woman in paradise, Lilith and also the holy name of God IEVE.

ADAM is supposedly the name of the first man created by God, but actually it is the generic name for man and woman. The word consists of the three words *A* meaning "Father," the word *DA* meaning "Know," and *AM* meaning "Mother." As the word *ADAM* cannot be complete without the word *AM*, then it should be remembered that man would not be complete without the woman AM. Hence, if man loves himself, then he should treat the woman with love and respect for she is a part of him. Thus, it is not only the story about the woman being taken from the rib of a man that makes a woman a part of man, but from his very composition and essence as shown by the letters composing the name ADAM.

	A	B	C	D	E	F	G	H	I	J	K	L
1										M		
2									D			
3								A				
4												
5												
6												
7												
8												
9												
10												
11												
12												
13	L	H			A	V	E					
14	A	L	T		V							
15			D	E								
16	I	I	M									
17												

Fig. 72 Names of IEVE, ADM, EVE, LILITH.

In the grid, there are two names of ADAM that are located at the upper right corner of the grid and the lower left corner of the grid. The upper name ADM starts with the letter *A* at H-3 with ELS of ten letters between the encoded letters. Reading diagonally upwards the letters *A*, *D*, and *M* are side by side without ELS. The name ADM is alone without the name of EVE around. This would seem to imply that during the time that ADM was alone, the focus of ADM was to be with God and the ELS of ten letters between the letters of his name showed his desire to be like God. His name in its defective form is spelled ADM without the letter *A*; thus, the numeral value of his name is 8, which needs an *A* or God to become ten. Near his name is the word *ISh* that means "MAN."

Compare this with the position of the name ADM at the lower portion of the grid, which starts at A-14 and going in the right direction has ELS of twelve (12) letters between the encoded letters. Reading diagonally downward, the letters are side by side without ELS. The letters of the supposed first woman named LILITH envelope the name of ADAM, which seems to encourage the story of the Gnostics that Lilith came first before Eve. While the name EVE is located between the letters *D* and *M* at C-15, as if to imply that she came from the BLOOD or DNA of ADM. It starts with the letter *E* at C-15 going diagonally upward and has ELS of nine letters. Now, ADM is going down while Eve is going up, aspiring to be like God. The word *DM* or *DAM* means blood that comes from the bone marrow. Thus the biblical story about the taking of the rib actually could mean the taking of the DNA of man and transforming it into a woman or in other words cloning of humans. The placement of the name EVE between the letters *D* and *M* symbolically implies that the woman was taken from the side of the man or from his rib or blood. The defective form of ADM whose numeral value is nine (9) hides the God within man. The addition of the letter *A* or GOD to the blood of man makes ADAM. Unless man reveals the God in him, then he cannot become ADAM whose numeral value is now ten (10), the number of God. Incidentally the numeral value of the word *DNA* is ten (10). Thus, man has in his blood or DNA the ability or capacity to become a GOD. The theory of Sitchin[5] about the ape-men being given the "essence" of the gods to create the present humans seems to be backed up by the grid. The ELS of twelve (12) letters between the letters of ADM connotes the twelve (12) tribes of Israel coming from ADM and EVE. Thus, from the grid one can see the history of man. Also *M* the last letter of the word *ADAM* is the initial letter of the word *MAN* at C-16, C-13 and C-10 with an ELS of two letters between the encoded letters.

		A	B	C	D	E	F	G	H	I	J	K	L
1		A											
2													
3													
4												S	
5													
6										K	A	I	N
7		B										E	
8													
9										S			
10											E	Th	
11										S			
12													
13		L											
14													

Fig 73 Sons of ADM, SETH, KAIN, and ABL

The name of ABL, the son of Adam, starts with the letter *A* at A-1 and reading vertically downwards has ELS of five (5) letters between the encoded letters. The letter *A* the first letter of the name ABL is the last letter of the name EVA, a variant form of EVE. It shows the connection of ABL with his mother EVE. *L* the last letter of the name is above the letter *A* that is the first letter of ADM. This also shows the connection of ABL with his father ADM. It would seem that ABL was really very close to his parents unlike KAIN whose name is isolated.

The name KAIN, the other son of Adam, is located in I-6 with the letters side by side without ELS. One will notice that the name is isolated and is far from the names of his parents Adam and Eve unlike that of ABL. This would suggest that KAIN was not close to his parents. The Gnostics implied that KAIN was the son of the Demiurge, the false god, thus the statement of EVE that she has gotten a son from the Lord.

The name SETH, another son of Adam, starts with the letter *S* at K-4 and going vertically downward has ELS of two letters between the encoded letters. According to the genealogy of Adam, SETH was the firstborn and made in the image and likeness of Adam. This statement creates controversies as it implies that KAIN was not the firstborn and that the teaching of the Gnostics that KAIN was the son of the Demiurge had a basis for KAIN was not made in the image and likeness of ADM. According to the Bible, it was only SETH who was made in the image and likeness of Adam, not ABL or KAIN. The seeming conflict as

to who was the firstborn could be resolved if one would treat KAIN as the first physical son while SETH was the first spiritual son from whom supposedly came the sons of gods who married the daughters of men.

g) DNA

When I was writing this section, I was wondering if there would be any word that would suggest something about DNA. I was surprised by what I found. There were two examples of the word. From the name ADM, the word *DNA* figuratively came out like a tree going vertically upward branching out into the words *AB*, which means "Father," *AM* meaning "Mother," and *BAR* meaning "Son." It would seem to convey that from the DNA of ADM came the family of man. They have as common letter, the letter *A* that symbolizes GOD. It would seem that God and DNA have a very intimate relation.

In the Kabalah, the letter *A* and the number 1 represent or symbolize God. Thus, any word or number that has a numerical equivalent of 1 can be connected to God. The word *DNA* has a numeral equivalent of "4 + 50 + 1" or a sum of 55 or 1. Even the basic units of life called adenine, thymine, guanine, and cytosine that form the DNA bases have their initial letters with the following number correspondences: A= 1, T= 4, G= 3 and C= 2 with a sum of 10 or 1. Thus, the word *DNA* can be said to refer to God. The other example of DNA went creeping in the right direction as if to give support to the DNA tree. There are only two examples of the word *DNA* in the grid that seems to imply that there might be a splitting of the DNA, which could result in something we could not handle in the future.

There is a saying that "what God has put together let no man put asunder." This is a saying based on a very, very ancient law when yet there was no man. This was the first violation of the law by angelic beings when they separated the atoms that resulted in the separation of the genders that created infinitissimal problems. This is a saying that has been erroneously referred to the institution of marriage. Religious leaders have made this saying as a commandment against divorce despite the saying of Jesus to the contrary. This saying actually refers to natural order of things like atoms being fused together or genes being together. But not man and woman who are born separately and not fused to one another. The manner of birth of human has never been two Siamese twins being born for that is an anomaly in birth. Thus what is alluded to refers to the natural order of things. It has never been natural for man to be born like Siamese twins. But it is natural that matters are fusion of atoms. It is the splitting of the natural order of things that we are being warned about. Angelic beings separated the atom that resulted in the separation of the genders and uncontrollable emotions. Man has split the atom and created the greatest fear of all—a nuclear war. Let us not create

another phobia by messing with the genes and molding man in the image and likeness of the robot without emotion. Man would like to create supersoldiers with incredible strength and endurance that could be used in future wars and the conquest of enemy territories.

	A	B	C	D	E	F	G	H	I	J	K	L
6	A		M									
7		B	A	R								
8		+										
9		+										
10		+										
11		N	‖									
12		+										
13		+										
14	- A	+										
15		D	+	+	N	I	- S	A				
16			M									
17		- I										

Fig. 74 Words about ADM, FATHER, SON, and ISA.

Note that there are two examples of the name ISA in the grid.

The first example starts at A-17 and going in a reverse direction to G-15 has ELS of seventeen letters between the desired letters. Its final letter *A* is the initial letter of the name ADM. It would seem to convey that from this entity called ISA descended ADM.

The second example is on B-15 and within the word *DNA* is the word *ISA* as if to imply that ISA is in the DNA of ADM. Again as before, the question is, who is ISA?

In the book *The Cosmic Code*, Zecharia Sitchin[6] discussed the four nucleic acids given the code A, G, C, and T that composed the whole DNA. These four letters, the genetic language of the DNA can be expressed in the following formation: "CGTAGAATTCTGCCCGAACCTT" and so on in a chain of DNA letters. A three-letter word combination of these letters is the core of all life forms on earth. Thus, when the three-letter word is combined with any of the twenty amino acids, protein is produced. Researches are being made to find which gene or group of genes in the DNA affect the functions of the different

organs of the body. The gene related to obesity has already been discovered. Now they are looking for the gene that affects ageing. I have cited the chain of DNA letters quoted by Sitchin because of the unbelievable connection to the grid as shown in figure 75.

In the example cited the letter sequence "TAGAAT" excites me for that sequence is in the grid. Why is this sequence in the grid? What is so important about it that it should be in the grid? It even shares the letters *G* and *A* with the word *GAL*, which means "REDEEMER." Is this a gene of the "REDEEMER"?

	A	B	C	D	E	F	G	H	I	J	K	L
7		A										
8		+										
9		+										
10		+				T						
11		N	|		A		E					
12		+		G	A							
13		+	A		V							
14	A	+	T									
15		D	E	+	N	+	+	A				
16			M									
17												

Fig. 75 Words about ADM, EVE, DNA, and the letter sequence TAGAAT.

Another interesting observation is that the name of EVE is going diagonally parallel to the letter sequence of the DNA as if to imply that there is another kind of DNA found only in the woman, which the scientists called Mitochondrial DNA (mtDNA). This mtDNA does not break or fuse with the male DNA. This discovery in the late 1980s enabled the scientists "to trace the mtDNA in modern humans to an EVE who had lived in Africa some twenty-five thousand years ago."[7] This special DNA coming from the woman is considered the reason why royal families in ancient times intermarry to keep the mtDNA in the family. Thus, the royal families are exempt from the law on incest. Ancient writings show that the royal families of Sumer, Egypt, Babylon, and Mesopotamia even Israel practiced these incestuous marriages. As a matter of fact, Abraham married his stepsister, Sarah, the daughter of his mother.

There was a time when our DNA was that of a God. We were immortals like Adam and Eve who only experienced death after they violated God's law. Due

to intermarriages with the sons of gods and other species, our DNA regressed. Sumerian documents also said that the gods manipulated our genes, introduced plagues and diseases to eradicate man. Due to these reasons, the characteristics of an immortal man like telekinesis, bilocation, clairvoyance, etc., disappeared. Materialism has so overcome us that we have forgotten our spiritual origin. It is time to reclaim our ancient heritage by transforming ourselves to become more positive as behooves a child of God and overcome the spreading negativity that is overcoming the world.

h) E.Din

After man was created, the Bible[1] said that God placed him in the Garden of Eden:

> And the Lord God planted a garden eastward in Eden; and there he
> put the man whom he had formed.

	A	B	C	D	E	F	G	H	I	J	K	L
7												
8												
9							M	U	S			
10												E
11							E	R				A
12											N	
13		L								U		
14			L		V				N			
15			D	E	N			A				
16			I	H								
17			N									

Fig. 76 Names of Anu, Enlil, E.A., Ninveh, E.Din, and Sumer.

This verse in the Bible is based on the Mesopotamian text called the Myth of Cattle and Grain."[2]

> After Anu, Enlil, Enki (E.A.) and Ninveh had fashioned the
> black-headed people, vegetation that is fruitful they had tilled the land.
> In the E.Din, they placed them.

What is this Eden? Where is it? The word *Eden* comes from the Sumerian words E and Din, which mean "abode" and "righteous" or "abode of the righteous." The word *righteous* refers to the deities or divine beings of Sumer and not to Adam and Eve. It is obvious that the garden was just part of Eden where the deities lived. But where is Eden? The Bible[3] said the Garden of Eden is located where four rivers meet.

> A river went out of Eden
> to water the garden;
> and from there it was parted
> and became four principal streams

The Bible describes Eden as the source of a great river that divided into four principal streams or rivers. These four rivers are

> The name of the first is Pishon. Xxx And the name of the second river is Gihon. And the name of the third river is Heddekel and the fourth river is Euphrates.[4]

Two of the rivers still exist today, Hiddekel known presently as the Tigris River and Prath called today as the Euphrates River. However, up to the present the location of Eden could not be pinpointed due to the other two rivers that are missing. The Gihon River is believed to be the present Karun River due to the similarity of its course as described in the Bible. However, the fourth river called the Pishon has completely disappeared. Another reason why it is difficult to pinpoint Eden is the mistaken notion that Eden is a dry land. We are forgetting who these beings are. Myths and legends of all ancient civilizations from Sumer, Mesopotamia, Egypt, India, China, and South Americas have described our ancestors as coming from the seas or having fishlike or reptilian features. Terra-cottas dating 3,000 BC show humanlike forms with reptilian features while terra-cottas dating 5,900 BC showed lizardlike faces. One of the Sumerian gods was called E.A, which means "He whose abode is water." He was the god who told Zuisudra (Noah) to build an ark to escape from the coming deluge. If E.DIN is the abode of the gods like E.A, then this abode must have been watery. The only place in Sumer where there is a big body of water until now is the Persian Gulf. This is also the place where three rivers confluence. A look at the map of the Persian Gulf will show that the Tigris, the Euphrates, and the Karun rivers meet at the Persian Gulf. But the question still is, "Where is the fourth river?" This question was resolved in 1993 when the Center for Remote Sensing at Boston University[5] announced the discovery of a lost river that

flowed under the Arabian Peninsula for more than 530 miles up to the Persian Gulf where it confluences with the other three rivers. The river was more than fifty feet deep with a width of three miles. According to the Boston University, during the last Ice Age between eleven thousand and six thousand years ago, the Arabian climate was wet and rainy that produced a mighty river that supported a lush forest and vegetation in the area. This would relate to the saying of Isaiah that there were forests in Arabia:

> In the forest in Arabia shall ye lodge.[6]

The only possibility that Arabia has forests was during the last Ice Age when there was a river running across the Arabian Peninsula that watered its surrounding. If this is the case, the river Pishon must have existed before the river dried up some five thousand years ago and disappeared according to Boston University. The river was found through the use of landstat satellites. With the discovery of the fourth river and the four rivers confluence in the Persian Gulf, then it could be said that EDIN is the Persian Gulf and its seashore is the Garden. Could this discovery lend credence to the myth that our ancestors lived in the waters? Could this also be one reason why they chose earth because it is a watery planet?

With respect to Isaiah, it is amazing how Isaiah knew that there were forests in Arabia before which were nonexisting in his time and was only confirmed scientifically to be true in 1993? How could Isaiah talked about the altar of God in Egypt, the sacrifices offered by the Egyptians to the God of Israel, and the blessings bestowed by God to Egypt that happened thousands of years before Isaiah's time? Isaiah was a remarkable prophet.

i) Amphibious Ancestors

All ancient civilizations like Sumer, Egypt, Mesopotamia, Babylon, Akkad, India, China, and the South Americas have stories about theirs ancestors and gods as coming from other planets and amphibious in nature. Most of us do not believe these stories and regarded them as myths and legends. Despite terra-cottas dating 3,000 BC and ancient drawings and paintings of amphibious beings, we accepted these artifacts as based on fantasies. What is strange about these stories is that it was prevalent in all parts of the world despite the distance of the places and different cultures of the people. Credible historians wrote seriously about these amphibious beings and considered them not as fantasies.

Robert Temple discussed these amphibious beings extensively in his book *The Sirius Mystery*[7]. He said that ancient historians like Berossos (290 BC), who was a friend of Aristotle wrote about the amphibious beings like Oannes who supposedly founded the earliest civilization on Earth, Sumer in 6,000 BC. Although the

Babylonians honored their amphibian founders, they described them as abominable and repulsive because of their fishlike features. They have scales and fishtails; they could not walk like humans. If the Babylonians have not actually seen these beings, why would they describe their founders in derision as repulsive and abominable? They could have described their founders and gods with more respect and reverence.

Another historian Appolodorus wrote about another fishlike god called Odacon who came from the Erythracean Sea that is now divided into the Red Sea, the Persian Gulf, and the Indian Ocean. He criticized another historian Abydemus (fourth BC) for not writing about the other amphibian gods existing at that time. The ancient historians were very serious in their narrations about the amphibian gods. They could not just be telling tall tales.

The Dogon tribe of Mali that knew the Sirius constellation long before modern men discovered the Sirius constellation claim that their ancestors were fishlike creatures that came from Sirius. The Egyptians have also long association with Sirius with the legend that Osiris, Isis, and Nepthys come from Sirius and were also amphibious beings. There were ancient paintings about Osiris and Isis with intertwined fishtails.

Robert Temple[8] quoted the descriptions made by another ancient historian, Alexander Polyhistor of Militus (105 BC) about these fishlike creatures:

> The whole body of the animal was like that of a fish; and had under a fish's head, another head, and also feet below, similar to those of a man, subjoined to the fish's tail. His voice too, and language, was articulate and human; a representation of him is preserved even to this day . . . When the sun set, it was the custom of this being to plunge again into the sea, and abide all night in the deep, for he was amphibian.

In a fourth to third millennium Sumerian text quoted also by Robert Temple,[9] Enki was described as:

> Enki, in the swampland, in the swampland, lies stretched out.

Only an amphibian would lie stretched out in the swampland unafraid of the snakes and the crocodiles.

According to a Sumerian poem that antedates Genesis and the Babylonian version of creation by one thousand years when the gods mutinied against En.lil, they complained to En.Ki, but En.ki or E.A. could not hear them because he "is lying asleep in the deep and fails to hear them."[10] "Lying sleep in the deep" means E.A., god of the sea, was sleeping in the bottom of the sea. The name E.A. also means "He whose abode is the water." E.A. did not know about the mutiny because he was at the bottom of the sea.

Plutarch recounted an Egyptian tale about Zeus not being able to walk for his legs were grown together maybe like fishtail.

The Greeks have many amphibious gods like Neptune (Posoidon), Cecrop (who came from Egypt and founder of Athens), Erichtonious (son of Cecrop), Nereus, Proteus, and Scylla. The others were Triton, Glaucos, Phorkys, Palaimon, and Negaion all called Old Men of the Sea.

India has fishlike gods like Trita and Aptya. It has also the story of Vishnu reincarnating as a fishman called Matsya while China has Fu Shi (3322 BC) and Nu Gua/Nu Wa/Nu Kua. During the Han Dynasty, around 2,000 BC, Fushi and Nu Gua were pictured as having intertwined fishtails.

	A	B	C	D	E	F	G	H	I	J	K	L
1					U						A	I
2				Y							Sh	Sh
3												
4												
5												
6			M	A								
7					Tz							
8					Y							
9				A								
10			N	U								
11		N		K	A			R	S			
12		N	U	G	A		A		A			
13			A	Y								
14										U		
15									Y			
16												
17												

Fig. 77 Matzya, Yu, Shia, Gun, Nu Gua, Nu Kua and Asar.

Other amphibian Chinese gods were Emperor Yu/Hsia, 2,205 BC and Gun. The Chinese have always maintained that their civilization was founded by an amphibian with a man's head and a fishtail. In a bass relief in Cyzicus, a city opposite Byzantium, Osiris and Isis known in ancient times as As-ar and As respectively were shown as half-human and half fish.

These very prevalent stories would further explain why the location of E.Din could only be the Persian Gulf as the Anunnakis were amphibian in nature as

suggested even by the name of the god E.A. that means "He whose abode is water" and the god EN.KI that laid stretched out in the swampland. The seashore of the Persian Gulf where the four rivers of E.Din confluenced, was a swampland.

These legends and myths would further bolster the reason why during this time the annihilation of man was done not through fire, but by water—the *deluge* for the gods were amphibians. They have nothing to fear, for they will not drown!

j) Deluge

There are many flood myths around the world. The most ancients are the Sumerian, Akkadian, Mesopotamian, Babylonian, Assyrian, Jewish, Hindu, and Chinese stories of the flood. The oldest version that is around 2,100 BC is the Sumerian version that is the basis of the Genesis story in the Bible. The story is the same; the details, the expression and style of narration are similar. So as not to be said as a copycat, some changes were made like the name of the hero, the mountain where the boat landed, and the creatures that were boarded to the ship. This is a case of different retellings of an essentially the same story. The reason for the flood, however, is the same. It is the story of a being that is angry and cruel. One capable of genocide unlike the Father whom Jesus said could love you and forgive you seventy-seven times. It is very obvious based on ancient writings and the actions of the gods that we are not dealing with a god but advanced beings with their own failings and anger. Thus, the Gnostics called that god as a Demiurge, the false god! However in this story, there is also the good god E.A., spouse of the goddess Nin.Mah the maker of man, who saved mankind from the deluge.

	A	B	C	D	E	F	G	H	I	J	K	L
9												
10									U			
11				I		A			R			
12						A	M	A				
13					Y				Y			
14												

Fig. 78 Deluge.

Figure 78 shows the Sumerian word *AMARU* meaning "deluge" in the pattern of a boat with the Sumerian words *YAM* meaning "sea" underneath the pattern.

In Genesis, the name of the god who was angry was not mentioned nor the name of the god who saved humanity. The hero in his story was Noah who was told to.

> And of everything of all flesh, two of every sort shalt thou bring into the ark, to keep them alive with thee.
> And take thou unto thee of all food that is eaten, and then shalt gather it to thee and it shall be food for them, and for thee.[1]

In obeisance with God's command, Noah brought two of every fowls after their kinds, two of every cattle after their kinds, and two of every creeping things of the earth after its kind. He brought along his immediate family sans relatives and friends.

When I read these verses I could not help criticizing Noah for being selfish. For sure there were other people besides relatives and friends who were also good, maybe not as perfect as Noah but at least good. Yet he did not even invite them or save them. It is for this reason that I always said that Abraham and Moses were greater than Noah for they always interceded for the failings of their companions. However, the Sumerian texts have corrected my view of Noah, for he did ask his neighbors, friends, and the poor to be with him.

	A	B	C	D	E	F	G	H	I	J	K	L
5										O		
6										A		N
7			A	R						Ch		
8				K								
9				H	A						A	
10			O	N						E		
11									S	O		
12									A	Ch	N	
13												
14												

Fig. 79 Noah and the Ark.

Other things that made me wonder about the deluge were the gigantic tasks that were given to Noah. How could Noah in so short a time perform such tremendous tasks? How could he possibly collect two kinds of all living flesh and

put them in the ark? Just collecting the animals and birds, leading them to the ark and placing them in their proper places would be an impossible task. Good that there were no dinosaurs. Then this matter of bringing the food and feeding all the creatures are unthinkable. Then the cleaning of the animals and their wastes would be horrendous. How could this be done? And that is not all. How do you remove all that wastes and the smell? The ark was supposed to be closed and the window was only opened after forty days at sea. How did Noah and his family survive the stench and the accumulating wastes? These are the questions that are difficult to answer. Yet we believe this story.

k) Different Deluge Stories

The Sumerian and Babylonian deluge stories are the oldest in the world ranging from 2,100 BC to 1,700 BC. The *Epic of Gilgamesh* found at Niniveh is contained in twelve clay tablets with the eleventh tablet containing the deluge story. The name of the hero was Utnaphistim who was a shipbuilder whose ship landed at Mt. Nisir. The god E.A. told Utnaphistim:

> Put aboard the seed of all living things, in the boat.[2]
> Loaded her with all the seeds of living things, all of them.[3]
> Aboard the ship take thou the seed of all living things.[4]

Utnaphistim also brought along with him not only cattle and wild animals but also his kin and all kinds of craftsmen. This portion was deleted from the Genesis story.

In another Chaldean story, the god HEA told the hero Sisit:

> Cause to go in the seed of life, all of it, to preserve them.
> All I possessed I collected of the seed of lie, the whole.
> Cause to go in the seed of life all of it, to preserve them. All I possessed
> I collected of the seed of life, the whole. I caused to go up into the ship,
> all my male and female servants, the beasts of the fields, the animals of
> the field and the sons of the army all of them, I caused to go up.[5]

Again the hero Sisit did not only bring the beasts and animals of the field but also his male and female servants and the sons of his army. Again this part of the story was deleted from Genesis. The god E.A. was the same god HEA.

In another flood story, the Epic of Atra-hasis dated 1,750 BC, the hero was called Atra-hasis while in another version it was Atram-hasis. The hero was not a shipbuilder. He brought into the ship birds, cattle, and field animals. In

this version the birds are already included in the cargo but not the quadrupeds. Atra-hasis, however, brought along the elders, the carpenters, workers, children, and the poor. This again was deleted from the Genesis version. Again the god who warned Atrahasis was E.A. The flood was not global as the city of Sippar survived as also narrated by Berossus.

In 300 BC, Berossus[6] narrated the story of the deluge based on the Sumerian story. He said,

> Take friends, different animal, both birds and quadrupeds.

This time the quadrupeds are included in the cargo. The taking of friends, however, is still not included in Genesis. In this story, the city of Sippar survived the flood.

In a Sumerian text approximately 2,100 BC that was found in Nippur, the hero was called Ziusudra and landed at Dilmun when the flood subsided. As I have said before I have a problem with the Genesis deluge story about the collecting of the animals, placing them in the ark, feeding them, cleaning them, and taking out the wastes. In the Sumerian creation story that was the basis of the biblical story, there was no such problem. The *Epic of Gilgamesh*, which is a thousand years older than the Genesis story, said that the god EN.KI/E.A. told Ziusudra (Noah):

> And into the boat take seed of all living creatures.[7]

It is apparent that there is a big difference between the Genesis flood story and the Sumerian flood story. In this story, Ziusudra took aboard the boat "the seed of all living creatures," not the physical living flesh consisting of two of its kind of fowls, cattles, and creeping things. What Ziusudra took was the "SEED" or "ESSENCE" of all living creatures. In the Akkadian language, the word *seed* means "ZERU," which refers to that matter from which living things sprout. In the Sumerian language the word is "NUMAN,"[8] which refers to the essence from where human comes from. The seed can therefore refer to the "sperm or essence" of living creatures from whence the offsprings come. In the Egyptian language, "DA" means "Seed," thus "Da Adam" means "Seed of Adam."

	A	B	C	D	E	F	G	H	I	J	K	L
1										M		
2									D			
3								A				
4			U									
5		R	E	Tz		N		A		M		
6								M		A		N
7		A							E			
8		+								N		
9		+										
10		+	N									
11		N	|									A
12		+				M	A	N				
13		+	A									
14	A	+										
15		D	+	+	N	+	+	A				
16		M									N	
17										N	U	M

Figure 80 shows the words that refer to ADAM, AM (means "Race/specie") MAN, ZERU, NUMUN, and DNA.

The Sumerian version would seem to be a more plausible and believable story as the tasks to be accomplished are more doable. Although there will be a question as to how the seeds and essences were taken and contained, however, the scientific knowledge of the gods could easily have helped in the collection and preservation of the seeds. Although the Sumerians considered them gods, their origin and failings showed that these gods were just highly advanced beings and not a God as our concept of a God is now.

Ian Wilson[9] said that during the last Ice Age, ice sheets covered 70 million cubic kilometers of the earth's surface. Presently there are 25 million cubic kilometers covering the earth more particularly Arctic and Antarctica. If these 25 million cubic kilometers of ice will melt, the present day sea level will rise up to 210 feet covering most of all the cites of the world except Mexico City.

1) Abraham

Most people know Abraham as a shepherd with many flocks and the father of many nations. Not only the Jews but also the Muslims and Christians honor him. The Bible said that he left Ur because God told him so. The Koran, however, gave a further reason why he left Ur. Abraham could not accept the idolatry practiced by the people. The Koran in 21'53 said:

> (Abraham) said to his father and to his people, "That are those images to which you are so devoted? They replied, "They are the gods our father worshiped." Abraham said, "There you and your fathers are in greatest error. I am no idolator."[1]

Terah, the father of Abraham, fearing for the lives of Abraham and the clan, left Ur and went to Canaan. However, Terah continued to practice his idolatrous way. Abraham who believed in just one God began to have conflict with his father. The Koran in 21'63 narrated this conflict:

> (Abraham said,) "Ask them if they can speak." They said to Abraham, "You know they cannot speak." Abraham answered, "Would you worship that which can neither help nor harm you? Shame on you and your idols?[2]

	A	B	C	D	E	F	G	H	I	J	K	L
4												
5			R									
6		A		M								
7		B	A	R								
8		H										
9												
10						T	H					
11							E	R	S			
12						M	A		A			
13					A	V						

Fig. 81 Names of Abram, Avram, Abraham, Terah, and Sarah.

Because of this religious conflict, God told Abraham:

> Get thee out from thy kindred, and from thy father's house.[3]

King and Pharaoh

In obeisance with God's command, Abraham left his father's house and those who still believed in the idols. Abraham had many followers, for he was not an ordinary shepherd. Actually he has 318 armed, trained servants for he was a king.[4] He held a vast territory. According to Genesis 15-18:

> In that same day, the Lord made a covenant with Abraham saying unto thy seed have I given this land, from the river of Egypt unto the great river, the river Euphrates.[5]

The land that was given to Abraham was a vast tract of land extending from the Nile to Euphrates River covering the Sinai Peninsula, Syria, Arabia, and part of Sumer. An ordinary king could not possibly control such vast territory, for it would require enormous resources and manpower. Yet he was given the vast territory, for he was a Hyksos pharaoh.

Due to his stature, Abraham was mentioned in the *War of the Kings* where he allegedly defeated the kings of Sodom, Ellasar, Elam, and the king of all nations. The king of Salem, Melchizedek gave him homage and blessed him. Because of his royal status, Abraham was married to a Sarai, which means "a princess." His marrying his own sister Sarah further shows the royal status of Abraham. It was the tradition of Sumer, Mesopotamia, Babylon, and Egypt that stepbrothers and sisters could intermarry to produce the heirs to the throne. Children from these kinds of marriages have priority even over the firstborn from other marriages. Thus, Isaac was given the leadership even if Ishmael was the firstborn. There was no such thing as incest for the royal blood. Thus Abraham said,

> Sarah is indeed my sister; the daughter of my father, but not the daughter of my mother."[6]

Abraham was not an ordinary king. He was a Hyksos king and was considered the Pharaoh Mam-ayb-re of Lower Egypt in acknowledgment that he was from Mam-bre. The Hyksos kings ruled Egypt for five hundred year.

It has been suggested by Ralph Ellis[7] based on the writings of the ancient historian Josephus that the Pharaoh Sheshi who lived at the time of Abraham was actually Abraham. The Pharaoh Shesi had his throne name as May-eb-ra that later became as Mam-aye-bra. The evolution of the name May-eb-ra has similarity with the transformation of the name of Abram to Abr-ah-am. There was just the insertion of the words *AM* and the rearranging of the letters to transform May-eb-ra to Mam-aye-bra. In the case of the name Abram, there was the insertion of the word *AH* to transform the name Abram to Abr-ah-am. The

word *AM* means "mother goddess or race" while the word *AH* means the moon god. Thus the Pharaoh Sheshi became connected to the mother while Abraham became connected to the moon god who later on evolved as the moon goddesses. Actually by adding the word *AH* to the name Abram that contained already the name RA, the sun god, Abraham became connected both to the sun god and the moon god that made him more powerful and complete. By the method of gematria, it can be shown that the Pharaoh Sheshi and Abraham had something in common. When Abraham came to Mam-bre, his name was still Abram. Later on this name was changed to Abraham by the insertion of the letters *AH*. The word *AH* is the Egyptian moon god and the Sumerian moon god Sin. The word *Mam-aye bra* was just a transformation of the word *Mam-bre*. The letter *A* and *E* in Hebrew and Egyptian are interchangeable; hence, there is no problem in interchanging them. In the Hebrew language, the letter *E* is always written in the script form as Aleph. The letter *E* is just another way of pronouncing the letter *A*. Thus in gematria, the word *Mam-bre* is also Mam-bra. With the insertion of the word *aye*, the word *Mam-bra* becomes Mam-aye-bra. One can see the similarity with the changing of Abraham's name.

By gematria and temurah, one will see the transformation of the word *Mam-aye-bra* to *Y Abraham*. As stated before the letter *A* is sometimes written as an *E*, but they have the same numeral correspondence of 1; hence, they can be interchanged. The letter *H* has a numeral value of 5; thus, *H* is equal to *A* (1) + *M* (4) = 5. Based on the preceding, the word *Mam-aye-bra* can be transformed to Abr-ah-am.

> Mam-aye-bra
> If E (1) = A(1) then *A* can replace *E*; hence, Aye becomes Aya.
>
> Mam-aya-bra
> If Am (1+4) = H (5), then "mam" can be "Mh"
> MH-aya-bra by means of temurah becomes
> Y—Abr-ah-am

I believe that the name Mam-aye-bra was actually written originally as Mam-ay-bra for the letter *E* could be deleted if a word is written in its defective form. Also if there is truth that the Pharaoh Mam-aye-bra was Abraham, then the word must be written as Mam-ay-bra. Gematria will show why. The name Mam-ay-bra has a numeral value of (4+1+4) + (1+1) + (2+2+1) or (9) + (2) + (5) or a total of sixteen. The name Abr-ah-am has numeral correspondence of (1+2+2) + (1+5) + (1+4) or a total of sixteen also. As Mam-ay-bra is equal to Abr-ah-am, there is therefore a relationship between Mam-ay-bra and Abr-ah-am. They could be one person.

Why was the word *AH* inserted to Abraham's name? If we will dissect the name of Abraham and show the root words, it will appear as Ab-Ra-Am. Ab means "father," Ra means the sun god while Am means "mother or race." It can be literally interpreted as "Father Ra and the Mother" or "Father Ra of the Race." If this is a title, to whom is it being addressed to? For sure it is being addressed to Abram, the father of all nations. What then is the reason for the insertion of the word *AH* to Abr-am? AH is the name of the moon god, the son of Ra. If the word *AH* will be added to the name Abram to become Ab-ra-ah-am, then it is impliedly being revealed that there was a transformation of Abram for the sun god and the moon god are now in him. Four thousand years ago, the moon god known also as Thoth was very central to the Hyksos beliefs. There was a legend that Ra made Thoth his successor on earth. This story might have a connection to the belief of the ancient Egyptians that the moon was the sun shining at night. Thus at night Thoth as the moon ruled earth. To completely evolve, Abraham must have also the symbol of the son of Ra, Thoth. Thus the name Abraham can now be literally interpreted as Ab (father), Ra (sun god), Ah (moon god), Am (mother). This is now a complete family for there is the father and the mother and the son. Abraham is now completely transformed. He has now become highly evolved with the masculine and the feminine powers in him. He has now wisdom for the name AH also known as IAH is also YA or YAH, the God of Wisdom of the Israelites and E.A. the god of wisdom of the Sumerians.

PART IV

REVELATIONS

The Gnostics were right in their allegations that Jesus taught secret doctrines unmentioned in any Christian teachings. Jesus's teachings showed he was a Kabalist and a Baal Shem Tov (Master of the Holy Names).

CHAPTER VI

THE SECRET DOCTRINES

Despite the many miracles and teachings of Jesus, the New Testament never mentioned Jesus teaching secret doctrines to the apostles although St. John said that if all the things Jesus did would be written, even the world could not contain the books that would come out from these writings. According to the Gnostic writings, Jesus allegedly taught the apostles secret teachings, which were very opposed to the traditional teachings of the church. These hidden teachings were Kabalistic and Gnostic in nature that were antagonistic to the church interests, hence considered heretical; thus, there was no mention about these teachings in the church writings.

As some of these secret doctrines are contained in this code, it is only logical to discuss the same. However, in our search for the truth, we have to transcend our beliefs to learn. One has to abandon his biases, prejudices and accepted concepts in order to learn and appreciate intelligently new ideas especially if they are avant-garde or revolutionary. Thus, the first step is to set aside our set of ideas and beliefs. Forget them temporarily. Like a glass filled with water, empty the glass first so that fresh water can be placed. A filled glass cannot take in additional water that will just spill over. Clear our minds so new ideas can enter. We must journey into the world of the Kabalah, free from any intellectual and emotional biases and fanaticism with faith in the wisdom of God to guide us to the truth that we may be set free of our fears and be what we are supposed to be, made in the image and likeness of God and not robots.

Fear is the greatest enemy of man, thus our deterioration. Reading this book will not make us infidels or devil but will make us what we deserve to be in the twenty first century, children of God and not slaves of others with their contorted interpretation of the Bible. God gave us a free will. He wants us to ask questions and not just follow. He could have created robots if He wanted one. Instead, He created man with all his imperfections, for only from imperfection can perfection be a reality.

Let us remember what Matthew said.[1]

> And the disciples came up and said to Him, "Why dost thou speak to them in parables?" And He answered and said, "To you it is given to know the mysteries of the kingdom of Heaven, but to them it is not given . . . That is why I speak to them in parables, because seeing they do not see, and hearing they do not hear, neither do they understand."

Also in Matthew,[2] it is said,

> All these things Jesus spoke to the crowds in parables and without parables He did not speak to them; that what was spoken thru the prophets might be fulfilled, I will open my mouth in parables, I will utter things hidden since the foundation of the world.

Thus, the masses were taught in parables, but the apostles were taught differently. What are these things hidden since the foundation of the world? Why could they not be mentioned in the Bible? Why were these teachings only taught to a chosen few? Could the reason be what Jesus[3] said?

> Do not give to the dogs what is holy, neither cast your pearls to the swine, lest they trample them under their feet, and turn again and rend you.

This is a reminder not to teach the sacred matters to the unworthy, for they will not understand. Jesus taught the Lord's Prayer to the apostles according to his interpretation, but the apostles were the ones who taught the masses according to their interpretations hence the difference in the teachings. So let us not be surprised with what we will find in this code. Even the Lord's Prayer was taught differently to the apostles as will be shown by the code.

According to the Secret Book of James[4] written approximately in the second century AD, it is stated,

> Since you have asked me to send you a secret book revealed to me and Peter by the Lord, I could not turn you down or refuse you. So I have written it in Hebrew, and sent to you and only you. But, considering that you are a minister for the salvation of the saints, try to be careful not to communicate this book to many people, for the Saviour did not even want to communicate it to all of us, his twelve disciples. Nonetheles, blessed are those who will be saved through the faith of this treatise.

It is very obvious that the teaching of Jesus was not given to all, and even to his disciples, they were each taught differently according to their spiritual evolutions. In one of the scrolls called the Secret Book of John,[5] the apostle John narrated the mysteries and secrets of heavens that Jesus revealed to him, which was very different from that contained in the Bible. According to the Gnostics, Jesus taught a cosmology very different from what the Old Testament was saying. In the secret teachings, Jesus talked about several worlds and heavens. This actually relates to the saying of Jesus about the Father having many mansions that unfortunately the Christian writers have never elucidated. They only talked about one hell and one heaven while St. Paul talked about several heavens. If ever matters foreign to Christian doctrines are discussed in this book, rest assured that they are relevant and related to the contents of the grid. So let us not be surprised if we will find Kabalistic, Gnostic, Egyptians, and other matters discussed in this book.

a) The World of Unity

In the Kabalah, it is taught that before the beginning when time was not and space was nonexistent, the world of unity existed where everything was at one. There was, is, and will be only One Infinite Being who has no name, no sex, nor form and is beyond the comprehension of man. From the Secret Book of John[6], Jesus described the Infinite Being to the apostle John as:

> It is illimitable, since there is nothing before it to limit it.
> It is unfathomable, since there is nothing before it to fathom it.
> It is immeasurable, since there was nothing before it to measure it.
> It is unnamable, since there is nothing before it to give it a name.

Since the Infinite Being is incomprehensible, the Kabalists mentally drew a veil to that point, which the mind cannot possibly reach. The veil became a concept corresponding to human limitations and has become known as the Veil of Negative Existence. For want of words, the term *Negativity* was used to imply a being or existence of a nature, which was incomprehensible and beyond man's realization. No words can possibly explain *it*. It is unity beyond unity, higher than the Creator. The Kabalists classified this negative existence into three levels of unmanifestation, namely:

"AIN"	=	which means "Nothingness"
"AIN SOPH	=	which means "Infinite"
"AIN SOPH AUR"	=	which means "Limitless Light"

It is said that Ain Soph contracted into "Itself" into a point, withdrawing its infinite light thereby creating a void around the point. As the point is a circle, it is evenly getting light from the Infinite One. If it was a square; then some points will be getting more light than the others. From Ain Soph Aur, which is the universe of infinite brilliance, a single ray of light was projected into the point, the center of the void, which transformed into ten lights or emanations, which became known collectively as the Sepheroth. From these initial emanations countless universes were formed, which ultimately culminated into the four worlds of Emanation (Atziluth), Creation (Beriyah), Formation (Yetzirah), and Making (Asiyah). Each Sephera is a phase of evolution containing the potentialities of all that comes after it in the scales of down floating manifestation. The Sepheroth are always shown in the form of a tree called the Tree of Life.

Veils of Unmanifestation

As the veils of un-manifestation are considered the world of unity, it only follows that it is above the Tree of Life that is the world of duality. In the World of Unity, there is only One Being who has no name, for there is no one to give IT a name; sexless for it has no constraint and formless for IT has no limitation and is beyond the comprehension of man. For distinction and reference purposes, we will refer the Holy Entity as the INFINITE ONE. This Kabalistic concept about the veils of un-manifestation can only be found in Kabalistic books. Since the Lord's Prayer is not supposed to be Kabalistic in nature, can this concept be found in the grid? Unbelievably, yes! The three levels of un-manifestations are contained in the grid, which will only confirm that a Kabalist has written this code, and the Lord's Prayer is a Kabalistic teaching in the guise of a prayer but actually a code containing secret doctrines only taught to a selected number of apostles.

The first veil of unmanifestation called AIN can also be written down in another form AYN as the letter I and Y are numerically equal and can be interchanged.

The second veil of unmanifestation called AIN SOPH can be found in the grid in the initial form AS. A look at figure 82 shows that the letters $A.S$ are printed horizontally, vertically, and diagonally without ELS as the letters are side by side.

The third veil of unmanifestation called AIN SOPH AUR is found in the initial form ASA in the grid.

The holy names AIN, AIN SOPH, and AIN SOPH AUR are used by the Kabalists to differentiate the Infinite One from the gods known by man. They are considered the highest names of God according to the Kabalah and are above the Tree of Life. The veils of unmanifestation are shown in figure 82.

	A	B	C	D	E	F	G	H	I	J	K	L
1				N								
2					I					A		
3						A						A
4								A	S	S		
5							A					
6										A	I	N
7												
8												
9												
10												
11												
12							A					
13			A					Y				
14				I			A	Y	N			I
15					N		S	A				
16												

Fig. 82 Three levels of Unmanifestations.

These holy names are usually not the subject of meditations, for they are beyond the comprehension of man. It is said that the highest plane that a man can reach in the meditation or spiritual level is the fourth Sephera of Hesed. To go to the third Sephera Binah might be very risky, for one might not be able to return to the physical world as one will pass the abyss or death before reaching Binah. But legend has it that Ezekiel was able to reach the highest heaven, Kether where he saw the chariot thrones of God.

Actually it is in the Sephirah Binah that diversity begins; thus, understanding is needed to comprehend the diversification of things.

As stated before in the Jewish esoteric tradition called the Kabalah, the highest realm or heaven is Ain—Nothingness. As it is beyond the comprehension of the human mind, it is hardly discussed. If ever there is a discussion of Ain, it is elucidated as to what it is not.

From where I came from, I was told that this heavenly abode of Ain was also the realm known as the realm of Divine Silence. This is the highest heaven where silence rules, nothing moves, everything is stillness. There is no movement, for there is no space to move around. Without space, there is no distance, measures, or numbers. Time does not exist. Without movement, there is no energy; thus, there is no vibration or frequency. There is no change or evolution or transformation

for energy does not exist. Without energy, the Newtonian and the Einstein theories of gravity and relativity do not apply. The world of duality does not exist. Nothing created is there. There is no form, for there is nothing to shape. There is no dissolution, for there is nothing to dissolve. If energy cannot be destroyed for it would just be transformed into another kind of energy, Ain cannot even be transformed, IT is just IS. Transformation means change. Ain is permanent and unchanging. It IS, it IS, it IS! It is a world of paradox. It exists yet does not exist. It is there yet not there. It is like the "missing mass" in space that man's instruments fail to detect yet exists. It is not even the world of unity for what is there to unify where nothing exists.

All the teachings of the mystics about the steps to undertake to reach union with the Holy One are only steps up to unity. All these steps of knowing oneself, detachment, unconditional love, understanding, forgiveness, and wisdom are for unity with the Holy One. All teachings say that unconditional love, understanding, forgiveness, and wisdom are above the world of emotions, for they are under the mental world. Yet they are still emotions, controlled, disciplined, and fueled by positive energy to reach the Highest Being of emotions known as Kether where the highest realm of emotion, Holiness is. Yet there is a higher realm known as the world of Ain where there is no love, wisdom, holiness, or thought. This is the world where there is no movement, no vibration, no frequency nor energy; thus emotion and thought do not exist. Without emotion, there are no feelings of love, hate, anger, depression, or loneliness. Without thought, there are no desires, greed, ambition, or ego; there is eternal peace, no conflict, war, or oppression. There is no karma. Look at the rock. It is alive. If you kick it, does it kick you back? If you curse it, does it curse you back? Does it want to be president? For sure no, for it does not have emotion or desire. Who is more evolved? If we came from "nothing" and not from the dust; then our ultimate aim is nothingness.

In the world of divine silence, where stillness rules, nothing moves, nothing breathes for oxygen is not needed; nothing eats, for there is no digestion. And nothing dies, for there is no transformation of energy. It is eternal peace. There is no law, for there is no act. There is no fear, for there is no emotion.

From this vast ocean of nothingness, a stirring occurred. Energy was born. Movement came about. Thought came to be. Desire was born, the desire to create. A portion of the vast ocean of nothingness contracted, forming space. Duality came to be. In that space, energy found a home. Energy filled the space. Creation began. The big bang occurred everywhere. With space, time, and distance came into being together with numbers and measurements. Expansion started. Particles of energy began to group together forming diverse fields of energy masses. Area, volume, and weight came into existence. Universes were formed with their galaxies, planets, stars, and solar systems. Diverse beings and things were created.

Although there is diversity, there is unity for everything is neutral. There is balance everywhere. The color is brilliance. It is a sexless or genderless system. Procreation is by thought, budding, or fission. There is no masculine or feminine energy. In this system of existence, the law was "what the Infinite One has put together let no one put asunder." This was the law for millions of years until the highly evolved beings known as angelic began thinking of separating energy into yin and yang, male and female. They experimented in far-flung universes. Thus, the first omission was the separation of energy or the atom. This is the basis of the biblical story about the making of Eve from Adam's rib, which is actually the separation of the masculine and feminine energy and the basis of the future conflict between the genders. The separation of the energy paved the way for the creation of more diverse, incredible beings and creatures and the appearance of extreme emotions like envy, greed, ambitions, etc. Different species came into existence. This caused the conflict between those for and against separation. The conflict became known as the war of the cosmos involving several universes. The experimenters were defeated and were banished into outermost universes deprived of their power to create. After millions of years of peaceful existence, the effect of the separation of the atoms came to be. There came the question about the superiority of the genders. Several universes became involved in this conflict that became known as the angelic war. The propatriarchal forces won over the promatriarchal forces. Since that time there had been a conflict between the two forces. Due to the aggressive and expansive tendencies of the masculine energy, more conflict and misunderstanding came about that resulted in more negative energy. To prevent further conflict, a force of angelic beings from different universes was formed to maintain peace.

However, more experimentations and interbreeding of races and species still continued that brought more diverse, aggressive, and uncontrollable creatures with extremes emotions. Due to this interbreeding the powers that the beings possessed before began to deteriorate and be lost. Procreation through thoughts, budding, and fission had been lost. The energy bodies became more and more dense and physical, losing its crystalline and liquid qualities. Due to this sad consequence, a new edict was promulgated prohibiting interbreeding with different species—"to each, his kind"—animals with animals, spirits with spirits, etc. Some beings had to look for new galaxies to suit the vibrations of their new bodies. The denser the bodies became, the farther the beings traveled. They went to lower dimensions that could sustain their vibrations. The travelers became more and more separated from their ancestors. To adopt to their new environments, changes in the energy bodies started. The travelers became more diverse and different from their ancestors. As time went on, they forgot their ancestors and where they came from. They even digressed. The ancestors, regretful of their experimentations, agreed to form a new race that would help supervise, monitor and guide the inhabitants of these

far-flung universes. Some ancestors did not agree. This is the source of the story about Lucifer not agreeing to the creation of man. For several million years, the new race evolved peacefully. But several races envied the new race and tried to block the evolution of the new race by schemes, manipulations. and even conflicts that resulted in planetary and galactic wars. The sequel to this story can be found in the writings of Ashayana Deane, author of the Voyagers.

b) The World of Duality

After the veils of un-manifestation comes the Tree of Life. And with the creation of the Tree of Life with its different hierarchies of angels and the different spirits, the world of duality came into being and plurality came into existence and the Infinite manifested in many forms appropriate to the state of evolution of the beings in the created world. It is said that the ten names of God contained in the Tree of Life were used in the creation of the world. Each name is a manifestation of God's power and traits. Thus the God of love and compassion is called El while the God of war is called Alhim Gibor. The Creator is called Elohim, or is it the Creatress as stated previously? As there are ten names of God, so there are ten heavens and ten hierarchies of angels. St. Paul[7] enumerated several hierarchies of angels, namely, Thrones, Domination, Powers, Virtues, Principalities, and Angels that is an implied admission that there are several heavens as commensurate the number of hierarchies of angels. It leaves no doubt that Paul was a Kabalist. It is even said that Paul was a student of a great Kabalist. The church did not elaborate on this doctrine about the several heavens but instead the church taught about only one heaven that actually contradicted the saying of Jesus that God has many mansions where the deserving souls correspondingly go according to its spiritual evolutions. There are findings now that Paul was also a Gnostic, and many of his supposed letters were forged like the letters to Timothy and Titus to support the contention of the church that Paul was anti-Gnostic. Of the thirteen (13) letters of Paul,[8] only seven (7) are now accepted as genuine although their authenticities are still in doubt.

c) The Tree of Life

We now come to the Sepheroth that is illustrated in the form of a tree hence its designation as the Tree of Life that is supposed to be in the Garden of Eden.

AIN

AIN SOPH

AIN SOPH AUR

0

Kether

| Binah | 0 | 0 | Chockmah |

| Geburah | 0 | 0 | Chesed |

0

Tiphereth

| Hod | 0 | 0 | Netzach |

0

Yesod

0

Malkuth

The Tree of Life

The ten branches are called Sepheroth or divine emanations. The Sepheroth are not gods, but the manifestations of the traits or essence of the INFINITE ONE. In the illustration given, the veils of un-manifestation are above the Sephera Kether that is the beginning of the Tree of Life.

Figure 83 shows the words *Otz* and *Etz ChI* both meaning "Tree of Life."

	A	B	C	D	E	F	G	H	I	J	K	L
1												
2					I							
3					Ch							
4					E							
5				Tz	O							
6												
7												
8												

Fig. 83 The Tree of Life.

For convenience, a table of correspondences was made to show the Hebrew names of the Sepheroth, their corresponding English translations, and the planets symbolically representing each Sephera:

NAME OF SEPHEROTH	TRANSLATION	PLANETS
1) Kether	Crown	
2) Chockmah	Wisdom	
3) Binah	Understanding	Saturn
4) Chesed	Mercy	Jupiter
5) Geburah	Strength	Mars
6) Tiphereth	Beauty	Sun
7) Netzach	Victory	Venus
8) Hod	Splendor	Mars
9) Yesod	Foundation	Moon
10) Malkuth	Kingdom	Earth

The Sepheroth

The Tree of Life is composed of ten Sepheroth with each Sephera having its own set of laws, conditions, times, and ethics.

The first Sephera is called Kether or Crown. which is the first impulse of Ain Soph Aur toward manifestation in this world of creation. In Kether, all things are together in peaceful union. There is no form only a monad of pure energy in which is contained the power of opportunities in unity. Kether contained all that was, is, and will be. It is the source of everything, and everything will return to it. The divine name of God in this Sephera is Eheieh equivalent to I Am, which is part of the name Ahih Ashr Ahih equivalent to I Am that I Am.[9] Kether is also a part of Creation, an extension of the unmanifest Ain Soph Aur and is represented by a point.

From Kether comes the second Sephera called Hokmah or Wisdom. where the will to create first manifested. Here the concept of creation began. Pure thought has not yet been broken up into differentiated ideas. Wisdom is the level above all divisions where everything is simple unity. Only below this level does the division between good and evil exist. He is the Planner. He is the Father who created all things, for it is from this will that all came about. He is the all-knowing, all-powerful Supernal Father called ABBA or ABA or AB, the father of Yehoshuah or Jesus. Hokmah, the great stimulator of the universe can be represented by straight line.

	A	B	C	D	E	F	G	H	I	J	K	L
4												
5										M	O	
6									K	A		
7	B									Ch		
8												
9												
10					E	T	H					
11				K			R					
12			N									
13												
14												
15												
16												
17				H								

Fig. 84 The Sepheroth: Keter, Chokma, and Binah.

The third Sephera is Binah or "understanding" in whose womb all that was contained in wisdom becomes finally differentiated. Here division exists. She was the spirit that hovered over the water, and she was called in Hindu esoteric teachings as Narayana. She is the Supernal Mother called AMA or AIMA or AM coequal with the Father. The divine name associated with Binah is ELOHIM, the implementor of the will of wisdom. Elohim is a plural word since understanding implies plurality of forces. It is the name Elohim that is used throughout the entire first chapter of Genesis as the Creator of the world.[10] According to the Bible, the name of the Creator is Elohim, which was mentioned thirty two times in Genesis. Binah is the feminine counterpart of Hokmah. It is the sphere that builds forms.

The translator of the Bible did not realize that the name Elohim refers to the feminine entity IHUH ELOHIM of the third Sephera, Binah. These statements have serious connotations as they infer as to who is the Creator. Had the translators of the Bible known this fact, would they have used the name? Esoteric teachings of other religions have stated that it was the feminine entity who created the world. This is against the Christian doctrine.

With the appearance of the father and the mother, duality came into existence, and the differences of the sexes became established. There can be no manifestation without differentiation. Without the spirit, matter cannot exist. Without matter,

spirit cannot manifest. In this world of duality, spirit and matter must be together, for they will be useless without the other.

	A	B	C	D	E	F	G	H	I	J	K	L
6												
7										Ch		
8												
9												
10												
11						Sh						
12												
13												
14												
15			D									
16												
17												

Fig. 85 Sephera, Chesed.

The fourth Sephera is Chesedor "mercy," the first sphere of the physical universe, which is capable of comprehension by the human mind. Chesed is the benevolent, loving, and protective father, unselfish and loving. This is the result of the union of wisdom and understanding. The holy name associated with this Sephera is EL, the generous and merciful Father. This sphere symbolically represents the first day of creation when God created light, which was different from the sun and the moon.

The fifth Sephera is Geburah or "justice." The benevolence, mercy, and form-building qualities of Chesed is now balanced by the severe, destructive actions of Geburah. The form issued by Chesed is now cleansed and purged by the cleansing fires of Geburah. It burns away all that is outmoded and useless. This is necessary for evolution. While Chesed is expansive, Geburah is constrictive. Geburah is feminine and limits the abundance of Mercury. The divine name associated with this Sephera is ELOHIM GIBOR, the dispenser of justice. This Sephera represents the second day of Genesis when God separated the waters by causing a firmament to appear between them.

The sixth Sephera is Tiphereth or "beauty" and receives all powers of the Sepheroth. It is the point of transmutation between the planes of force and form. It lies within the range of human experience. As the top sphere, it is the mediator for the other five Sepheroth. This is the place of the Mediator or Redeemer, which includes Christ, Buddha, and Osiris. It reconciles what is above with what is below. Here God has a manifestation. This sphere mediates between Mercy and judgment. If Kether is metaphysical, Tiphereth is mystical. The divine name in this Sephera is ELOAH VAU DAAT. Tiphereth represents the third day of creation when God gathered the waters in one place and dry land appeared.

The Sepheroth Gevurah and Tiphereth can only be found by permutation.

The seventh Sephera is Netzach or "victory." This is the sphere of human instincts, emotions, and desires. Art, music, dance, and poetry are expressions of Netzach energy. All emotions are here. This sphere controls nature and elemental forces. The divine name in this Sephera is IHVH TZABAOTH. This sphere represents the fourth day when God created the sun and the moon.

		A	B	C	D	E	F	G	H	I	J	K	L
5													
6													N
7						Tz					Ch		
8													

Fig. 86 Sephera Netzach.

The eight Sephera is Hod or "splendor." This represents the left brain, the rational mind, which organizes and categorizes. All expressions of writings, languages, communications, and magic are from Hod. All words and names of power originate from here, which are necessary in ceremonial magic and occultism. Netzach represents the right sphere where the emotions and instincts take form and come into action. Intellect needs emotions to drive it. ELOHIM TZABAOTH is the holy name in this Sephera. Hod represents the fifth day when God created the creatures of the sea and the moon.

	A	B	C	D	E	F	G	H	I	J	K	L
1												
2									D			
3												
4												
5					O							
6												
7												
8	H											
9									S			
10												
11												
12												
13												
14												
15												
16									Y			
17												

Fig. 87 Sepheroth: Hod and Yesod.

The ninth Sephera is Yesod or "foundation." It is the sphere of the astral light also known as the Akasha. The blue print is made in the astral light, which materializes in the physical plane. All things if natural or man-made occur in the astral plane before they occur in the physical plane. Ideas first appeared in the Yesodic part of the inventor's mind. Yesod is the seat of intuition. Magical operations take place here before occurring in the physical plane. SHADDAI EL CHAI is the divine name in this Sephera. Yesod represents the sixth day of creation when God created Adam and Eve.

The tenth Sephera is Malkuth or "kingdom," the ultimate sphere of form and of final manifestation. This is the Sephera where the four elements air, water, fire and earth are. Malkuth symbolically represents God's feminine counter-part, the "SHEKINAH." It is thru Her that divine grace passes to the other Sepheroth. The divine name in this Sephera is ADONAI MELECK. It is in this sphere that the presence of God, the Shekinah is in exile. Malkuth represents the seventh day of creation when God rested.

	A	B	C	D	E	F	G	H	I	J	K	L
1												
2												
3											M	A
4	L	K	U	T								
5												

Fig. 88 Sephera Malkut.

With the presence of the Sepheroth in the grid, it could truly be said that the author of the code had knowledge of the Kabala. It would not have been possible for a non-Kabalist to discuss the esoteric doctrine of the Tree of Life. Further discussion will also show that the author of the code was a Baal Shem Tov, a master of the secret, holy names of God or Semiphoras.

d) The Law of Opposites

In this world of duality, the law of opposites applies. Thus, there are always two opposing forces, the positive and the negative, yin and yang, light and darkness, male and female, father and mother. Thus, if one talks about God the Father, it only follows that there is a God the Mother. It is intriguing why it is heretical to talk about a God the Mother when it is the most natural thing in this world of duality? There is a mystical law that says, "What is above so is below." We are supposed to be a reflection of the above. If in this world of duality there is always a mother to have a child, how come that above there is only a Father and a Son but no Mother and the Holy Spirit is an "It," a neutral? In the old Jewish religion, which was very much influenced by the Babylonian religion, the Jews acknowledged the God the Mother. They called Her the Queen of Heaven,[11] and cakes were being offered to her.[12] She was well-known to the Hebrews of biblical times who worshipped in the groves of the goddess Asherah,[13] and the Jews bowed down to her images.[14] The Jews also honored Astarte, the goddess of the Phoenicians and Philistines.[15] The name of the goddess Anath survives in the Bible as that of Shamgar's mother[16] and of the priestly village Anathot, Jeremiah's home now—Anatha—north of Jerusalem. She had become so dear to Jews of both sexes that those who escaped to Egypt vowed to serve her with libations and cakes made in her image.[17]

A transformation, however, in the Jewish religion from matriarchal to patriarchal took place when Moses received the Ten Commandments, and as a consequence the Queen of Heaven was discarded, and God the Father was put in Her place. Despite this turn of events, however, the Kabalists still maintain their belief that in this world of duality, male and female divinities exist and who are equal with one another. If there is a God the Father, there is a God the Mother. Thus, if there is a mention about the Mother, it does not only refer to Mary, but to the Supernal Mother, the God the Mother.

Figure 89 shows the dual nature of the physical world with the presence of the following words:

Hebrew words:

AB—means "Father"
AM—means "Mother"
BN/BAR—Son
BATh/BET—Daughter
ABA—name of God the Father
AMA—name of God the Mother

	A	B	C	D	E	F	G	H	I	J	K	L
1							B	A		M	A	
2								A		A		
3											M	A
4								A		S		
5											O	B
6	A											N
7	B-	A	R	E-			T-					
8												
9												
10							H					
11												
12					A	M	A					
13												

Fig. 89 Words Father, Mother, Son, and Daughter.

The Father

Presently in this world of duality, the highest God is called the Father and considered the creator of the world. But there was a time, eons ago when the

Mother was the highest entity. The Father is called by many names as there are religions. To the Jews, He is called IHVH, a name so sacred that no Jew except the high priest can pronounce it. When the name is encountered in any reading, it is substituted by the name ADONAI or TETRAGRAMMATON. However, Jesus addressed this God not as IHVH, but as ABBA to instill in his followers that God should be considered as a Father who loved and cared for His children. Jesus pictured God as a loving and forgiving God who was very different from the God of Israel who was very strict and unforgiving for those who violated His laws. Thus the question arose as to whether the God of Israel was the same God the Father that Jesus was talking about. The God of Israel was a jealous God who generously rewarded those who obeyed His law but severely punished those who disobeyed Him, even ordering the massacres of enemies and the destruction of their cities while the Father of Jesus was forgiving and merciful to the enemies and even loving them. Was the God of Israel the Father of Jesus? If the first Christians, the Gnostics, would be asked, they would say no! For the Gnostics considered the God of Israel as the Demiurge, the false god. While the present Christians out of blind faith never bothered to ask. This attitude cannot settle the question as to who is the God of Israel. Jesus's Father is very different from the God of Israel as the apostles did not even know His name. Jesus[18] said,

"I have declared to them Thy Name."

What is this name of the Father that Jesus has declared to the apostles? It could not have been IHVH, for the Jews knew that name, and Jesus did not use said name in the New Testament. It could only have been a new name given only to the disciples to fulfill what Jesus said that He had given the Father's name to them. This is one secret that seekers of knowledge should try to discover. Jesus said, "the Father and I are One."[19] If they are "One," then their names are equal to one another. The different names of God are found in the chapter on Semiphoras or names of God.

The Mother

In the discussion of the code, it would seem inevitable that the focus of discussion would be the masculine aspect of God since it is about the Father. Thus, the appearance of the feminine aspect in the grid was very surprising as the teaching of the church has eliminated the goddess doctrine. However, it seems to follow the natural law or the law of duality that when one talks about the Father, one cannot simply evade the question about the Mother. As this is the world of duality, we therefore cannot just leave the feminine entity out of the picture. This study will just be half-truth without the inclusion of the Mother. Although

the feminine entity was left out in the Old Testament, however, in other ancient writings older than the Old Testament the feminine entity was the focal point of discussion. There was a time when the Mother was the highest spiritual being worshipped by men.

There was the temptation not to include the Mother in this study to evade the possible controversy that might be created, but this would result in a dishonest and unfair exposition for the code contained many doctrines about the Mother, which were not revealed in the Gospels. There might be a repetition of the mistakes committed by the early church fathers who decided not to include the writings about the Mother like the "Evangelium of the Hebrew/Gospel of the Hebrew" where Jesus said, "the Holy Spirit, my Mother."[20] Thus, for the sake of the truth, we will now talk about the Mother as pointed out in the code.

In the world of unity (the highest heaven), All is One and One is All. Everything is at One with the Supreme Being who exists without form for the One has no constraint; without sex for the One has no limitation; without name for no being exists before the One to give It a name. The One God is the God of all; hence, there is no question as to whether one is a Catholic, Protestant, Muslim, Hindu, Buddhist, or a pagan to be saved.

e) Apocryphal Writings

Most ancient writings that refer to the Mother are called Apocryphal writings because they are not included in the Bible when it was being collated. The Gnostics or the Knowers wrote most of the Apocryphal. They were the Christian followers of St. John the Beloved who believed in a God the Mother. This belief can be attributed to the close relationship between the disciple "Behold, thy mother" and Mary "Behold thy son" and the supposed teachings imparted by Jesus to a select group of apostles. The Gnostics prayed to the Mother. They believed in the duality of God, the masculine and feminine aspects of God. The followers of St. James, the apostle and Mary Magdalena were also Gnostics who prayed to the Father and Mother. The Gnostic followers of Mary Magdalene later on became the Cathars who were the cause for the formation of the Inquisition that massacred the Cathars of France including women and children.

Existence of the Mother

In the world of duality (the material world), God has to manifest with a form, sex, and a name in order for man or created beings to comprehend and to allude to. This manifestation appeared in different forms—humanlike and animal-like. Being the world of duality, "they come in pairs" the one the opposite of the other.[21] Hence there is the law of opposites, light and darkness, black and

white, spirit and matter, male and female, father and mother. In this kind of world, the absence of one renders the other inutile. The bow without the arrow is useless. Hence if there is a God the Father, it follows that there must be a God the Mother or Goddess. The Christians do not accept this obvious and glaring fact and would rather keep blind. The problem is what if there are names of God the Mother in this code, will they condemn this code and this study as devilish? I hope not. Because of the code's Kabalistic nature, it should not be surprising that there are many names of the Mother in this code. Doctrines about the Mother were Kabalistic teachings that were hidden and not given to the masses but only to the apostles. Even in the Gnostic writings, it is alleged that Jesus taught the secret of secrets to John, James, and Mary Magdalene but not to the other apostles who were taught secret doctrines according to their spiritual evolutions. So let us not be surprised specially those who are strangers to the Kabalah about the many names of the feminine entity and the corresponding doctrines therein. An extensive explanation about the Mother is made because of its controversial nature, a controversy that is hard to understand considering that this is the world of duality, and it is very natural to have a mother. Centuries of brainwashing have made it easier for man to accept a physical mother but not a spiritual mother. It is ironical that man can accept God appearing as a dove, a flame, or a lamb but not as a woman.

What Is Above, so Is Below

Besides the Gnostic writings, there is a mystical law relevant to the doctrine about the existence of the Mother that says, "What is above so is below." We are supposed to be just a reflection of what is above. In this material world, there is always a father and a mother to have a child. If these representations exist in this world, then there must exist also in this world of duality the entities being represented, God the Father, God the Mother, and God the Son or the Daughter. And this principle is shown by the different Trinitarian beliefs of the different religions. Hinduism has Brahma, Vishnu, and Siva as the Trinity while the Egyptians have Osiris, Isis, and Horus as the Trinity. It is only the Catholic Trinity that is different, for while there is a God the Father and a God the Son, the feminine aspect is missing. There is no God the Mother, but an IT—a dove. This is violative of the natural law, the law of Duality and the mystical law stated above.

The Kabalist recognized the third Sephera called Binah (understanding) as the highest feminine entity. The divine name associated with this Sephera is IHVH ELOHIM pronounced "Adonai Elohim" or "Tetragrammaton Elohim" in deference to the nonpronunciation of the name IHVH. The feminine entity in this Sephera is also called AMA, the dark Mother and sometimes also addressed

as AIMA, the fertile Mother who is always conjoined with the Father. The words *AM* or *EM* also mean "mother."

	A	B	C	D	E	F	G	H	I	J	K	L
1	A.										A/	
2												
3												A
4												
5												
6			M.					M/				
7												M
8												
9												
10												
11					A./							A
12					A	M	A					
13												

Fig. 90 First to the fourth examples.

As if to emphasize the doctrine about the Mother, the author of the code had given many examples in the grid with different ELS, and most of them with short intervals that would more than satisfy the rigid requirements imposed by Israeli researchers on ELS. I did not show anymore the other examples that could have been given if I used the permutation method as there are already many examples shown through the method of the ELS. Below are fifteen examples with different ELS.

Number of Examples			Coordinates		ELS
1st example	A = A-1	M = C-6	A = E-11		61 letters
2nd example	A = K-1	M = H-6	A = E-11		56 letters
3rd example	A = L-3	M = L-7	A = L-11		3 letters
4th example	A = E-12	M = F-12	A = G-12		None

	A	B	C	D	E	F	G	H	I	J	K	L
1								A				
2			M					A		A		
3		M				A		A				A
4												

Fig. 90-a Fifth, sixth, and seventh examples.

5th example	A = H-1	M = C-2	A = J-2	6 letters
6th example	A = H-2	M = B-3	A = H-8	5 letters
7th example	A = J-2	M = B-3	A = F-3	3 letters

	A	B	C	D	E	F	G	H	I	J	K	L
5												
6	A											
7												M
8												
9											A	
10												

Fig. 90-b Eighth, ninth, and tenth examples.

177

8th example	A = F-3	M = G-9	A = H-15	79 letters
9th example	A = L-3	M = H-6	A = D-9	31 letters
10th example	A = G-4	M = G-9	A = G-14	4 letters
11th example	A = H-5	M = C-6	A = J-6	6 letters

	A	B	C	D	E	F	G	H	I	J	K	L
4												
5								A				
6			M						A			
7												

Fig. 90-c Eleventh example.

12th example   A = D-6   Y = F-6   M = H-6   A = J-6   ELS = 1 letter

	A	B	C	D	E	F	G	H	I	J	K	L
5												
6				A		Y		M		A		
7												

Fig. 90-d Twelfth example.

13th example   A = A-6   M = L-7   A = K-9   22 letters

	A	B	C	D	E	F	G	H	I	J	K	L
5												
6	A											
7												M
8												
9											A	
10												

Fig. 90-e Thirteenth example.

| 14th example | A = B-7 | M = G-9 | A = L-11 | 28 letters |
| 15th example | A = D-9 | M = F-12 | A = H-15 | 37 letters |

It is intriguing that the total number of examples is 15 that in numerology is equal to 6, the number of the Mother—AMA. With the appearance of the many holy names of the Mother with different ELS, the only conclusion is that this is a very deliberate act and not a coincidence. This will emphasize the acceptance by the author of this code about the existence of God the Mother who is known in Kabalah as AMA or AIMA.

	A	B	C	D	E	F	G	H	I	J	K	L
6												
7		A										
8												
9				A			M					
10												
11												A
12						M						
13												
14												
15								A				
16												
17												

Fig. 90-f Fourteenth and Fifteenth examples.

	A	B	C	D	E	F	G	H	I	J	K	L
1										M	A	
2		I	M							A		
3	E	M	E								M	A
4	L											
5	H		E					A		M		
6	A		M	A			I	M		A	I	
7		A		E							E	M
8												
9												
10										E		
11					A		E			L		
12				G	A	M	A			A		
13			A		A		E			Th		
14												
15			E									
16		I	M									
17				A								

Fig. 91 Other Hebrew names of the Mother.

It is unfortunate that many people were prosecuted and killed, more particularly the Cathars in France for the perceived heresy of believing in the Mother. The Inquisition was primarily put up because of the Cathars, and there is a big possibility of another Cathar crisis in the millennium if the church will acknowledge Mary, the Mother of Jesus, as Coredemptrix with Jesus.

Figure 91 shows the other Hebrew names of the Mother like AM, EM, IM, ELHA, which can be read as ELOHA and ELATh. The letters are side by side without ELS.

Equality with the Father

The position of the third Sephera, Binah in the Tree of Life is opposite the second Sephera, Chokmah not below it. This only affirms the doctrine that the Father and the Mother are equal, and not as believed by others that the Mother is inferior to the Father. Even the word *ABBA* that means "Father" and the word *AMA* that means "Mother" have both the numeral equivalent of 6 meaning they are equal and one. Further, the verse in Genesis about the simultaneous creation of man and woman show that there is equality in the sexes. The creation story about Eve being created from the side of Adam was not meant to prove the inferiority of women but to allegorically narrate the separation of the sexes.

In most religions of the world, past and present like the religions of India, Egypt, Babylon, Persia, Greece, Rome, Africa, China, Tibet, North America, the Incas and the Mayas, the feminine entity or goddess had always been acknowledged.

Dove as Symbol of the Mother

Only in the Christian religions (Catholic and Protestant) is there so much masculinity that even in the doctrine of the Trinity—Father, Son, and the Holy Spirit—the female aspect is missing. The Holy Spirit is neutral with the dove as a symbol forgetting that in the Hebrew language the word *YONAH* meaning "dove" is "feminine" in gender. Ironically in ancient times, the dove was the symbol of the Mother worshipped by the Jews before and during the Exodus. This symbolism has been carried over in the Bible without the Christians realizing that the symbolism represents the Mother whom we now address as the Holy Spirit. During the baptism of Jesus, the Bible narrated,

> And Jesus when he was baptized, went up straightway out of the water; and lo, the heavens were opened unto him, and he saw the Spirit of God descending like a Dove, and alighting upon him; and lo a voice from heaven saying "This is my beloved Son in whom I am well please,"[22]

Who descended? Not God but the Spirit of God? Who is the Spirit? Who else but the Mother! Yet the Christians made the Mother an "It." Thus, the Christians have the most unnatural and illogical Trinity—a Father, Son, and an It (Holy Spirit) while all religions have their Trinity as the Father, the Mother, and the Child or Son.

The Unnatural Trinity

The reason for the unnaturalness of the Christian Trinity is the error in the use of the Greek word *Pneuma* in the interpretation of the Hebrew word *Ruach*, which means wind or spirit. Although both words *Ruach* and *Pneuma* can mean spirit, however there is a great difference between the two because of genders. Ruach is feminine in gender while Pneuma is neutral in gender. In layman's term Ruach is a she while Pneuma is an "It." Since Pneuma is a neutral, it was translated into Latin as a neutral and retranslated into English as an "It." From a she, Ruach became an "It," resulting in an erroneous doctrine that is illogical and violative of natural laws; thus the Christian Trinity is the Father, the Son, and "It" instead of the Father, the Mother, and the Child as revered in other religions.

	A	B	C	D	E	F	G	H	I	J	K	L
7		A	R									
8	H	U										
9			H	A								
10		O	N									
11	Y											
12												
13												
14									N			
15								A		O		
16									Y			
17												

Fig. 92 The Dove.

The mistake made resulted in a doctrine that completely eliminated the feminine aspect and created a belief that the Holy Spirit could appear as a dove but not as a "woman." Despite this glaring error, the Christian religions could not correct their doctrines about the Trinity and the Mother. This reminds us of what Jesus said:[23]

They have eyes but cannot see, they have ears but cannot hear neither do they understand.

Holy Spirit—A She

Some Gnostic writings dating AD 100 to 300 spoke about the Mother. One of these books, the secret book also commented in the differences between the words *Ruach* and *Pneuma*. The Jews who believed in the secret book acknowledged the Holy Trinity as the Father, Mother, and Child. The secret book described the Mother as:

The image of an invisible, virgin, perfect spirit. She became the Mother of everything, for She existed before them all, the Mother-Father.[24]

As stated in the Gospel of the Hebrews, Jesus himself admitted the gender of the Holy Spirit by using the expression "Even so did my mother, the Holy Spirit."[25] This explains the saying of Jesus that blasphemy committed against Him can be forgiven, but not blasphemy against the Holy Spirit. This reminds us of our common saying, "You can curse me but not my mother for that I will never forgive you."

Another Gnostic book is the Gospel of Thomas[26] where Jesus differentiated "His earthly parents, Mary and Joseph with His divine Father, the Father of Truth and His Divine Mother, the Holy Spirit."

These Gnostic writings cannot be included in the Bible as they speak about the existence of the Mother. However, some writings in the Bible like Wisdom, Proverbs, Sirach, and Baruch talk about the feminine entity known as Wisdom. However, Wisdom, which talks lengthily about the feminine entity has been deleted from the Protestant Bible. Maybe in this millennium, the Protestants may reconsider the deletion of the entity known as Wisdom.

Holy Spirit—Second Person of the Trinity

Another illogical concept emanating from the Christian concept of the Trinity is the idea that the Son is the second person of the Trinity that gives the Son a higher position than the Mother. This implies that the Son came first before the Mother that would result in a queer and illogical situation. In the Kabalah and other religions of the world, the Mother is the second person of the Trinity. In the Tree of Life, the position of the third Sephera, Binah, the Mother, is opposite the second Sephera, Chokmah, the Father that shows the correct doctrine about the Trinity. The Mother is first before the Son. In the physical world, there is always a father and a mother to have a child. If this is very logical in the material

world, the more it should be in the spiritual world. If we are just a reflection of what is above, should this not be also the order of things? But because of the Jewish tradition that male is superior to women, even the son is given higher position than the mother, a woman. Even by royal succession, the male heir was given the priority to succeed the king. This is another chauvinistic feature that has become a religious concept.

Creatress of ADAM

Another mistranslation that will be difficult to remedy for the correction will affect the very foundation of the Christian religion is the seventh verse chapter 2 of Genesis. The Hebrew words used in the creation of man or Adam were *VIITzR IHVH ALHIM ATh HADM* pronounced "Va-Yeyetzer Tetragrammaton Elohim Ath Ha-Adam." As can be seen, the holy name IHVH ALHIM was referred to as the creator of Adam. Unfortunately IHVH ELOHIM was just translated as God without deference to the meaning the holy name connotes for it refers to the name of the Mother in the third Sephera, Binah. This will again confirm the mistranslations committed by the translators of the Bible. If the Bible were only translated according to the meanings contemplated by the writers of the Bible, maybe there would not have been much religious conflict in this world and women would have been accorded the respect they truly deserve.

This theory about the Mother being the Creatress of the world is in consonance with other religious beliefs and the mystical law "What is above, so is below." Here, in the physical world, the source of birth is the mother. Cannot the spiritual Mother be also the source of birth of the universe?

Further evidence as to this theory about the Mother as the Creatress is the use of the word *ELOHIM* or *ALHIM* thirty-two (32) times in Genesis. *ELOHIM* is the plural word of the singular word *ELOHAY*, which is feminine in gender. It is the combination of two words *EL* meaning "God" and *IM* meaning "they," "them," or "theirs."[27] Together Aleph and Mem make AM, which is the Hebrew word for "MOTHER"; thus, another reason why ELOHIM is considered feminine.[28] In Hebrew, AM can be interchanged with the word *IM* because numerically they are the same.

f) Who Created the World?

In the creation story of the world, there are as many versions as there are religions or beliefs. The Christians believe that God the Father is the creator of the world while many ancient religions acknowledged that God the Mother was the creator of the world. As the Christian belief is based on the Old Testament

more particularly Genesis, then it is only proper that we examine the verses on creation in Genesis.

Traditional Interpretation

Previously, we have discussed some interpretations of the phrase, "Berashit Bara Alhim Ath Ha-Shamym Vath Ha-Aretz," which was traditionally interpreted as "In the beginning, God created the heavens and the earth." Some have objected to the said interpretation and offered alternative interpretations. On my part, I have arrived at a very different interpretation from the traditional and the alternative interpretations. Figure 93 shows the letters of the first verse of Genesis in the grid, and which by permutation, the verse is formed.

In the translation of the Hebrew phrase, the English translation should as much as possible faithfully follow the structure of the Hebrew phrase. It would seem, however, that the traditional translation has a flaw and does not follow the Hebrew structure and makes assumptions that are questionable, hence the objections.

Some of the assumptions are the following:

1) In the phrase "Berashit Bara Alhim Ath," the translators assumed the word *Alhim* as the subject of the verb "Bara" as there is no noun preceding the word *Bara* to be the subject matter. Hence the phrase was translated as "In the beginning, God (Elohim) created," which if translated into Hebrew would have been "Berashit Elohim Bara." The word *Ath* meaning "and" would seem to have no place in the sentence. For if one has to place the word *Ath* before the word *Ha-Shamym*, then the phrase as translated would become "In the beginning, God created and the heavens and the earth." This would result in an illogical and senseless phrase. Thus, the English translation eliminated the word *Ath* or "and." Thus, the translation became "In the beginning, God created the heavens and the earth" without the word *and* in front of the word *heavens*.

2) The translators assumed the word *Elohim* as meaning "God." They did not realize that the word *Elohim* can mean the heirarchy of angels in the seventh Sephera. If this is the case, then the phrase "let us make man in our image and likeness" would become logical and not refer to an individual God who should have said, "I will make man in my image and likeness." For to use the words *let us* connotes talking to somebody and asking permission to create which should not be for one who is supposed to be God and alone. Thus, an explanation of the word *Elohim* is necessary for further enlightenment. The word *Elohim* is a combination

of the words *EL* meaning "God" and *Im* meaning "they or them." Thus, the word *Elohim* implies many or a group or heirarchy of divine beings and not God. Unfortunately, the word *Elohim* was translated as God. This matter has also been explained previously.

	A	B	C	D	E	F	G	H	I	J	K	L
1		V										
2												
3												
4		L			T							
5		H	R	E	Tz							
6		A	Sh	M	A	I	Y	I	M			
7		B	A	R	E	Tz						
8												
9												

Fig. 93 The first verse of Genesis.

The discussion on the Sumerian version of the creation story would further elucidate the reason for the use of the phrase "let us." The Sumerian creation story that dated more than 2,000 BC narrated the gods who discussed the creation of mankind. Many biblical stories are based on Sumerian myths and legends.

3) Since there was no apparent subject before the verb *Bara*, the translator assumed Elohim as the subject and therefore the "Creator." Thus, Elohim became God, and therefore could not be the subject of creation. Actually, the Creator was named, but the word was so intricately hidden that it escaped the attention of the translators. This is the focus of the alternative interpretation.

New Interpretation

The new interpretation being offered will resolve the validity of the assumptions made by the translators.

The word *Berashit* is actually composed of two words *Bet*, which means "daughter" and the word *Reshit*, which means "In the beginning." Thus, the word *Berashit* can be translated or interpreted as "the daughter, in the beginning" or "in the beginning, the daughter." Thus, this interpretation will resolve the first question about the missing subject of the phrase "Berashit Bara Alhim." Here Bet

is the subject while Alhim/Elohim is the predicate. Thus, the interpretation will become "In the beginning, the daughter created the Elohim." Bet as the subject is more logical than Elohim as it precedes the verb *Bara*. This will further explain why the name of the Mother in the third Sephera, Binah is IHVH ELOHIM, which means "GOD of the ELOHIM" for she is the creatress of the Elohim.

This interpretation also resolves the question as to the right interpretation of the word *Elohim* as the heirarchy of angels and not as God. Secondly, this will also clearly show and settle the controversy as to when the angels were created. As the word *Elohim* precedes the words *Ha-Shamaym* and *Ha-Aretz*, then it follows that the heirarchy of angels were created before the creation of the heavens and the earth. It will also resolve the question why the conjunctive word *Ath*, which means "and" is between the words *Elohim* and *Ha-Shamaiyim*, which if translated would mean "the Elohim and the heavens." Thus, the translation should be "In the beginning, the daughter (mother) created the Elohim and the heavens and the earth." For if one will translate the Hebrew phrase "Berashit Bara Elohim Ath Ha-Shamaiyim Vath Ha-Aretz" as "In the beginning, created God and the heavens and the earth," the translation will be illogical and ungrammatical.

The Jews are very meticulous in their writings, and they just do not place a word without a reason. Eliminating a word to suit the translator is not the solution. One must look for the reason why the word was used. Thus, I do not agree to some translators who just eliminated the word *Ath* and translated the phrase as "In the beginning, the Elohim created the heavens and the earth." In their search for the solution of the problem, some Kabalists proposed that the word *Ath* should mean the planets, the stars, etc., but this would be stretching the imagination too much as one would not find any translation of such import in any Hebrew dictionary for the word *Ath* is a conjunctive meaning "and." However, if one would insist that Ath could mean the planets, then we offer a more plausible alternative. Ath should refer to the choir of angels attendant to the Elohim. The use of Ath here is different from the use of the word *Vath* before the word *Ha-Shamaiyim* although both words can be considered conjunctive. The use of the letter Vath was meant to emphasize that the said word *Vath* should be used only as a conjunctive and not any other else.

The interpretation will also enlighten us why the phrase "Let us make man in our image and likeness" was used instead of the phrase "I will make man in my image and likeness," for the phrase refers to a hierarchy of angels and not a personal God who can be jealous and strict.

This interpretation will also explain the use of the holy name Elohim as the Creator of the world. The said name was used thirty-two times in Genesis to emphasize the message being conveyed so that there would not be an error made in the translation or interpretation of Genesis. The translators of the Bible

not being Kabalists but orthodox Christians did not realize that the name being used as the Creator was the name of the feminine entity in the third Sephera, IHVH ELOHIM who was addressed as God the Mother. It therefore follows that the Creator was not a male entity but a Goddess who should be known as the Creatress. The holy name IHVH ELOHIM means the "God of the Elohim." If there is a God of the Elohim, then it means that the Elohim is not a god, and that there is a higher entity than the Elohim. Who can this God of the Elohim be but the Creatress of the Elohim or the heirarchies of angels? Unfortunately this interpretation will not be accepted by the Orthodox Christians no matter how logical it is, for it would mean changing the traditional interpretation and belief about the Creator of the world that would adversely affect organized religions, which are very patriarchal in nature. An acknowledgement of the feminine entity as the Creatress would destroy this belief and the doctrine about the superiority of the patriarchal form of religion. The present chauvinistic religions cannot accept this interpretation. However, this new interpretation will validate the sayings in Wisdom, Sirach, and Proverbs that Wisdom was present in the creation of the world, and that the spirit of God who hovered over the water was the Creatress.

For those who insist that the Creator was a he and not a she, there is another alternative interpretation. When Moses descended from Mt. Sinai carrying the tablet of Commandments, he saw the idolatry of the Israelites who were worshipping the golden calf. Moses was very angry at the spectacle that he destroyed this first tablet of Commandments. When God gave Moses the second tablet of Commandments, there were already differences between the two tablets. Instead of the Torah beginning with the letter *A* like in the first tablet, the second tablet started with the letter *B*. The letter *A* representing God disappeared and became concealed. Due to the idolatry and transgressions of the Israelites, *A* became hidden; thus the Torah started with the letter *B* instead of the letter *A*. Despite the unworthiness of the Israelites, God still blessed them; thus, the Torah started with the letter *B*, the first letter of the word *Berachah* meaning "blessing." The first verse of Genesis should have started as ABRShT, ABEREShIT, or AVEREShIT. Thus the first verse of Genesis should have read as "ABRShT BRA ALHM AT H-ShMYM VATH H-ARTz" meaning "The Father in the beginning created the Elohim and the heavens and the Earth."

Another interpretation that is not very controversial but also logical is the interpretation that the word *Berashit* comes from the word *Berachah*, which means "blessings." Thus, the Hebrew phrase "Beracha It Bara Elohim Ath Ha-Shamym Vath Ha-Aretz" can be translated as "Blessed art Thou who created the Elohim and the Heavens and the Earth." However, this interpretation also implies that someone created the Elohim.

According to the famous Kabalistic book *Bahir*, the "beginning" is "wisdom" and that "wisdom is feminine." This statement just supports what is stated in the biblical books like Wisdom, Sirach, and Proverbs that state that Wisdom is a feminine entity. Thus, in the footnotes on Wisdom in the New Jerusalem Bible, it is also said that Wisdom is a divine feminine entity. If the *Bahir* interprets the word *beginning* as Wisdom, then it is right to interpret the phrase "Berashit" as the "daughter Wisdom," thus it can be said that Wisdom (the daughter) created the Elohim and the Heavens and the Earth.

g) MARY, the Christian Symbol of the Mother

In the discussion of the Mother, it would be a great mistake if Mary, the mother of Jesus who is the Christian symbol of the mother, will not be included. The feminine entity in this dualistic world is known in many names as there are religions. To the Assyrians, she is known as Innana; to the Egyptians, Isis; to the Hindus, Shiva; to the Buddhists, Tara; to the Chinese, Kuan Yin; to the ethnic Filipinos, Poong Bato; and to the Christians, the feminine entity is known as Mary although she is not considered as a goddess like the others, but the Catholics treat her almost as one to the chagrin of the other Christian sects. Are the Catholics right in their treatment of Mary? Who is Mary? According to the Bible, Mary is the most blessed among women, the Mother of the Messiah.

"Blessed are you among women"[29]
"ASHER AT GUASH"

	A	B	C	D	E	F	G	H	I	J	K	L
9												
10					T							
11					A	Sh	E	R				
12			U	G								
13												

Fig. 94 "Blessed art thou among women."

Why is she the most blessed among women? Is it because she is the mother of Jesus, or is there a deeper reason for making her the most blessed among women? In the New Testament Jesus supposedly said,

"Among those born of women, John is the greatest."[30]

188

What does Jesus mean? Is John greater than him? Is Jesus not also born of a woman? If Jesus is greater than John, then Jesus was not born of a woman. If this is so, who then is Mary? According to Gnostics and Filipino occultists, Mary is not an ordinary woman. She is a divine entity who came down into this world to take care of Jesus.

Origin of Mary

A Gnostic writing says she was a power in heaven sent to earth, taking human form to take care of Jesus:

When Christ wished to come upon the earth to men, the God Father summoned a mighty heavenly Power, called Michael, and entrusted Christ to his care. And the Power came into the world, and it was called Mary; and Christ was in her womb seven months.[31]

In *Karunungan*[32] it is said that the mother who would take care of Jesus had already been chosen even before her appearance on earth. It was related that God "FOOC" told the Trinity:

Huag na kayong magpagod sa gagawing Ina na mananaog sa lupa na magbabata ng madlang hirap sapagkat wala pa kayo ay nilikha ko na ang magiging Ina na magbabata at magtitiis ng lahat ng hirap upang pagkatapos ay bihisan siya ng walang hanggang kaluwalhatian. (Do not tire yourself in the making of the Mother who will descend on earth to endure much sufferings because even before you existed, I created the entity who will become the Mother who will carry and endure all sufferings so that afterwards she will be clothed with eternal bliss.)

The above stories compliment the story relayed in a vision to a thirteen-year-old Filipino boy in the Philippines in 1984 who wrote it down. This vision will be narrated as a matter to ponder and not as a dogma or truth.

Infinite One and Father, I have come down from the heaven and has taken the form of flesh and blood. I will start now your Divine Plan to save these mortals whom you love dearly, who are the descendants of the imperfect Adam. I will raise my Brother, your Son, the Messiah of your people. He will grow up according to Your ways, and be baptized as Your Son on this earth. Then He will preach all the things You want Him to preach. And he will choose 12 men whom You have already chosen whom Your Son and Daughter will instruct. And then

will come the day when men will be saved, when they will kill Your Son and My Brother whom I love dearly. Then, He will rise on the 3rd day and the people We have instructed will continue Our work. And I'll see to it that all these come to pass which I know will come to pass, for it is Your will. Then I'll once again go home to that heavenly abode which I love.

After the sins of the imperfect Adam, his descendants inherited his will and therefore sinned against the Infinite One. The Infinite One knew this would happen and was ready to carry out His Divine Plan. As the Infinite One has planned, there would be one man and one woman who could not bear a child and who would offer burnt sacrifice in order to have a child and chosen to be the temporary parents of His beloved Child, God the Daughter. For these two were faithful to the Infinite One. Then He sent Sts. Gabriel and Michael to the temple disguised as priests and talked to the two to go to the mountain or Mt. Sinai and there they would find a child. The next morning, before the sun has risen, the two were on top of the mountain, praying. Then the most beloved Daughter of the Father and one of the most beloved Children of the Infinite God went down from the heaven with a blinding light in the dazzling colors of the rainbow which was beyond description. Then, the heavens opened and shone upon the Child. For the God the Daughter descended from Heaven as a seven year old Child. Then, the voice of the Infinite One was heard from heaven saying to the couple "This is My beloved Child, take good care of Her as I have taken care of you. For I love Her very much." Then the God the Daughter said to the Infinite One, "I am here to do Your will, and I love You. I will wait for my Brother to come. I love You, Infinite One." Then the Infinite One watched as the couple descended from the mountain with the God the Daughter.

After descending from Mt. Sinai, the foster parents and the God the Daughter or Mary had to cross a barren field which stretched to the valley and homeward. While walking on the fields, the parents decided to rest for a while. While resting, three men appeared and offered gifts to the Child Mary and bowed down on the ground and worshipped Her. The God the Daughter was pleased with them. The 1st man who was the king of the people of _____ said to the God the Daughter "I humbly offer these small offerings of incense and a

metal with the symbol of Your people living outside this solar system, who are devoted to the Infinite One, God the Father, God the Son, God the Daughter and the Holy Spirit." Then the 2nd man who was the priest of the survivors of the people of Mu who were now living outside this galaxy, offered incense and a crown of valuable metals and rocks which were much more valuable than gold and diamonds, said "I humbly offer this crown which I know is nothing compared to You, but please take it, for we also offer to You the prayers and labors spent during the making of the crown." Then the 3rd man offered incense and jewels which were not found on earth and said "I offer humbly these incense and jewels which represent the unity of the people of Mu and the people of my planet who are living together in harmony. And I would like to thank You, God the Daughter, God the Father, God the Son, the Holy Spirit and most of all the Infinite One for everything." And the God the Daughter to show how pleased She was, gave them wisdom and knowledge in their hearts before they return to their rightful places. After the visitors left, the parents woke up. (for they were asleep when it happened), and continued their journey home with the Child Mary. And the couple, upon reaching their place, announced (as planned by the Infinite God) to the people that they have a child and called Her, Mary.

The above stories are identical with stories about the mothers of Krishna and Zarathustra who descended into this world to take care of Krishna and Zarathustra respectively.

There is a legend that the Shekinah, the feminine aspect of God, out of her great love for man, voluntarily went into exile to be with Adam and his descendants and will not return to the Father as long as there is a single soul in this world. That is how much she loves us.

Immaculate Conception

Another reason why the Catholic church regards Mary highly is the belief in Mary's Immaculate Conception. It is said that pure energy can only be contained in a pure energy container, not an alloy or else it will be destroyed. If one believes that Jesus is holy and pure not considering anymore His being a God, can the container be of less than the same quality. Hence, the Catholic church considers Mary as conceived without original sin, for how can a sinner conceive a sinless person. How much more if you consider Jesus as God, who is then Mary?

	A	B	C	D	E	F	G	H	I	J	K	L
3												
4						Ch						
5						N	Ch					
6												
7										Ch		
8										N		
9												
10												
11		N										
12	Ch	N								Ch	N	
13									N			
14												

Fig. 95 Immaculate.

According to the Gospel of the Pyramids, a son of God cannot have human parents. The Hebrew word *CHN*, which means "without stain or immaculate," is written seven times in the grid. As stated before, the number 7 relates to spirituality and being immaculate is the apex of spirituality.

First Disciple

Due to the chauvinistic attitude of the writers, editors, and revisionists of the Bible, women were hardly mentioned and sometimes made to appear as inferior. There are verses in the Bible being cited to demean Mary like Matt. 12:48-50 wherein Mary was portrayed as being rebuffed and denied by her son, Jesus when Jesus after being informed of the presence of his mother and brothers supposedly said, "Who is my mother, and who are my brothers? And stretching out His hands towards His disciples He said, "Here are my mother and brothers, and sisters."[33] Could it be possible that Jesus, a holy man, would put to shame His own mother? I don't think so. Further, a continuation of the verse would show to whom Jesus was referring to as his mother, brother, and sister "for whosoever shall do the will of my Father who is in heaven, the same is my sister and mother."[34] Mary was the first disciple who obeyed the will of the Father when she said in the annunciation:

Be it done unto me according to Thy word.[35]
Y'asseh retzoncha Thy will be done[36]

She obeyed the will of the Father in utter disregard of the Jewish law about being stoned to death if a woman became pregnant without a husband. She accepted the

will of God without fear of any consequences unlike some of the apostles who denied Jesus thrice, betrayed Him, and deserted Him in the crucifixion. God the Father exalted Mary by making her the mother of His only begotten son; the Holy Spirit honored her by conceiving the son in her womb, and the son glorified her by being in her womb. If the Trinity can honor her, why cannot mere mortals do the same?

	A	B	C	D	E	F	G	H	I	J	K	L
1												
2												
3												
4								Y	A	S	S	E
5	H	R	E	Tz	O	N	Ch	A				
6												

Fig. 96 "Thy will be done."

The magazine *Newsweek*[37] aptly commented.

> Mark, the earliest Gospel, suggests that Mary did not understand or approve of what her son was up to. Matthew is more benign, mentioning the virgin birth. Luke pays her the most attention presenting Mary as the obedient handmaiden and spokeswoman for the outcast. It is only in Luke that Mary is hailed "as full of grace" and promised that all generations will call you blessed. In John, the latest of the Gospels, a request from Mary prompts Jesus to turn water into wine, the first miracle of his public life. And unlike the other Gospels, John places Mary at Jesus crucifixion—thus signaling that she was after all, a disciple of her son.

She was not only a disciple but also the mother of Jesus who could request Jesus to perform a miracle even if it was not time to perform one. She was not accused as Satan. She did not betray Jesus nor deserted him. She stayed at the crucifixion. No wonder the Trinity honored her.

h) SEMIPHORAS (Names of God)

The names of God are very important to the Jews, for they believe that miracles could be performed if one knows the correct names of God. Thus, Judaism has many names of God (Semiphoras) according to the different powers and attributes of God. Christians have been taught only few names of God like Yaweh, Jehovah, and Abba; but the Jews and the Kabalists were taught differently and the Infinite One in its masculine and feminine aspects has many names.

The Powers of Names

The book Sixth and Seventh Books of Moses[38] discusses the powers and uses of the names of God. According to the said book, King Solomon supposedly said that

> To obtain all that which is asked of God, . . . the name and prayer must agree, and no strange name must be used unnecessarily if anything fearful or wonderful is intended to be accomplished.

> Therefore, this name must be held in the highest honor and should be hidden from all frivolous and unworthy persons, since God says himself in Exodus: Out of all places will I come unto thee and bless thee, because thou rememberest my name.

The book also said that the names of God can only be taught and understood in the Hebrew language. With proper understanding and use of the names, one can perform supernatural things.

Thus, according to King Solomon, if one does not know the name of God, God will not hear him. Some people would say that is foolishness. All you have to do is pray. This may be correct. But have you ever tried calling somebody by phone without his numbers or his name? And even if you have his name but not his numbers, can you be connected? And even if you have the numbers and the name but you do not have a phone, can you have a phone call? No. And even if you have the phone but not the security code, will there be an answer? No. We can liken this to the billions of people praying to Jesus, yet their prayers remain unanswered? They know the name of Jesus, yet why are they still poor, hungry, sickly, homeless, and unemployed with so many problems? What is wrong? True they know the name of Jesus, but do they have love in their hearts to make a connection? To call the God of love, one must have love in his heart, and that is the security code. And that is also the secret of the Semiphoras. Not just the physical name and the right pronunciation but also the esoteric code.

As this code is Kabalistic in nature, we will encounter many different names of God, some are familiar others may be strange, but they all refer to One God, whose powers and attributes are encoded in the different names.

Names of the Father

In the Christian religion, the highest entity is God the Father known as YAWEH but whom Jesus addressed as ABBA or ABA. However in Judaism and in the Kabalah, God is known in many names in His masculine aspect as

the Father. If these names of God can be found in this code, it can only mean one thing that the author of this code was also a Kabalist—facts that were not taught to the Christians. However, there are verses in the Bible that imply about the secret name of God when Jesus said:[39]

> I have manifested Thy Name to them whom Thou hast given Me out of the world. Holy Father, keep in Thy Name those whom Thou hast given me, that they may be one even as We are. While I was with them, I kept them in Thy Name.

This name could not have been IHVH, ELOHIM, or YAWEH, for the Jews knew these sacred names. It could only be a new name that was given only to the apostles and not to the masses.

One of the most revered names of God is the name given to Moses AHIH AShR AHIH, which is known under the initials AAA and translated as "I Am that I Am."[40] This is the divine name of God in Kether, the first Sephera. The name as shown in figure 97 is written horizontally, vertically, and diagonally in sequence or with ELS. These facts show that the name has been deliberately placed and not just a coincidence. There is so much repetition of the name that one cannot escape the importance it is being given.

	A	B	C	D	E	F	G	H	I	J	K	L
1	A							A				
2								A	A			
3					A		A					A
4						A		A				
5							A					
6	A			A					A			
7		A										
8												
9				A						A		
10												
11					A							A
12					A		A	A				
13			A	A								
14	A						A					
15								A				
16					A							
17						A						

Fig. 97 Examples of the name AAA.

Why the emphasis? One reason maybe is that the name should be seen in tridimensional level—the physical, the spiritual, and the divine as when we were told to love God with our heart, our soul, and our mind. *A* in the physical world means "one" or the "start of a count" or "unity." *A* in the spiritual world means "one nation or race." And *A* in the divine world means "one God." Considering that the word *Ach* is written three times and near the name, it can be implied that *Ach*, which means "brother" is connected with the name. Thus in the physical world it can be interpreted that unity can be achieved through brotherhood of men. And once this is achieved, then there can be one planet with one God that is the aim of all saviors.

The name of the Father has been written sixteen (16) times as if to emphasize that this is truly a prayer for the Father. The number 16 when reduced to a single digit by adding the numbers 1 and 6 produces a sum of 7, which is a sacred number to the Jews, for it connotes spirituality.

Different Meanings of AAA

The Filipino occult book *Karunungan ng Diyos* by M. Sabino enumerates some of the explanations about the initials or name:

> AAA = ABISTE ABITE ABITEM
> These are the three names at the top of the crown of God which the archangels recite in unison.

> AAA = ARAM ACDAM ACSADAM
> These are the names of the three archangels supporting the world. They are also the names written on the three fishes the Holy Trinity saw.

> AAA = ADAM ARDAM ARADAM
> These are the three names that go in and out of the chair throne of God and also the names embedded in the rocks.

> AAA = AINSOPH AENSOPH AYENSOPH = The Infinite
> AAA = *AHAJAH ASAR AHAJAH* = The Alpha and Omega

When I opened the computer, I was surprised to find the two holy names in a different format and italicized, for I inputted the names without

accentuations or italics. It was unbelievable that the two highest names of God were the ones italicized when there were other names around. They just appeared as if to emphasize the importance and sacredness of the two holy names, so I just let them be. So many unexplainable things have happened in the preparation of this code as if an unseen hand was manipulating the whole thing.

Other Forms of AAA

Again, the holy name AAA is written in other forms to hide the holy name from the noninitiates. By replacing the three As with letters of the same numerical values, the name is hidden. And only by the method of gematria or temurah can the holy name be unravelled. As stated previously, the letters *A*, *Y*, and *I* have the same numerical values of one (1); thus, they can be interchanged with one another as shown by the following examples which all mean AAA.

AAI AAY AIA AYA AYY AYI AII AYY
YAA YYA YIA YII YIY IAY

The Unpronounceable Holy Name IHVH

To the Jews, the holiest name of God is IHVH. It has been given so much respect by the Jews that in ancient time it was blasphemy to pronounce the name, and it could mean the penalty of death. The sacred name was only uttered during the benediction of the temple[41] and on the day of the atonement when the name is spoken ten times by the high priest before the worshipping Jews.[42] The name can only be pronounced in a holy place like the temple and if only one is truly holy and endowed with wisdom.

As early as the fourth century before Christ, the pronunciation of the holy name was forbidden too. To utter the sacred name was a serious blasphemy that entailed death. When the name is encountered while reading a book, another name of God like ADONAI or ADNI, which meant "Lord" replaced it. Thus, the Jews forgot the right pronunciation of the holy name. Traditions say that only Adam, Eve, Noah, Abraham, David, Solomon, and eventually the high priest knew the correct pronunciation of the holy name, which if uttered correctly could allegedly cause massive earthquakes.

.	A	B	C	D	E	F	G	H	I	J	K	L
1	A	V	E									
2	Y				I							
3	E								V			
4					E							
5												
12												
13				Y	A	V	E					
14					V							
15			E									
16	I											
17												

Fig. 98 IEVE

There have been debates as to what the correct pronunciation of the holy name is. Even the different versions of the Bible have different enunciation of the name. Some writers have suggested that the right pronunciation of the holy name was JEHOVAH, but most Kabalists say that it was the wrong pronunciation. Others have suggested YAHWEH or YAVE. There are scholars who opined that the correct pronunciation could be based on the Greek writing of the name, namely, IEVE with the letter *H* replaced by the letter *E*. I scanned the grid for any information about the pronunciation and found the following:

No. of Examples		Coordinates			ELS
1st example	I = E-2	E = A-3	V = I-3	E = E-4	7 letters
2nd example	I = A-16	E = C-15	V = E-14	E = G-13	9 letters

The grid would seem to favor the Greek version of the pronunciation.

There are also two examples of the word *YAVE*.

Before I was wondering what was so special about this holy name IHVH. Why did the Jews make it the holiest of names besides the reason that it was given to Moses? There were many names of God given to the different prophets of Israel. Why this name whose gematria was not even 1 but 26. I was thinking that the number 1 should be the gematria of the highest name of God since number 1 always referred to God until I learned that numerically the number 26 is the most unique of numbers as it is the only number between a perfect square and a perfect cube for 26 is between number 25, a perfect square and number 27, a perfect cube. As a square denotes "space" and a cube implies "volume," then number 26 transcends space and volume. There is no number in mathematical

science that is between a perfect square and a perfect cube like number 26. As there is not any number like 26, hence it is the number of God for God is without comparison. This is how I learned to understand why the holy name IHVH is the highest.

Customarily when one reads the holy name IHVH, what comes into mind is the highest name of God. But is that all? Do we understand the meaning of every letter in the name and the esoteric secrets that it carries? This has been the mistake of the English translators of the Bible where every Hebrew name of God was only translated as plain God not knowing that in the Kabalah every letter and name has an esoteric meaning and like a computer diskette carries many details and information about the name. An example is the *unpronounceable* name IHVH. In the Kabalah, the name IHVH or YHVH refers to the entities, world, names as shown in table 6.

Entities		World		Names	
I	—	Father	Atziluth	Archetype	ABBA
H	—	Mother	Briah	Creation	AIMA
V	—	Son	Yetzirah	Formation	ZAUIR ANPIN
H	—	Daughter	Assiah	Action	MALKUTHA

Table 6

When I was scanning the computer, I was surprised to find the word *unpronounceable* underlined. I only know basic computer but ignorant about underlining a word or removing such underline. However, since it appeared mysteriously, I did not ask my secretary to remove it. I considered it as a reminder from above to respect the holy name. This event was just the start of other mysterious happenings.

It can also be said that the name of God is in man. If we look at the chemical composition of man, man is of more than 75 percent water or H_2O. The symbol of water, H_2O can also be written as HOH. If we look at the symbol of the DNA helix, it looks like an intertwined snakes or the letter *Y* or *I*. If we put together the DNA helix and the water symbol HOH, it becomes YHOH, which is the name of God. The Hebrew letter *U* is sometimes written as an *O* for pronunciation purposes. Thus YHOH is actually YHUH.

The Holy Name YH

One of the most revered names of God is YH, IH, YAH, or JAH, which is the divine name of God in Hockmah or Wisdom in the second Sephera. He is

the Supernal Father called AB, ABBA, or ABA, the name that Jesus wanted us to address the Father.

	A	B	C	D	E	F	G	H	I	J	K	L
5												
6				A		Y						
7												
8												
9			H	A	Y							
10												
11												
12												
13		H	A	Y								
14												
15				Y								
16		I		H								
17			H									

Fig. 99 The holy name IH or Yh or YAH.

If Jesus was a Kabalist, His suggestion in the use of the holy name ABBA had a very serious implication for He was referring to the Father in the second Sephera and not the manifestation of God in the ninth Sephera—"SHADDAI EL CHAI," the God of Israel. This would explain why Jesus talked about a loving, forgiving, and merciful God and not the strict and jealous God of Israel whom the Gnostics called the Demiurge.

The Breath of Life O'JAH

In *Karunungan*,[43] it is said that the letters in the name YAH or JAH are the initials of the names of the Holy Trinity. The letter *J* means JO-HAOC, which refers to the Son while the letter *A* means AB-HA referring to the Father, and the letter *H* means "HICAAC" or the Holy Spirit.

The holy name JAH can also mean "JAH AHA HAH" by Notarikon. This was supposedly the holy name breathed to man and became the spirit of man. Together with the letter *O* or *U*, the name becomes O'JAH or U'JAH or UHAH, which is the sound cried out by a newborn baby *"uha or waa,"* which reminds us of Matthew 8:3,[44] which states,

Out of the mouths of babes and sucklings, you have fashioned praise.

The Egyptian word *UAH* means "to live long" while the reverse of the word *UHA*, which becomes the Egyptian word *AHU* means lifetime. Thus it is said that a baby who does not cry out the holy name of God upon birth is a dead baby.

	A	B	C	D	E	F	G	H	I	J	K	L
1												
2	Y			Y								
3												
4												
5												
6				A								
7												
8												
9				A								
10							H					
11												
12												
13												
14												
15												
16				H								
17												

Fig. 100 Yah, the God of Wisdom.

There are five (5) examples of the name written here as YAH, namely,

Number of Examples		Coordinates		ELS
1st example	Y = A-2	A = D-6	H = G-10	50 letters
2nd example	Y = D-2	A = D-9	H = D-16	6 letters
3rd example	Y = F-6	A = E-11	H = D-16	58 letters
4th example	Y = E-9	A = D-9	H = C-9	None
5th example	Y = D-13	A = C-13	H = B-13	None

		A	B	C	D	E	F	G	H	I	J	K	L
5													
6							Y						
7													
8													
9					H	A	Y						
10													
11							A						
12													
13				H	A	Y							
14													
15													
16						H							
17													

Fig. 100-a Third, fourth, and fifth examples of the name.

Relevant to the above is the esoteric teaching about the speech of babies that most people do not understand including the learned translators of the Bible, hence our discussion on the matter.

The Holy Name EL

The holy name EL is one of the most revered names of the God of Israel that is older in use than the unpronounceable name YHVH. It was a carry over of the Phoenicians and the Canaanites names of God also called EL.

The name is supposed to be based on the Egyptian word *ALI* meaning the "associate gods." Before, the name EL used to imply the male and female gods, but later on it referred only to the male gods. It is the holy name of God in the fourth Sephera of the Tree of Life that refers to a benevolent and generous Father. He is the Father called by Jesus in the crucifixion ELI, ELI, which means "My God." "My GOD". The name EL is written many times in the grid as shown in figure 101. Sometimes the name is written as AL, but more oftentimes as EL. In gematria, its numeral value is 31 or 4. Its feminine counterpart is the holy name Eloah.

	A	B	C	D	E	F	G	H	I	J	K	L
3	-E											
4	L											
5												
6												
7								L	E		E	
8									E		L	
9										L	A	
10	-L									E		E
11											L	A
12												
13	L		A									
14	A	L										
15												
16					A	L						
17	-I					A						

Fig. 101 The holy name EL.

In this grid, the word *AVE* means the "Father." The letter *B* is sometimes written in V form to show the needed pronunciation of the letter. Also for pronunciation purposes and the sign that the letter *A* is being used as a vowel, the letter *A* is written as an *E*. Thus, "Our Father" in this grid is equivalent to the Hebrew word *AVENU*. The word *AVE* is written four (4) times as if to emphasize that the holy name ABA has a numerical value of four (4). AVE in reverse is the name of EVA or EVE.

	A	B	C	D	E	F	G	H	I	J	K	L
1	A	V	E									
2												
3												
4												
5												
6												
7												
8									E			
9											A	
10									V			
11							E					
12									A			
13					A	V	E					
14												
15												

Fig. 102 The holy name Ave.

Names of the Mother

As there are many names of the Father, so are there many names of the Infinite One in its feminine aspect as the Mother. Figure 103 shows the names of the Supernal Mother in Binah, namely AMA written in ELS of two (2), three (3), and four (4) letters interval. There are fifteen examples with different ELS. The number refers to the Mother, for if the number is reduced into a single digit, it becomes number 6. The numeral value of the name AMA is six (6). Another way the name of the Mother is written as AIMA or AYMA, which is written in ELS of one (1) letter. All the words cited here have the same skip intervals or ELS whether going on the right or left direction or downward or upward direction.

The number of examples given here and the many short intervals would more than satisfy the rigid requirements imposed by Israeli researchers on ELS. I did not show anymore the examples that could have been given if I used the permutation method.

	A	B	C	D	E	F	G	H	I	J	K	L
1	A.										A/	
2												
3												A
4												
5												
6			M.					M/				
7												M
8												
9												
10												
11					A./							A
12					A	M	A					
13												

Fig. 103 First to fourth examples.

Number of examples	Coordinates			ELS
1st example	A = A-1	M = C-6	A = E-11	61 letters
2nd example	A = K-1	M = H-6	A = E-11	56 letters
3rd example	A = L-3	M = L-7	A = L-11	3 letters
4th example	A = E-12	M = F-12	A = G-12	None

	A	B	C	D	E	F	G	H	I	J	K	L
1								A				
2			M					A		A		
3		M				/A		A				.
4												

Fig. 103-a Fifth to seventh examples.

5th example	A = H-1	M = C-2	A = J-2	6 letters
6th example	A = H-2	M = B-3	A = H-3	5 letters
7th example	A = J-2	M = B-3	A = F-3	3 letters

	A	B	C	D	E	F	G	H	I	J	K	L
1												
2												
3						A						A
4							A					
5								A				
6			M					M	A			
7												
8												
9				A			M					
10												
11												
12												
13												
14							A					
15								A				
16												
17												

Fig. 103-b Eighth to eleventh examples.

8ᵗʰ example	A = F-3	M = G-9	A = H-15	72 letters
9ᵗʰ example	A = L-3	M = H-6	A = D-9	31 letters
10ᵗʰ example	A = G-4	M = G-9	A = G-14	4 letters
11ᵗʰ example	A = H-5	M = C-6	A = J-6	6 letters

In Fig. 103-c are 12th to 14th examples

	A	B	C	D	E	F	G	H	I	J	K	L
5												
6	A,											
7		A.										M,
8												
9				A-			M.			A,		
10												
11												A.
12						M-						
13												
14												
15							A-					
16												

Fig. 103-c Twelfth to fourteenth examples.

12th example	A = A-6	M = L-7	A = K-9	22 letters
13th example	A = B-7	M = G-9	A = L-11	28 letters
14th example	A = D-9	M = F-12	A = H-15	37 letters

	A	B	C	D	E	F	G	H	I	J	K	L
5												
6				A		Y		M		A		
7			.									,

Fig. 103-d Fifteenth example.

15th example   A = D-6 Y = F-6 M = H-6 A = J-6   1 letter

It is intriguing that the total number of examples is 15, which in numerology is equal to six, the number of the Mother, AMA. With the appearance of the many holy names of the Mother with different ELS, the only conclusion is that this is a very deliberate act and not a coincidence. This will emphasize the acceptance by the author of this code about the existence of God the Mother who is known in Kabalah as AMA or AIMA. It is unfortunate that many people were prosecuted and killed more particularly the Cathars in France for the perceived heresy of believing in the Mother. The Inquisition was primarily put up because of the Cathars, and there is a big possibility of another Cathar crisis in the millennium if the church will acknowledge Mary, the Mother of Jesus as Coredemptrix.

Other Names of the Mother

Figure 104 shows the other Hebrew names of the Mother like AM, EM, IM, ELHA, which can be read as ELOHA and ELATh. The letters are side by side without ELS.

The word *AM* or *EM* or *IM* means the mother or source or beginning while the word *AH* is the title of the tenth (10th) Sephera, Malkuth where the daughter or SHEKINAH is in exile.

Another name of the Mother has the letters *A* and *G* as the initials, which means ALHIM GIBOR, the holy being in the fifth Sephera who is in charge of the dispensation of justice. This is reflected in our justice system where the female is the representation of justice holding the scale of justice.

In *Karunungan*[8] the letters *A* and *G* means "AMPHILAM GOAM," the Holy Spirit. Again in *Karunungan*[9] the letters *E* and *M* means "EMERENCIANA MITAM," the name of God the Mother.

	A	B	C	D	E	F	G	H	I	J	K	L
1										M	A	
2		I	M							A		
3	E	M	E								M	A
4	L											
5	H		E					A		M		
6	A		M	A			I	M		A	I	
7		A		E							E	M
8												
9												
10										E		
11					A		E			L		
12				G	A	M	A			A		
13			A		A		E			Th		
14												
15			E									
16		I	M									
17				A								

Fig. 104 Other Hebrew names of the Mother.

Another name of the feminine entity is SHEKINAH. According to the Zohar, the Shekinah is the intermediary between man and God. She is the channel through which influence is transferred from the upper world to the lower world. It is said that whoever seeks the king must inform her first. The Shekinah is also known as NUKVA, the female.

There are three examples of the holy name SHEKINAH or ShKN, which means "the presence of God." The three examples remind us of the third Sephera Binah, the Mother. If Jesus sacrificed Himself to redeem the world, according to legends, the Holy Daughter Shekinah sacrificed Herself by telling the Father that she would not return to heaven as long as there is one soul still remaining in this world. It is also said that she was the entity who assumed the form of Mary and took care of Jesus, for there was no human being worthy to contain the Son of God.

The first example of ShKN starts with the letters Sh on L-2 and going diagonally downward, there is ELS of 33 letters between the letters Sh, K and N.

The second example is ShKEEN with the letter Sh on B-6 and going to the right direction has ELS of six letters between the encoded letters.

The third example is ShKN with Sh on F-11and going t the right direction has ELS of six letters between the encoded letters.

	A	B	C	D	E	F	G	H	I	J	K	L
1												
2												Sh
3												
4												
5									K			
6		Sh							K			
7				E							E	
8						N						
9												
10												
11		N		K		Sh						
12												

Fig. 105 Shekinah

i) The Speech of Babies

There are many Christians who believe that God dictated every word in the Bible, forgetting the many revisions, editions, and deletions undergone by the different writings composing the Bible that changed and transformed the context and substance of the Bible. After the Bible was collated, it underwent again several revisions, editions, and deletions sometimes to suit the intentions of the translators or the editors or the religious group concerned. The Roman Catholic Old Testament contains forty-six books while the Protestant Old Testament contains only thirty-nine books with the writings on Wisdom, Sirach, and Baruch deleted. The said books contain the most writings about a divine feminine entity called Wisdom.

In my unpublished manuscript "God, the Mother," I extensively discussed Matthew 11:25 to show the defects in the translation and interpretation of the Bible that can lead to its wrong interpretation. The following illustration will show how the choice of words used by the different translators without taking into considerations their intentions can change the meaning and substance of one verse like Matthew 11:25 resulting in mistranslation.

Matthew wrote,

> I thank Thee, O Father, Lord of heaven and earth, because Thou hast hid these things from the wise and prudent, and has revealed them unto BABIES.[1]

> Father, Lord of heaven and earth, to you I offer praise, for what you have hidden from the learned and the clever, you have revealed to the merest CHILDREN.[2]

> Father, Lord of heaven and earth, I thank you for you have shown to the UNLEARNED what you have hidden from the wise and learned.[3]

Three English translations of the same verse but with three different meaning and substance because of the choice of words used, namely, *BABIES, CHILDREN,* and *UNLEARNED.*

At first glance, one may comment, "What is wrong with the words used in the translation, do not they mean the same?" No, for there are many differences between the three categories of human beings enumerated above like age and capacity to learn. BABIES can become CHILDREN and UNLEARNED, but not the other way around. Also, the CHILDREN and the UNLEARNED can become prostitutes or beggars or vagrants but not the BABIES. Also, BABIES

---

don't lie, cheat, or curse. Thus, the three categories cannot just be interchanged and be deemed to mean the same thing.

Many of the translators of the Bible have been misled to change the word *BABIES* to CHILDREN or UNLEARNED because of their mistaken notion that BABIES cannot be the recipient of a secret teaching because of their ages and capacities to learn without realizing the great errors they have committed. People who are ignorant of the esoteric meaning of the word *BABIES* maybe tempted to commit the same mistake, but to those who are privy to the secret teaching will know that the right word to use is *BABIES*. Babies are innocent, children, maybe! Babies and children are also different from the unlearned, for the unlearned may range from a baby to an old person.

Most of the modern translators do not know the esoteric or hidden meaning of the word *BABIES* as used in the Bible. They can only see the exoteric meaning the word implies, the physical newborn baby with still little capacity to learn, hence the doubt as to the use of the word *BABIES*. However, most of us do not realize that once born, the babies whether Filipinos, Asians, Americans, Europeans, or Africans cry out one secret name of God. It is a secret name or word of praise for the Creator not a word of anger, hate, or slander. Every time a baby cries, it is a cry of praise O'JAH, UHA, or WAA. Thus, it was said,

> Out of the mouths of the babies and sucklings, you have fashioned praise.[4]

> Because wisdom opened the mouths of the dumb, and gave ready speech to infants.[5]

And what is this ready speech of babies and sucklings but the wonderful sound of a newborn baby crying out in praise the holy name of God O'JAH, UHA, or WAA. This name of praise is also known by initiates called also as *BABIES* for their innocence and considered as true disciples to whom the secret about the kingdom of heaven were given. It is a powerful name, the nonutterance of which means death. All the babies in the world come out in praise of God in one language while children and the unlearned cry out in different languages and most often in anger and blasphemy. This is the reason why Jesus said in Matt. 11:25:

> I thank Thee, O Father, Lord of Heaven and Earth, because Thou hast hid these things from the wise and the prudent, and hast revealed them unto "BABIES."[6]

In the Philippines, the word *UHA* refers to the cry of a newborn baby. Thus, any newborn baby who does not utter this holy name is dead. To the Filipino

occultists, *UHA* is a power word equivalent to the Hebrew name of God O'JAH, O'YAH, or O'HAH. The holy name UHA is used in Philippine amulet or talismans. For other occultists, the power word might seem strange and new but to the Filipinos' UHA is a part of their occult tradition. A baby's cry may sound as UAH, UAA, WAA, or OAA. If one will be observant, all babies whether Asians, Americans, Europeans, or Africans cry out but one language—the language of praise—"Out of the mouths of babies, you have fashioned praise."[7] Maybe this is the only universal word that was left after the destruction of the Tower of Babel to remind us when the whole world had but one language because the world believed in one God and not in the egos of men. Not only the babies but the birds and the dogs say the same language. The crow is called in the Philippines UAK because of its cry "UAK" in praise of God. Listen to the dogs; they bark "BAW UAW UAW." In Egypt there was a goddess called BAU that was connected to the dogs.

We will only illustrate the examples of the name UHA with different ELS as shown in figure 106 to show that this was a deliberate act of the author of the code. There are seven examples as if to denote the great spirituality of the holy name.

Number of Examples	Coordinates			ELS
1st example	U = G-8	H = G-10	A = G-12	1 letter
2nd example	U = G-8	H = C-9	A = K-9	7 letters
3rd example	U = B-9	H = C-9	A = D-9	None

.	A	B	C	D	E	F	G	H	I	J	K	L
5												
6				.A								
7												
8							U-					
9		U,	H-	A							A-	
10							H.					
11			U.									A,
12			U				A					
13		H										
14	A									.U		
15												
16												
17												

Fig. 106 The cry of a baby—"UHA"

4th example	U = B-9	H = G-10	A = L-11	16 letters
5th example	U = C-11	H = G-10	A = K-9	7 letter
6th example	U = C-12	H = B-13	A = A-14	10 letters

Going diagonally downward, the letters are side by side without ELS.

7th example	U = J-14	H = G-10	A = D-6	50 letters

There are three other examples which by permutation the word *UHA* can be formed. The total ten examples of the name implies that the name refers to God as the number 10 is the number of God, the Alpha (1) and Omega (O).

The reverse of the word *UHA* is *AHU*, which in the Egyptian language means "LIFETIME."

There is also an Egyptian saying "UA HUA," which sounds like the cry of a baby that means "WE ARE ONE." Could this be what the babies all over the world are saying to the elders? "BE ONE." If that is so, then there will be meaning to the Egyptian word *UAH*, which means "TO LIVE LONG."

Maybe if the translators of the Bible had an inkling as to the esoteric meaning of the word *BABIES* as stated in the Psalm and in Wisdom, they would not have changed the word *BABIES* to *CHILDREN* or *UNLEARNED*. If mistranslation of this kind can be committed in one language, how much more from one language to another like the translation of the Bible from Hebrew to Greek to Latin to English and now to Filipino. It is doubtful if one in all sincerity and honesty can say that nothing in the Bible has been changed, added, or subtracted, and that God dictated every word. Already many Christian scholars have found forgeries in the Bible. With the many revisions, editions, deletions, wrong choice of words, and mistranslations, without taking into consideration the intention of the translators and editors, only the mindless could say there was no change. One thing in the New Testament that has not changed is the essence of the teaching "LOVE ONE ANOTHER" like the cry of a new born baby "UA HUA"—"WE ARE ONE."

Figure 107 shows the variations of the name UHA based on the sound coming from a crying baby.

VAH = the Sanskrit word for LOGOS
Coordinates: V = B-1 A = B-7 H = which starts with the letter *V* on
        H-1 and V-2 and going vertically downward has an ELS of
        five letters between the encoded letters *V*, *A*, and *H*. In the
        Kabalah, the letters *V*, *W*, and *U* can be interchanged as they
        have the same numerical value of six.

UAH = The Egyptian word for LIVE LONG
Coordinates: U = E-1 A = D-9 H = C-17 ELS = 94 letters

VAA = a variant of the word *UAA* or *WAA*
Coordinates: V = I-3 A = J-2 A = K-1 ELS = 10 letters

.	A	B	C	D	E	F	G	H	I	J	K	L
1		V.			U,			A			A	
2									A			
3						A		A	V	O		
4									A			
5								A				
6												
7		A.										
8												
9				A,								
10												
11												
12					A							
13		H.			A							
14					V							
15												
16												
17				H,								

Fig. 107 Variations of UHA.

OAA = another variant of the word *UAA* or *WAA*
Coordinates: O = J-3   A = H-3   A = F-3   ELS = 1 letter
             O = J-3   A = I-4   A = H-5   ELS = 10 letters

.	A	B	C	D	E	F	G	H	I	J	K	L
4												
5	H											
6												
7												
8												
9		U	H	A								
10				U			H					
11			U		A							
12												
13		H	A			V						
14												
15												
16					A							
17												

Fig. 108 Several examples of HUA.

HUA = another variant of the word *UHA*, which means in the Egyptian language "WE ARE." There are several examples with different ELS. The examples are side by side with the Filipino word *UHA* that is the sound of a baby's cry.

.	A	B	C	D	E	F	G	H	I	J	K	L
5												
6												
7	B											
8		U										
9		U	H	A	Y							
10				U								
11					A							
12												
13												
14												

Fig. 109 Filipino words *Buhay* and *Uha*.

Figure 109 shows two Filipino words that should not be appearing in a Hebrew grid, and they are even near each other. The words are even related to the subject matter of discussion. It is uncanny that the Filipino word for BUHAY that means "LIFE" is near the Filipino word *UHA*, which the Filipinos consider as the cry of a newborn baby. The words are even using the same letters comprising the Egyptian words *Hua* (We are), *Ua* (One), *Uah* (Live long), and *Ahu* (Lifetime).

PART V

THE LORD'S PRAYER AND
THE ANCIENT CIVILIZATIONS

The Lord's Prayer is supposed to be a short Jewish prayer, yet it contains data and information about Sumer. Egypt, China, and the Meso-American civilizations, their religions and gods, why?

Chapter VII

ANCIENT CIVILIZATIONS

After the controversial issue about the Mother, another intriguing surprise is about the appearance of the names of ancient civilizations and their religions in the grid. They are Egypt, Sumer, Meso-Americans, and China. This is unexpected as this is supposed to be a Hebrew grid concerned about Christian and Jewish cultures and beliefs and not anything Egyptian, Sumerian, Meso-American, or Chinese more particularly their religions, which are very alien to Jewish and Christian religions. The Lord's Prayer is supposed to be about Christian doctrines and its Jewish heritage. Yet the grid mentions these ancient civilizations more particularly Egypt and Sumer and their religions. How can the Lord's Prayer be related to these ancient civilizations?

The sudden appearance of these ancient civilizations on earth is still an enigma. No one can explain satisfactorily how primitive tribes suddenly developed advanced civilizations. From stone tools using primitives, the natives suddenly became knowledgeable in agriculture, mathematics, and astronomy. The primitives became suddenly *Homo Sapiens*. They have similar mythologies and beliefs about beings from heaven teaching them the art of civilization. These were civilizations from different parts of the world that were very far apart. Yet they have the same techniques of pyramid buildings and aligning these pyramids with the stars. They have knowledge of the Siriun constellation consisting of the three Siriun stars that modern man learned only recently. Our astronomers learned about Sirius C only last 1995.[1] They knew the polar and equatorial fields of the sun that became known only to man by the use of the satellites. The Mayans calculated the solar year as 365.24 days. The modern calculation is 365.242 days. The Mayans were off only by .08 seconds or an error of .000000003%.[2] Where did they get this knowledge? Before the ancient world was using the 360 days calendar; then suddenly they synchronized their calendars to 365 days. Why did they do it? How were they able to synchronize their calendars when their civilizations were far apart? How were they able to plot the continuous movements of the stars for hundred thousands of years? A modern computer program reaches only up

100,000 BC, and it confirms the findings of the ancients. What made these civilizations so advanced in science and mathematics could not be explained. Up to the present, none can build a pyramid the way it was built before, not even with modern equipment.

Ancient Sumerian and Hindu documents spoke about terrible weapons that could destroy the enemies beyond recognitions and described as creating pillars of smoke and halos of dusts. The Hindus, Chinese, Chaldeans, and Babylonians (offsprings of the Sumerian civilization) wrote about "flying machines." An ancient document of Chaldea called the Sifrala contained one hundred pages of technical details on how to build a flying machine. It spoke about crystal indicator, vibrating spheres, angles of flight, etc. How could they possibly give details about how to construct a flying machine unless they have built one and experienced operating the machine?

While the Hakatha (Laws of Babylonians) said,

> The privilege of operating a flying machine is great. The knowledge of flight is among the most ancient of our inheritances. A gift from "those from upon high." We received it from them as a means of saving many lives.[3]

The admonition implies so many things: (a) the presence of flying machines, (b) the knowledge of flight is a very ancient one, (c) beings from heavens or other planets imparted that knowledge, and (d) the knowledge was used to save people and not to destroy as we are doing now. However, modern man will just dismiss these beliefs about ancient gods or beings coming from heaven as myths and legends? How can one explain how the ancients developed? It is against logic and the rule of evolution. It is impossible that overnight, a primitive people transformed into expert engineers, architects, astronomers, and scientists.

The Talmud that contains the Oral Torah says that during the time of King Saul, Doeg, the head of the Sandhedrin could recite three hundred legal decisions on the subject of a migdal (a vehicle) that flew through the air. Nine hundred years ago, a Jewish sage named Rashi, who could explain the whole Torah and the Talmud, had difficulty explaining the flying vehicle for he had never seen one. Even the prophet Isaiah (60:8) said,

> Who are these that fly as a cloud and as the doves to their windows?

What was Isaiah referring to? Was he talking about angels or flying machines?

With that background about ancient civilizations, let us begin with the great civilization of Egypt whose relation with the Jews was highlighted in the Bible by the Jewish story of Moses.

A) THE LAND OF EGYPT

The appearance of Egypt, its deities, the Pyramids, the Sphinx, and the river Nile in the code is very puzzling. It is unbelievable that in a Hebrew code, there is so much data about Egypt. What is so important about Egypt that it should be discussed in the same breathe as the Christian and Judaic matters? This is almost akin to the readings of Edgar Cayce relating Jesus to the Pyramids and the Sphinx. What is the mystery behind Egypt's prominence in the code? With this premise, I tried to unravel the mystery.

Because of the cinemas and the television programs that portrayed the sufferings and oppressions undergone by the Jews under the hands of the Egyptians during the time of Moses, people remembered Egypt as an enemy of Israel, forgetting the other biblical stories about the special relationship between Egypt and Israel; how Egypt became the second home of Abraham, where Moses was made a prince of Egypt and learned the magic and rituals of the Egyptian esoteric teachings, where Joseph was given a high position that enabled Joseph to save his countrymen from starvation and death, where Jesus hid during His childhood, and where according to legends the unaccounted eighteen lost years of Jesus from age twelve to thirty were partially spent, and where He studied the esoteric teachings of the adepts.

a) Geography of Egypt

Presently, a burning desert (Tesher) surrounds Egypt that made the ancient people called Egypt BSH or House/ Land of the Sun. The Tesher was a blessing in disguise as it protected Egypt from foreign invaders; thus, leaving the people to live in peace and security. This resulted in the flourishing of a civilization for 2,500 years unabated that up to now is unequalled in human history. After the unification of Egypt, it was divided into three kingdoms, namely, (a) the Old Kingdom from about 2,700 BC to 2,200 BC when the pyramids were supposedly constructed, (b) the Middle Kingdom around 2,000 BC to 1,800 BC when there were political and economic prosperity, and (c) the New Kingdom around 1,600 BC when Egypt greatly expanded through conquest of neighboring lands.

Another blessing of Egypt is the Nile. The annual flooding of the Nile enriches the soils causing the proliferation of farms on the banks of the Nile. Thus, it is said that the Nile is the life of Egypt. Without the Nile, Egypt is barren. It flows for more than four thousand miles across Egypt. Two rivers converge to form it—the Blue Nile coming from Ethiopia and the White Nile from Uganda. They join at Khartoum to become the Nile proper. The part near the Mediterranean Sea (Uatch Ur) known as the Ta Meh (Delta) is called Ati (Lower Egypt) while the part south of the Ta Meh is called the Upper Egypt.

223

The Nile annually inundates the surrounding land, depositing rich fertile silt that makes the land appear black; thus, the ancients refer to Egypt as the Black Land or KMT, which has been written in many ways like "Khemit, Khemet, Kemet, Khem."[1] Egypt is known in many names during ancient times depending on the period of time in the past.

Egypt was also called Musur[2] and Magan.[3] It was the Greeks who started calling the land as Aegyptos.[4] The Greek historian Herodotus wrote in the fifth century BC that when the Nile overflowed, Egypt became like a sea with only the towns remaining above the waters like the islands of the Aegean Sea.[5]

	A	B	C	D	E	F	G	H	I	J	K	L
1												
2			M									
3												
4		K		T								
5							Ch		K			
6			M					M				
7							T			Ch	E	M
8												
9							M	U	S			
10									V			
11							R					
12		N		G	A	M						
13			A									
14												

Fig. 110 Ancient names of Egypt, KMT, ChM, Musur, and Magan.

During the inundation of the Nile, people traveled by boat, sailing past the pyramids. There are around twelve Egyptian words like *BAH* and *URT* both meaning "flood" that are in the grid to remind us not only about the annual inundation of the Nile, but the abundance of water in ancient Egypt, which resulted in lush vegetation and forest. However, there was a change in the weather causing the disappearance of the forest and the resulting deserts. Thus, the ancient names of Egypt like BSH, CHM, or KMT referred to Egypt when there were no more forests but an abundance of sand or desert.

Although there is now the Sahara Desert, geologists believe that several million years ago, there was an ocean in Egypt that Herodotus in his writings called as the Triton Sea. This ocean later on disappeared because of the severe weather changes leaving a vast desert of sands. As to where the water went nobody

knew. Although there is a possibility that the water created the Mediterranean Sea that geologists said did not exist several million years ago. There was a report compiled from an international meeting in Egypt in 1963 that provided information about the many observations and investigations by various geologists about the ground water in the Western Desert. The report[6] said that there was enough ground water under the Western Desert of Egypt to supply all of Middle East with fresh water for many years. This report would seem to confirm the presence of abundant supply of water underneath the desert that was once an ocean before.

Whenever one talks about CHM/KMT, the ancient name of Egypt, the things that come into mind are ON or INNU presently called the Sphinx, the MER or HR, the mountain called the Pyramids, or the House of Mountain (E. KUR) as known by the Sumerians, the river YR or the Nile, the desert (TESHER or HA), and the scorching sun (HER). If letters/words to these effects are found and grouped together in this code, could these be coincidences, or did the very wise author of this code deliberately place these words?

It is amazing to find clusters of Hebrew letters that can be formed into Egyptian words that are interrelated and descriptive of Egypt. They are in a quadrant composed of F-5, G-5-6-7, H-6-7, and I-5 and 8. To find these interrelated words in a small quadrant composed of four vertical rows and four horizontal rows is truly amazing. Figure 111 shows the following words related to Egypt, namely:

ChM = An ancient name of Egypt which according to Herodotus was the gift of the Nile. The name starts with the letter *Ch* G-5, and reading diagonally downward the letters *Ch* and *M* are side by side without ELS.

	A	B	C	D	E	F	G	H	I	J	K	L
4												
5						N	Ch		K	M		
6							I	M	K			
7							T	L		Ch	E	M
8									E			
9												
10												

Fig. 111 The word *Nile* with the ancient names of Egypt, KM, KMT, ChM, or ChEM.

KMT = another ancient name of Egypt, which refers to the silt deposited by the Nile during its inundation making the land looks black. The name starts with the letter *K* on I-5, and reading diagonally downward, the letters *K*, *M*, and *T* are side by side without ELS. The names *ChM* and *KMT* share the same letter *M* in the grid. The other variants of the name are KM and ChEM. This is a deliberate attempt to emphasize the presence of Egypt in the grid.

NILE = It is intriguing that in a pattern consisting of the Hebrew alphabet one will read the word *NILE*, which in biblical Hebrew is called YR or YEOR. Could this be a coincidence? As stated previously, nobody talks about Egypt without mentioning the pyramids or the River Nile that provides life to Egypt. The word is side by side with the ancient names of Egypt, ChM, and KTM. It starts with the letter *N* on F-5, and reading to the right direction has an ELS of twelve letters between the encoded letters *N* at F-5, *I* at G-6, *L* at H-7, and *E* at I-8. Reading diagonally downward, the letters are side by side without ELS.

As I am not a mathematician, I wish I could give the mathematical ratio or probability of the words *CHM*, *KM*, *KMT*, and *NILE* being lumped together side by side without ELS and even sharing some letters in a quadrant composed of only sixteen squares. It is amazing the way the author of this code has sent his message about the importance of Egypt in this code. This is one of the most beautiful illustrations of words, which are interrelated, sharing even letters without ELS and being lumped together. Examples like these are very difficult to refute.

As I became more interested in Egypt, I tried to learn what the other name of the Nile was like searching for the other names for Egypt, the Pyramids, and the Sphinx. Geologists believe that millions of years ago, an ocean covered a portion of Egypt that was cited by Herodotus in his book *The Histories* as the Triton Sea. When the waters receded, islands were formed and the huge ancestral Nile appeared. The *National Geographic* magazine[7] wrote that 5.5 million years ago, the Mediterranean Sea was dry and the ancient Nile emptied to the dry seabed. Around 800,000 BC, the Nile delta expanded. According to Stephen S. Mehler,[8] the ancient Nile still existed between 60,000 to 20,000 BC, and the scientists called the river UR NIL. There are several examples with different ELS in the grid.

UR NIL = the name given by scientists and geologists for the primordial Nile

	A	B	C	D	E	F	G	H	I	J	K	L
1							B					
2												
3												
4	L-											
5						N			K			
6							I-					
7			R					L				
8		U							E			
9	N-										A	
10												
11												
12		N										
13	L.											
14		L		I		I.						
15						I					N.	
16						L			N			
17												

Fig. 112 The Nile River.

Coordinates					ELS
U = B-8	R = C-7	N = A-9	I = G-6	L = A-4	29
		N = B-12	I = D-14	L = F-16	25
		N = K-15	I = F-14	L = A-13	16
		N = J-16	I = F-15	L = B-14	15

AKB/AKBA = celestial Nile which refers to the Milky Way and the
  Orion Constellation

Coordinates: A = K-9   K = I-5   B = G-1 ELS = 49 letters.

There are scientific and geological evidences to show that the Nile in very ancient time was a huge river, and that when the rainfall receded around 10,000 BC, it shrunk in size with a large portion of its riverbeds drying up. Thus, it has moved from its original path. Isaiah also prophesied this event.

The waters of the Nile will dry up, and the riverbed will become parched and dry . . . . and the streams of Egypt will dwindle and dry up.[9]

This is also happening now to the Dead Sea, which according to a newspaper report[10] will disappear in a period of fifty years if nothing is done as it drops three feet a year.

There are many other words with different ELS like Sphinx (ON), Pyramid (HR), House of the Sun (BSH), desert (HA), or hot (TA), which are in the grid. Figure 113 shows the different examples written several times with different ELS maybe to emphasize that the examples were deliberately placed there in the grid.

ON = Ancient names of Heliopolis and the Sphinx, which is written several times in the grid.

	A	B	C	D	E	F	G	H	I	J	K	L
1						Sh	B					
2						T						
3						A	T	A				
4												
5	H	R			O	N					O	
6	A											N
7		A										
8	H					N						
9				H	A	O						
10		O	N					H				
11		N							R		O	
12											N	
13		H	A									
14	A								N			
15											O	N
16				H	A					N		
17				H	A	R						

Fig. 113 Heliopolis and the Western Desert.

HA = the hieroglyphic symbol of the Western Desert. It is intriguing that the word *HA* appeared eight times on the western part of the grid, which symbolizes the exact location of the desert in the western portion of Egypt. I considered the eastern part of the grid as that part of the grid where the words *SOL, OM, ON,* and *CHO,* which all mean "SUN" are placed.

TA =   means "hot," which is another reference to the "Land of the Sun." The word is written several times in the grid.

BSh =   means "House of the Sun" or more figuratively "The Land of the Sun" as Egypt is known due to its burning sun and scorching desert. The word is also found on G-1 and F-1 with the letters side by side.

With respect to the other words related to Egypt, I have separated them into two groups—those with ELS and those that can be formed by permutation.

ANU = another name for Heliopolis or On;
Coordinates: A = L-11   N = K-12   U = J = 13 ELS = 10 letters
             A = G-15   N = I-14   U = J = 13 ELS = 10 letters

	A	B	C	D	E	F	G	H	I	J	K	L
1								A		M		I
2												
3												
4									A			
5		H								M		
6		A.		M.		I.		I.			I	
7		B										
8												
9							M.					
10												
11												A
12							A.				N	
13										U		
14									N			
15								A				
16												
17												

Fig. 114 Words related to Egypt.

AMI =   dweller in Ausek; the letters are in H-1, J-1 and L-1 with an ELS of one letter between the encoded letters. There are other examples with different ELS.

	Coordinates			ELS
A = H-1	M = J-1	I = L-1	1 letter	
A = I-4	M = J-5	I = K-6	12 letters	
A = A-6	M = C-6	I = I-6	1 letter	
A = G-12	M = G-9	I = G-7	2 letters	

BAH = to be flooded; starts on A-7 and going vertically upward without ELS.

	A	B	C	D	E	F	G	H	I	J	K	L
1												
2		I				T				A		
3												
4												
5					O	N					O	
6												N
7												
8						N						
9	N					O						
10			O	N								
11					A	Sh	E	R		O		A
12											N	
13										U		
14								N				
15							A			O	N	
16										N		
17												

Fig. 115 Words still related to Egypt.

NO = another ancient name of Thebes, which is written several times in the grid

ASHER = name of an ancient city in Egypt

Coordinates: A = E-11 Sh = F-11 E = G-11 R = H-11
ELS = None

ATI = ancient name of Lower Egypt, the kingdom of the Hyksos

	Coordinates		ELS
A = J-2	T = F-2	I = B-2	3 letters
A = I-4	T = G-3	I = E-2	13 letters
A = E-12	T = C-14	I = A-16	21 letters

	A	B	C	D	E	F	G	H	I	J	K	L
1												
2		I			I	T				A		
3							T					
4								A				
5												
11												
12					A							
13												
14			T									
15												
16	I											
17												

Fig. 116 Lower Egypt.

Figure 117 shows the following word:

AAT = kingdom of Osiris

	Coordinates:		ELS
A = K-1	A = I-4	T = G-7	33 letters
A = J-2	A = H-2	T = F-2	1 letter
A = H-2	A = F-3	T = D-4	9 letters
A = H-3	A = L-3	T = D-4	3 letters
A = G-12	A = E-13	T = C-14	9 letters

	A	B	C	D	E	F	G	H	I	J	K	L
1											A	
2						T		A		A		
3						A		A				A
4				T					A			
5												
6												
7							T					
8												
9												
10												
11						A						
12												
13					A							
14				T								

Fig. 117 AAT: Kingdom of Osiris.

ABU = the island of Elephantine
Coordinates: A = J-2 B = L-5 U = B-9 ELS = 37 letters

UNNU = another name for the ancient city, Hermopolis, the city of Thoth.

Coordinates: U = B-8 N = F-8 N = J-8 U = B-9 ELS = 3 letters

	A	B	C	D	E	F	G	H	I	J	K	L
1												
2								A		A		
3												
4												
5												B
6												
7		B										
8		U				N				N		
9		U										
10						T						
11												

Fig. 118 Cities of Hermopolis and Elephantine.

ABT = eastern region of Egypt
Coordinates: A = H-3   B = A-7 T = F-10   ELS= 40 letters

	A	B	C	D	E	F	G	H	I	J	K	L
1												
2												
3		E						A-				
4		L										
5												
6												
7		B-					L	E			E	
8								E			L	
9										L		
10						T-				E		E
11									S		L	
12									A			
13									N			
14			L									
15				E			S					
16					A							
17				H								

Fig. 119 Constellation of Orion and the stars.

SAH = refers to the constellation of "ORION," the constellation of Osiris.

Coordinates: S = G-15 A = E-16 H = C-17 ELS = 9 letters

EL = means "stars"; there are many examples in the grid.

SAN = means "stars"; the word is found in J-11, and going vertically downward, the letters are side by side without ELS.

The following Egyptian words all refer to the Pyramids and can be found by permutation.

ChEOCh = In the Egyptian desert stands one of the most beautiful pyramids in the world called Cheop. In this illustration, the word *ChEOCh* appears. One may say that there is no pyramid in Egypt called Cheoch for the greatest pyramid in Egypt is called Cheop. This is correct, but by the method of gematria, the letter *Ch* and the letter *P* can be interchanged for they have the same numerical value of 8; hence Cheoch can become Cheop. The word is found in a cluster of letters on E-3-4-5 and F-4. The Pyramid was also called in ancient times as EAKU or YAKU.[11]

E.KUR = means "the house of mountain," the Sumerian term for the Pyramid.

	A	B	C	D	E	F	G	H	I	J	K	L
1												
2												
3					Ch							
4		K	U		E	Ch						
5		R	E		O							
6												
7		U	R	E								
8			K									
9												
10				U	E							
11				K	A							
12			U		A							
13					Y							
14												

Fig. 120 The ancient names of the Pyramid.

MER = also the name of the Pyramid in ancient time found at J-10, I-8, and H-11 with ELS of thirty-four letters going in the right direction; two examples are grouped with the word E.Kur in the grid.

	A	B	C	D	E	F	G	H	I	J	K	L
1												
2												
3					Ch							
4		K	U		E	Ch						
5		R	E		O					M		
6			M									
7		U	R	E								
8			K						E			
9												
10												
11							E	R				
12						M						
13												
14												

Fig. 120-a The ancient name Mer.

b) The Alien Connection

The civilization of Egypt is a paradox. The older the civilization is, the more advanced it becomes. Thus it is said that the civilization of Egypt was not an internal development but was a legacy from the fabled Lemuria or Atlantis or from an alien civilization, more particularly from the constellations of Orion and Sirius. There is a legend that the gods of Egypt came from these constellations; thus, the ancient Egyptians' fanatical attachment to Orion (SAH) and Sirius (SOTHIS). The shafts from the king's chamber and from the queen's chamber in the Pyramid of Cheop respectively point to the stars of Orion and Sirius. Even the layout of the three pyramids at Giza is an exact replica of the positions of the three stars of Orion in the heavens. The Egyptians even have the word *SAH*, which does not only mean "Orion," but also "Star People" in the Egyptian language. Why do they have such a word? Are the ancient Egyptians being literal in talking about the "Star People" or people coming from the stars? They even believe in a boat that the god Ra used in traveling around the universe for million of years. What boat could travel millions of years in space? This boat was called UAA EN HEH—"the boat of millions of years." How could a boat last for millions of years? What need is there for this kind of words unless they are used only for story telling? But the actuations of the ancient Egyptians contradict this supposition. Orthodox Egyptologists who opposed this theory about an alien connection maintain that the civilization of Egypt is the result of its internal development. There is doubt, however, as to how for just several centuries, a country with primitive people using flint stones only as tools could transform into an intelligent and sophisticated people with knowledge of mathematics, science, astronomy, and engineering. They became preoccupied with the movement of the stars and the planets, and they were extremely accurate. The Egyptians were so advanced in technology that even up to the present time nobody could perform their mummification method and pyramid building techniques.

Egypt can be called the ancient of the ancients. For it was already a great nation two thousand years before the civilizations of the Minoans, the Israelites, the Greeks, and the Romans. Allegedly, three groups of migrants moved into the Nile area around 10,000 BC. They were the Africans from Africa, an unknown group from Asia and a group from Libya. The people were ordinary farmers and peasants. Around 4,000 BC, there was a migration of a race of broad headed people who were different from the indigenous population of long-headed people. According to the historian Diodorus Siculus[12] of the first century AD, the Egyptians were strangers who settled at the bank of the Nile coming from the west where the ancient immigrants settled. Prof. U. B. Emery[13] in his book "Archaic Egypt" commented that these foreigners were of greater size and larger than the natives. However, around 3,100 BC there was a unification of Lower and Upper Egypt under the Pharaoh Narmer or Menes. The unified Egypt was

called Tameru. Hieroglyphic writings and the calendar were invented. In less than three hundred years, an agricultural people were suddenly transformed into a very literate people with knowledge of medicine, mathematics, and astronomy. Later, around 2,700 BC, the Egyptians supposedly constructed the pyramids, a technological wonder up to the present. How the Egyptians were able to evolve in so short a period of time is a puzzle up to now. The orthodox Egyptologists cannot accept the Pyramids and the Sphinx as older that 2,500 years BC because at around 3,000 BC Egyptians historically were still using just flint stones as their tools. However if we will believe the oral tradition of Egypt as narrated by Herodotus, the fifth century BC Greek historian and Manetho, the third century BC Egyptian historian, Egypt had a very ancient oral tradition. According to Manetho[14] based on ancient stele, tablets, and papyrus, the gods ruled Egypt for 13,900 years; the demigods ruled for 1,255 years then 1,818 years and finally 350 years. The spirits of the dead ruled also for 350 years. The total reign was 24,925 years. Herodotus[15] on the other hand said that the written history of Egypt went back as far as 11,340 years before his time or around fourteen thousand years prior to the present time. During the unification of Egypt around 3,000 BC under Menes, Egypt was already a civilized country. These allegations might strain the credulity of many as this would place the civilization of Egypt from 15,000 BC to 25,000 BC; however, archeological findings like that in Hohlenstein, West Germany, where a thirty-two-thousand-year-old statuette of a carved body of a man was excavated would serve to confirm the possibility of such allegation. A beautifully carved ivory lion muzzle was later found at the same site that fitted the statuette perfectly.[16] This archaeological find could substantiate this claim that there was already an advanced civilization at the time. There were also other archeological findings in other sites like the thirty-two-thousand-year-old statuettes of the mother figure. Sumerian records would seem also to point to a more ancient Egyptian civilization.

The ancient Egyptians had Solar, Lunar, and Sothic calendars. The Sothic or Siriun calendar is based on the heliacal rising of Sirius that always takes place when the sun is in the constellation of Leo. It has 365 ¼ days that is equal to the Julian calendar year of 365 ¼ days. This calendar also known as the Pharaonic Calendar was said to be in use since 4,240 BC.

c) Legendary Powers of Moses

In ancient times, Egypt was the source of esoteric teachings and magic. Much of the magic and rituals practiced in Egypt had been conveyed to us through the ancient texts called the Book of the Dead that contained the greatest Egyptian collections of magical formulae, spells, incantations, hymns, and rituals. The high priests (Urma), keepers of these sacred esoteric traditions, supposedly taught Moses these secret traditions, Moses being considered an Egyptian prince. Thus

he became great in magic. Still, the pharaoh could not believe that Moses, only a student of the Urma, could be more powerful than the teacher—the Urma. Thus, when Moses confronted and threatened the pharaoh, he told Moses:

> Have you come to drive us from our land with your sorcery, Moses?
> Know that we will confront you with sorcery as powerful as yours.[17]

The pharaoh ordered the Urma and the Egyptian priests (Aata) to overcome the magical powers of Moses. He commanded the Urma and the Aata to counter Moses magic by magic. Moses said to the Pharaoh:

> O King, I do not myself despise the wisdom of the Egyptians, but I say that what I do is much superior to what these (priests) do by magic and tricks.[18]

The pharaoh, however, did not believe what Moses said. He did not know that Moses was taught not only by the Urma but by Aarat, the serpent goddess whom according to legend, Moses was able to defeat in battle when Moses sought to get the SHAT (Book of Thoth), which contained the supreme esoteric teachings of the Egyptians. As nobody has ever defeated the immortal serpent goddess Aarat, the guardian of the Shat except Moses, the goddess taught Moses the Shat. As Moses learned the supreme esoteric traditions of the Egyptians, he became twice great in magic and defeated the Urma. Another reason for the supremacy of Moses in magic was when God appeared to Moses in Mt. Sinai where for forty days God taught him the esoteric secrets of the Kabalah and the ten names of God that created the world and the basis of the Ten Commandments. Thus, Moses was able to perform miracles beyond the capabilities of the Egyptians. He became thrice great or trimegestus in magic. Moses supposedly taught Aaron and the Jewish high priests the secret teachings he had learned, which evolved into what is now known as the Kabalah.

Figure 121 shows three examples of the Egyptian words *SHTA*, which means "SECRET or HIDDEN" and the word *SHAT,* which means "BOOK." The words can be formed into the phrase "SHTA SHAT," which means "SECRET BOOK." The word *TAT* is an ancient name of "Thoth." Was this the secret book of Thoth that contained the wisdom and knowledge of Thoth that made the pharaohs very powerful? The existence of the words in the grid would seem to confirm the story about the legendary secret Book of Thoth. As to whether Moses was able to possess it, is something else. It is the subject of many legends.

> The first example of the word *SHTA* starts with the letter *SH* on F-1 and going to the right direction has ELS of eleven letters between the desired letters. The letters are side by side without ELS when read vertically

downward. In this example, the word *SHAT* has to be mentioned because of its intriguing connection with the word *SHTA*.

The word *SHAT* starts with the letter *SH* on I-1 and going in the right direction has ELS of ten letters before reaching the letter *A* at H-2 and the letter *T* at G-3. What is intriguing is the last two letters of the word *SHTA* and the last letter of the word *SHAT*, *T* forms the word *TAT*, which is the ancient name of THOTH. Is this the confirmation that the code is referring to the secret book of Thoth?

.	A	B	C	D	E	F	G	H	I	J	K	L
1						Sh		Sh				
2						-T		A				Sh
3						-A	-T	A.				
4			U	T.								
5		R		Tz								
6	A		M	A								
7		A	R				T					
8												
9												
10												
11												
12												
13					A							
14												

Fig. 121 The Book of Thoth (Shta Shat Tat),
Aarat, Urma, and Aata.

The second example of SHTA starts again at F-1 and going in the right direction has ELS of thirty-three letters between the desired letters *T* at D-4 and *A* at B-7. What is amazing about this example is that the final letter *A* of SHTA forms part of the semicircle pattern of the word *AARAT(z)*, which is the name of the serpent goddess who taught Moses the art of magic.

The third example of SHTA at I-1 and going in the right direction has ELS of sixty-nine letters between the encoded letters *T* at G-7 and *A* at E-13. The letter *SH* of SHTA is also the initial letter of the word *SHAT*, which has ELS of ten letters between the encoded letters. Thus, the words *SHTA SHAT*, which mean "Secret Book" have the letter *SH* as its common letter.

The last example of the word *SHAT* starts with the letter *SH* on H-2 and L-2 and going to H-3 has ELS of Seven letters between the encoded letters.

d) Egyptian Religion

Generally, a man separates his religion from the other aspects of his life. But in Egypt, religion permeates his social, political, and economic existence. His ruler was the pharaoh who was also god. Thus, state and religion are fused.

Trinity of Gods

In the unified Egypt, there were many tribes, each with its own local deities or gods. Usually, the town gods were composed of a principal male god, his wife or the goddess, and the son who had the powers of the father. This is the triad concept that became later on the Trinity concept of the Christians, the only difference being that the third person of the Christian Trinity was an "IT" and not a "SHE" as in olden times. The chapter on the Mother contains an extensive discussion about the matter.

This Trinity concept is shown in the principal cities of Egypt. In the city of Abydos, the Trinity is composed of Osiris, his wife, Isis, and the son, Horus. While at Memphis, the triad is composed of Ptah, Soker, and Tem. The one at Thebes was composed of Amun, Nuet, and Khoms. The most popular Trinity was that of Osiris known as AS-AR, his wife Isis known as AST, and their son Horus known as HERU. Figure 122 shows the ancient names of the popular Trinity.

From the three different religious centers in Egypt, three religious systems emanated, namely, Heliopolis, Hermopolis, and Memphis.

	A	B	C	D	E	F	G	H	I	J	K	L
1												
2												
3							T					
4										S		
5												
6		A										
7			R									
8			U	E								
9			H									
10												
11								R	S			
12							A		A			
13												
14												

Fig. 122 The Trinity Osiris, Isis, and Heru.

The principal Gods of Heliopolis are Tem-Ra/Atum (the creator God), Geb (Earth), Nut (Sky), Osiris, Isis, Nepthys, Set, and Tefnut while those of Hermopolis are Nu (the primordial ocean), Hehu (eternity), Kekui (darkness), Amun (air), Naunet, Hehret, Kekuit and Amaunet. The main Gods of Memphis are Ptah (supreme god) Nauet, and Tem-Ra who created the gods worshiped in Heliopolis, Shu, Geb, Osiris, Isis, Seth, Nepthys, Nut, and Tefnut.

The first appearance of the name RA, the sun god, was around 2,865 BC (Second Dynasty, Archaic period), carried by King Ra-Neb at Heliopolis and the cult of Ra worship accelerated, peaking at around the time of the great pyramids—2,500 BC.[1]

Gods of Egypt

The number of gods and goddesses that the Egyptians worship, more particularly the forms the deities are represented like the sphinx, the snake, the bull, confuses many people. Thus, there is a misconception about the Egyptian religion because of the animalistic features of its deities and the number of deities worshipped. However, in reality the Egyptians believe in just one powerful God, and all these deities are just manifestations of His powers like the Kabalists who believe in just One God but have many names and symbols of God. There are so many names of the Egyptian deities enumerated in the grid; thus, the necessity of discussing them. There is a quadrant composed of only sixteen squares consisting of four columns and four rows where there are twenty-seven names of Egyptian deities. The names can also be found in other parts of the grid. For convenience and easy reference, I have grouped together the names with ELS and separated them from those that could be found by Permutation. Figure 123 shows the name of the Egyptian God RA/RE while figure 124 shows the name of the Egyptian God, AMN/IMN/AMEN.

	A	B	C	D	E	F	G	H	I	J	K	L
4												
5		R	E									
6	A			A								
7		A	R	E								
8				E								
9												
10												
11							E	R				
12							A		A			
13												
14												
15												
16					A							
17				A	R	A						

Fig. 123 The sun god Ra.

RA/RE—Sun God; the name is written twelve times in the grid as if to imply that RA or the SUN travels the twelve signs of the Zodiac yearly.

AMN/AMEN = Great Father; the name is written many times in the grid with different ELS.

	A	B	C	D	E	F	G	H	I	J	K	L
1												
2				N						A		
3												
4												
5										M		
6				A				M				N
7		A										M
8										N		
9												
10												
11					A		E					A
12					A	M		N				
13					A		E					
14												
15					N			A				
16			M							N		
17	I											

Fig. 124 The name Amen.

IMN = a variant of "AMN" with ELS of nine letters between the desired letters *I* at A-17, *M* at C-16, and *N* at E-15. The god Amun was also known by this name.

Figure 125 shows the other names of the Egyptian gods.

ATUM = the Creator; the name is at the center of the grid starting at
      E-12 and going diagonally upward has an ELS of twenty-two
      letters each before reaching the encoded letters.

ShU = Lord of the Sky and Air, Brother of Tefnut, separated heaven
      and earth; the name is found at F-1 and E-1.

AAT = great one; the word is written several times in the grid.

HORUS/HERU = The son of Isis and the third person of the Egyptian
      Trinity.

SAA = Shepherd, a title of Osiris

Coordinates: S = K-4 A = I-4 A = G-4 ELS = 1 letter
                    S = I-14 A = G-12 A = E-13 ELS = 9 letters

	A	B	C	D	E	F	G	H	I	J	K	L
1					U	Sh						
2						T		A		A		
3								A				
4							A		A		S	
5												
6								M				
7			R									
8		U		E			U					
9			H					U				
10						T						
11									S			
12					A		A					
13					A							
14												
15												

Fig. 125 Several names of gods.

AMU/AAMU = gods of fire

Coordinates: A = I-4 M = H-6 U = G-8 ELS = 22 letters
A = H-3 M = H-6 U = H-9 ELS = 2 letters
A = J-2 A = I-4 M = H-6 U = G-8 ELS= 22 letters

	A	B	C	D	E	F	G	H	I	J	K	L
1												
2												
3												
4							A					
5	H											
6	A			A								
7		A										
8	H						U					
9												
10							H					
11												
12							A					
13												
14							A					
15												
16				H	A							
17			H	A								

Fig. 126 Names of the moon god Thoth.

AH/AAH/AAHU = names of the moon god Thoth

	A	B	C	D	E	F	G	H	I	J	K	L
9												
10						T						
11					A		E					
12					M							
13			A									
14			T									
15			E									
16			M									
17												

Fig. 127 The name Atem.

ATEM/TEM = God of night; the name starts on C-13, and going vertically
downward, the encoded letters *A, T, E,* and *M* are side by side
without ELS. The name is also found at the center of the grid.

244

Figure 128 shows the name of the god AUA.

	A	B	C	D	E	F	G	H	I	J	K	L
3								A				
4							A		A			
5												
6												
7		A										
8							U					
9								U				
10												
11												
12			U		A		A					
13												
14							A					
15								A				
16												
17				A								

Fig. 128 The name Aua.

AUA = god of the extended arms

Coordinates: A = H-3   U = H-9   A = H-15   ELS = 5 letters

A = G-4   U = G-8   A = G-12   ELS = 3 letters

A = B-7   U = C-12   A = D-17   ELS = 60 letters

Figure 129 shows the other names of the Egyptian deities with ELS.

	A	B	C	D	E	F	G	H	I	J	K	L
1								A				
2								A				
3								A				
4							A		A			
5						N						
6	A											
7		A										
8												
9				A						N		
10				N							A	
11					A							A
12		N			A		A	N	A		N	
13			A		A				N			
14									N			
15					A			A				
16					N							

Fig. 129 The gods.

AA = Great One; the name is written several times in the grid.
AN = Name of a god that is written several times.
SIA = God of knowledge; the name is found on G-15, F-14 and E-13 with ELS of twelve letters between the encoded letters
AUI = Gods

Coordinates;   A = D-6   U = C-4   I = B-2   ELS = 24 letters.
            A = L-11   U = L-12   I = L-13   none
            A = H-2   U = G-8   I = F-14   70 letters
ShAY = male guardian angel
Coordinates: Sh = F-11   A = G-12   Y = H-13   ELS= 12 letters
                Sh = F-11   A = E-12   Y = D-13   ELS= 10 letters

	A	B	C	D	E	F	G	H	I	J	K	L
1												
2		I						A				
3												
4				U								
5												
6					A							
7												
8							U					
9												
10												
11						Sh						A
12					A		A					U
13				Y	A			Y				I
14						I						
15							S					
16												
17												

Fig. 130 Other names of the gods.

HAH = God of Infinity

Coordinates:

H = A-5	A = B-7	H = C-9	ELS=24 letters
H = A-8	A = D-9	H = G-10	ELS = 14 letters
H = C-9	A = C-13	H = C-17	ELS =3 letters

	A	B	C	D	E	F	G	H	I	J	K	L
4												
5	H											
6				A								
7		A										
8	H						U					
9		U	H	A								
10							H					
11												
12							A					
13			A									
14												
15											N	
16	I		M	H								M
17	I	N	H	A								

Fig. 131 HAH, AHU, and MIN.

MIN = God of Fertility

Coordinates: M = C-16   I = A-16   N = K-15   ELS = 1 letter
              M = L-16   I = A-17   N = B-17   ELS = none

AHU = god connected with offering; the name is written several
     times

Figure 132 shows the other names with ELS.

	A	B	C	D	E	F	G	H	I	J	K	L
1												
2		I										
3												
4				T						S		E
5		R										
6						Y	I					
7							T					
8							U					
9			H	A			M					
10												
11					A	Sh	E	R				
12												

Fig. 132 More names of gods.

ITY =   god of music; the name is found in B-2 and going in the right
         direction has an ELS of twenty-five letters

SER =   Osiris—the name can also be found in the quadrant starting
         with the letter *S* on J-4 and reading from left to right direction
         has an ELS of one letter between the encoded letters

ITUM/ATUM = the Creator; the name is found on G-6 and reading
         vertically downward, the letters are side by side without EL

ASHER = name of a god; the name is found on the eleventh horizontal
         rows with the letters side by side without ELS

ATON = One God; the letters can also be found on rows 8 to 11 and
         columns E and F, and reading vertically upward, the letters
         are side by side without ELS.

	A	B	C	D	E	F	G	H	I	J	K	L
1	A											
2												
3												
4		K										
5										M		
6												
7			R									
8		H	U			N			E			
9		U	H			O						
10				U		T						
11					A		R					
12												

Fig. 133 Additional names of gods.

HU = God of Food; the name is written many times in the grid.

REM = a god symbolizing the tears of Ra; starts on H-11 and going in the reverse direction has an ELS of thirty-four letters between the desired letters

AKERU = ancestor gods of Re; starts at H-1 and V-1 and going in the right direction has an ELS of thirty-six letters.

BES = God of the Dwarfs; the name is at G-1, C-3, and K-4 with ELS of nineteen letters between the desired letters

	A	B	C	D	E	F	G	H	I	J	K	L
1							B					
2												
3			E									
4											S	
5												
6												

Fig. 134 Seb and Bes, gods of the earth and the dwarfs.

SEB = Husband of Nut, God of Earth; the name is found on K-4, C-3, and G-1 with ELS of nineteen letters between the desired letters.

	A	B	C	D	E	F	G	H	I	J	K	L
3												A
4									A	S	S	
5										M		
6						I					I	
7												M
8						O	U	U				O
9							M	O				
10												
11										S		
12							A	A				
13												
14												
15							S	A				
16												
17												

Fig. 135 More names of gods.

SA =   god of Knowledge; the name is written several times in the
            grid.
AMI-MU/MO = "He who is in the water"; the name is found in I-4
            with ELS of twelve letters.
ASHM = forms in which gods appear before men.

	A	B	C	D	E	F	G	H	I	J	K	L
1								A	Sh	M	A	
2										A	Sh	Sh
3		M									M	
4												
5								A				
6		Sh						M				
7												
8												
9							M					
10												
11						Sh						
12					A	M	A					
13					A							
14												

Fig. 136 Ashm: Forms that gods tak.

The Goddessess

As this is the world of duality, if there are gods, there must also be goddesses. At least in the Egyptian pantheon of deities, there is equality of the sexes and the goddesses are acknowledged. Female gods or goddesses are taboo in the Christian and Islamic religions. But in most religions of the world, the Goddesses are very powerful deities. It is an accepted fact that the matriarchal form of religion is older than the patriarchal form of religion that started during the time of Moses. Goddess worship is considered to be thirty-five thousand years old. Stone Age sculptures representing the Mother more particularly the Venus figures date back to the time of the Cro-Magnon between 35,000 to 10,000 BC. Thus, earth, nature, space, and the universe are called Mother Earth, Mother Nature, Mother Space, and Mother Universe respectively. The oldest statue of the Madonna and Child is not that of Mary and Jesus, but of Isis and Horus.

Among the goddesses of Egypt, the most popular and respected is the goddess ISIS. She was known in ancient times in many names and was represented by the cobra, the fiercest of the snakes. She was the daughter of RA, the wife of OSIRIS, the mother of HORUS, and the Great Mother of the Egyptians. One of her ancient name was AST sometimes also called AS.

The first example of the name AST is found at A-6, J-4, and G-3 with ELS of fourteen letters between the encoded letters.

The second example of AST is at B-7, K-4, and F-2 with ELS of twenty-seven letters between the desired letters. The name shares the letter *S* with the Hebrew word *SMK*, which symbolizes the "snake biting its tail" and the other name of Isis, AS.

	A	B	C	D	E	F	G	H	I	J	K	L
1												
2						T						
3							T					A
4									A	S	S	
5										M		
6		A							K			
7			A									
8												
9												

Fig. 137 AST, ancient name of Isis.

The name KADASH, which means "the goddess of love" can be found on G-2 with the letters side by side without ELS going to the right direction while the name of the "goddess of destiny," ShAI is at K-2 and going in a reverse direction has an ELS of two letters between the encoded letters.

	A	B	C	D	E	F	G	H	I	J	K	L
1												
2					I.		K	A.	D	A	Sh	
3												

Fig. 138 Goddess of Love.

Many names of the other goddesses can be found in the grid with different ELS and in beautiful patterns. As it will be difficult to find the letters forming the words, several illustrations were made for convenience and easy reference.

MAA = The Mother, Wife of Thoth, Daughter of Ra; MAA shares
a common letter *A* with *AS*.

Coordinates:	M = J-1	A = H-2	A = F-3	ELS =	9 letters
	M = C-2	A = H-1	A = A-1	ELS =	6 letters
	M = J-5	A = I-4	A = H-3	ELS =	12 letters
	M = J-5	A = A-6	A = D-6	ELS =	2 letters
	M = H-6	A = I-4	A = J-2	ELS =	22 letters
	M = L-7	A = J-6	A = H-5	ELS =	13 letters
	M = G-9	A = E-11	A = C-13	ELS =	21 letters

MAAT = the Mother; the name is found at J-1, H-2, F-3 and D-4
with ELS of nine letters between the encoded letters

	A	B	C	D	E	F	G	H	I	J	K	L
1	A							A		M		
2			M					A		A		
3						A		A				A
4				T					A			
5								A		M		
6	A			A				M		A		
7												M
8												
9							M					
10												
11					A							
12												
13				A								
14												

Fig. 139 Maa and Maat.

AAT = two ancient goddesses, Isis and Nepthys; the name is written several times in the grid.

Coordinates:

A = H-2	A = F-3	T = D-4	ELS = 10 letters
A = J-2	A = H-2	T = F-2	ELS = 1 letter
A = H-3	A = L-3	T = D-4	ELS = 3 letters
A = G-12	A = E-13	T = C-14	ELS = 9 letters

	A	B	C	D	E	F	G	H	I	J	K	L
1												
2						T		A		A		
3						A		A				A
4				T								
5												
11												
12							A					
13					A							
14				T								

Fig. 140 Isis and Nepthys.

MUT = World Mother, Giver of Life, Queen of Heaven, Wife of Amen-Ra; the name is at G-9-8-7, the letters are side by side without ELS.

NU = Great Mother; the name is written several times in the grid.

NUT = Life Giver, Mother of Gods and of all living symbolized by a cow; the name is found on F-8, G-8, and H-8 with the letters side by side without ELS.

NUN = Goddesses of the Ocean; the name is written several times in the grid.

NET/NIT = Mother of the Gods, Great Goddess; the name is found on J-8 with the letters side by side without ELS and sharing the same letter *T* with the name NUT. It is also found on H-12 and reading diagonally upwards the letters are side by side without ELS.

	A	B	C	D	E	F	G	H	I	J	K	L
6												
7							T					
8						N	U	T	E	N		
9		N	U				M					
10				N	U	E	T					
11							E					
12								N			N	
13									N	U		
14									N	U		
15											N	
16												

Fig. 141 Names of the Mother.

SKMT/SEKMET = Lion headed Goddess, "the Powerful"; the name starts at J-4 with ELS of ten letters between the desired letters.

ShAYT = female guardian angel; the name starts with the letter *Sh* at F-11 with ELS of ten letters between the encoded letters. Reading diagonally downward, the letters are side by side without ELS.

		A	B	C	D	E	F	G	H	I	J	K	L
3													
4												S	
5										K			
6									M.				
7								T					
8													
9													
10													
11							Sh						
12						A							
13					Y								
14				T									
15													

Fig. 142 Lion-headed goddess and female guardian angel.

The names of the goddesses are not only shown in unbelievable ELS but in beautiful formations like the stars in heaven. It seems as if this is an Egyptian grid and not a Hebrew grid. We started with the Father and now the names of the Mother overwhelm us. It is unbelievable. There are other names of the goddesses that can be permutated, but we did not include them anymore because of the numerous examples already.

Angels and other Spirits

In the spirit world of the Egyptians, there are other spirits that the Egyptians acknowledge besides the gods and goddesses. These are the angels, deified human beings, elemental spirits, watchers, guardians, and spirits in the forms of animals.

Most people since childhood have been enamored by the stories about their guardian angels. They thought this was an original Christian teaching unaware that this was based on the teaching of the magi, the ancient Persian religion. This doctrine of angelology has now become very popular. Although Egypt is well-known for its many deities and spirits, however, there is very scarce material about its belief in angels. It is therefore surprising that there are many examples of the words *SHAY* meaning "male guardian angel" in the grid. The ancient Egyptians have even distinguished them into male and female guardian angels as shown in figure 143.

Number of Examples	Coordinates			ELS
1ˢᵗ example	Sh = F-1	A = K-1	Y = D-2	4 letters
2ⁿᵈ example	Sh = I-1	A = K-1	Y = A-2	1 letter
3ʳᵈ example	Sh = L-2	A = H-2	Y = D-2	3 letters
4ᵗʰ example	Sh = K-2	A = H-5	Y = E-8	32 letters
5ᵗʰ example	Sh = L-2	A = H-2	Y = D-2	3 letters
6ᵗʰ example	Sh = L-12	A = I-4	Y = F-6	20 letters

	A	B	C	D	E	F	G	H	I	J	K	L
1						Sh			S		A	
2	Y			Y				A			Sh	Sh
3				Y								
4								A				
5						A						
6		Sh		A		Y						
7												
8					Y							
9												
10												
11						Sh						
12					A		A					
13				Y				Y				
14			T									
15												
16												
17												

Fig. 143 Male guardian angel.

7ᵗʰ example	Sh = B-6	A = D-6	Y = F-6	1 letter
8ᵗʰ example	Sh = B-6	A = I-4	Y = D-3	16 letters
9ᵗʰ example	Sh = F-11	A = E-12	Y = D-3	10 letters
10ᵗʰ example	Sh = F-11	A = G-12	Y = H-13	12 letters

ShAYT = female guardian angel; the name contains the name of the male guardian angel Shay.

11ᵗʰ example	Sh = F-1 A = E-12 Y = D-13 T = C-14	10 letters

The ten examples of guardian angels composed of ten Shay and one Shayt would seem to agree with the Kabalistic version of the ten heirarchies of angels with the Shekinah sometimes being referred to as the feminine angel. It would imply that in the ten hierarchies of angels discussed previously in the section on Sepherotic angels, there are angels who are assigned to protect highly evolved individuals whose spirituality have reached certain levels of the Sepherotic tree. L. W. de Laurence[2] enumerated the different archangels of the Sepheroth who guided and protected the following holy men of Israel, namely:

ARCHANGELS		HOLY MEN
RAZIEL	=	ADAM
ZAPHKIEL	=	NOAH
ZADKIEL	=	ABRAHAM
KAMAEL	=	SAMSON
RAPHAEL	=	ISAAC
HANIEL	=	DAVID
MICHAEL	=	SOLOMON
GABRIEL	=	JOSEPH
MERATTRON	=	MOSES

I was surprised to find the doctrine about the guardian angels under Egypt instead of under the Christian or Judaic matters. This seems to imply that this doctrine emanated from Egyptian teachings and not original Judeo-Christian teaching. It would have been enough to give just one example in the grid, but to give ten examples with the implication about a female guardian angel is unbelievable for there is a legend that among the ten archangels is a female one who is usually referred to as the tenth angel from Malkut who protected Moses.

After the angels, the most well-known elemental spirits are the dwarfs, the small people known as the leprechauns or elves, and the fairies. Among the elemental spirits, the Egyptians believe in the dwarfs. It is uncanny that the word *BES*, which means "god of the dwarfs" is beside the word *NM*, which means "dwarfs." Is this a coincidence? The Egyptian word *ASBIO*, which means "fiery spirits" is also besides the two words. Even the Hebrew word *AOB*, which means "familiar spirits" is also there. Figure 144 shows the following words:

	A	B	C	D	E	F	G	H	I	J	K	L
1							B-					
2												
3			E-									A
4											S-	E
5											O	B
6										A	I	N
7												M
8												

Fig. 144 Bes, god of the dwarfs.

BES =   God of the Dwarfs; the name is found at G-1, C-3 and K-4
        with ELS of nineteen letters between the desired letters. It is
        also found in the cluster of letters at L-4-5 and K-4.

NM—dwarfs; the word can be found at L = 6-7 with the letters side
        by side without ELS.

ASBIO = fiery spirits

Figure 145 shows the other names of the spirits.

	A	B	C	D	E	F	G	H	I	J	K	L
1												I
2					I							
3						A						A
4							A		A			
5							A					B
6	A			A			I					
7												
8												
9												
10												
11												
12			U				A				N	
13												
14												
15						I						
16					A							
17				A								

Fig. 145 Divine being.

BAI = divine soul;

Coordinates: B = L-5   A = L-3   I = L1   ELS =   1 letter
               B = A-7   A = J-6   I = G-6   27 letters

AAI = three divine beings connected with RA

Coordinates:	A = G-4	A = F-3	I = E-2	ELS = 12 letters
	A = A-6	A = D-6	I = G-6	2 letters
	A = D-17	A = E-16	I = F-15	10 letters

NAU = serpent with seven heads; the word is found at K-12, G-12, and C-12 with ELS of three letters.

ARI = guardians

Coordinates:	A = D-9	R = H-11	I = L-13	ELS = 27 letters
	A = E-16	R = H-11	I = K-6	56 letters

Fig. 146 Guardians.

RAU = divine companion of RA; the word is found at H-11, I-12, and J-13 with ELS of twelve letters between the desired letters.

AAR = serpent

Coordinates:	A = E-11	A = D-9	R = C-7	ELS = 24 letters
	A = L-3	A = G-4	R = B-5	6 letters

UASH = watchers; the word is found at B-8-7-6, and reading upward, the letters are side by side without ELS.

	A	B	C	D	E	F	G	H	I	J	K	L
1								A				
2							K	A				
3					A			A	A			
4								A	K			
5									K	A		
6		Sh										
7		A	R									
8		U										
9					A							
10												
11								A				
12												
13												

Fig. 147 Other divine entities.

KA = Divine Bull; the word is written several times in the grid.

AMU = divine beings

Coordinates:	A = L-11	M = F-12	U = L-12	ELS =	5 letters
	A = H-3	M = H-6	U = H-9		2 letters

ANT = solar boat; the word is found at C-13, I-13, and C-14 with ELS of five letters. It is also found at E-13, F-8, and G-3 with ELS of fifty-eight letters.

	A	B	C	D	E	F	G	H	I	J	K	L
1												
2												
3								A				
4												
5												
6								M				
7												
8												
9								U				
10												
11												A
12						M						U
13			A						N			
14			T									
15												

Fig. 148 Ant: Solar boat.

Book of the Dead

There is a collection of ancient Egyptian texts containing spells, incantations, prayers, hymns, rituals, and magical formulae for the benefit of the dead called the Book of the Dead. These texts were found in the pyramids and tombs carved, engraved, or painted on the walls, coffins, sarcophagi, or rolls of papyri. The Book of the Dead has become the source of numerous books on the Egyptians spells, incantations, amulets, talismans, and magic formulae.

Sir E.A. Wallis Budge wrote the most authoritative book about the Book of the Dead.[3] However, Patrick Geryl and Gino Ratinckx[4] have challenged the traditional translation by advocating the translation made by Albert Slosman that the Book of the Dead was actually the story about the destruction of Atlantis or the END TIME. They supported their theory by mathematical calculations based on the translation of Slosman.

It is the belief among the Egyptians that the spirit world is inhabited by nefarious and horrifying entities that even the gods were afraid of them. Thus, words of power, spells, and magic formulae were carved or painted in the sarcophagus or rolls of papyri with spells and incantations were placed in the tomb to protect the dead in his travel to the spirit world.

The Book of the Dead is composed of the following collection of texts, namely:

1) Heliopolitan Recension—It is also called the Pyramid Texts for the hieroglyphics were found in the walls of the chambers and tombs of certain pharaohs in the fifth and sixth dynasties around 4,266 BC.

2) Theban Recension—The hieroglyphic writings in papyri and on the coffins, which were used from eighteenth to twenty-second dynasties around 3,333 BC to 3,166 BC.

3) Saite Recension—Hieroglyphics orderly written in papyri and on the coffins and used in the twenty-sixth dynasty around 600 BC to 30 BC.

The Pyramid Text is the oldest form of the Book of the Dead; certain sections of which were written three thousand years before Christ. Some writings were around 4,266 BC. The longest papyrus about the Book of the Dead is dated 1,420 BC for the benefit of Ani, a royal scribe.

During the time of the Old Kingdom around 2,700 BC, it was the belief that only the pharaoh was entitled to an afterlife. However, by the time of the New Kingdom around 2,040, everybody from the highest to the lowest person was believed to have an afterlife. Thus, special care was taken to mummify (Uahtu) the body of the dead. The embalming ritual might take seventy-days days to complete if the deceased was a wealthy person and only a day or two for a poor man. Since the dead would be using again his physical body, the embalmers sought to preserve the body for eternity. The ritual of the opening of the mouth (Aba Ru) was performed so that the dead could eat, drink, and speak in the other world. The burial usually took place on the west where supposed to be the sun began its nightly journey. From the east to the west, the mummy (Sah) was brought by a barge along the Nile and then by ox-drawn hearse in the form of a boat to the tomb. Shaven-headed priests (Aata) who prayed and chanted along the way led the funeral procession. At the door of the tomb, the last funeral rites were performed, including a solemn ceremonial dance and a feast. They brought plenty of offerings (Uten) and gifts (Anu) that are delivered to the one in charge of the offerings called Ani, the treasurer of the offerings.

It was believed that the dead remained in his tomb during daytime, but at sunset, he would sail on his solar boat, the Aa to accompany the sun Ra who nightly

journeys in his boat Uaa through the underworld. Ra traverses the universe for millions of years through his boat called the Uaa En Heh or "boat of millions of years." The deceased in his journey could visit the Field of Reeds (Sekhet Aaru) to work. In this place, he could perform the work he was accustomed to do on earth. At dawn, he returned to his tomb for the food and rest that even the dead needed. Thus, the reason for the many offerings of food, beers, and wine placed in the tomb for the benefit of the dead who was treated as if he was still alive. It was believed that the paintings of food and wine could be converted into real food, which could also be eaten by the dead, hence the many paintings of food and drinks. The importance of the offerings (Kau) and presents (Aab) can be gleaned by the repetition of words in the grid referring to food offerings (Atu). Figure 149 shows the words with ELS while figure 150 shows the words that can be formed by permutation.

AHU = god connected with offerings   ANU = gifts, offerings

AU = offerings   UTEN = bring offerings

ANI = Treasurer of offerings; there are fifteen examples shown in figures 23, 24, and 25.

	A	B	C	D	E	F	G	H	I	J	K	L
1												
2												
3												
4							A					
5						N						
6					I							
7		A										
8		U					U	T	E	N		
9		U	H	A								
10							H					
11												
12							A.					
13										U.		
14									N.			
15								A.				
16												
17												

Fig. 149 Words about offerings.

AKHAB = to give   AAB = offerings, presents

KAU = offerings   ANTU = pure offerings

ATU = food offerings   NEB KAU = Lord of food

ABSHE = monster crocodile that eats hearts of lost souls

AMAM = monster beast that eats the hearts of sinners

SHAT EA SHAU = known as the Book of the Pylons that deals with
           Osiris and Tuat, the underworld

	A	B	C	D	E	F	G	H	I	J	K	L
1					U	Sh	B	A	Sh	M	A	
2								A		A		
3						A	T				M	A
4				T	E							
5			E									
6		A	Sh		A							
7		B	A									
8			U	K								
9												
10												
11												
12			N	U								
13			A									
14			T									
15												

Fig. 150 Other words related to offerings.

Some of the rituals performed for the dead are the following:

1) Opening of the mouth (Aba Ru)—This is one of the most important rituals performed on the deceased. For the opening of the mouth would enable the deceased to speak, eat, and drink in the other world. The words *Aba Ru* can be found in the quadrant composed of A-6-7, B-7-8, and C-7. The letters are lumped together and are side by side without ELS. It shows the importance of the ritual.

2) Giving of word of power for protection in the other world against evil spirits. Even the gods fear the many nefarious spirits. Thus the deceased needs words of power and talismans for protection.

3) Ritual for the dead to remember his name. This is important for the deceased to be recognized in the other world. The word Ren or name is found at C-7, G-11 and K-15.

4) Getting a heart for use in the other world. Without a heart, the deceased cannot see Osiris.

5) Spells against losing the heart, head, etc. The deceased is given the spells/formula to protect his spirit body.

6) Spells so as not to decay or to eat filth in the underworld and drink polluted water; also to gain power over the water and fire.

7) Power to change into animal forms. To enable the deceased to travel fast, protect himself; and for other purpose, he is given the power words to change form.

All these rituals are only effective if the deceased has passed the test in the hall of truth.

Weighing of the Heart

One of the rituals mentioned in the Book of the Dead is the "weighing of the heart," the purpose of which is to verify the purity of the heart so that one can be with Osiris. It is a beautiful story that is said to be the basis of the Sermon on the Mount by Jesus who said, "Blessed are the pure of heart for they will see God."[5] As will be noted, this saying of Jesus is based on a very ancient tradition of the Egyptians to weight the heart.

It was the belief among the followers of Osiris that the physical body (Khat) of a dead man was sacred and should not be desecrated, burnt, or dismembered. The preservation of the Khat was necessary for from the dead body would spring the glorious, translucent, and transparent shell (Sahu) in which the spirit soul (Khu) of the dead would take up its abode with all his mental and spiritual attributes.

To the Egyptians, AB (the heart), BA (the soul), KA (the spirit), and the KHU (the spirit-soul) are very important, for they are the vehicles to the spiritual world. The heart is considered the seat of life and the fountain of good and evil, hence the greatest care of the heart by the Egyptians. It is uncanny that the words are found side by side at G-1-2 and H-1-2 and also at A-6-7, B-7, and C-8. In the embalmment (Utu) and mummification of the dead, the Egyptians take special care of the heart, for it is supposed to be weighed in the balance scale to see the worthiness of a dead person. On the other hand, the Ka is the abstract individuality or personality endowed with the deceased characteristic traits. The Ka has an independent existence and can travel anywhere separating and joining with the Khat at will. It was considered a double like the astral body as presently known today. The Ka was supposed also to eat and drink the offerings of food and drinks. It was also believed that offerings painted on the tomb could be converted into nourishments by prayers of the living, thus the many paintings of food and drinks in the tomb. Another body of man was called Ba, the soul or heart-soul

that was considered as eternal. It would revisit the Khat, animate, and talk to it. It could take any shape. It also partakes of the funeral offerings. Another body of man is the Khaibit or his shadow that can separate itself from the body or moves where it pleases. It also partakes of the offerings. Another part of man is the Khu, which means the "shining or translucent spirit soul."

From the preceding, it could be said that the Egyptians consider the whole man as consisting of a physical body, a spirit body, a heart, a double, a heart soul, a shadow, a spirit soul, and a name (ren). For the well-being of the spiritual bodies, it was necessary to preserve the physical body, thus the outmost care in mummifying the physical body. The Egyptians believe in the resurrection of the dead upon which the Christian doctrine is founded.

According to the Egyptian Book of the Dead, when one dies, the deceased enters the hall of truth (Maati) where the heart is weighed by the god Anubis in the balance (Ausu) against an ostrich feather emblematic of "Truth or Law" while the deities, Meskhenet, a nurturing birth deity and Renutet, controller of destiny and life span, look on. The deceased makes a confession of what he has done on earth. Thoth records the confession while a beast called the Devourer waits for the verdict. If the verdict is guilty, the Devourer eats the heart of the deceased who will be vanished to hell. Those who are judged worthy with pure hearts will be with Osiris in heaven or abode of the gods.

	A	B	C	D	E	F	G	H	I	J	K	L
1							B.	A.				
2							K.	A.				
3							T.	A.				
4							A.		A			
5					.			A	K			
6	A.								K	A		
7	B.	A	R									
8			K									
9				A								
10							H					
11				K	A		E					
12					A							
13												
14					V							
15											N	
16							E					
17					R							

Fig. 151 The words *AB*, *BA*, *KA*, *KHU*, and *REN*.

It is intriguing that many words related to the spiritual world and the rituals mentioned in the Book of the Dead are found in the grid. Again for easy reference, I have grouped together the words with ELS and those that can be found by permutation.

Figure 152 shows the words related to offerings given upon the death of a person.

ANI =   treasurer of holy offerings
AHU =   god connected with offerings
AAB =   offerings, presents
ANU =   abode of the dead; gifts offerings
ATU =   food offerings; the word is found at E-12, F-10, and G-8 with
        ELS of ten letters
AU =   offerings
TH =   gift
UTEN = bring offerings

	A	B	C	D	E	F	G	H	I	J	K	L
1							B	A				
2								A				
3												
4							A					
5						N						
6	A.		.		I							
7	B.	A										
8							U.	T.	E.	N.		
9			U.	H.	A.							
10						T					Th	
11												A.
12				U	A				A.	N.		
13				A						U.		
14												

Fig. 152 Words related to offerings.

Figure 153 shows the words related to the dead.

TA = to pass away	UT = abode of Anubis
SAH = mummy	SEK = to decay

	A	B	C	D	E	F	G	H	I	J	K	L
1							B	A				
2						T		A				
3						A	T	A				A
4						A						
5									K			
6	A											
7	B	A					T		E			M
8							U					
9							M		S			
10						T						
11					A	Sh	E					A.
12			U								N.	
13			A							U.		
14			T									
15							S				N	
16					A			E				
17			H		R							

Fig. 153 Words related to death.

REN = name of the dead

SHE = chamber of embalmment of Osiris

AAU = portion of the abode of the blessed

Figure 154 shows another group of words with different ELS.

UASH = to worship   AAU = to praise
AMA = priest   MUT = weights
AAAU = incarnations of spirits praising the rising sun

	A	B	C	D	E	F	G	H	I	J	K	L
3												A
4												
5												
6		Sh										
7		A					T					M
8		U					U					
9		U					M					
10												
11												A
12			U		A		A	A				
13												

Fig. 154 Words still related to the dead.

The inclusion of the Egyptian gods and goddesses, other spirits and rituals in the grid is very surprising as they are anathema to the Christian and Judaic religions. It is unbelievable that the author of this code can infuse these matters in a Hebrew code. What does it imply? Do Egypt and its religion have a special place in the heart of the supposed author of this code, Jesus? Can it be true that he truly spent some of his adolescent years in Egypt where he studied the secret esoteric teachings of the adepts like Moses, thus his knowledge of the Egyptian practices? The religious practices of Egypt are very alien to Christian religion especially if the gods assume the forms of animals. Thus, there is a misconception of the Egyptian religion as animalistic in nature. But why is it included in this code? Does the inclusion of Egypt and its religion in the code a reminder to the Christians to respect the beliefs of others and to love one another? Is this the attitude expected by Jesus of His disciples, thus his saying:

If they are not against us, they are with us?[6]

This also reminds us of what Krishna of the Hindus supposedly said in the Bhagavad Gita:

> Even those who worship other Gods with devotion, full of faith, they also worship Me.[7]

This liberal attitude runs counter to the Christian fundamentalist fanaticism, which brings to mind the story I heard when I was still young about what Mahatma Gandhi supposedly said when he was being converted to Christianity that he believed in Jesus Christ but not in Christians.

I placed another illustration to show the Egyptians' emphasis on the importance of the heart not only physically but also in the spiritual world. The words speak for themselves.

	A	B	C	D	E	F	G	H	I	J	K	L
1							B	A			A	
2								A	A			
3					A			A				
4							A					
5				Tz				A				
6	A						I					
7	B	A	R									
8												
9		U										
10												
11					A							
12					A		A		A			
13			A		A							
14	A						A					
15								A				
16					A							
17				A		A						

Fig. 155 The importance of cleansing the heart.

AB = means "heart"
URT(z) AB = He whose heart is still
AA = means "Wash the Heart"
AM AB = "What is in the Heart?"
ABA = heart soul
AMI AB = "He who is in the Heart"

	A	B	C	D	E	F	G	H	I	J	K	L
1							B	A		M		I
2										A		
3												A
4							A		A			
5										M		B
6	A		M		I		I				I	
7	B	A										
8												
9							M					
10												
11												
12							A					
13												

Fig. 156 He who is in the heart.

AB = means "Heart"   ABA = heart soul
TAT AB = means "Heart's desires"

	A	B	C	D	E	F	G	H	I	J	K	L
1							B	A				
2						T		A				
3						A	T	A				
4						A						
5												
6	A											
7	B	A										
8												
9												

Fig. 157 Pure Heart.

TA-AB = pure heart   AAAB = means "Great Heart"
AAB = great heart

Looking at the illustrations, it would seem that much importance is given to the heart. Based on the words mentioned, an opinion or idea can be formed. What is in the heart? What is the heart's desire? Is it to be pure? How? Is it by washing the heart and thereby cleansing it of all the hurts, pains, disappointments, and

anger? Then we must still the heart by meditation and prayers for only the pure of heart can see God. God is in the heart. If we will not find God in our hearts, then we will not find Him anywhere. The Egyptian words show the high spiritual teachings of the Egyptians. There are other words related to the weighing of the heart that can be permutated, but because of the substantial examples already in the grid, I did not include them anymore.

e) Hidden Records

The discovery of the different texts of the Book of the Dead has enabled us to look at the funerary rites and religious beliefs of the ancient Egyptians. Other ancient Egyptian documents speaking about some events in the Bible have given us additional and different insights based on the Egyptians' versions of the story like the Exodus that has been discussed on the later parts of this book about Egypt. Could it be possible to discover other ancient writings and records about Egypt as envisioned by Cayce and other visionaries who have narrated about hidden records in the secret chambers within and under the Pyramids and the Sphinx? Although recent diggings near the Pyramids have revealed new findings, however the Egyptian government had been very strict in allowing excavations.

Maybe it is time for the Egyptian government to reconsider its position about allowing more research and excavations in the Giza area as there are still so many matters to be discovered and studied. Even the grid would seem to suggest that a further exploration and survey of the Giza area is needed.

HO = search
HR = pyramid
SHETAIT = hidden place
SHETA = hidden, mystery
SOD = Hebrew word for secret

	A	B	C	D	E	F	G	H	I	J	K	L
1						Sh						
2					I	T		D				
3					A	T		O				
4					E					S		
5		H	R									
6		A										
7												

Fig. 158 What is the secret?

Figure 159 shows the hidden places and chambers to be searched.

AMI = chamber
AKIT = chamber

MENU = chamber
AT = hall, palace

	A	B	C	D	E	F	G	H	I	J	K	L
1			E	N	U			A		M		I
2			M		I	T	K					
3						A	T					
4						A		A.				
5								A.		M.		
6	A		M		I		I.	M.		A	I.	
7												
8												

Fig. 159 Words denoting chambers.

The grid says that there are hidden chambers in the Pyramids that confirmed the readings of Edgar Cayce and the vision of the Filipino visionary. In figure 160 are additional words suggesting that there are underground streams and hidden entrances to the Pyramids and Sphinx. These underground streams and hidden chambers are now the subject of many books.

There had been reports last October 2002 that at the end of a shaft inside the Pyramid was discovered an entrance to chambers still unexplored.

	A	B	C	D	E	F	G	H	I	J	K	L
3												
4											S	E
5								A				B
6	A						I	M		A		
7	B	A	R				T		E			
8		U					U	T		N		
9												
10						T						
11			U	K.	A.	Sh	E	R				A
12			U			M		N	A.			U
13			A							U		
14			T							U		
15												
16				H	A							
17				A	R	A						

Fig. 160 Passages and entrances.

KAS = chamber   AMT = chamber
UAR = passage   UA = path
UAU = waterway   ABA = entrance
UAT = path   BES = enter UTIT = chamber
ATER= canal, stream   AMENT = hidden place, to hide

The cluster of words that are found in the grid would seem to suggest that there is a need for further exploration and excavations near the Pyramids and the Sphinx and that the visions of Edgar Cayce and the Filipino visionary have in fact a basis.

It has been the esoteric tradition of the Egyptians to search (HO) for the truth. In this search, they have built an unequalled monument called the HR or Pyramid that is considered the Bible in Stone, the symbol of man's aspiration to be one with God.

It is intriguing that the words enumerated are lumped together side by side in the cluster of letters found at F-9, G-10-12, H-10-11, and I-12. Their proximity and their interrelationship show deliberateness in putting up the words especially if the words when formed show the following sentence "HO HR RA," which when loosely translated means "Search for the Pyramid of RA." What does it mean? Is there something hidden in the pyramid of RA, which up to now is undiscovered?

And which is the pyramid of RA? Is it the pyramid of Cheop or a buried pyramid still undiscovered? There are documents and legends that spoke about pyramids that are now nonexistent. Herodotus[8] in the fifth century BC described a labyrinth that he said was more impressive than the pyramids and Greek buildings. Yet this labyrinth could not be located now. It had disappeared, thus the necessity for further explorations in the area. The words *HO* and *HR* have been written three times. Does this imply that the three Pyramids, namely, CHEOP, KAFRE, and MENKAURE have to be searched for hidden chambers? The words *AMI*, *UTIT*, *AMT*, *MENU*, *KAS*, and *AKIT*, all meaning chambers have been written many times as if to emphasize that there are hidden chambers in or below the Pyramids and the Sphinx. The words *SHETA*, *SHETAIT*, and *AMENT* meaning "HIDDEN PLACE" have been written several times. What do we do?

	A	B	C	D	E	F	G	H	I	J	K	L
8												
9			H			O						
10		O					H	O				
11								R				
12							A		A			
13												
14												

Fig 161 Search for the Pyramid of Ra.

There have been rumors about undiscovered chambers in the Pyramids and Sphinx. In 1983, a young clairvoyant Filipino boy related to me his mental travel inside the Pyramid of Cheop and the Sphinx where he was shown by a guide with golden complexion and golden robe the ancient records about the fabled Lemuria or Mu. Is this message in the code a confirmation of the boy's mental travel? In 1999 and the first half of the year 2,000 Egyptian authorities have revealed some interesting archeological finds near the Pyramids. The words *AMI, UTIT, AMT, MENU, KAS*, and *AKIT*, all meaning "CHAMBERS" have been written many times as if to emphasize that there are many hidden chambers. The word/s *SHETA, SHETAIT*, and *AMENT* all meaning "HIDDEN PLACE" have been written many times. The repetition of the words suggests that an exploration of the Pyramids and the Sphinx be undertaken.

In the book *Keeper of Genesis* by R. Bauval and G. Hancock cited a reading of Edgar Cayce, namely:

> References and clues (which) indicate Egypt as a repository for records—records of Atlantis and ancient Egypt during the time of Ra-Ta, which may someday be found. They also mention again and again tombs and pyramids yet to be uncovered in Egypt, and give specific dates for the building of the Great Pyramid.[9]

In the Discovery Channel, it was reported in February 2000 about the successful digging in the vicinity of the Sphinx, which yielded a sarcophagus thirty (30) meters underground.

The authors of the book *Fingerprints of God*[10] commented that Cayce also said that at around 10,500 BC, a vast underground repository was established containing a library of wisdom from the lost civilization of Atlantis: "This in position lies, as the sun rises from the waters, the line of shadow (or light) falls between the paws of the Sphinx . . . . Between, then, the Sphinx and the river." In another reading Cayce gave even more specific directions: "There is a chamber or passage from the right forepaw (of the Sphinx) to this entrance of the record chamber." According to the readings, the Hall of Records is to be rediscovered and re-entered when "the time has been fulfilled," which Cayce suggested would be at or just before the close of the twentieth century, perhaps in 1998. The readings allude frequently to the Old and New Testaments of the Bible with frequent references to Jesus and depict the rediscovery of the lost Halls of Records.

The young Filipino visionary also related how a man with golden skin guided him through the corridors and chambers under the Sphinx where he saw voluminous records of Lemuria or Mu. Edgar Cayce's references about Jesus might have answered the reason why in the code Egypt had been mentioned and it further gave insight as to who could be the real author of the code.

There was a time when high technology equipment like ground-penetrating radar was used to locate the hidden chambers in the Pyramid. The results of the tests were very promising showing some cavities and chambers beneath the Sphinx; however, the Egyptian authorities have discontinued the test.

f) The Pyramids

In the discussion of Egypt, it is inevitable that the subject about the Pyramids will always crop up for Egypt is equated with the Pyramids. Presently, the Pyramids are the only ancient wonders still existing in the world. The Pyramids have amazed people now, how much more in ancient time? Yet there is a lack of records about the Pyramids and the Sphinx in ancient Egyptian documents, in the Bible, or even in the Koran. Why? Was it forbidden to write about them like in medieval times when it was forbidden to paint the image of God the Father? Due to the lack of information about the Pyramids and the Sphinx, they have become subject of debates as to who built them and when. If ever there are references about them, these are just implied. What could be the reasons? Are there hidden references in the Bible about the existence of the Pyramids? Yes!

In Exodus[1] the Lord said,

> An altar of earth thou shalt make unto me. And if thou wilt make me an altar of stone thou shalt not built of hewn stone: for if thou lift up thy tool upon it, thou has polluted it. Neither shalt thou go up by steps unto mine altar, that thy nakedness be not discovered thereon.

These verses are intriguing, for God was giving instructions and pattern as to how the Jews would make an altar. God even specified the kind of stones and tools to be used. This must be a special altar, not just heap of stones filed on top of another. The Jews were told neither to cut the stones nor to use man-made tools in fashioning them. How could this kind of stone altar be possibly built without cutting the stones to fit them together? And how could the stones be fashioned into pieces without using man-made tools? This was an impossible task. Yet this was accomplished. How? An ancient Sumerian text showed how it was done.

> In the land of the Na-stone, the large Na stones of the mountains will be cut up into slabs for you.

> To the mountain of (mountain) of stone not for men to enter,
> Did for the Lord Ningursa, Gudea bends his steps cutting in slab forms its great stones.[2]

Based on these verses, there was a mountain where a special kind of stones called the Na-stones were quarried and processed. However, humans were not allowed to enter this mountain. Only the gods were allowed to go there and cut the stones. Why were humans forbidden to enter the mountain? Was it to keep secret the cutting and processing of the stones? If the gods were the ones who fashioned the slabs of stones and supervised the construction of the altar with the manual labor provided by men, then indeed the construction of the altar was possible. Without the help of the gods, the construction of the altar would have been impossible. Just the ferrying of the heavy stones from the mountain to the site was an impossible task. There were approximately 2.5 million stone blocks weighing from one to seventy-five tons each. Presently, there is no modern heavy equipment like cranes or haulers that can carry the fifty to seventy-five tons of stone slabs. Then there were the 144,000 casing stones with an average weight of twenty tons that were placed at the sides of the pyramids. Orthodox Egyptologists suggested that rolling logs and substantial manpower were used to install the slabs precisely on top of one another to form the Great Pyramid that had a height of 481.4 feet.[3] This theory is untenable. How could the stones be brought up to such a height and piled on top of one another with such precision? How could the casings be installed sideways? How was the altar or the pyramid built?

Who Built the Pyramids?

It would seem that an ancient Sumerian text called "Ninurta Myth Lugal—E" written around 2,150 BC contains the secret of how the altar was built, to wit:

> He made a bank of stones against the highland—like drifting clouds
> they (come floating on) outstretch wings.[4]

The stones were like drifting clouds that came floating on outstretched wings. What is the meaning of this verse? Does it mean that the stones were floating like drifting clouds? How could this be possible? Was an antigravity machine or a sonic device used to lift the heavy stones? Only aliens could have this kind of scientific devices. If they were able to fly here, they would also have other scientific knowledge to do supernatural things. But we do not want to believe in aliens despite mounting evidences. Further discussion on the builders of the pyramids could be found in the chapters about Sumer.

Another problem in the construction of the altar was the prohibition to build steps in going to the altar. As there would be steps, for sure the altar would be tall or in a high place, yet there was the instruction not to build steps so that the nakedness of the workers would not be shown. But how would one go up the altar without steps? How did the builders prevent the people from going

up the altar and showing their nakedness? With respect to the steps, casings were made over the steps to cover them. Because of the casings' smoothness, people could not climb and step on them. This altar was very tall and steep like a mountain and became known in ancient times by many names. The Jews called it as HR while the Egyptians addressed it as MR, both words meaning "Mountain." The Sumerians called the altar E.KUR, which means "House of Mountain." The ancients were calling the altar as mountain when actually they were all referring to the Pyramids. They used also other words like *mount* or *mountain* to hide the existence of the Pyramids. Why do we say that the words refer to the Pyramids?

Josephus, the Jewish historian of the first century AD wrote that the "children of Seth" in order that their wisdom and inventions might not be lost due to the predictions of their ancestor Adam that the world would be destroyed by fire and then by water:

> They made two pillars, the one of brick and the other of stone. They described their discoveries on both, that in case the pillar of brick shall be destroyed by the flood, the pillar of stone might remain, and exhibit their discoveries to mankind, and also inform them that there was another pillar of brick erected by them. Now this remains in the land of Syria or Seirad to this day.[5]

Murry Hope in her book *The Sirius Connection* also quoted the verse in this manner:

> The patriach Seth, in order that Wisdom and Astronomical Knowledge should not perish, erected in prevision of the double destruction by fire and water predicted by Adam, two columns, one of brick, the other of stone, on which this knowledge was engraved, and which existed in the Siridic country[Egypt].

Syria is known for its bricks and the imposing ziggurat made of bricks whose ruins could still be traced in Syria. Josephus also pointed to Syria as the place where the pillar of bricks was located. But where is the Siridic country? Murry Hope and Robert Temple suggest Egypt. What does the grid say? Where is the pillar of stone?

	A	B	C	D	E	F	G	H	I	J	K	L
1												
2			M.									
3		M			Ch							
4		K	U		E	Ch						
5	H	R	E.		O		Ch		K	M		
6			M					M				
7			R	E			T			Ch	E	M
8			U	K.								
9												
10												

Fig. 162 Egypt and the Pyramids.

Figure 162 shows the ancient names of Egypt KM, KMT or ChM, and the E.KUR Figure 163 shows the ancient name of Sumer SHUMER and the ancient names of the Pyramids. The ancient name of the Pyramid Cheop was EAKU or YAKU,[6] while the pyramid Kafre was known as UR and the pyramid Menkaure as HAR.[7] It is intriguing to find these ancient names of the places and pyramids in the grid. We can only conclude that the pillar of stone is in EGYPT. Unfortunately the casings where most of the ancient knowledge has been engraved have already been lost.

The Greek historian Herodotus[8] in 450 BC claimed that he saw the inscriptions on the casings of the Pyramids. He was the one who wrote that the Pharaoh Cheop built the Great Pyramid. Manetho, the foremost Egyptian historian in the third BC said that it was Suphis 1 of the fourth dynasty around 2,720-2,560 BC who built the Great Pyramid. Ibn Abd Hokam,[9] a nineteenth-century Arab historian said that the Pyramids were built by Sured Ibn Salhouk, King of Egypt who lived three hundred years before the deluge because of a dream about an impending catastrophy. He ordered the buildings of the pyramids with all the knowledge deposited in the pyramids. Arab historians and writers up to the Middle Ages wrote about this story regarding the writings in the casings of the Pyramids This story is similar to the Sumerian story of the the Cylinder of Gudea[10] written about 2,125 BC. It was about the dream of King Gudea who was told by the gods to build an E.Kur for the god Ningursu.

	A	B	C	D	E	F	G	H	I	J	K	L
3												
4			U									
5	H	R										
6	A											
7		A	R									
8	H	U										
9							M	U	S			
10				U	E		H					
11					A		E	R				
12			U		A							
13				Y								
14												
15												
16				H	A							
17				A	R							

Fig. 163 Sumer and the ancient names of the three Pyramids.

Manetho also wrote that it was Nitocris, daughter of the Pharaoh Mycerinus around 2,560-2,420 BC, who built the third Pyramid. According to Eusebius, Nitocris was the noblest and loveliest woman of her time with fair complexion. The Armenian version of Eusebius said that Queen Nitocris was braver than all men, most beautiful of women, fair skinned with red cheeks. She was known also as Neith-okre {Neith is excellent} or as Queen Khentkawes.[11]

The Egyptians and the Hyksos (Predecessors of the Jews)

In Joshua,[12] the Jews were saying,

> Let us now prepare to build us an altar, not for burnt offerings nor for sacrifice:

> But that it maybe a witness between us, and you, and our generations after us.

> Therefore said we, that it shall be, when they should say to us or to our generations in time to come, that we may say again, Behold the pattern of the altar of the Lord, which our fathers made, not for burnt offerings, nor for sacrifices, but it is a witness between us and you.

And the children of Reuben and the children of Gad called the altar
ED for it shall be a witness between us that the Lord is God.

What is this altar that was built not for burnt offerings and sacrifice, but as a witness about the Jews relationship with each other and their God? What is this altar that would last for generations and generations and had a pattern that the builders were boasting about? This was not an ordinary altar. Where did the Jews build this altar? For sure not in Jerusalem nor in any part of Israel but in their original homeland—Lower Egypt in the plains of Giza—did the Jews build the altar. They were not called the Jews then but Hyksos who according to ancient historians Manetho and Josephus ruled Lower Egypt for more than five hundred years, and according to an ancient Egyptian document "Admonitions of Ipuwer,"

Foreigners have become people (Egyptians) everywhere.[13]

The foreigners being referred to in this statement are the Hyksos, the predecessors of the Jews, who became known in Egypt as the Hyksos Pharaohs of Egypt. The Jews had become assimilated with the natives and actually became Egyptians. This would be similar to Americans not being all native Indians, but most are combinations of different cultures. Only after the Exodus did the Jews become a separate nation.

There is a Gnostic text found at Nag Hamadi written supposedly by Seth, the son of Adam. The text is called the "Gospel of the Egyptians."[14] Why is the text considered a Gospel for the Egyptians when supposedly Seth wrote it, and he was not an Egyptian? This text must have originated from the Hyksos who have deified Seth whom the Egyptians equated with their god Seth. Considering that the Hyksos were also considered Egyptians, then the title of the Gospel had some truth in it.

However, the Hyksos, despite being assimilated and surrounded by Egyptian culture and religion, still practiced their own religion and not the Egyptian way. Isaiah said,

And the Lord shall be known to Egypt, and the Egyptians shall know
the Lord in that day and shall do sacrifice and oblation; yea, they shall
vow a vow unto the Lord and perform it.[15]

When have the Egyptians ever offered sacrifices and oblations to the God of Israel? When did they ever swear to the God of Jacob? This could only have happened during the time of the Hyksos.

The Egyptians (Hyksos) offered sacrifices and oblations to God during the Hyksos five-hundred-year reign. For obeying their God and building monuments that would last for generations as signs for their faith in their God, the God of Israel blest the Hyksos, the Egyptians Jews as Isaiah said in the Old Testament:

> In that day shall Israel be the third with Egypt and with Assyria, even a blessing in the midst of the land.[16]

> Blessed be Egypt my people, and Assyria the work of my hands, and Israel my inheritance.[17]

When was ever the time that in God's estimation, Egypt was first, then the Assyrian and lastly Israel? When did the God of Israel ever bless the Egyptians? Were not the Egyptians and the Assyrians the abomination of God? Without the history of the Hyksos, we would never have known why the God of Israel blessed the Egyptians first, then the Assyrians and then the Israelites. The sayings of Isaiah were mysterious as there were no documents/writings to show that these events have ever happened. The period of time of the occurrence of these events had never been mentioned. It is only Isaiah who said that the God of Israel blessed the land of Egypt and its people considered the people of the Lord. Why did Isaiah say these things? What was his basis? When was this time? Could this unknown period of time be the reason why Egypt is contained in this code? Is it because it is time to know the truth? Even the formation of the words "KMT AMI" in the grid is in the form of a pyramid.

Isaiah[18] even said that there were five cities in Egypt speaking the language of Canaan and swearing by the Lord of Hosts.

	A	B	C	D	E	F	G	H	I	J	K	L
1												
2			M			I	T					
3												
4		K		T					A			
5							Ch	K	M			
6	A		M		I		I	M		I		
7	B	A	R				T			Ch	E	M
8		U	K									
9							M					
10												
11												
12							A					
13												

Fig. 164 Baruk Kmt Ami (Blessed be Egypt my people).

Isaiah further said that in the midst of the land of Egypt was an altar of the Lord:

> In that day shall there be an altar of the Lord in the midst of the land of Egypt, and a monument of the Lord at the border thereof.
>
> And it shall be for a sign and for a testament to the Lord of Hosts-in the land of Egypt.[19]

In Jeremiah,[20] it is stated,

> O most mighty, great and powerful, the Lord of Hosts is Thy Name—who hast set signs and wonders in the land of Egypt.

According to some Bible authorities, the verses of Isaiah and Jeremiah refer to the Pyramids and the Sphinx in Egypt that already existed during their time.

	A	B	C	D	E	F	G	H	I	J	K	L
1							B	A				
2							I	T				
3												
4										S		
5									K			
6		A										
7		B	A									
8												
9												
10												
11				K								
12				G								
13												

Fig. 165 The throne and altar of God.

The grid would seem to affirm the verses. There are two words in this illustration, namely, GK found on D-12-11 and KS located on I-5 and J-4, which mean "Thy altar" and "Throne of God." There are also two Egyptian words, namely, *ABTI* and *AB*, which mean "doubly holy place" and "altar," respectively.

	A	B	C	D	E	F	G	H	I	J	K	L
4												
5		R		Tz	O	N						
6					I							
7					Tz							
8												
9						O						
10						T	H				Th	
11								S	O			
12							N					
13												

Fig. 166 Signs and monuments.

There are also other words that would relate to the verses in the Old Testament. Figure 166 shows the following Hebrew words, which mean signs and monuments.

NTzR = means "monument"   TzION = means "signs"

NS = sign   OTh = signs

The words are shown with the letters in different ELS. It is unbelievable that the final letter *N* of the word *TZION* (monument) is the initial letter of the word *NTzR* (sign). This would seem to confirm the sayings of Isaiah and Jeremiah about the signs and monument in the land of Egypt.

The word *pyramid* comes from the Greek word *pyra* meaning fire or light and *midos* that means measure. The form of the pyramid is like a flame ascending to heaven. Its measurement has been the subject of much debate and prophecies.

In figure 167 are the Sumerian word *E. KUR*, the Hebrew word *HR*, and the Egyptian word *MR* that all mean the "PYRAMID." It is unbelievable that the three words are near each other and even share the common letter *R* as shown on B-5 and C-7. The Hebrew word *HR* is uncannily placed near the three symbolic pyramids that are discussed in the succeeding paragraphs. The quadrant composed of rows 4 to 8 and columns A, B, C, and D contains the words *HR*, *MR*, and *E. KUR* while the word *SHETA*—which means hidden, mystery, and the word *SHETAIT*—which means a hidden place are found in the quadrant composed of rows 1 to 4 and columns E, F, and G. What could be the mathematical probability of the said words that are interrelated being lumped together near one another?

	A	B	C	D	E	F	G	H	I	J	K	L
1						Sh						
2					I	T						
3						A	T					
4			K	U		E						
5		H	R	E								
6				M								
7				R	E							
8				U	K							

Fig. 167 What is hidden in the Pyramids?

In the city of Giza are located the three Pyramids, namely, Cheop with its three satellite pyramids, Kafre with the Sphinx, and Menkaure with its three satellite pyramids. If all the said structures are symbolically represented in the grid, will this not be mind-boggling? And if the actual locations of the structures are symbolically represented in the grid, will this not be fantastic? Truly it is unbelievable.

According to Stephen S. Mehler,[21] the first pyramid that was not constructed by a king was the middle pyramid known as Kafre. Based on his research, the pyramid was known then as the Great Pyramid and not the present Great Pyramid known today, and that it was built on a mound, which had the highest elevation in the place. It was constructed on the top of a mound to make it the highest point in the place and to fuse it with the earth to make it solid and stable.

What is fascinating with this finding is that it relates with what Isaiah[22] said, namely:

> And it shall come to pass in the last days, that the mountain of the
> Lord's house shall be established in the top of the mountain, and shall
> be exalted above the hills, and all nations shall flow into it.

When one reads the phrase "the mountain of the Lord's house," for sure there will be confusion especially if one is not aware of the meaning of the word *mountain* as used by the ancients. The reason why the words *mountain* and *house* are together is because the holy mountain means it is the house or temple of the Lord. It is not really a mountain but an altar. As it looks like a mountain, the Sumerians called it E.KUR, the house of mountain while the Jews called it as HR and the Egyptians called it as MR all meaning "mountain" but actually referring to the Pyramid. Thus, the phrase the "mountain of the Lord's house" shall be

placed on top of a mountain will not be confusing anymore. It only means that the altar or temple of God is being constructed on top of a mountain and not a mountain being placed on top of another mountain.

The verse also said that the mountain "shall be exalted above the hills and all nations shall flow into it."[23] Being constructed in the highest point in the place besides being the tallest structure, for sure it will be exalted above the hills. People will go and see it not because it is a mountain but because it is an extraordinary altar to the Lord.

> And many people shall go and say, come ye, and let us go up to the mountain of the Lord, to the house of the God of Jacob.[24]

It is very clear from the verse that the mountain is the house of the Lord as the Sumerians called it. But what is intriguing is that the mountain was in Egypt; thus how could it be the house of the God of Jacob? Well, the history of the Hyksos will explain this matter for Jacob was supposed to be a Hyksos Pharaoh in Lower Egypt.

In figure 168 are the names of the famous pyramids of Egypt, Cheop, Menkaure, and Kafre. To find them in a cluster of letters near each other is very intriguing. In the cluster of letters found at E-3-4-5 and F-4 are the letters *CH*, *E*, *O*, and *CH*. As previously explained, the word *CHEOCH* can be replaced by the word *CHEOP*, the name of the greatest pyramid in Egypt; thus, it can be assumed that the letter formation symbolically represents the pyramid Cheop (the First Pyramid). Right in front of the said pyramid are the letters *A, A,* and *A.* with the letter *Y* enclosed, which seemed to represent three small triangles or the three small pyramids besides the pyramid CHEOP. The letters are found on the square composed of G-4, H-4-5-6, and I-4. Someone may say that there is no pyramid by the name of CHEOCH; true, but remember by gematria the letter *CH* can be replaced by the letter *P* because both letters have the same numerical value of eight (8), hence they are interchangeable. Thus, CHEOCH can become CHEOP; the real name of the biggest Pyramid in Egypt called also in ancient time as EAKU (YAKU). The three small pyramids are located in the eastern portion of CHEOP, which coincides with the actual configurations of CHEOP and the three small pyramids in Giza. And to think that the symbolic pyramid is named CHEOP.

I have made the symbolic Second Pyramid as composed of the letters *A, A,* and *A* on the eastern side or at E-11-12-13 and the letters *A,Y,* and *A* on the southern side or at C, D, and E-13 as the letters formed a triangle. The letters *K* and *A* on the north side or on row 11 would seem to signify that it is the symbolic pyramid called KAFRE also known as UR in ancient times. The symbolic Sphinx composed of the letters *R, A, Y,* and *A* with the letter *N* enclosed is found at

G-12, H-11-12-13, and I-12 in its eastern side, which is the actual location of the Sphinx in Giza.

	A	B	C	D	E	F	G	H	I	J	K	L
1								A				
2								A				
3					Ch			A				
4		K	U		E	Ch	A	Y	A			
5	H	R	E		O			A				
6	A	Sh	M	A								
7		A	R	E								
8		U	K									
9												
10				U	E		H					
11				K.	A			R				
12			U.		A.		A	N	A			
13			A	Y.	A			Y				
14												
15				E	Y	N						
16				M	H	A						
17				A	R	A						

Fig. 168 The positions of the Pyramids in the grid.

As to the Third Pyramid I have designated the letters forming a triangle composed of the letters *A*, *A*, and *A* with the letter *R* enclosed and found at D-17, E-16-17, and F-17. Near the symbol are the letters *MEYN* found in a cluster of letters at C-16-15, D-15, and E-15 as if to imply that the Pyramid is the one called MENKAURE. It is uncanny that beneath the word *MEYN* was the word *HAR* meaning "mountain," which according to Ralph Ellis[25] was the original name of the Pyramid Menkaure in ancient time. At the side of the symbolic Pyramid are the three letter *Is* found at A-16-17 and B-16, which I designated as the three small pyramids. In front of the third Pyramid is the symbolic figure composed of the letters *Y* and *Y* found at I-15-16 that symbolizes the Valley Temple. What is amazing about the patterns appearing in the grid are that they almost conform to the actual plan of the structures found in Giza.

The letters REARAA enclosing the letters *ShM* is a circular structure that is at the back of the symbolic Pyramid of Cheop. In the actual site, there are structures at the back of the Pyramid of Cheop the underground portion of which has never been investigated or dug. REARAA is found at A-6,

B-5-7, C-5-7, and D-6. Besides this symbolic structure are the words *E.KUR* meaning "a house like a mountain," which the Sumerians used in describing the Pyramids. The Egyptian words *HR* and *MER*, which also mean "mountain" are used to describe the Pyramids. The word *AMI*, which means chambers and the words *SHETA* and *SHETAIN*, which mean "Hidden Place" surround the Pyramid Cheop. This seems to imply that there are hidden chambers in the pyramid. Also the word *HO*, which means "Search" is near the words *UAR* meaning "passage," UA meaning "path," and ABA meaning "entrance." What does this imply?

In the said pattern, I included the letter *E* considering that by gematria the letter *H* can replace the letter *E* to form the word *HR*, which means pyramid. This pattern created another mystery as the letters enclosed the word *ShM* that means "name." The question is, Whose name are we looking for? Is this name very important that it has to be encircled or enclosed? Is it really a name we are to look for? Is it the ancient name of the Sphinx? I leave this mystery for others to unravel. If we reverse the letters from *ShM* to *MSh*, it would now mean essence, touch, or search for worldly affairs or guardians. Are we to search for the essence or the physical facts about the guardians? Are the records underneath these structures? Or thus, it tells us who built the pyramids, the guardians whom the Egyptians called the SAH or the "star people." It is really intriguing to find words like *star-people*. Are the Egyptians being literal in their description about these beings as coming from the stars like Orion and Sirius? The word *SAH* is found at G-15, E-16, and C-17 with ELS of nine (9) letters between the encoded letters *S*, *A*, and *H*.

Another set of letters in the form of a square is found at the back of the symbolic pyramid Cheop and consists of the following letters, namely, E. KUR, which in Sumerian means "a house of mountain" or a pyramid. The word is found in the square composed of rows 4 and 5 and columns B and C.

Is Mt. Sinai the Pyramid?

According to Herodotus,[26] when he visited Egypt in the fifth century BC, the most impressive structures in Egypt were not the Pyramids, the great temples at Karnak, and Heliopolis—but the labyrinth. Yet ancient Egyptian and Jewish writings never mentioned them. Why? We can understand the Jews not writing about the grandeur of Egypt, but for the Egyptians themselves not to write about them is puzzling. Why was the intimate relation between Egypt and Judah suppressed when the Jews were considered Egyptians? Even the chronological events were messed up. Even the most important mountain in the world where God appeared to Moses and where the Ten Commandments were given could

not be pinpointed exactly up to the present. The Bible was able to enumerate unimportant towns in Israel yet did not mention the wonders of ancient Egypt. Locations of towns like Galilee, Bethsaida, and Nazareth that were in western Arabia suddenly were found in Palestine. Ralph Ellis[27] has pointed out that the mountains Horeb, Hor, and Seir would seem to point to the same mountain "Sinai."

	A	B	C	D	E	F	G	H	I	J	K	L
14						I						
15					N	I	S					
16				H	A							
17												

Fig. 169 Mt. Sinai.

Why confuse the people about Mt. Sinai? What is the purpose? Is there something about Mt. Sinai that has to be concealed? Is the spelling of the name Sinai not actually Sinah? The moon god of Sumer is called Sin while the moon god of Egypt is Ah. Could it be possible that the ancients were talking about the mountain or temple of the moon god Sin/Ah that became phonetically Sinai? Is Mt. Sinai really a mountain?

In Exodus,[28] God supposedly said,

> And thou shalt set bounds unto the people round about, saying, Take heed to yourselves, that you go not up into the mount, or touch the border of it; who ever toucheth the mount shall be surely put to death.

Again, in Exodus[29] it is said,

> And Moses said unto the Lord. The people cannot come up to Mount Sinai: for thou chargedst us, saying, Set bounds about the mount and sanctify it.

What kind of mountain can be encompassed and surrounded so easily? Was there a very distinct border between the mountain and the adjacent ground? Was Mt. Sinai a very small mountain, yet according to Josephus it was very steep and caused pain to the eyes when one looked up to it? How could it be

detected that a person has really touched the border of the mountain? Was there a line around the mountain, or was the mountain so constructed that it had borders that differentiated it with the ground? Remember, the penalty is death for anyone who touches the border of the mountain. The mountain must have been so delineated with its surrounding that one could easily detect if somebody touched the mountain. What kind of mountain is this?

According to Exodus,[30] when God descended and ascended in Mt. Sinai, there was smoke and great fire and "the whole mount quaked greatly." Mt. Sinai must be a very small mountain or a hill or a platform that it would quake greatly upon the descent and ascent of God. Could this be the secret why the location of Mt. Sinai has been hidden and nothing is written about the Pyramids in ancient writings? Additional reading materials on this matter are the books of Ralph Ellis *Tempest and Exodus* and *Jesus the Last of the Pharaohs*.

g) The Sphinx

The Pyramids and the Sphinx are like twins; the discussion of one necessitates the discussion of the other. In the city of Giza where the pyramids Cheop, Kafre, and Menkaure are located is another famous edifice known as the Sphinx that was used as a target practice by Napoleon's soldiers thus, the destruction of its nose. It is two hundred forty feet long, thirty-eight feet wide across the shoulders, and sixty-six feet in height. Oftentimes, it is buried under the sun with only its head protruding. Its majesty and grandeur since antiquity are unmatched until now.

Ancient Names of the Sphinx

Around 2,000 BC, the Egyptians worshiped the Sphinx as a god called HUL.[1] The Sphinx gazes patiently to the east as if waiting and watching for something. Its eyes are focused on the exact position of sunrise at dawn on the spring equinox.

HUL = ancient name of the Sphinx

Coordinates:			ELS =	
H = G-10	U = D-10	L = A-10		2 letters
H = C-9	U = H-9	L = A-10		4 letters
H = B-13	U = J-14	L = F-16		19 letters

		A	B	C	D	E	F	G	H	I	J	K	L
8													
9				H					U				
10		L			U			H					
11													
12													
13			H										
14											U		
15													
16						L							
17													

Fig. 170 Hul: ancient name of the Sphinx.

In ancient times the Sphinx was considered a "She," thus her association with the goddesses Tefnut, Sekmet, Mut, Nut, and later on Hathor. Although it has now the face of a man, it is believed that before it had the face of a lioness representing the goddesses. If this is the case, then the Sphinx is older than the age espoused by the traditional Egyptologists. It is said that the present head of the Sphinx was not proportionate to the body because someone recarved it to have the face of Kafre whom the orthodox Egyptologists believed as the builder of the Sphinx because of the face. In 1993, a senior forensic expert named Lt. Frank Domingo of the New York Police Department whose work was to prepare "identikit" portraits of suspects for more than twenty years made a comparative study of the Sphinx and the statue of Khafre. Domingo reported that based on schematics and measurements that the two works were different. The proportions in the frontal view and especially the angles and facial protrusion in the lateral view convinced Domingo that the Sphinx was not Kafre.[2]

If the grid will be given the appropriate directions, the east direction is the right side of the grid when one is looking at it and the west direction is the opposite side at the left while the north will be the topside of the grid and the south at the bottom of the grid. The actual location of the Sphinx is on the eastern side of the Pyramid Kafre that is the same location as the symbolic Sphinx in this grid. I considered the symbolic Sphinx as composed of the following letters R, A, Y, and A with the letter N enclosed for the following reasons:

1. The symbolic Sphinx is located on the eastern side of the symbolic Pyramid Kafre.
2. It is in front of the Pyramid Kafre that is the actual location of the Sphinx.
3. In front of the Sphinx is a pattern composed of the letters *L*, *E*, and *O*, which symbolizes the Sphinx Temple and the direction as alleged by some Egyptologists and scientists where the Sphinx was supposed to be gazing at 10,500 years ago, which was the Zodiac sign of Leo shown in figure 172.

	A	B	C	D	E	F	G	H	I	J	K	L
4												
5					O	N					O	
6												N
7												
8	H					N						
9		U	H			O		U				
10		O	N	U			H					
11		N								O		
12											N	
13												
14												I
15										O	N	
16										N	U	
17												

Fig. 171 Ancient names of the Sphinx.

4. And lastly due to the proximity of the following words to the symbolic Sphinx as shown in the succeeding figures.

HU = ancient name of the Sphinx; the name is written many times in this grid.

ON = another ancient name of the Sphinx and Greek word for the sun; the name shares a common letter *O* with the words *LEO*, *SOL*, and *CHO*.

INNU/YNNU = another ancient name of the Sphinx; the word is found on rows 14, 15, 16 and columns L, K, and J.

Sphinx in Relation to the Sun/Leo

As the Sphinx is connected to the zodiac sign Leo and the lioness goddesses, I looked for the words referring to LEO and LION. In figures 173 to 176 are the words all relating to LION.

	A	B	C	D	E	F	G	H	I	J	K	L
6												
7								L-			E	
8				E-							L	O-
9										L		
10								O.		E		
11										O	L	
12												
13						E.						
14												
15												
16						L.						
17												

Fig. 172 The zodiac sign Leo.

LEO = the zodiac sign of the lion, the Sphinx was gazing at 10,500 years ago. Three examples are with different ELS while the others are found by permutation.

Coordinates:	L = H-7	E = D-8	O = L-8	ELS =	7 letters
	L = J-9	E = J-10	O = J-11		None
	L = F-16	E = G-13	O = H-10		34 letters

AB/AV = refers to the Hebrew zodiac sign LEO; the word is written several times in the grid.

ARV = means lion in Hebrew; the word is found on G-12, H-11, and I-10 with ELS of ten (10) letters between the encoded letters.

MAA = Egyptian word for lion; there are many examples of the word for lion that means "power."

Fig. 173 Hebrew words for Lion.

Coordinates:			ELS =	
M = J-1	A = H-2	A = F-3		9 letters
M = C-2	A = H-1	A = A-1		6 letters
M = J-5	A = I-4	A = H-3		12 letters
M = J-5	A = A-6	A = D-6		2 letters
M = H-6	A = I-4	A = J-2		22 letters
M = L-7	A = J-6	A = H-5		13 letters
M = G-9	A = E-11	A = C-13		21 letters

Fig. 174 Maa: the lion symbolizes power in Egypt.

MAU = another Egyptian word for lions; the word starts with the letter *M* on H-12 and V-6 and going to the right direction, has an ELS of two letters between the encoded letters. The word is written several times in the grid.

	A	B	C	D	E	F	G	H	I	J	K	L
7												
8												
9										L		
10					U					E		
11					A					O		
12						M			A		N	U
13												
14												

Fig. 175 Mau and Leon.

LEON = another term for LION, which starts with the letter *L* on J-9-10-11 and K-12

ARI = another name for LION

	A	B	C	D	E	F	G	H	I	J	K	L
5												
6											I	
7												
8												
9				-A								
10												
11								R				
12												
13												I
14												
15												
16					A							
17												

Fig. 176 Ari

In figure 177 are the words for the SUN in different languages.

ChO = Heavenly Sun in Hebrew; the word is written several times with the letters side by side without ELS. One example shares the letter *O* with the words *LEO* and *SOL*.

	A	B	C	D	E	F	G	H	I	J	K	L
3												
4						Ch						
5					O							
6												
7												
8												O
9												Ch
10												
11								R		O		
12						A		A	Ch			
13									U			
14												

Fig. 177 Hebrew and Filipino names for the sun.

SU = Sunlight in Egyptian; the word is found on I-9 and H-9 with the letters side by side without ELS.

OM = Greek word for the sun; the word is written several times in the grid one of which is besides the symbolic Sphinx.

	A	B	C	D	E	F	G	H	I	J	K	L
3												
4												
5					O	N				M	O	
6												N
7												
8						N						
9							O	M	U	S		
10			O	N				O				
11			N						S	O	L	
12										Ch	N	
13										U		
14												
15										O	N	
16										N		
17												

Fig. 178 Names of the sun in other languages.

SUN = the English word for SOL, OM, ON, ChO, and ARAO; the word starts with the letter *S* on I-11, *U* at J-13, and *N* at K-15 with ELS of twenty-four letters between the encoded letters.

SOL = the Latin word for sun; the word is found on I-11, J-11, and K-11 without ELS.

ARAO/ARAU = the Filipino word for SUN is found on G-12, H-11, I-11-12, and J-13.

ON = Egyptian and Greek word for the sun.

Why does the author of this code keep repeating the words relating to LION and SUN in different languages? What is the purpose? Is it to guide us in solving the mystery of the Sphinx?

RA/RE = Egyptian sun god; written several times in the grid

HER = ancient name of the sun; the word is found in the quadrant composed of G-10-11 and H-11 sharing the letter *R* with the symbolic Sphinx.

	A	B	C	D	E	F	G	H	I	J	K	L
1									Sh	M		
2											Sh	Sh
3											M	
4												
5			R	E								
6		A	Sh	M	A							
7			A	R								
8					E							
9												
10							H					
11						Sh	E	R				
12						M	A		A			
13												
14												
15												
16					A							
17					A	R	A					

Fig. 179 The sun god.

MSH = means guardians; the word is found on F-12-11, and going vertically upward, the letters are side by side without ELS. The

word *MSH* is found between the symbolic second Pyramid and the symbolic Sphinx. The word is written many times in front of the three (3) small pyramids near the symbolic pyramid Cheop. The Sphinx is the symbol of the guardian keeping watch over Egypt.

The words about the Sphinx are lumped together and so interrelated that to consider the placement of the words as a coincidence is very remote. The use also of different languages to refer to the Sphinx would seem also to emphasize the importance of the Sphinx as a subject matter off this grid. The author of this code is truly a superintelligent person especially if the discussion about the Sphinx will help resolve the conflicting theories about the age of the Sphinx.

Age of the Sphinx

The age of the Sphinx has been the object of considerable debate between the orthodox Egyptologists on the one hand and the scientists and geologists on the other hand. Orthodox Egyptologists have always maintained that the Sphinx was constructed during the time of Kafre around 2,500 BC. However, recent findings by scientists and geologists about the Sphinx have shown very extensive erosion of the Sphinx body due to water pressure. However since 3,000 BC onward, there had been not enough rain in Egypt to cause said erosion of the Sphinx by means of water. The scientists believed that it was only around 10,000 BC that Egypt had a wet climate to account for the massive water erosion of the Sphinx. If the Sphinx was constructed during that time, then the Sphinx must have been constructed by an advanced civilization and not by primitive Egyptians. G. Hancock[3] citing John West said that the Sphinx had been left untended often during historical times, and that it could be proven by a combination of textual references and historical extrapolations that during the 4,500 years since its supposed construction it's been buried to its neck for as much as 3,300 years. Thus it could have been susceptible only to wind erosions for only a cumulative total of just over one thousand years, and the rest of the time it's been protected from the desert winds by an enormous blanket of sand. If wind erosion was the cause, then the Sphinx should also show the same weathering suffered by the other structures in the area; but in the case of the Sphinx, it was water that had caused the erosion.

Professor Robert Schoch, a Boston University geologist and specialist in rock erosion said that "the weathering of the Sphinx—and of the walls of its

surrounding rock-hewn enclosure—had not been caused by wind-scouring at all but by thousands of years of heavy rainfall long ages before the Old Kingdom came into being." At the 1992 Annual Meeting of the American Association for the Advancement of Science (AAAS), Mr. Schoch pointed out to the delegates that

> As Santha Faiia's photographs of the Sphinx and the Sphinx enclosure indicate, this weathering takes the distinctive form of a combination of deep vertical fissures and undulating, horizontal coves—"a classic textbook example." In Schoch's words, "of what happens to a limestone structure when you have rain beating down on it for thousands of years . . . . It's clearly rain precipitation that produced these erosional features."[4]

Scientific findings show that the erosions of the Pyramids are different from the erosions of the Sphinx; thus, the ages of the Pyramids and the Sphinx are different. The annual inundation of the Nile could not have caused the entire body of the Sphinx to weather or erode.

Mr. Robert Temple[5] agreed with Prof. Schock that it was water that caused the erosion of the Sphinx but advocated another theory that the ditch surrounding the Sphinx, which was in a deep pit, was used to hold vast reservoir of water, thus the erosion of the Sphinx by water. Even in the present time, digging under the Sphinx showed presence of water.

Based on the preceding, it is startling to discover that the code would contain something very relevant to the question about the age of the Sphinx. This is unexpected. It is only a recent development in Egyptology that the age of the Sphinx is the center of debate among scholars and Egyptologists. Some Egyptologists enunciated the theory that the Sphinx had the body of a lion because at the time it was being constructed, the zodiac sign was LEO; thus, the gaze of the Sphinx was supposed to be at the direction of the zodiac sign LEO in the east when it was made. Since the zodiac sign LEO was directly in the gaze of the Sphinx around 10,500 BC, then the Sphinx could not just have been made 2,500 years BC when the zodiac sign was TAURUS, as alleged by orthodox Egyptologists, but ten thousand years ago when the zodiac sign was LEO. For if it were true that the zodiac sign at the time was TAURUS, then the Sphinx should have the body of a bull and not a lion, for it had been the tradition of the Egyptians to construct statues and images according to the prevailing zodiacal signs.

	A	B	C	D	E	F	G	H	I	J	K	L
6												
7								L-			E	
8				E-							L	O-
9										L		
10							O.			E		
11										O	L	
12												
13						E.						
14												
15												
16						L.						
17												

Fig. 180 Zodiac sign of Leo.

This grid seems to confirm the theory that the Sphinx was made around 10,500 years ago, and that it had the body of a lion because it was gazing at the zodiac sign LEO at around 10,500 BC before the deluge. To confirm this, the word *LEO* was written three (3) times near the symbolic Sphinx. One LEO was placed in front of the symbolic Sphinx. The other two LEO words were near the symbolic Sphinx. One LEO, which starts with the letter *L* at F-16, *E* at G-13, and *O* at H-10 with ELS of thirty-four (34) letters between the letters *L*, *E*, and *O*. The other LEO starts with the letter *L* on H-7 with ELS of seven (7) letters between the encoded letters *L* at H-7, *E* at D-8, and *O* at L-12.

Before, I was wondering why the word *LEO* was in the grid until I read the recently published books about this new theory on the age of the Sphinx. This fact convinced me further that the author of the code was not an ordinary person.

Another word related to the zodiacal sign LEO is the Hebrew word *AB/AV*, which means the zodiacal sign LEO in Hebrew. The word is written several times near the symbolic three small pyramids and in front of the symbolic pyramid Cheop.

	A	B	C	D	E	F	G	H	I	J	K	L
6												
7		A										
8	H	U										
9												
10							H					
11					A							
12			U									
13		H	A									
14												

Fig. 181 Period of Time—Hau.

In the quadrant composed of A-8 and B-7-8, B-13 and C13-12 are two examples of the Hebrew word *HAU* which means "period or time." The third example is found at G-10, E-11, and C-12 with ELS of nine letters between the desired letters.

	A	B	C	D	E	F	G	H	I	J	K	L
1												
2			M									
3		M	E									
4			K	T								
5		H	E									
6		A	M									
7			A									
8		H	K						T	E	N	
9									U			
10						T	H		O	V	Th	
11				K	A		E		S	O		
12						M			N	A		
13												

Fig. 182 Ten thousan—Met Kha

There are two examples of the English words *ten thousan*, one is at F-10, G-11, and H-12 and at F-10, G-10, H-10, I-10-11-13, and H-12 while the other phrase "ten thousan" is at H-8, I-8, and J-8 and at K-10, J-11, I-11-12, and J-12. To find these English words in a Hebrew grid is fantastic. At first, I could not understand why this period of time of "ten thousan" was written in the grid until I read this matter about the age of the Sphinx wherein it is being suggested that the true age of the Sphinx was not 2,500 years but around 10,000 years.

Considering also that the Egyptians words *MET KHA* which means ten thousan is also in the quadrant, could it be possible that these two sets of words in Egyptian and English both refer to the age of the Sphinx or to the sinking of Aha Men Ptah (Atlantis)? Why would the author of this code put these words specially the English words that were nonexistent at the time?

Floods in Egypt

Another observation to support the theory that there was much rain or flooding which caused the erosion of the Sphinx is the presence of the numerous words relating to rain or flood in the grid. These words should not have been mentioned in the grid if these flooding did not occur. Yet we find so many words relating to floods.

AATEB= flood, rainstorm	AKB = flood
BAH = flood	SMEHIT = flood
HEBT = flood	MEHIT = flood
NHR = storm	YOHR = storm
NUT = large collection of water	

	A	B	C	D	E	F	G	H	I	J	K	L
1						B						
2												
3						A	T					
4				T	E		A					
5	H		E									
6	A			E								
7	B	A		E								
8	H		K		Y	N	U	T				
9	N	U	H			O						
10			N				H					
11								R				
12												
13												
14			T	I								
15			E		N		S					
16			M	H								
17					R							

Fig. 183 Rains and floods in Egypt.

The author of the code did not use only the words meaning flood, but also the words referring to the submersion of the land. The erosion of the Sphinx that has a height of sixty feet from head to paw implies heavy rains and severe flooding that covers the whole Sphinx. Considering the lush vegetation when there was no desert yet in Egypt, the possible heavy rains and flooding would have been possible. The erosion of the Sphinx attests to this.

It is intriguing that the words MEH and SMEH, which both mean "to be submerged" are closed and almost covering the symbolic Sphinx RAYA.

	A	B	C	D	E	F	G	H	I	J	K	L
9												
10							H					
11							E	R	S			
12						M	A		A			
13							Y					
14												

Fig. 184 Submersion of the Sphinx.

The repetitions of the words meaning flood, rain, or submersion would seem to emphasize that there was really much rain or water causing flood during ancient times. This will support the theory why there was lush vegetation and forest in Egypt before and which unfortunately disappeared, resulting in the appearance of the surrounding deserts.

Another proof that the area was flooded besides the observation of Herodotus in fifth BC was the discovery of twelve five-hundred-year-old royal ships buried in the desert thirteen kilometers from the Nile.[6] The royal ships that were unearthed were the same ships that were depicted in mural paintings that were 1,500 years old. The discovery of the ships attests to the time that there was plenty of water in the vicinity of the Nile.

Another logical observation made was that if the Sphinx was built during the time of the fourth dynasty, why was there no text or writing speaking about the Sphinx that could have been a favorite topic for discussion considering its colossal size? Maybe the reason why it was not the topic of discussion anymore was because it has been there since time immemorial, and it was taken for granted for its antiquity. Or as suggested by John West, the Sphinx was fully covered by the sand that there was no Sphinx to see and talk about. It is unbelievable that Herodotus who wrote about the Pyramids and the labyrinth never mentioned the Sphinx. Maybe during his visit in 5 BC, the Sphinx was nowhere to be seen. It could have been covered by the sand or under water.

Orthodox Egyptologist cannot accept the possibility that the Sphinx was made around 5,000 BC to 7,000 BC as the population then of the Nile was composed of herdsmen and primitive hunters whose tools were only sharpened flint stones and sticks. Acceptance of this theory would create an impression that the civilization of Egypt was just a legacy and not an internal development in Egypt. What is wrong if it is a legacy? Why pretend?

Is there a need to discuss lengthily Egyptian matters? Yes! Because there are many things about Egypt contained in this code that not to discuss them would be unfair and would keep hidden the unbelievable intelligence of the author of

this code, the special relationship between Egypt and Israel and the interesting theories about the Sphinx.

h) Why Egypt Is in the Grid?

The presence of the Egyptian words in the Hebrew grid is fascinating, but the extensive discussion about the Egyptian gods and goddesses is not only intriguing but puzzling. To the Jews and the Christians, the Egyptian gods and goddesses are anathema to them. A blasphemy. Yet why are they extensively discussed in the Lord's Prayer? What could be the reasons? Why is Egypt given so much importance in a Hebrew grid? Strange as it may seem, there are several reasons that could be presented, namely:

1. Despite the negative presentation of Egypt as the oppressor of the Jews, yet the Egyptians and the Jews had a long intimate relationship. Egypt became a home to Abraham, Joseph was made a ruler of Egypt saving Israel from famine, and Jesus was given sanctuary when Herod was searching for him. Jesus like Moses studied the Egyptian religion with its practices and rituals during the lost years as alleged by some writers.
2. Another reason could be that the story of Jesus is actually the story of Horus?
3. The Lord's Prayer is more ancient than we think it to be and is also the story of Egypt because it is also the homeland of the Jews, and the Egyptians and the Jews were but one people.

Although it could be said that Egypt had a special relation with Israel, however, that said relationship could not be enough reason for Egypt to merit a special part in the grid. There must be a deeper reason. Even Edgar Cayce kept on relating Jesus to Egypt and the Pyramids and the Sphinx. To resolve this question, maybe it is time to discuss the uncanny similarities between Jesus and the Egyptian god Horus the son of Isis and Osiris and the story of the Jewish people.

Heru and Jesus Christ

Acharya S[1] said that the story of Jesus was just a myth with the possible connection to the Egyptian story of Horus due to the unbelievable similarities between Horus and Jesus; to quote,

1. Horus was born of the virgin Meri, an ancient name of Isis, on December 25 with his birth being announced by a star in the east and attended by three wise men.

2. He was of royal descent and during his infancy was also hidden by his mother for his uncle would like to kill him.
3. He performed miracles, exorcised demons, and raised El-Azarus (EL-Osiris) from the dead.
4. His personal epithet was Iusa, the ever-becoming son of Ptah, the Father. He was thus called the Holy Child. The name Iusa almost sounds as Yeshua. Even the name Hesu is almost similar to Heru, the ancient name of Horus.
5. He died and resurrected.
6. He was also the Way, the Truth, the Light, the Messiah, God's Anointed Son, the Son of Man, the Good Shepherd, the Lamb of God, the Word made flesh, the Word of Truth, etc.
7. He was the Fisher and was associated with the Fish (Ichthys), Lamb and Lion.
8. He was called the KRST or Anointed One.
9. Like Jesus, "Horus was supposed to reign one thousand years."

	A	B	C	D	E	F	G	H	I	J	K	L
3												
4			U									
5	H	R	E	-								
6												
7			R									
8		U		E								
9			H				M	U	S			
10							H	O				
11							E	R	S			
12												
13												

Fig. 185 The names Heru, Horus, and Hesus (Jesus).

As if the comparison was not enough, the following observations were also given, to wit:

Furthermore, inscribed about 3,500 years ago on the walls of the Temple at Luxor were images of the Annunciation, Immaculate Conception, Birth and Adoration of Horus, with Thoth announcing to the Virgin Isis that she will conceive Horus, with Kneph, the "Holy Spirit,"

impregnating the virgin, and with the infant being attended by three kings, or magi, bearing gifts. In addition, in the catacombs at Rome are pictures of the baby Horus being held by the virgin mother Isis—the original "Madonna and Child."[2]

Acharya S compiled the cited similarities between Horus and Jesus from the different scholarly researches and writings by Doanne, Jackson, A. Churchward, Walker (EMS), Massey (EBD), and Higgins. Questions may be raised as to the veracity of the many similarities cited and the credibility of the researches made, but this can be attributed to that part of the human psyche that followers or disciples of different religions usually make up stories that present their gods as better or greater than the gods of other religions. We cannot discount the possibility of the findings being questionable. Be that as it may, it would be very encouraging if someone can present evidences to the contrary.

Even a few similarities between Horus and Jesus would already be a shocking revelation especially to fundamentalist Christians, but let us face it, the story of Horus was several thousand years before Jesus. Let us not make the same mistakes made by the missionaries and the early Christian fathers in India and Mexico in saying that the devil concocted the similarities between the ancient saviors Krishna and Quetzacotl and Jesus in order to confuse the faithful. The extensive data about Egypt in the code would seem to indicate the special relationship between Jesus and Horus. Are they one? Is Jesus the reincarnation of Horus? Is the story of Jesus based on the story of Horus that is why Egypt is in the grid? It is difficult to answer, but let us proceed and find out what the code says about these comments on the similarities of Horus and Jesus.

	A	B	C	D	E	F	G	H	I	J	K	L
3												
4			U	T								
5	H	R	E	--	O							
6		Sh	--	A								
7		R										
8		U		E								
9			H					U	S			
10						T-	H	O				
11					A-	Sh	E	R	S			
12						M						
13												

Fig. 186 Heru Messu.

Figure 186 shows two quadrants with the name of HERU/HORUS mentioned four times, once as HORUS and three times in its ancient form as HERU. What is intriguing is the mention of the English word *AUTHOR* besides the name of Horus in both quadrants and also the presence of the Egyptian word *SHAT*, which means "BOOK."

Why mention the name of Horus four times, the English word *Author* two times, and the Egyptian word *Shat* two times? What is the implication? Besides the name HERU/HORUS is the Egyptian word *MESSU*, which means "MESSIAH." Based on the illustration, it would seem that the Egyptian god Heru or Horus has a connection with the supposed author of the code, Jesus.

	A	B	C	D	E	F	G	H	I	J	K	L
6												
7			R									
8		U		E								
9			H					U	S			
10							H	O				
11							E	R	S			
12						M						
13												

Fig. 187 Messu: Heru, Horus, or Hesus.

Another intriguing possibility is that Heru and Jesus are just one person whose stories intermingled that is why Heru is in the Lord's Prayer code. Figure 187 shows the names of Heru and Hesus, a variant of the name Jesus in a cluster and sharing common letters with respect to their names and the word *Messu*.

Hyksos—Egyptian Pharaohs

Another plausible reason why Egypt or the Egyptians are very much part of this Hebrew grid is the possibility that the Egyptians and the Jews were but one people. According to Josephus,[3] an ancient Jewish historian, the Hyksos or the Shepherd Kings of Egypt who established Jerusalem were the predecessors of the Israelites. They were a Semitic people whose origin could not be ascertained but believed to be Asiatic. They were so feared by Upper Egypt for their fierceness that they conquered Lower Egypt without a blow. They razed and destroyed cities and massacred enemies. According to Manetho, an ancient Egyptian and Graeco historian, some of the predynastic pharaohs of Egypt were Hyksos. Josephus said that the pharaohs Mamembre and Yakuber were actually Abraham and his son Jacob. What does the Bible say about these conclusions?

Based on the Bible, it would appear that Abraham was not an ordinary person chosen by God to be the source of many nations. He left Ur with many men around him. His trained servants alone numbered to 318.[4] He married a princess; that was why her name was Sarai meaning "princess." She was not only a princess but also a sister of Abraham.[5]

> She is indeed my sister; she is the daughter of my father, but not the daughter of my mother.

This statement is significant, for it shows the royal lineage of Abraham. Only members of the royal family in ancient times could intermarry without violating the law on incestuous relation. It was an ancient tradition to keep intact the royal lineage; thus brothers can marry sisters and vice versa. This statement reveals the royal status of Abraham. His royal standing could also be inferred from the people he dealt with. He fought and defeated many kings like the Kings of Elam, Shinar, Eliasar, and King Tidal. Other kings respected him. The priest king of Salem Melchizedeck blessed him. Thus, Josephus the ancient Jewish historian considered Abraham who lived in Mamre as the Hyksos Pharaoh Mam-embre of Lower Egypt. Look at the similarity between the name of Abram that became Abr-ah-am and the name of the place where Abraham lived, Mamre and the name of the Pharaoh Mam-emb-re. Somebody just inserted the letters *emb* to Mam-re.

Another person considered by Josephus as a Hyksos Pharaoh besides Abraham was Jacob, for there was a predynastic pharaoh named Yakuber according to Manetho.[6] Again, observe the addition of the letters *Er* to the name Yakob. The Bible would seem to confirm also the royal standing of Jacob, not only as being a descendant of Abraham but based on his dealing with other people. In Genesis,[7] it was said that Jacob blessed the pharaoh of Egypt. Who is Jacob to bless the pharaoh of Egypt who is considered a god unless the pharaoh recognizes him as an equal or higher than him?

	A	B	C	D	E	F	G	H	I	J	K	L
6												
7												
8			K									
9					Y				S			
10							H	O				
11									S			
12												
13												

Fig. 188 Hyksos, the shepherd kings.

During this time, Egypt was divided into Lower and Upper Egypt with both parts ruled by a separate pharaoh. And to affirm the pharaoh stature of Jacob, during his funeral, all the servants of the pharaoh and all the elders of Egypt attended, an honor befitting a pharaoh.[8] The people said that the Egyptians would be mourning the passing of Jacob.

> And when the inhabitants of the land, the Canaanites, saw the mourning in the floor of Atad, they said, "This is a grievous mourning to the Egyptians."[9]

How could the death of Jacob be a grievous mourning to the Egyptians? Why were the Canaanites referring to Jacob and his clan as Egyptians and not their own? Jacob was a foreigner in Egypt. This could only have happened during the five-hundred-year rule by the Hyksos of Egypt.

In the text "Admonition of Ipuwer,"[10] it is said:

> Foreigners have become people (Egyptians) everywhere.

Due to the five-hundred-year rule by the Hyksos, they became assimilated with the population and became Egyptians. Thus Jacob and his clan were considered Egyptians and justified the saying of the Canaanites about the Egyptians mourning the passing of Jacob. This would relate to the sayings of Manetho and Josephus about the Hyksos that would in turn clarify the sayings of Isaiah.

Although the Hyksos were considered Egyptians, they however believed only in the major gods like Ra and their ancestors Seth. This belief led into a religious dispute with the Thebans of Upper Egypt who believed in a plethora of gods.

In Exodus it is said,[11]

> And I appeared unto Abraham, unto Isaac and unto Jacob, by the name of God almighty, but by my name Jehovah was I not known to them.

Thus, in the time of Abraham and Jacob, they did not know the name of God YHVH. Abraham and Jacob called God as El' Sadai, the God Almighty, a general appellation for God or any god. Actually Abraham venerated the sun god Ra and the moon god AH or Thoth. But he did not adore the other gods. He destroyed their images:

> He broke them all (their idols) in pieces, except their supreme god, so that they return to him.[12]

Abraham wanted the people to return to the supreme god Ra and not to worship the lesser gods. This was the reason why he destroyed the images of the lesser gods. He wanted the Egyptians to return to the sun god Ra whom Abram worshipped. His very name showed the god he worshipped. The word *Ab* in Egyptian means "heart" or "priest." Thus the name Abram could be interpreted as "The Heart of Ra or the Priest of Ra." Abram could have been the high priest of Ra in his clan. This was the reason why the name Abram contained the word *Ra* for Abram worshipped the sun god:

> When Abraham beheld the rising moon, he said: "that's my god." But when it set, he said, "If my Lord does not guide me, I shall surely go astray." Thus, when he beheld the sun shining, he said: "that must be my god, it is the largest (heavenly body)."[13]

Prophecies of Isaiah

This belief by Abraham and his descendants led to the disputes between them and the Egyptians from Upper Egypt. This event would now relate to the very puzzling and intriguing sayings of Isaiah:

> And I will set Egyptians against Egyptians; and they shall fight every one against his brother; and every one against his neighbors; city against city, and kingdom against kingdom.[14]

This is the only verse in the Old Testament that talks about the Egyptians fighting one another, brother against his brother, city against city, and kingdom against kingdom. Was Isaiah talking about a future event in his time? Or has it already happened? If so, when?

An Egyptian New Kingdom script called "Prophecies of Nefertiti" talked similarly about what Isaiah has uttered,

> I show you the son as an enemy, the brother as a foe, as man slaying his father. The land is quite perished, no remnant is left.[15]

Both writings could only have referred to the most violent period of Egyptian history when Egypt was still divided between two kingdoms, the Lower Egypt ruled by Hyksos pharaohs and the Upper Egypt ruled by the Theban pharaohs. As the Hyksos have ruled Lower Egypt for more than five hundred years, they were also considered as Egyptians. But their religion was different from the Thebans, for they believed only in the major gods and their ancestor Seth, hence their dispute with the Thebans who believed in a plethora of gods.

As Abraham and his clan were already considered Egyptians at the time for there were no Jews yet, then the Egyptians were actually fighting one another—brother against brother, city against city, and kingdom against kingdom. The Hyksos only left Egypt around 1,600 BC in what was considered the real Exodus when according to Egyptian historian Manetho, around three hundred thousand Jews left Egypt for Canaan and founded Jerusalem out of the town of Shalem where Melkezedeck was king and high priest. Even the naming of Shalem to Herusalem was suspicious. Why would the Jews name their most holy city in honor of HERU, the ancient name of Horus unless they were Egyptians?

This would also give light to the saying of Isaiah[16] that

> The land of Judah shall be a terror into Egypt.

This saying of Isaiah is intriguing for there are no records whether Jewish or Egyptian that speaks about Judah being a terror to Egypt. How can a small unknown nation terrorize a large powerful nation like Egypt? When has Judah ever become a terror to Egypt? It could only be if Isaiah was referring to the Hyksos, the predecessors of the Jews.

According to the text of the Tempest of Stele erected at around 1,570 BC and the account of the ancient Egyptian historian Manetho, the Hyksos:

> They forced the priests and prophets to slaughter the (sacred) animals and then they turned them out naked, set villages and cities on fire, not only did they pillage the temples and mutilate the images of the gods, but not content with that, they habitually used the very sanctuaries as kitchens for roasting the venerated sacred animals.[17]

The cruelties, savagery, and sacrilegious acts of the Hyksos forced the pharaoh of Upper Egypt to pay tribute so that the Hyksos would not attack and pillage Upper Egypt. The Egyptians bribed the Hyksos to leave Lower Egypt. This was the time that Judah terrorized Egypt. It will also be noted that the name used was Judah and not the name Israel.

Again Isaiah[18] said,

> In that day shall five cities in the land of Egypt speak the language of Canaan, and swear to the Lord of Host.

> In that day shall there be an altar to the Lord in the midst of the land of Egypt and a pillar at the border thereof to the land.

These are again puzzling sayings of Isaiah. There are no historical records whether Jewish or Egyptian that the language of Canaan had been spoken in five cities in Egypt. There is no evidence that the Egyptians ever swore to the God of Israel. How can there possibly be an altar to the God of Israel in Egypt? When has the God of Israel ever been worshipped in Egypt? All these things could have happened only during the time of the Hyksos pharaohs who ruled for five hundred years in Egypt. Why are there no records of these events? The reason is that the Egyptians hated the Hyksos so much that they did not want to be reminded of them. The Hyksos on the other hand said that they were the oppressed people. These utterances of Isaiah were also significant for the altar and pillar referred to the Pyramids and the Sphinx. This would mean that the Pyramids and the Sphinx are older than the ages being given them for the Hyksos ruled Egypt for more than five centuries, and they were the pharaohs of Egypt from the fifteenth to the sixteenth dynasties, which were around 1,780 BC to 1,560 BC.

Also, there were actually two instances when an Exodus occurred in Egypt involving the Jews. The first was when the Hyksos Pharaoh Yakuber with three hundred thousand people left Lower Egypt after being paid tribute by the pharaoh of Upper Egypt to leave them in peace and went to Canaan and founded the city of Jerusalem. The ancient Jewish historian, Josephus[19] described another Exodus led by the high priest Onarseph who changed his name to Moses. This is the Exodus of those Jews who were left behind in the first Exodus. This could be the Exodus that Isaiah[20] was talking about when he said that God again for the second time collected his people to leave Egypt.

> And it shall come to pass in that day, that the Lord shall set his hand again the second time to recover the remnant of his people which shall be left.

It is very clear from the verse that there was a second exodus. This could only refer to the Exodus led by Jacob that happened earlier. This was the time when the pharaoh of Upper Egypt asked the Hyksos to leave Lower Egypt and bribed them by giving much gold and silver. In both instances God performed a miracle by separating the sea for the Jews to cross the waters.

In Isaiah[21] it was said that

> And the Lord shall utterly destroy the tongue of the Egyptian Sea, and with his mighty word shall he shake his hand over the river, and shall smite it in the seven streams, and make men go over dryshod.

In the Dead Sea Scroll Bible, the same verses were given as follows:

> The Lord will utterly destroy the tongue of the Egyptian Sea, and with a scorching wind he will wave his hands over the River and split it into seven streams, so that people can march over in sandals.[22]

If one will look at the ancient map of Egypt, one can see that the only sea inside Egypt is the Red Sea, and that the river Nile has seven tributaries going to the Mediterranean Sea. There is a stretch of dry land separating the Red Sea and the Mediterranean Sea that resembles a tongue. The dry land is between the Gulf of Suez and the Gulf of Aqaba. In olden times, this land was an island surrounded by the Mediterranean Sea and the two gulfs. The only sea that Isaiah could be referring to could be the Red Sea that may have been known as the Egyptian Sea during that time. There is also a possibility that at that time the Egyptian Sea exited to the Mediterranean Sea as shown by ancient maps that showed also the streams of the Nile exiting to the Mediterranean Sea. The island that was surrounded by the Mediterranean Sea and the two gulfs became the tongue of the Egyptian Sea that God dried up so that the Jews could cross over to Canaan. The once huge and mighty river Nile also flowed over this land and exiting to the Mediterranean Sea, but God split it into seven streams that still exist today.

Isaiah lived in the middle of the seventh century BC, yet he talked about events that happened thousands of years before his time. Again Isaiah said,[23]

> And the waters shall fail from the sea, and the river shall be wasted and dried up.
> And they shall turn the rivers far away; the brooks of defense shall be emptied and dried up.

In the Dead Sea Scroll,[24] the authors gave the verses in Isaiah as follows:

> The waters of the Nile will dry up, and the riverbed will become parched and dry . . . . and the streams of Egypt will dwindle and dry up.

Could Isaiah have been privy to ancient Egyptian documents that narrated these past events? In the Prophecy of Nefer-Rohu that was written around the Middle Kingdom (2,000 BC-1,800 BC), it was said:

> The rivers of Egypt are empty, [so that] the water is crossed on foot. Men seek for water for the ships to sail on it. Its course is (become) a sand bank.[25]

There are scientific and geological evidences to show that the Nile in very ancient time was a mighty river that has shrunk in size and moved its path.

If Isaiah was correct in his predictions that are now being backed up by scientific evidences, then there must be a revision of the dating of the Exodus. Due to the lack of written records, events that happened several thousand years ago could not be ascertained. Recent records and findings have already put in doubt many dates in the Bible.

With that history of the Hyksos and its pharaoh, maybe it is not surprising anymore if this grid is about the Jews and the Egyptians and Jesus and Horus. There are so many mysteries in this world.

B) SHUMER (SUMER)

After Egypt, I thought this book was already finished. But I was mistaken, for there were other names of ancient civilizations that came up in the grid that could not be deleted and must be revealed. One of these civilizations is a mystery, for it came out of nowhere and around 3,800 BC was already a great civilization, older than the recorded civilizations of Egypt, India, and China. It was called SHUMER but now mistakenly known as SUMER because of wrong translation. The ancient Sumerians also called it as KI. It is said that the culture, technology, art of writing, and pantheon of gods of Egypt are derived from Sumer. Even the Bible spoke about Sumer and called it Shinar.[1] The Bible described its first king named Nimrod as "a mighty hunter by the grace of the Lord."[2] His kingdom consisted of Babylon, Erech, and Akkad where he built Nineveh, Rehoboth-Ir, and Kalah. He built also the city of Resen between Nineveh and Kalah.[3] Except for Resen, all the cities have been excavated confirming the story of the Bible about the existence of the said cities. Archaeological findings have shown that the Akkadian, Babylonian, and Assyrian civilizations were based on Sumer. The reference by the Bible to Sumer and its first king is an acknowledgment even by the author of the Genesis that Sumer is an older civilization than Egypt. It is astonishing to find the places enumerated in the Bible in the grid. Figure 189 shows the different names of Sumer while figure 190 shows the places mentioned in the Bible.

a) Names and Places in Sumer

SHINAR/SINAR = name given by the Bible to Sumer; the word is found at G-15, F-14, E-15-16-17.

	A	B	C	D	E	F	G	H	I	J	K	L
1								A				
2							K		D			
3								A				
4												
5												
6												
7												
8												
9							M	U	S			
10												
11						Sh	E	R				
12							A	N				
13												
14						I						I
15				N			S					K
16			H	A								
17				R								

Fig. 189 Different Names of Sumer.

KI = ancient name of Sumer

SUMER/SHUMER = an ancient civilization reputed to be older than Egypt or India; the word is found at I-9, H-9, G-9-11, and H-11.

AKKAD/AKAD = part of the Kingdom of Sumer; the word is found at H-1, G-2, H-3, and D-1-2 with the letters in the form of a cross.

	A	B	C	D	E	F	G	H	I	J	K	L
4	L	K	U									
5	H	R										
6	A											
7		A	R									
8		U										
9												
10												
11							E	R	S			
12								N				
13							E					
14												

Fig. 190 Cities of Ancient Sumer.

	A	B	C	D	E	F	G	H	I	J	K	L
3												
4			U									
5		R										
6	A	Sh										
7		A	R									
8		U										
9												
10												
11					A	Sh						
12				G								
13			A									
14		L							I			
15					N	I	S					
16												
17												

Fig. 190-a Ashur, Lagash, and Isin.

KALAH = another city of Sumer; the word is found at B-4-7 and
    A-4-5-6.

RESEN = a city between Nineveh and Kalah; the word is found at
    G-11-13, H-11-12, and J-11

UR = the city where Abraham came from

ASHUR = another ancient city of Sumer

LAGASH = one of the first five cities in Sumer

ISIN = another ancient city of Sumer

NINEVEH = a city of Sumer; the word is found at B-17-16, C-15,
    D-16, E-14-15.

	A	B	C	D	E	F	G	H	I	J	K	L
8												
9												
10							H	O	V		Th	
11							E	R	O			
12												
13												
14				I	V							
15			E		N							
16		I		H								
17		N										

Fig. 190-b Nineveh and Rehoboth.

319

REHOBOTH = another city of Sumer; the word is found at G-10-11, H-10-11, I-10, J-11, and K-10.

b) Deities of Sumer

The deities of Sumer although coming from another world have human characteristics with feeling of love, hate, anger, envy, and other human traits. They reward those whom they love and punish those whom they hate. Although they can be hurt or be killed, they can be considered immortals as their planetary year is equal to 3,600 earthly years. All succeeding deities of the world like the Egyptians, Greeks, Romans, and Hindu are patterned after the Sumerian gods. Their highest GOD is known as AN, who is always addressed as the Father, and the highest feminine entity is known as the Mother sometimes called MAMI that created "Man." Usually there is the son or the daughter. The most famous daughter goddess is INANNA that became the model of later goddesses like Ishtar, Astarte, and Isis. Zecharias Sitchin[4] opines that the gods of Sumer came from Niburu, an outer planet of Sirius A that Sitchin considers the twelfth planet in our solar system. The Niburians were referred to as the Nephilims of the Bible.

Figure 191 shows the highest god of Sumer.

AN/ANU = the highest god of Sumer who is considered the Father; the name is written many times in the grid.

ENLL/ENLIL = eldest son of An, lord of the airspace; he destroyed the earth with flood; the name is found at J-8-9 and K-6-7-8.

	A	B	C	D	E	F	G	H	I	J	K	L
3												
4							A					
5						N						
6												
7												
8										N		
9				A				U			A	
10			N	U								
11												A
12		N	U				A	N	A		N	U
13			A						N	U		
14									N			
15								A				
16												

Fig. 191 An or Anu, the highest Sumerian god.

NINLL = wife of Enlil; By permutation the name is found at L-7, K-6-8, and J-8-9.

YNANNA/INANNA = daughter of Anu; the source of the goddess cult, the name is found at I-15-14-13-12-11 and H-12.

SIN = moon god; the name is found at G-F-E-15 with the letters side by side without ELS.

NANNA = moon god

AIA = wife of the sun god

BA-U = wife of Nin-Urta; the name is at A-7 and B-7-8.

	A	B	C	D	E	F	G	H	I	J	K	L
4												
5						N						
6					I		I				I	N
7	B	A									E	
8		U				N	T			N	L	
9										L		
10												
11					A	Sh	E	R	A			
12						A	N		A			
13									N			
14									N			
15					N	I	S		Y			
16												

Fig. 192 Pantheons of Sumerian god.

ASHERA = Mother goddess; the name is at row 11 with the letters side by side without ELS.

NIN-TI = Lady-life, title of Ninhursag; the name is at E-6, F-5-8, and G-8-6.

EA = second son of An, the god of wisdom who saved mankind from the flood; the name is written several times in the grid.

	A	B	C	D	E	F	G	H	I	J	K	L
2												
3						A						A
4					E							E
5				E								
6				A						A		
7				E					E		E	
8												
9				A							A	
10					E					E		E
11					A		E					A
12							A					
13							E					
14												
15								A				
16								E				
17												

Fig. 193 Ea, the god who saved mankind from the flood.

c) Cosmology of Sumer

There are cuneiform writings about the planetary system known in Sumer. In a well-researched series of books by Zacharias Sitchin,[5] he opined that there were twelve planets known to Sumer. One of these was Tiamat that supposedly collided with the planet Marduk resulting in the splitting of Tiamat into two parts that became the earth and the moon. He said that Marduk had an orbit of 3,600 years and most often was out of our solar system and thus, could not be seen from earth. This orbit results in making one year of Marduk equivalent to 3,600 years of earth time. Thus, the inhabitants of Marduk appear to be immortals. There have been legends in Hindu mythology of men living up to sixty thousand to one hundred thousand earth years. The Bible spoke of ancient people living up to almost one thousand years old like Methuselah. It is said that the planet Marduk would be visiting again earth and many catastrophes would occur because of the tremendous gravity and pull of Marduk.

This belief of the Sumerians about our solar system having twelve planets is intriguing. How they learned about the positions and the orbits more particularly of the outer planets without the aid of the telescope is puzzling. Where did they get their information? Up to now, this is a mystery. Presently, there have been claims by astronomers about the discovery of a tenth planet that has an orbit of 560 years. It is uncanny that the names of the planets mentioned by Sitchin in his series of books are found in the grid that seems to agree with the theory of Sitchin about the twelve planets. The planets according to the Sumerians are the following:

> MARDUK = the name of the chief god of the Babylonians whose name was given to the twelfth planet. The name is written here as MARTUK; as explained before, the letter *T* can be interchanged with the letter *D* as both letters have the numeral values of 4. Thus MARTUK can become MARDUK. The word is found at C-6, A-6, B-5, D4, C-4, and B-4.

MARUKA/TUTU/ASAR: other names of Marduk

	A	B	C	D	E	F	G	H	I	J	K	L
3												
4		K	U	T								
5		R										
6	A		M									
7		A	R				T					
8		U	K				U	T				
9				A				U				
10												
11								R	S			
12							A		A			
13												
14												

Fig. 194 Marduk: the twelfth planet.

> KISHAR = is the planet Jupiter in Sumerian; the word is found at C-8, B-6-7, and C-7. By permutation, the word is formed.

UTU = the sun god

	A	B	C	D	E	F	G	H	I	J	K	L
3												
4		K										
5		R										
6	A	Sh										
7		A	R									
8		K					U	T				
9								U				
10												
11												

Fig. 195 Kishar and Utu.

EA =   the word refers to the planet Neptune; the word is several times written in the grid.

GAGA = refers to the planet Pluto; the word is found at D-12 and E-11-13.

	A	B	C	D	E	F	G	H	I	J	K	L
1												
2												
3						A						A
4					E							E
5												
6				E						A		
7				A							E	
8				E								
9				A							A	
10					E					E		E
11					A		E					A
12							A					
13												
14												
15								A				
16								E				
17												

Fig. 196 The planet Ea.

KI =   the planet Earth; the word is found at L-15-14 with the letters side by side without ELS.

	A	B	C	D	E	F	G	H	I	J	K	L
3												
4	L		U									
5		H										
6		A	M									
7			A									
8												
9												
10												
11					A							A
12				G							N	
13					A				U			
14								N				I
15							A					K
16												
17												

Fig. 197 The planets: Lahmu, Lahamu, Anu, Gaga, and Ki.

LAHMU = the planet Mars; the word is found at A-4-5-6 and C-6-4.

LAHAMU = the planet Venus; the word is found at A-4-5-6, B-7, and C-6-4.

ANU = which refers to the planet Uranus; the word is written several times in the grid.

The other planets are shown in figure 198.

ANSHAR = refers to the planet Saturn; the word is found at I-12, H-12-11, G-12, and F-11.

MUMMU = means the planet Mercury; the word is found at C-6-4-2 and B-3-1.

APSU = here the name is written as ACHSU; as explained before, the letter CH can be interchanged with the letter P as both have the numeral value of 8, thus, ACHSU can become APSU which means the sun. The word is found at I-10-11-12, and J-12.

KINGU = the planet Moon; the word is found at D-11-12 and C-10-11.

	A	B	C	D	E	F	G	H	I	J	K	L
1		V										
2			M									
3		M.										
4			U									
5												
6			M									
7												
8												
9												
10			N									
11			U	K		Sh		R	S			
12				G.			A	N	A	Ch		
13										U		
14												

Fig. 198 Other planets.

d) Sumerian King's List

A text excavated from ancient Sumer contained a schematic list of kings who supposedly ruled before and after the deluge. The Greek historian Berossus copied the list that enumerated the ruling kings, years of their reigns and their dynasties. There were ten kings before the deluge and nineteen dynasties between the deluge and the third dynasty of Ur. The reign of the antediluvian kings was 241,200 years. Another list said that the reign was 456,000 years. The kings after the deluge numbering twenty-three ruled for 24,510 years, 3 months, and 3 ½ days. This period of around 24,510 is almost similar to the total reign of 24,925 years for Egyptian kings narrated by Manetho. There are other ancient documents that confirmed the historical character of the first dynasty of Ur.[6]

Scientists cannot accept these periods of time for the civilizations unearthed showed only a dating of 7,000 BC at most. Usually the carbon method dating is used although there are now several methods of dating that are more accurate than carbon dating. These new methods of dating are revealing artifacts dated hundred thousand years old that orthodox archaeologists could not accept. However, there are artifacts dated 32,000 years BC or more showing a civilized society. There were the thirty-two-thousand-year old Madonna and Child and a nonplayable flute dated forty-five thousand years old. These are artifacts not for primitive people, but civilized ones. Further, scholars could not believe the long reign attributed to the kings. They could not accept the claim that ten kings

before the deluge have ruled for 241,200 years or 456,000 years. This is similar to the unacceptability of Adam and his descendants living up to almost a thousand year. The ancient Sumerian documents, however, mentioned a period of time called the Saroi one year of which is equivalent to 3,600 years of earthly time. Thus, one year for these advanced beings would be equivalent to 3,600 earthly years. A period of 36,000 earthly years would only be equivalent to ten Saroi or Sars, which for these deities would only be considered a short period of time.

There are other Sumerian words in the grid, namely:

> E. DIN = "Home of the Righteous Ones," which became the basis of the Christians' "Garden of Eden." The word is found at C-15 and B-15-16-17.
>
> ARALI = place of the Neters of the Shining Lodes; the word is found in the cluster of letters at D-16-17 and F-17-16-15.

	A	B	C	D	E	F	G	H	I	J	K	L
14												
15			D	E		I						
16			I			L						
17			N		A	R	A					

Fig. 199 Garden of Eden.

MUL = star

TI = the Sumerian word for life; the word is written several times in the grid.

E.KUR = "House like a Mountain" the name given by the Sumerians to the pyramid. The word is at C-3-4 and B-4-5.; also at D-8, C-8-7, and B-8.

	A	B	C	D	E	F	G	H	I	J	K	L
1					U	Sh						
2					I	T						
3												
4		K	U									
5		R	E									
6			M				I					
7			R				T					
8		U	K	E			U					
9							M	U	S			
10	L						H					
11												
12												

Fig. 200 Ekur, the Pyramid.

SHU = means "seven"; the word is found at F-1 and E-1.

SHUMU = seven shining ones, the word is found at I-9, H-9, G-10-9-8.

A. (T)ZU = means water physician; the word is found in the cluster of letters at D-6-5 and C-4.

IA. (T)ZU = oil physician; the word is found in the cluster of letters at E-6, D-6-5, and C-4.

AMARU = deluge; the letters are in the form of a boat.

YAM = the sea; underneath the word *Amaru* are the words *Yam*.

NI-SI = mankind; the word is underneath Amaru.

MAR = son

BARU = seers

HAY = rain

ARU = conceive

MAH = hig

KEBAHNU = the Ark

	A	B	C	D	E	F	G	H	I	J	K	L
3												
4			U									
5		R		Tz								
6		A		M	A	I						
7		B	A	R								
8		H										
9												

Fig. 201 Physician.

	A	B	C	D	E	F	G	H	I	J	K	L
6												
7	B	A		E								
8	H	U	K									
9	N		H	A	Y							
10									U			
11					A			R				
12					A	M	A					
13		H	A	Y				Y				
14						I						
15					N	I	S					
16												
17												

Fig. 202 Deluge and mankind.

EN = lord
ENU = change, replace
HA = fish
A = water

ME = Divine force
AB = cow
KA = mouth
NAG = drink

SHE = barley

e) Sumer and Egypt

Presently there are no extant documents, records, or writings about the link between Sumer and Egypt. Although it is said the cultures, religious practices,

and beliefs of Egypt are a legacy from Sumer. Maybe it is more appropriate to say that the later Sumerian civilizations like Akkad, Mesopotamia, and Babylon particularly under Sargon in 2,350 BC were the ones that made an influence in the Egyptian civilization. Archeological evidences show that Sumer at around 6,000 BC was already a flourishing civilization while Egypt only started developing at around 3,000 BC. However, based on Sumerian records, it would seem Sumer and Egypt almost developed at the same time. Yet this important matter escaped the eyes of the Sumerologists and the Egyptologists. Why? Nobody knows. Maybe one reason is that Egypt in ancient times is known in another name. Or could it be that orthodox Egyptologist would not touch the subject as it would destroy their paradigm about Egypt? Sir W. Budge, the foremost Egyptologist, may be correct in his observation that the religion of Egypt was not a legacy from Sumer but developed from a common source:

> It is surprising therefore to find so much similarity existing between the primeval gods of Sumer and those of Egypt, especially as the semblance cannot be the result of borrowing. It is out of the question to assume that Ashurbanipal's editors borrowed the system from Egypt, or that the literati of Babylon or Assyria. And we are therefore driven to the conclusion that both the Sumerians and the early Egyptians derived their primeval gods from some common but exceedingly ancient source. The similarity between the two companies of gods seems to be too close to be accidental.[7]

This observation of Sir Budge could radically change the paradigm about Egyptology. Actually in the book *The Land of Osiris*,[8] Mehler is advocating a change in paradigm in Egyptology including changing the name of the study of Egyptian civilization from the name Egyptology to Khemetology out of respect to the very ancient name of Egypt, KM, KMT or Khemet that means "the black land" of which Egypt was known in more ancient times.

Mehler has talked about a certain man named Abd El Hakim whom he called as a Khemetologist, who knows many ancient indigenous traditions of ancient Khemet or Egypt. Hakim said that Sumer was just a part of ancient Egypt in olden times. However, he has no record to back him up. Sumerian records however say otherwise. Although Hakim may be correct in saying that Egyptian and Sumerian civilizations are older than the dates accorded to them.

	A	B	C	D	E	F	G	H	I	J	K	L
4												
5									K			
6								M	K			
7							T			Ch	E	M
8												
9							M	U	S			
10												
11							E	R				
12												
13												

Fig. 203 Sumer and Egypt.

The Countries Magan and Meluha

As I personally believe that Sumer had a hand in the development of Egyptian civilization and that the observation of Sir. W. Budge is tenable, I searched for materials and information about Egypt in ancient Sumerian writings. As the word *Aegyptos* was a Greek name for Egypt, I looked for more ancient names of Egypt in Sumerian documents. The writings of the foremost Sumerologist, Samuel Noah Kramer became my guide in searching for the names. In the different books Kramer wrote, he said that the word *Magan* was a Sumerian name for Egypt.[9] Based on this observation, I looked for verses in Sumerian writings about the word *Magan*.

	A	B	C	D	E	F	G	H	I	J	K	L
3	E	M										
4	L		U									
5	H		E									
6	A		M									
7												
8												
9												
10												
11												
12		N	U	G	A	M						
13		H	A									
14		L										
15		D	E									
16		I	M									
17												

Fig. 204 Magan, Meluha, and Dilmun.

In a Sumerian text "Enki and Ninhursag-Affairs of the Water Gods," Enki, the Sumerian water god told Ninhursag:

Let Nintul be the Lord of Magan.[10]

This verse confirms the authority of Enki to appoint the King or Lord who would rule Magan or Egypt. This authority is further confirmed in another ancient text called "Enki and the World Order" where it is said:

The lands of Magan and Dilmun looked up at me [Enki].
The ships of Dilmun brought wood.
The ships of Magan are loaded sky-high.
The magilum boats of Meluhha, transport gold and silver.[11]

This verse is very revealing, for it shows that the land of Magan [Egypt] looked up at Enki; and to show its obeisance, the ships of Magan brought shiploads of tributes to Enki. This shows the connection between Magan [Egypt] and Sumer in a time when Egypt was not yet recording its history. This brings up the question as to why there are no Egyptian records, artifacts, stele, or monuments about these dealings with Sumer. Did the Egyptians destroy the records? Or the Egyptians did not want the world to know that the Sumerians were more advanced or superior to them? Or could the Egyptians been considered also as Sumerians thus only Sumerian records exist?

There are two ancient Sumerian texts that mentioned the words *Magan* and *Magilum*, namely, *The Epic of Gilgamesh* and *Enki and the World Order*. In the Epic of Gilgamesh[12] dated around 2,000 B.C., there was a description of the boat the hero Gilgamesh used. It was a Magan boat called the Might of Magilum.

> After the Magan boat had sunk
> After the boat "Might of Magilum" had sunk.

In the text *Enki and the World Order*, it is said,

> The ships of Magan are loaded sky-high.
> The magilum boats of Meluhha, transport gold and silver.[13]

In both texts the words *Magan* and *Magilum* were used. In the epic, the word *Magan* was used to identify where the boat was made, and the word *Magilum* was used as the name of the boat. In Enki, the word *Magan* was used to identify where the ships came from while the word *Magilum* was used to identify the kind of ships Meluhha used. Although Kramer said that the meaning of the word *Magilum* is unknown, however, their uses in the two texts implied a connection between Magan and Meluhha. These words *Magan* and *Meluhha* can both refer to Egypt, or one of them could be a city in Egypt like Ur was the capital of Sumer.

Then again in the Sumerian text, it is said,

> It is Enki, however who actually organizes the earth and especially that part of it which includes Sumer and its neighbors into a going concern.
> He decrees the fates of Sumer, Ur and Meluhha.[14]

Again this verse shows that Enki ruled over not only Sumer and its capital Ur but also Meluhha, for he was the one who decreed their fates. Although Sumer and Meluhha were already flourishing civilizations at the time, however, Enki ruled Meluhha. But where is Meluhha? What country is it? Two Sumerian texts

Curse of Agade and *Enki and the World Order* are the links as to the whereabouts of Meluhha. The texts show the connections between Magan and Meluhha.

Kramer opined that Meluhha could be in the northeastern coast of Africa, possibly Ethiopia or Somaliland. However, in the Sumerian text *Curse of Agade*[15] there was a description of Meluhha that contradicts the opinion of Kramer:

> To it [Agade] came the "Meluhhites", the people from the "black land."

This verse is very important for it pinpoints the location of Meluhha. The people of Meluhha were called Meluhhites, who came from the "black land." Present studies and researches have pinpointed "the black land" as Egypt for the term refers to the rich black soil deposited by the inundation of the Nile thereby giving the appearance of black to the land. Egypt is the only land in Africa since ancient times to be called "the black land." This is the reason why Egypt in more ancient time was called KM, KMT, or Khemet meaning "black land." This is also the reason why some scholars would like to change the study of Egypt from Egyptology to Khemetology. Egypt is also in the northeastern coast of Africa. Hence, Meluhha could also refer to Egypt or one of the ancient cities of Egypt. Again, it is said:

> Enki then comes to Meluhha, the "black mountain."[16]

This referral to Meluhha as the "black mountain" also relates to Meluhha being called the "black land" with "black mountains." According to Kramer,[17] during the organization of earth, Enki went first to Sumer, then to its capital UR. From there, Enki proceeded to the distant lands Meluhha, the "black land" and Dilmun and blest them. Kramer said that Enki was fond of Meluhha as if it was Sumer itself. He usually blest Meluhha and its people, and from there he proceeded to the Tigris and Euphrates rivers and filled them with fresh life giving water. The verses cited would show the parallel development of the Sumerian and Egyptian civilizations.

Underground Passages, Tunnels, and Canals

This section should have been discussed under the chapter on Egypt, but because of the relation between Sumer and Egypt that answers the question who are the ancient Khemetians and the builders of the ancient passages and canals and the Great Pyramids, this particular section has to be discussed under Sumer.

In the Bu Wzr area composed of Giza, Sakkara, Abusir, Abu Roash, and Zawiyet El Aryan is an elaborate and intricate system of interconnecting tunnels, water channels, wells, aqueducts, and ditches that extends up to twenty-five to thirty miles underground in the whole area. The right angles and smooth walls cut through solid rocks in a serpentine way. The constructions simulate the flow of a river that defies explanation. Why were these structures constructed in such a pattern? What was the purpose? Who constructed them? These structures could only have been made through the use of advanced machining techniques. The indigenous Khemetian tradition says these structures were constructed by ancient Khemetians to bring in water not from the present Nile but from the more ancient Nile located in the western portion. Some of the shafts in the Giza Plateau are estimated to be as deep as three hundred meters (over 1,000 ft.). One can only imagine the difficulty and hardship to drill through limestone rocks especially if only primitive tools like copper would be used as suggested by orthodox Egyptologists. According to Khemetians tradition, the tunnels extend for miles throughout the Bu Wzr area and then to the ancient Nile in the west. These tunnels may extend up to twenty-five to thirty miles north to south and are as old as ten thousand years as tradition goes. The tunnels were intrinsically connected to the Great Pyramid. The tunnels have been known since the 1920s and the 1930s. A shaft called the Reisner's shaft goes down to 1,000 ft.[18] One of the sons of the American Egyptologist George Reisner drowned in the shaft trying to discover the depth of the shaft. There was a report in 1940 that a tunnel was discovered in 1938-1939 leading from the Sphinx to the Great Pyramid. In 1995-1996, a number of water conduits were excavated.

Underneath Sakkara is an elaborate tunnel system going down hundreds of feet into the bedrocks. The tunnels and channels were bored in different layers of bedrocks with rectangular, smooth, solid serpentine passages going for miles under the limestone bedrocks. These passages were not natural formations but man-made. The orthodox Egyptologists do not comment on these tunnels as it will destroy their contention of copper tools and stone ponders as the technology used. These passages could only have been made through the use of advance machining techniques using sophisticated concepts of engineering. Mehler said that these tunnels according to Hakim were drilled by ancient Khemetians to draw water from the ancient Nile in the west. If this is true, then Sakkara would already be around ten thousand years old. Hakim[19] said that when he was still seventeen years old, he wandered in one of the tunnels; and after several hours, he emerged out of a tunnel in the Giza Plateau some eight to ten miles away.

In Abusir and Abu Ghurob, two miles north of Sakkara, there are plenty of water channels and extinct lakebeds. There are also remnants of aqueducts. The two towns were around since 2,450 BC.

In Dashur, fifteen miles south of Giza, there are many man-made canals, remains of docks, and also extinct lakebeds. This is the site of the Red and Brent Pyramids that are six to eight miles from the present Nile River. Yet around the Pyramids were man-made canals.[20] The Pyramids were made of limestones, basalt, and granite while the other pyramids in ruins were made of mud-bricks. The ruined pyramids were of later constructions; thus they were made of inferior materials.

The Pyramids and Water

The ancient Khemetians drilled holes of tunnels through limestones and bedrocks while above ground they constructed aqueducts and water channels out of limestones, granite, and basalt. The tunnels, channels, and passageways were constructed in undulating serpentine pattern to create the phenomenon of running water in rivers. They wanted to mimic the natural flow of waters in rivers in order to create sound and vibrations that will enhance the harmony of water as discussed in the book *The Land Of Osiris* where the connection of water power and the Pyramids was extensively discussed.

There is an Egyptian legend that describes a sacred lake that measures 440 by 440 cubits. There is only one structure in Egypt with such measurement of 440 by 440 cubits, the base of the Pyramid of Cheop. In the myth, the Pyramid is the source of the mythical Nile.[21]

Herodotus[22] in the fifth century BC narrated a story about an artificial lake called Lake Maoris whose size matched the whole seabed of Egypt with a depth of ninety meters with two ninety-meter pyramids above the waters in the middle of the lake. It was supposed to be located in the City of Crocodiles. The whereabouts of the site, the lake, and the pyramids are uncertain up to now. Herodotus even said that there was an island in the Giza plateau surrounded by the Nile. All these structures have vanished, and they are all connected with the water.

The Roman historian Ammianus Marcellus (AD 330-400) wrote this:

> There are also subterranean passages and winding retreats, which it is said, men skillful in the ancient mysteries, by means of which they divined the coming of the Flood, constructed in different places, lest the memory of all their sacred ceremonies shall be lost.[23]

The Khemetian tradition about the intrinsic connection between the Pyramids and water is further bolstered by the ancient Sumerian texts about the battle between the gods and the Kur. Although these are supposed to be only stories, however, they seem to imply as to how some structures in Egypt were built.

Builders of the Pyramids

This text also touches on who the possible builders of the pyramids are. There are three versions of this story with different characters. The oldest story was the story of Enki and his battle with the Kur. Then the next story also based on the first story was the battle of Ninurta and the Kur, and the last was the battle between Inana and the Kur (Mountain Ebih). The importance of this story is that the second version gave the reason why the Kur was made, who made it and its relation to water. The story about the relation of the Kur with water tallies with the new findings and researches on the Pyramid. It is reported that the pyramids are related to water control and not to the entombment of pharaohs. This version known as "The Feats and Exploits of Ninurta"[24] tells about the battle between Ninurta, son of Enlil and the Kur. When the Kur was defeated, a calamity occurred. The primeval water that Kur held in check rose to the surface, preventing the fresh water from irrigating the farms. So Ninurta put up heaps of stones over the dead Kur like a wall to hold the water, and as a result, the waters of the lower region could not rise up to the surface anymore. The waters that had flooded the land, Ninurta collected and channeled to the Tigris River. This story connected the Kur to water. In another version of the story called "The Ninurta Myth Lugal E" written around 2,150 BC, it was narrated:

> He made a bank of stones against the highland-like drifting clouds they (came floating on) outstretched wings—and placed it as a bar before the country like a great wall. At hundreds of places he set up well-sweeps—the warrior was shrewd, accorded the cities equal importance—and the mighty waters followed along the stones.[25]

Where did all the stones come from? According to the Cylinder of Gudea:

> From the mountain of stone, great stones of the foothills will be cut for you in slab forms[26]

> In the land of the Na-stone, the large Na-stone of the mountain will be cut up into slabs for you.[27]

> To the mountain of (mountain) of stone not for man to enter

> Did for the Lord Ningursa, Gudea bends his steps
> Cutting in slab forms its great stones.[28]

The stones came from the mountain of stones where man could not enter and where the gods cut the stones into slab forms. Why were men not allowed to enter

the mountain? Was it to keep the method secret from men? How were the big slabs of stones weighing in tons carried out? They were brought floating like drifting clouds in outstretched wings.[29] Was antigravity equipment involved in carrying out the tons of stones? Many will say that is impossible. How can the ancients have such equipment when presently these devices are still just in the planning stage? Why don't we visit a three-thousand-year-old temple at Abydos where there are images of modern helicopters, airplanes, and "star wars gliders"? Ancient documents dating from hundred years to 1,500 years BC like the Mahabharata and Ramayana (1,500 BC) talked about flying machines Vimanas while the Vaimanika Sastra (fourth century BC) had eight chapters with diagrams describing three types of flying machines: the Samara Suthradhara with 230 stanzas about construction of flying machines, take-off, and flight; the Sifrala of Chaldea; and the Hakatha of Babylon contain about one hundred pages of instructions on how to build a flying machine and admonitions about responsible flying respectively. How could these ancient documents talk about antigravity devices unless they existed?

Returning to the Sumerian verses, they did not only narrate where the stones came from and how they were brought but also how they were used in setting up well sweeps; the implied tunnels and canals that the waters followed and the involvement of several cities. Where are these places and towns? This story seems to relate to the Khemetians' traditions about the underground tunnels and canals in the Bu Wzr area composed of several towns with an elaborate network of tunnels, canals, and wells whose constructions nobody could explain. The Sumerian story has no connection with any construction that could be found in Sumer or any part of Africa. Could this story be relating to the Bu Wzr and its mysterious network of underground water tunnels, canals, and wells? This is not only the mystery contained in the Sumerian story but also about the story of the E.Kur. It has already been stated that the Sumerians have connected the word *Kur* to "mountain" and oftentimes describe the houses of the gods as E.Kur, another term for the Pyramid. In the third version of the story, the Kur was called Mountain Ebih and was said to be: the "mountain," its dreadful rays of fire, it has directed against all the lands.[30]

What kind of mountain has dreadful rays of fire that can destroy the lands except an E. Kur or a Pyramid? What kind of weapon has dreadful rays that can be directed against all the lands? This weapon must have very long distant range. Were not the weapons at that time only bow and arrows? Was the narrator talking about a laser weapon that up to the present has not yet been perfected and used?

It was narrated that Enlil told Ninurta:

[Let him] rain down fire [in the country], but he may not strike with the lightning those in whom I trust.[31]

How could Ninurta possibly choose whom the lightning would strike unless the weapon is under the control of Ninurta? What kind of weapon is this that shoots lightning and is at the will of the one firing it? It was further said:

The weapon going to reconnoiter the border areas, cast fire upon the highland.[32]

The flood storm weapon hurling fire upon the highland.[33]

The weapon even had the capability to reconnoiter the border areas and from its vantage position cast fire upon the highland. This could only imply that the weapon is in a high position or in the air for the weapon to reconnoiter the border areas and cast fire upon the highland. This weapon could not possibly be a sword, a bow and arrow, or a catapult. What kind of weapon is this?

Further from the "Ninurta Myth Lugal E," it was said,

His lion headed mace
birdlike it was flying off,
. . . it beats its wings . . .
it circled heaven's base . . .
untiring, it sat not down (to rest),
its wings going like a flood storm.

This weapon is also described in the Cylinder of Gudea as:

The mettu (mace) which out of the skies
like a gale, storm of battle,
is hurled heading at the highland.

A mace will appear like a long handle with a big rounded end filled with spikes. If it is flying it will look like a guided missile. By the ancient desription of its capability, the weapon would seem to have the capability to fly, circle the enemy position and hurled itself to the target unerringly like a smart bomb or a guided missile.

Some people will say that this is impossible for the ancients did not even know how to fly. They did not have airplanes, how much more guided

missiles. Yet why does the ancient document called the "Hakatha" (Laws of the Babylonians) declared:

> The privilege of operating a flying machine is great. The knowledge of flight is among the most ancient of our inheritances. A gift from "those from upon high." We received it from them as a means of saving many lives.

What were the Babylonians, the descendants of the Sumerians talking about? They were talking about flying machines that were given to them a long time ago by the gods whom presently we call as aliens. Maybe the only difference between those flying machines and our present airplanes is the purpose for their use. We use them for destruction and not for saving lives. The book of D. Hatcher Childress *The Anti-Gravity Handbook* about flying machines is a fascinating one.

> It was further narrated that the weapon created with winds having halos (of heat) it gathers the dust, rains down clay pellets for rains.[34]

In "Gilgamesh and Aka" quoted by Thorkild in his book *The Harp that Once* it was said:

> May a great fear of the fiery halo prove enough.

What is this weapon, just the mere idea of which makes the enemy tremble? What is this fiery halo that brings great fear to the enemy? Is this the mushroom cloud brought about by an exploding nuclear bomb? This description is similar to the story told in the *Mahābhārata*, an ancient poem in India that narrated:

> Gurkha flying in his swift and powerful Vimana hurled against the three cities of the Vrishis and Andhakas a single projectile charged with all the a power of the Universe. An incandescent column of smoke and fire, as brilliant as ten thousands suns, rose in all its splendor. It was the unknown weapon, the Iron Thunderbolt. A gigantic messenger of death which put to ashes the entire race of the Vrishini and Andhakas.

Is this not a description of the atom bombs explosions in Hiroshima and Nagasaki where there were created columns of smoke and fire, halos of dust and clouds, and brilliant lights that hid the sun? What ancient weapon could wipe out an entire race in just one instant? According to the *Mahābhārata*, the effects of this messenger of death were so devastating that the corpses were burned beyond recognition, the hairs and nails fell out and the birds turned white.

Potteries were broken, and all foodstuffs became infected. The survivors had to throw themselves into the streams to wash themselves and their equipment. How can one projectile wipe out an entire race? How can it produce a brilliance equivalent to ten thousand suns unless it is an exploding nuclear bomb? The city of Mohenjodaro, Pakistan, when excavated last century showed skeletons that rivaled those found in Nagasaki and Hiroshima in terms of radioactivity. How come that there is so much radioactivity there even after more than a thousand years? Fused stones and black lumps of glass were found, which turned out to be clay pots that had melted under intense heat, which only an atomic explosion could create. Although these stories are now being backed up by physical evidence, still modern men will dismiss them as myths and tall tales. Yet if they are myths, how come that that the radiation level in Mohenjodaro equals that of Hiroshima and Nagasaki despite the thousand years that have passed? Myths or not, still the descriptions of these ancient weapons are truly intriguing.

Builders of the Underground Passages and Canals

Going back to the exploits of Ninurta, the ancients talked about the relation of the Kur to water. Can the Sumerian story also be relating to the mysterious land of Dilmun where Enki was said to have a hand in the construction of its water facilities. The story of Dilmun might possibly resolve the questions as to who constructed the tunnels, water channels, wells, aqueducts, and the extinct riverbeds in the Bu Wzr area; why they were constructed and why there are no Egyptian records, steles, or monuments about their constructions including the Pyramids and the Sphinx. Actually the most logical reasons why there is a lack of information about their constructions are that these edifices and structures were made before the recorded civilization of Egypt around 3,000 BC. For sure the orthodox Egyptologist will vehemently disagree, for this will destroy their theories about Egyptian civilization like the age of the Pyramids and the Sphinx, the Pyramids as tombs for the pharaohs, and that the civilization of Egypt developed internally without outside help. If the Pyramids were constructed before 3,000 BC when there were no pharaohs yet, then it would be absurd to construct the Pyramids as tombs for nonexisting persons. Where can we find the answers to these questions about who, why, and when these structures were constructed?

Is there a Sumerian text that can help resolve these questions? There is a Sumerian story about a land that could be considered a paradise for the animals do not harm men and sickness and death are unknown. Even Enki resided there with his wife.

He who is alone laid himself there in Dilmun,
The place, after Enki had laid himself by his wife.[35]

But this paradise called Dilmun, whose whereabouts nobody knows, lacks one thing—"sweet water" or "freshwater." For this reason, the goddess Ninsikil pleaded with Enki, the water god to bring fresh water to Dilmun. As requested, EA ordered Utu, the sun god to bring in fresh water to Dilmun. As a result:

Dilmun drinks the water of abundance,
Her well of bitter water, behold they are become well of fresh water,
Her fields and farms produced crops and grains,
Her city, behold it is became the home of the banks and quays of the land.[36]

Based on the story, it would seem that Utu, the sun god like in Genesis just said the magic the words, and behold fresh water came to Dilmun. The truth is there was so much sweat and labor in bringing water to Dilmun. The so-called Sumerian gods are not really a "god" according to our present concept, more particularly the Igigi who were described like the hominids. The verses from "Atra-hasis" dated around 1,700 BC will show who these gods are. When the Annunakis and the Igigis first arrived on earth, they were compared to the hominids roaming Africa. They were said to be

Like mankind when first created,
They (the Annunakis) knew not the eating of bread,
Knew not the wearing of garments,
Ate herbs with their mouths, like sheep;
Drink water from the furrows.[37]

This comparison also includes the Igigis, the workhorse of the Annunakis. These would mean that those who came to earth were mostly the lower class that was also primitive in their ways. Why were they brought here? Well, they were brought here to do the works of the gods.

As stated before, there are no records or documents narrating the constructions of the waterworks, the Pyramids, and the Sphinx in the Bu Wzr area. It could only mean that like the Pyramids and the Sphinx, they were constructed before the art of writing came down to Egypt, or that these structures existed already at that time; hence there was no report about how they were erected. These are constructions that could have made any pharaoh proud, but nobody claimed the honor of constructing these structures and edifices. Who then constructed them? Sumerian texts answered these questions.

According to the Sumerian text "Atra-hasis":

> When the gods instead of men,
> Did the work, bore the loads;
> The god's load was too great
> The work, too hard, the trouble too much;
> The Great Anunnaki made the Igigi,
> Carry the workload sevenfold.
> Xxxx
> The gods had to dig out the canals,
> Had to clear channels, the lifelines of the land,
> The Igigi had to dig out canals
> The gods dug out the Tigris river[bed]
> And then dug out the Euphrates.
> Xxx
> For 3600 years they bore the excess
> Hard works, night and day.[38]

This is a very revealing story, for it tells about the nature of the gods. For 3,600 years, the Igigis although companions of the Annunakis, performed the manual labors of digging out the canals, constructing the channels, and clearing them for these were the lifelines of the land. These were the sources of the water going to the fields and the farms. They even dug out the Tigris River then the Euphrates River that ran across Sumer in a serpentine way. Although this can be compared to the construction of the Suez Canal, however, the construction of the Suez Canal pales in comparison with the constructions of the two mighty rivers. This heavy work instigated the Igigis to revolt against the Annunakis. It was only the intervention of Enki that prevented a bloody confrontation. He suggested to fashion workers from the hominids roaming Africa that would replace the Igigis from their heavy load. This resulted in the fashioning of "MAN," the hominids that were given the images of the gods so that they could speak and be intelligent. These humans became the workers of the gods who replaced the Igigis from their heavy loads.

"Atra-hasis" is an extant record about the gods constructing canals, waterways, channels, and rivers. If the gods were the ones who constructed these Egyptian aqueducts, waterways, channels and tunnels, then these structures must have existed before the creation of "man." This will give these structures incredible ages that are unacceptable. If these structures were constructed after the creation of man and before the flood that scientists said occurred around 6,000 to 10,000 BC, then these structures were constructed with the supervision and help of the

gods. No wonder their constructions could not be explained. These structures would then be at least ten thousand years old. Khemetians traditions say that these structures, the Pyramids and the Sphinx, are at least ten thousand years old. These new dates will destroy the theory of the orthodox Egyptologists who insist that the Pyramid was constructed around 2,500 BC based on the writings of Herodotus. It would not be surprising anymore that the constructions of these edifices and structures are not recorded in Egyptian documents, stelae, or monuments for historically writing came only to Egypt approximately 3,000 BC. Although an ancient Egyptian artifact with writings is dated around 3,250 BC.[39]

With respect to this mysterious land called Dilmun whose whereabouts is unknown and the only reference is that it is outside Sumer and according to the Epic of Atra-hasis, it is in the Orient or in the East. The East here could mean the eastern portion of Africa. Egypt is in the northeastern part. Could it be in any part of Bu Wzr where there are plenty of waterwork structures like well, water channels, and tunnels? Thorkild Jacobsen[40] suggested that Dilmun is the present Bahrain where Ziusudra, the Sumerian Noah supposedly lived.

Who then engineered the constructions of these edifices and waterworks? Sumerian records show that Enki, the water god, was responsible for the constructions of the waterways, canals, and rivers. Like in the story of Dilmun, it was Enki who

> He filled the dikes with water,
> He filled the ditches with water,
> He filled the uncultivated plains with water.[41]

Enki was known for building a magnificent EKUR (House of Mountain). In the blessing of a house that Enki built in Eridu that up to the present has not been unearthed, it is said,

> My son [Enki] has built a house, the King Enki;
> Eridu, like a mountain, he has raised up from the earth.
> In a good place, he has raised it.[42]

The E.Kur is described as:

> The Ekur, the lapis-lazuli house, the lofty dwelling
> Place, awe-inspiring,
> The awe and dread are next to heaven,
> Its shadow is spread over all the lands
> Its loftiness reaches heaven's heart[43]

Builders of the Great Pyramid

Has Enki any connection with the construction of the Great Pyramid in Egypt? Extant Egyptian documents or monuments do not contain any records about who and when the Great Pyramid was built. Herodotus in fifth century BC said the pharaoh Cheop built the Great Pyramid; however, the ancient Egyptian historian Manetho[44] in the third century BC said it was Suthis 1, king of the second dynasty around 2,720-2,560 BC who built the Great Pyramid.

Are there other sources that can show who was the possible builder of the Pyramid? There are evidences that can show who built the Pyramid and consequently also confirm the relation between Sumer and Egypt. These evidences can be found in the names of ancient places and edifices in Egypt. Unfortunately these ancient names have vanished and were substituted by other names. The ancient names of the Great Pyramid and the Middle Pyramid hint about that relationship too. The Pyramids have several ancients' names, but it would seem that the name EAKU and UR are more ancient than the Greek term *pyramidos* and the Hebrew term *HAR*.

The Great Pyramid Cheop was known also in ancient times as EAKU.[45] The name sounds very Sumerian as it is a combination of two Sumerian words *EA*, the name of the Sumerian water god EA who had authority over Magan (Egypt) and E. KUR meaning "House of Mountain," an ancient Sumerian term for the Pyramids.

	A	B	C	D	E	F	G	H	I	J	K	L
3			E									
4		K	U									
5	H	R	E									
6	A			A								
7		A	R	E								
8	H	U	K	E								
9				A								
10				U	E							
11				K	A							
12												
13												
14												
15												
16				H	A							
17			H	A	R							

Fig. 205 Ea, E. Kur, Ea, Ku, Ur, and Har.

Although the word *EA.KU* can mean "The land of EA," it is also possible that the complete name for the Great Pyramid was not EAKU but EAKUR, which means "The Mountain House of EA" or the "Pyramid of EA." Whether the name is "EA.KU" or "EAKUR," it shows the link between Sumer and Egypt. However, there will be a serious implication, for it means that the Great Pyramid is older than the age being attributed to it now; that the Pyramid was constructed in an earlier period beyond the recorded time of the Egyptian.

Another example is the ancient town of Kherara that was known in more ancient times in other names denoting Sumerian influences. Why these names have been shelved nobody knows.

One of its names were UAR or UR and was called Babylon of Egypt.[46] These names showed the connection of Sumer to this ancient town. It has been the custom of immigrating people in ancient times to name their new location or place with the names of their previous land to remember and honor their homeland.

Thus in western Arabia, there were the ancient towns of Bethsaida, Galilee, and Nazareth that became the Philistine towns of the same names where Jesus supposedly preached. Although the Arabian town of Nazareth already existed during the supposed time of Jesus, the Philistine town of Nazareth was still nonexisting during the time of Jesus. This custom added to the confusion as to the true locations of the towns or sites being referred to.

Another place referred to by the ancient Egyptians as UR was the "Red Sea" that the ancient Egyptians called the Sea of MR.

		A	B	C	D	E	F	G	H	I	J	K	L
3													
4				U									
5			R										
6													
7			A	R									
8			U										
9			U										
10													
11									R				
12								A		A			
13							V				U		
14													
15													

Fig. 206 Ur or Uar ancient names of Kherara and the Red Sea.

Again the town of Kherara is also called YABU,[47] which actually was EABU that means the "Land of EA," the Sumerian water god. EABU is a combination of the Sumerian word *EA* and the Khemetian word *BU* meaning "place or land." It is on the east bank of the Nile opposite the Giza Pyramids. Why the name EABU was shelved and changed to YABU nobody knows. Actually EA and YA are phonetically and numerically the same. EA, the Sumerian god of wisdom also became YA the Semitic god of wisdom. By eliminating EA, the Sumerian connection was eliminated and the Semitic connection was instituted; hence EABU became YABU. YABU is identified as the location of the "Twin Caverns" or the "Twin Breast,"[48] the source of the Nile or the water; hence, it was called EABU, land of the water god. The terms *Twin Caverns* or *Twin Breasts* could have referred to the Pyramids of Cheop and Kafre when the Pyramid of Menkaure was not yet built.

Another example of the changing of the names is Heliopolis whose more ancient names were EANU[49] (the "Abode of Anu," the god the Father of the Sumerians) or AN (Sumerian term for Heaven or Anu).

Even the Hyksos in ancient times were known as EAMU[50] meaning the "Waters of EA" or "Abode of the Divine Beings." The Hyksos became the hated "Asiatics." Thus, by eliminating the ancient names, the Sumerian connections were taken out.

Another name that has escaped the eyes of the researchers with respect to its connection to Sumer is the peninsula or the mountain called Sinai. By its very name, one can see the Sumerian link. The word *Sin* is the Sumerian or Mesopotamian moon god while the word *Ai* could have been the word *Ah*, the Egyptian moon god. Maybe through migration and conquest, the word *Ah* was changed to *Ai*. Actually the word *Ai* is also Ay or Ya in reverse, the Semetic god of wisdom.

	A	B	C	D	E	F	G	H	I	J	K	L
3												
4							A					
5						N						
6												
7												
8										N		
9				A							A	
10			N									E
11												A
12			N				A	N	A		N	U
13				A					N	U		
14									N	U		
15					N			A				
16					A			E				
17												

Fig. 207 An or E.Anu ancient names of Helopolis.

Another name that has escaped scrutiny is the name Haran where Abraham settled with his family. Actually the name Haran is composed of two words—*Har* that means "Mountain" and sometimes also a name of the third Pyramid and the word *An*, a Sumerian word for "Heaven" or An, the Sumerian god the father. Thus Har. An could mean "The mountain of An or Pyramid of An." As An is also the ancient name of Heliopolis, then Har.An can also mean the "Pyramid of Heliopolis." In this connection, the opinion of Ralph Ellis[51] that the migration of Abraham and his family was only from Kheraha to Heliopolis and not from Ur to Haran might be tenable.

Another link between the two countries that was bypassed was the architectural works in Egypt. In Sakkara, Egypt, where the Step Pyramid supposedly constructed around 2,600 BC was an enclosure surrounding the Step Pyramid. The style of architecture was Mesopotamian in nature. If this enclosure is older than the Step Pyramid as the tradition shows; then the civilizations of Sumer and Egypt are older than the 3,000 BC alluded to them.[52]

What does the Bible say about Sumer and Egypt? According to Genesis 10:6:

And the sons of Ham—Cush and Mizraim.[53]

The verse from the Bible says that Cush and Mizraim descended from Ham, the son of Noah. Cush is the father of Nimrod, the founder of the Sumerian civilization. If Cush is the father of Nimrod, then Cush also relates to Sumer that was called in the Bible as Shinar. The word *Mizraim* became the biblical name for ancient Egypt.

	A	B	C	D	E	F	G	H	I	J	K	L
2												Sh
3									U			
4					Ch							
5												
6												
7										Ch		
8												
9							M	U				
10												
11						Sh						
12												
13					A							
14												
15												
16												
17			H									

Fig. 208 Ham and Cush.

It is actually puzzling that the Jewish Old Testament would narrate the story of Nimrod and the establishment and the development of the first cities in Sumer instead of narrating first the development of Israel. Is this an acknowledgment that civilization started at Sumer, and that the Jews also relate to Sumer? By simultaneously speaking about Cush and Mizraim, it would seem that Sumer and Egypt developed if not simultaneously, one after the other. Since the Old Testament is a Jewish book, what was narrated was the genealogy of Shem that evolved into the Jewish nation of Israel instead of the genealogies of Ham that evolved into Sumer and Egypt. By the appearance of the names of Ham and Cush, the grid would seem to confirm the genealogy stated in the Old Testament.

Are we still surprised if Sumer is mentioned in the grid? I don't think so especially after the conclusion we have made as to why Egypt is included in a Hebrew grid. Due to the antiquity of Sumer, there is a scarcity of information about the country. But we know based on the Bible that Abraham came from Sumer, the biblical Shinar. His clan was from there. If this was the place where the Jews came from, was it not worth mentioning?

Maybe this is a way of acknowledging the contribution of Sumer or Assyria to the formation of the state of Israel. The Jews were part of the Semitic group that migrated and settled at Sumer; hence; they were first Sumerians or Assyrians. This would explain what Isaiah said:

> In that day shall Israel be the third with Egypt and with Assyria, a blessing in the midst of the land" Blessed be Egypt my people, Assyria the work of my hands and Israel, my inheritance.[54]

From these verses it would seem that God has placed Egypt first, then Assyria and lastly Israel. Why was the blessing of God in this order? It would seem that the blessings were made when Egypt was under the rule of the Hyksos kings who ruled for five hundred years. They became assimilated with the Egyptians and thus became Egyptians themselves. Despite being surrounded by people worshipping other gods, they remained faithful to their one God, Sadai El Chai. Hence the Egyptians were blessed first.

	A	B	C	D	E	F	G	H	I	J	K	L
1												
2			M			I	T					
3												
4		K		T					A			
5							Ch		K	M		
6	A		M	I			I	M		I		
7	B	A	R				T			Ch	E	M
8		U	K									
9							M					
10												
11												
12							A					
13												

Fig. 209 Baruk Kmt Ami (Blessed be Egypt my people).

God blessed Assyria next, for it was where Abraham came from and where he practiced his monotheistic belief. It was also the works of God's hand, for it is located near the Persian Gulf where the Garden of Edin was located. Thus in the blessing we should not be surprised that Israel was only third for it has not existed yet as a state, for it would still be an inheritance, an offspring from the Sumerians and then the Egyptians. It would not be surprising that there would be a story from Sumer about a Savior with similarities to Jesus like the ancient Saviors of Egypt, Arabia, India, Mexico, and Peru. Perhaps the Iranian stories of Zoroaster, the supposed founder of the Magi religion or Zoroastrianism and Mithra, Persian sun god can be the stories of the ancient saviors of Sumer. Again, it is very intriguing how the stories of Zoroaster and Mithra who existed thousands of years before Jesus would have very similar correspondences with Jesus. Let us see the similarities between Zoroaster, Mithra, and Jesus

Zarathustra, Mitra, and Jesus

According to Acharya S.,[55] Jesus has the following similarities with Zoroaster and Mithra:

ZOROASTER = founder of the Magi who lived thousand of years before Jesus and whose teachings have been adopted by the Christian Churches.

1. Zoroaster was born of a virgin and "immaculate conception by a ray of divine reason."
2. He was baptized in a river.
3. In his youth he astounded wise men with his wisdom.
4. He was tempted in the wilderness by the devil.
5. He began his ministry at age thirty.
6. Zoraoster baptized with water, fire, and "holy wind."
7. He casts out demons and restored the sight to a blind man.
8. He taught about heaven and hell and revealed mysteries, including resurrection, judgment, salvation, and the apocalypse.
9. He had a sacred cup or grail.
10. He was slain.
11. His religion had a eucharist.
12. He was the "Word made Flesh".

13. Zoroaster's followers expect a "second coming" in the virgin born Saoshyant or Saviour, who is to come in 2,341 CE and begin his ministry at age thirty, ushering in a golden age.

The saying of John the Baptist that after him would come one who would baptize with fire and the Holy Spirit came directly from the teaching of Zoroaster. Most of the Christian doctrines like heaven and hell, baptism by fire, Messiah, last judgment, good and evil, angels and demons, paradise, apocalypse, prophesy, Armageddon, the defeat of Satan came from Zoraoaster.

> MITHRA = He is a very ancient God known in Persia and India predating Jesus by thousands of years. During the early Christian era, Mithraism was the most popular and widely spread pagan religion. The Christians took advantage of the similarities between Jesus and Mithra in converting people to Christianity.

1. Mithra was born of a virgin on December 25 in a cave, and shepherds came bearing gifts. The Christians adopted this date as Jesus birth date.
2. He considered a great traveling teacher and master.
3. He had twelve companions or disciples.
4. Mithra's followers were promised immortality.
5. He performed miracles.
6. As the "great bull of the sun," Mithra sacrificed himself for world peace.
7. He was buried in a tomb and after three days rose again.
8. His resurrection was celebrated every year.
9. He was called the Good Shepherd and identified with both the Lamb and the Lion.
10. He was considered the Way, the Truth and the Light, and the Logos, Redeemer, Saviour, and Messiah.
11. His sacred day was Sunday, the Lord's Day, hundreds of years before the appearance of Christ.
12. Mithra had his principal festival on what was later to become Easter.
13. His religion had a euchrist or Lord's Supper, at which Mithra said, "He who shall not eat of my body nor drink of my blood so that he may be one with me and I with him, shall not be saved."

14. His annual sacrifice is the Passover of the Magi, a symbolical atonement or pledge of moral and physical regeneration.

	A	B	C	D	E	F	G	H	I	J	K	L
2												
3												
4				T								
5												
6			M	A	I							
7			R									
8												
9							M					
10						T	H					
11								R				
12							A					
13												
14			T	I								
15												
16			M	H	A							
17				R								

Fig. 210 Mithra, Mitra or Mtra.

Before when I was still young, I used to hear from religious people that the Christian doctrines were original and not copied from any pagan religion.

C) CHINA

Of the four civilizations mentioned in the grid, the one with the least information about the development of its civilization is China. This is due to the form of government that China has had since the beginning of its inception, from the emperors to the Cultural Revolution to the present government that have censored information about China. However, going back to its earliest beginning, it would seem that the earliest indices of human habitation in China dated around 1.7 million years ago at Yuanmon[1] in western China where remains of *Homo Erectus* with stone tools and knowledge of the use of fire were found. Remains similar to modern man were found at Zhou Koulian. There the stone tools, ornaments, and methods of burial were more refined.

	A	B	C	D	E	F	G	H	I	J	K	L
1				N								
2					I							
3					Ch	A						
4						Ch	A					
5						N	Ch	A				
6	A				I		I			A	I	N
7										Ch		
8						N				N		
9	N										A	Ch
10												
11												A
12	Ch	N								A	Ch	N
13			A							N		I
14												

Fig. 211 China

The name China is in ELS of two letters starting at A-12 going up to A-9 then to A-6. The other examples are in anagram.

The origin of the first Chinese civilization was around 3,000 BC about the same time as Egypt. It fully developed around 1,800 BC in northeast China and was called Shang due to the dynasty of kings who ruled during that time.

a) China and the Other Ancient Civilizations

There is a similarity between Sumerian, Egyptian, Latin American, and Chinese stories about ancient gods teaching mankind the art of civilization, agriculture, mathematics, and sciences. The Chinese have an ancient emperor called YU[2] who regulated the flood, built canals, and dredged the Yellow River like the Sumerian water god ENKI/EA who dredged the Tigris River, built the canals, and was responsible for the flood. Why do ancient civilizations have the same stories? Could the Sumerian and Egyptian stories about sending sages around the world after the flood to teach mankind the art of civilization be true? Could these sages be the gods, the Incas, Mayas, the Aztecs, and the Chinese were referring to as the ones who taught them the art of civilization? The Latin American and the Chinese civilizations came after the Sumerians and the Egyptians. The Chinese have a list of divine emperors who ruled before the first human ruler at around 2,300 BC. The Sumerians and the Egyptians have their own King's Lists of rulers before and after the flood.

The Chinese also have a creation story about a goddess named Nu Wa[3] who created the first human from mud like the story of the Sumerian goddess Nin. Mah called Mami. Nu Wa's creation was called black-haired, a common name for peasants. This is similar to the creation of Ninmah called black-headed people, for it referred to the laborers. Nu Wa was usually depicted as a human-headed snake like the Egyptian goddesses. She taught the people how to breed, so she would not be creating them all the time. This is the same reason of ENKI why he gave humans the knowledge to procreate so that the gods would be saved from the difficult tasks of creating humans from the laboratories. Another similarity between the Sumerians and the Chinese are their ancient names. The Bible calls Sumer as Shin-Ar while China in ancient times was known as Shin or Chin. Could China be under Sumer at that time like Egypt when it was still known as Magan?

	A	B	C	D	E	F	G	H	I	J	K	L
1		V			U							
2	Y			Y								
3				Y					V			
4			U					Y				
5												
6												
7		A										
8		U										
9	N	U		A	Y							
10			N	U								
11			N	U	A							
12			N	U								
13			A	Y								
14					V							
15				Y								
16												
17												

Fig. 212 Yu and Nu-Ua.

b) Pyramids in China

Another similarity between the four civilizations is their pyramids. Most people are unaware that there are more that one hundred pyramids in China.

This fact has been kept secret from the public. However, the United States government knew this information since World War II as U.S. reconnaissance planes took pictures of them. The U.S. satellites also took pictures, but these were never revealed to the public.

There are more than one hundred pyramids near the city of Xian[4] in the central plains of southwest of Beijing. Due to the restrictions imposed by the Chinese government, access to the area is prohibited especially since the Chinese space program facility is in the area. There was, however, a story about two Australian traders who one hundred years ago traveled through the area and saw the pyramids. They went to a monastery whose record keeping according to the custodian went back to 5,000 BC. The custodian said that the pyramids were built before they started keeping records and during the age of the ancient emperors who did not come from earth but from another planet on their "fiery metallic dragons."[5]

There was a German writer by the name of Hartwig Hausdorf[6] who was able to visit the area and took pictures and video of the pyramids that have an average height of one hundred to three hundred feet with the tallest said to be one thousand feet. Hausdorf said that the government prevented him from continuing his investigations. The area of Xian is famous as the site where the terra-cotta soldiers that guarded the tomb of the first emperor of China were excavated. The ancient race called Xian/Shian was said to be the builders of the pyramids. Xian/Shian/Chian is actually an anagram of the word *China*.

Besides the pyramids, there are mummies in China. In the Talamakan Desert in eastern China, one thousand mummified bodies have been unearthed from the 1970s to the 1980s. Dozens of bodies excavated are dated thousands of years. The mummies are known as the Tarim Basin people. There was a human skull that was determined to be five hundred thousand years old showing that people were in the area around five hundred thousand years ago. But the puzzling thing about the mummies is that their features were non-Asian or Chinese for they had blond, reddish, or yellow-brown hairs and long limbs.

c) Alien Presence in China

There was a news report from Reuters, Beijing dated June 6, 2002,[7] bearing the title "Tunnels, Pipes, Tower, from 'ET Launch Site' Found in China." It said that a team of Chinese scientists investigated an area where a "mystery pyramid" according to local legend was "a launch tower left by aliens from space." This site near a salt lake was described as containing a 180-foot pyramid and "rusty scraps, pipes, and unusually shaped stones" dubbed ET Relics. Soon after an investigative report was published in a local newspaper called *City Weekend*. It described a metallic pyramid between fifty and sixty meters tall. In front of the

structures lie three caves each with triangular openings. The two smaller caves have collapsed, but the largest central cave is still passable. Inside, on the ground lies a forty-centimeter-length pipe sliced in half. Another red-brown pipe is sunk deep into the earth with only its lips visible above the ground. Outside the cave, half pipes, scraps of metals, and strangely shaped stones are scattered along the southern bank of the lake. Some pipes run into the water; it is not known what may lurk in the salty depths. This area is a remote area in Quinghai province in a desolate barren desert near a salt lake. A U.S. scientist looking for dinosaur fossils first reported the ET Relics to the Chinese government in 1998. The report was ignored until another reporter wrote in the Henan Dahe Bao about the site. According to the Qinhua News Agency, results of the rocks and metal samples showed 8 percent of the samples as unidentifiable. The engineer who conducted the studies said the levels of silicon dioxide and calcium oxide point to the pipes having been on the mountainside for at least five thousand years. Iron smelting only dates back two thousand years ago. Maybe in the years to come before 2,012 more knowledge will be known.

There is a story cited by various writers like Von Daniken about strange skeletons found near the Chinese border with Tibet that do not resemble humans because of their thin bodies and large overdeveloped heads. Along with the skeletons was a stone disk with a grooved spiral of characters that Dr. Tsum Nui, a respected Chinese archaeologist said was a recording. However, the Peking Academy of Prehistory forbade him to reveal his findings. In 1965, 716 more disks were found in the same cave complex. The Peking Academy allowed Dr. Nui and his colleagues to publish their report, which was entitled "The Grooved Script Concerning Spaceship, Which, as Recorded in the Disc Landed on Earth 12,000 Years Ago."[8] Archaeologists are still studying the cave where crude pictures of the sun, the moon, unidentifiable stars, and Earth are encircled on the walls. The disks are said to be twelve thousand years old. Maybe in the future the Chinese government will share its information with the rest of the world concerning ancient artifacts discovered in China.

Several years ago the Chinese discovered some ancient Sanskrit documents in Lhasa Tibet that were sent to the University of Chandigarh for translation. Dr. Ruth Reyna of the university said that the documents contained directions for building interstellar spaceships for interstellar travels. The Chinese announced that they were including certain data in the documents for further study in their space program.

A report from Reuters, London dated September 22, 1999, said that archaeologists have found the world's oldest playable flute in China dating around nine thousand years old. This artifact would imply that China has a very ancient civilization. Flutes are played by civilized people and not by the Neanderthals.

D) South American Civilizations

After Egypt, Sumer, and China, the next civilization that will be discussed is the Meso-American civilization in South America generally composed of the Incas, the Mayas, and the Aztecs. Why are we going to discuss these ancient people? What is their connection to the Lord's Prayer or to Jesus? Their civilization is a mystery to many as their origin is unknown. Their knowledge in astronomy and mathematics rival that of Egypt, Sumer, and India. Where they got their knowledge is a puzzle. Yet they are mentioned in the grid, hence this portion about the Meso-American civilization. Even the great civilization of India is in the grid, but I might not be able to finish this book if I will include India. For now, let us take a peep at the ancient Meso-American people.

a) Legend of Jesus in Ancient South America

There is a legend that Jesus appeared and went around the South American countries before the Spaniards came. Descriptions of this mysterious man wandering in the Andes and teaching people about love and harmony fitted the description of Jesus.

According to the Incas or Indians of the Andes, this mysterious man whom they called in different names went in many places and taught them how to live, treating them with great love and kindness and entreating them not to harm one another but to love one another and show charity to all.

In some places, this man was called Viracocha who was also a teacher and a healer and helped those in need wherever he went. He healed all who were sick and restored sight to the blind.

When one reads these kinds of descriptions, one feels that he is reading the Bible. As if the story is about Jesus, the God of Love. Thus, the legend about this mysterious, holy man who was known in many names like Viracocha, Quetzalcoatl, Con, Kon Tiki, Illa, Huaracocha, Tupaca, and Taapac.

According to legends, Viracocha who was tall, bearded, and dressed in long cloak was a teacher who taught the savages who lived in caves to change into a cultured and civilized society. He treated everyone with kindness and had abjured the use of force.

In a Mayan myth, it was said that the principal deity of the Mayans Itzamana or Kukulkan, robed and bearded, came from the East and who healed by the laying of the hands and could revive the dead. He sailed again to the East, and he promised to return one day like Viracocha did.

According to Sumerian legends, EA, the Sumerian god of wisdom, sent seven sages throughout the world to teach the art of civilization. Likewise, Egyptian

legend says that Thoth sent seven wise men to the different parts of the world also to teach civilization. In the 1940s at La Venta, Mexico, a twenty-ton stele measuring fourteen feet high by seven feet wide and one foot thick was dugged up, showing two tall men wearing elaborate robes and wearing European-styled shoes. What was incredible about the stele was that it is dated four thousand years old. Who were these nonnatives roaming around Mexico four thousand years ago? The quarry from where the stele came from was sixty miles away. How was it carried to the site?

b) Pantheon of Gods

The olden gods of the ancient people of South America who are similar to the serpent gods of the Hindus can be found by permutation. They are

KUKULKAN = Plumed serpent god of the Mayas; the name is found at A-10, B-9, C-8-10, and D-9-10-11.

BOCHIKA = god of the Chibkas who supposedly caused the flooding of the earth; the name is found in the cluster of letters at L-5, K-5-6, J-6-7, and I-6.

CHIA = wife of Bochika; the name is found side by side with her husband Bochika.

	A	B	C	D	E	F	G	H	I	J	K	L
1												
2					I							
3					Ch	A						
4		L	K	U	T	Ch						
5			E	Tz	O						O	B
6				A					K	A	I	
7										Ch		
8			U	K								
9			U	A								
10		L		N								
11												
12												
13												

Fig. 213 Ancient gods of South America.

In figure 214 are the other names of the South American gods:

TAAPAC = another name of Viracocha, god of the Incas; the name is written here as TAACHAK. As previously explained, the letter *CH* can be interchanged with the letter *P* as both have the numeral value of 8. Thus, TAACHAK can become TAAPAK. The word is found in the quadrant composed of columns G-H-I and rows 2-3-4-5.

MONAN = creator god of the Tupinumba Indians of Brazil who destroyed the world with flood and fire. The name is found in the cluster of letters found at L-6-7-8, K-9, and J-8.

TUPAKA = another name for Virachocha; again the name is written as TUCHAKA, which can be written down as TUPAKA explained previously. The word is found in F-2, E-1, E-3, F-4 G-a, and H-2.

	A	B	C	D	E	F	G	H	I	J	K	L
1												
2						T						
3						A	T	A				
4						A						
5						Ch	A	K				
6												N
7												M
8										N		O
9											A	
10												
11												

Fig. 214 Other South American gods.

INTI= Sun god of the Incas; the name is found in the cluster of letters at E-6, F-5, G-6-7; it can also be found at F-E-15 and C-D-14. The word *INTI* can be transformed into INIT, the Filipino word for "HOT" or "WARM," a trait of the sun.

	A	B	C	D	E	F	G	H	I	J	K	L
1					U							
2						T	K	A				
3					Ch	A						
4												
5						N						
6					I		I					
7							T					
8												

Fig. 215 Tupaka and Inti.

ASIN = semidivine person of the Toba Indians of Paraguay, Argentina, and Chile who survived the great cold that enveloped and destroyed the world. The word starts with the letter *A* on H-15, and going to the left direction, the letters are side by side without ELS.

ILLA/YLLA = God of the Incas; the name is found in A-15-13, B-14, and A-14.

Another ancient people are the Olmecs who are supposed to be older than the Mayans and the source of Mayan knowledge. There is no knowledge about their beginnings. They just came about.

	A	B	C	D	E	F	G	H	I	J	K	L
12												
13	L											
14	A	L		I								
15	Y				N	I	S	A				
16												
17												

Fig. 216 Asin and Ylla.

In figures 217-218 are the ancient people who inhabited the South Americas. Their advanced civilizations that suddenly disappeared have baffled the scientists.

Their knowledge about mathematics, astronomy, and pyramid building was mind-boggling.

There is a temple in Sakkara, Egypt, attributed to a person named MAYA built around 1,300 BC. Maya in ancient Egyptian means "water." Bas-reliefs taken of the Maya in 1987 showed the original paint still evident after 3,300 years. (*The Sirius Mystery* page 86) These bas-reliefs were studied by Mayan scholars and were found to be Mayan in nature. The word *NAGA* came from the ancient Egyptian word *NG* or *NAG* that means "tribe." Naga Maya therefore can mean "Tribe from across the water." Egypt and South America are separated by the Pacific Ocean. Each one can be the "tribe across the water."

c) Ancient Meso-Americans

These ancient people were

MAYA = the ancient people of Mexico and Guatemala who came after
      the Olmecs two thousand years ago.
INCA = ancient people of Peru
AZTEC = ancient people of Mexico
TOLTEK/TULTECH = another ancient people of Mexico

	A	B	C	D	E	F	G	H	I	J	K	L
1												
2												
3						A		A				
4					E	C		Y				
5				TZ		N		A				
6				A	I		I	M				
7												
8			K	E								
9			H	A								
10												
11												

Fig. 217 Maya, Inca, and Aztec.

HAKE = means people

	A	B	C	D	E	F	G	H	I	J	K	L
6												
7							T	L	E	C	E	M
8							U	T			L	O
9												
10												

Fig. 218 Tultec and the Olmec.

OLMECH = an ancient people who started the civilization of Mexico

In figure 219 shows the other natives of South America and the continent Mu or Lemuria:

LEMURIAN = The legendary people living supposed to be in the first civilization on earth called Mu or Lemuria.

MU/MO = The legendary civilization located in the Pacific Ocean extending from Hawaii to the Himalayas, which was supposed to be the first civilization on earth with Atlantis its colony.

CHIBKAS = ancient people of Columbia

	A	B	C	D	E	F	G	H	I	J	K	L
1	A					SH	B					
2		I			I		K					
3	E	M			Ch	A						
4	L		U									
5		R										
6												
7												
8							U					
9						O	M	U				
10							O					

Fig. 219 Lemuria or Mu.

d) Count/Numbers

KIN =   means days; the word starts with the letter *K* at G-2, *I* at E-6, and *N* at C-10 with ELS of forty-five letters.

TUN = 360 days

KATUN = 20 Tuns; the word is found at G-2, F-3-2, E-1, and D-1.

BAKTUN = 20 Katuns; the word is besides "Katun"

	A	B	C	D	E	F	G	H	I	J	K	L
1				N	U		B	A				
2						T	K					
3						A						
4												
5												
6					I							
7												
8						N	U	T				
9												
10			N									
11												
12			U									
13												
14			T									
15												
16												
17												

Fig. 220 Tun: 360 days calendar

e) Why Are South America and Its Ancient Gods in the Grid?

This is a question that is difficult to answer, but it would seem that there are two principal reasons why they are mentioned in the grid:

1. The natives particularly the Mayans were Egyptians who in ancient time came to South America.

2. And the stories of the ancient gods are very similar to Jesus and might lend credibility to the legend that a person similar to Jesus was in South America before the Spaniards came.

When scholars of Mayan culture saw the bas-reliefs of unknown origins, they were very certain that those reliefs were Mayan in nature and could only come from South America. They were very surprised to know that these relieves were taken from a temple in Sakkara, Egypt, which was built in 1,300 BC way before the Mayan civilization was known to exist. The word *MAYA*, which was encircled meant "water" in ancient Egypt. Even the word *NG* or *NAG*, which means "tribe" came from ancient Egypt. Thus, the words *Naga Maya* could mean "tribe from across the water" that could refer to the Egyptians who came from across the water bringing with them the technique of pyramid buildings and the story of Iusa or Horus whose story is similar to Jesus could be the second reason. There is an Egyptian myth that Thoth sent wise men to other parts of the world to civilize mankind. Older Sumerian myths talked about EA the Sumerian god of wisdom who sent seven sages before the flood to different parts of the world to teach mankind the art of civilization. They were in the forms of "fish."[2]

	A	B	C	D	E	F	G	H	I	J	K	L
11												
12		N		G	A	M						
13			A		A							
14				Y								
15												
16												
17												

Fig. 221 Naga Maya

Quetzalcotl and Jesus

A pre-Columbian myth in Mexico described its principal deity Quetzalcotl or Virachocha as one who was fair with long hair and bearded. He wore a long white robe reaching to his feet. He abhorred sacrifices except for fruits and flowers. He was known as the God of Peace. He was worshipped as a savior born of a virgin who was told that she would bear a son without having carnal relation with a

man. His mother was called the Queen of Heaven. Quetzalcotl like Jesus was tempted and fasted for forty days. He was crucified. He descended into hell and rose again from the dead. He was slain for the sins of the world and was coming back to redeem the world. No wonder the natives thought the Spaniards as the returning savior.

Long before Christianity, the natives revered the cross and performed baptism. In existing codices, Quetzalcotl was shown bending under the weight of the cross. He was depicted in the cross with nail holes in his feet and hands. According to Doanne, quoted by Acharya S, the conquistador Cortes remarked,

> The devil had positively taught to the Mexicans the same things which God had taught to Christendom.

Due to the similarities between Jesus and Quetzalcotl, the natives readily accepted the Spaniards as the returning Savior. Due to this belief, the Aztecs did not fight the Spaniards under Pizaro, believing the Spaniards as their gods. This resulted in the unprecedented victory of only 160 Spanish soldiers over an army of eighty-thousand Aztecs killing seven thousand of them. This military victory has never been equaled in history. Thus, the natives were massacred, and their books and temples were destroyed by supposed to be more civilized people. It is unbelievable that even in South America that is very far from the Middle East, Europe, and Asia there is this myth of a savior with all the similarities of the Christian savior Jesus. How could this possibly happen unless there was only one source that could either be Zoroaster, Mithra, Horus, or Krishna? This might have been the time when there was only one civilization, one continent, one language, and one religion, which the deified beings destroyed for the people were becoming like them and might equal or even surpass them. Gods were not supposed to fear men, so why the destruction? Could the story of Jesus and the ancient saviors the story of a highly evolved spiritual man who resisted the deified beings before the destruction of the Tower of Babel? Why is the story so universal and timeless? Why do all races have similar stories? Could there have been just one story that became fragmented after the destruction of the Tower of Babel and the dispersal of the people to different corners of the world? According to the Filipino visionary, there was an original Christ who came from another galaxy and whose story his disciples preached when they landed in different parts of this world in different times.

PART VI

APOCALYPSE

Another fascination of man is about the future and the impending cataclysm we call the Apocalypse or the End Time. Many ancient documents, including the Bible speak about this Apocalypse. Does the Lord's Prayer also contain matters about the Apocalypse?

Chapter VIII

PROPHECIES

For centuries men have been fascinated by apocalyptic revelations more particularly the so called END TIMES and the consequent catastrophic events. This fascination started not only during biblical times, but also even during the times of the Sumerians, Egyptians, Incas, Mayas, and other ancient civilizations. The New Testament and the Apocalypse further encouraged this END TIMES fascination. Due to the depressing End Time messages I did not wish anymore to include these apocalyptic sections as there are already many distressing and horrible events happening in the world today, and according to Jesus[1] future events are only for the gods:

> But of that day and hour knoweth no one, not even the angels of heaven, neither the Son, but the Father only.

However, there will not be a true and faithful decoding of the LP code if only positive matters will be revealed and the negative matters are suppressed. So I scanned the grid and looked for the words saying END TIME or END of DAYS as mentioned by Daniel in the Old Testament. According to Michael Drosnin.[2] to find the words *END of DAYS* in the Bible, the computer had to make forty rows with 7,551 letters each out of the 304,805 letters of the Bible. Is it possible to find said verse "END of DAYS" in a grid composed of only 198 letters? I was surprised to find the following words in the grid.

HAYOM/YOM = day, the day; the word starts at C-9 at row 9 with
the letters side by side without ELS.

KETZ = end; the word crosses Hayom.

Coordinates: K = D-11   E = D-8   Tz = D-5   ELS = 2 letters

	A	B	C	D	E	F	G	H	I	J	K	L
1												
2	Y				I							
3												
4												
5				Tz								
6									K			
7				Tz								
8	H			E								
9			H	A	Y	O	M					
10												
11				K								
12					A				A			
13												

Fig. 222 End of Days/End Time

KTzH = end
Coordinates: K = I-6   Tz = E-7   H = A-8   ELS = 7 letters

YTzA = end; the word crosses over the word *Hayom*.
Coordinates: Y = A-2   Tz = E-7   A = I-12   ELS = 63 letters

ITzA = end; the word cuts across Hayom.
Coordinates: I = E-2   Tz = E-7   A = E-12   ELS = 4 letters

It is amazing to find all these words relating to the word *END*, and as if to emphasize their connections, the words are even crisscrossing each other. The words *Ketz*, *Ytza*, and *Itza* are even crossing the word *Hayom* meaning "Day." As if this is not enough, the grid by permutation shows other words that are also associated with the End Time.

The Egyptian word *NENTI*, which means END TIMES can be permutated as shown in figure 223.

	A	B	C	D	E	F	G	H	I	J	K	L
4												
5						N						
6							I					
7						E	T					
8						N						
9												
10												

Fig. 223 End Times in Egyptian.

In the quadrant composed of A-13-14, B-12-13, and C-13 shown in figure 224 are the letters, which when permutated form the words *NLH* in its defective form and its full form *NALAH* that means "END." It would seem that it was written in its full form so that there would not be any mistake in the interpretation of the defective form and the intention of the writer.

	A	B	C	D	E	F	G	H	I	J	K	L
11												
12		N										
13	L	H	A									
14	A											
15												
16												

Fig. 224 End

Besides this quadrant is another quadrant shown in figure 225 composed of C-14-15-16 and B-15-16-17, containing the letters that can be formed in to the English words *END TIME* to ensure the English-speaking people in getting the message. With the message in different languages how can we possibly miss the message? The interrelationship and proximity of the English, Hebrew, and Egyptian words are uncanny and intriguing. Even the Hebrew words *DIN* and *MET* mean "JUSTICE" and "DEATH."

	A	B	C	D	E	F	G	H	I	J	K	L
13												
14			M									
15		D	E									
16		I	T									
17		N										

Fig. 225 End Time

With the presence of many words relating to END TIMES, maybe it is time to take note.

a) The Number 666

As if the End Time prophecy is not enough, also mentioned is the number of the beast, MSO, MSU, or VSO that means 666, which reminds us of the following:

> Here is wisdom. He that has understanding, let him count the number of the beast; for it is the number of man; and his number is Six hundred and sixty and six.[3]

The words *MSO, MSU,* or *VSO* have the following numeral values:

M =   has a numeral value of either 40 or 600 or 6. As this is a code and the letter *M* is near the letters *O* or *U* and the letter *S*, I feel that the author was using the numeral equivalent of 600 for only by the use of this said numeral correspondence could there be a sense in the lumping together of the letters.

S =   has the numeral value of 60 or 6.

V or O = has a numeral value of 6.

Thus, if the numeral values of the word *MSO, MSV,* or *VSO* are added, the result will be "SIX HUNDRED SIXTY SIX" (666), the mark of the beast.

	A	B	C	D	E	F	G	H	I	J	K	L
1												
2												
3									V	O	M	
4										S	S	
5										M	O	
6												

Fig. 226 Number of the Beast

This verse has been the subject of much debate with diverse conclusions as to who is the beast ranging from Hitler, Stalin, Sadam, Bin Laden, and the Roman Catholic Church. As the verse states the number of the beast is the number of man, what then is the number of man? Man is said to be number 9 as the word *ADM*, which refers to man has a numeral value of 9. Also, esoterically man is number 9 because he is not yet perfect and yet he is only one number away to become a perfect number, which is 10, the number of perfection and of God. One can see the fascinating evolution opened to man. Man can turn from dust to gold, from imperfection to perfection and be a god. He can be a god or a beast that will destroy the world. Right now, he is more a beast destroying his fellowmen, the environment, and the world. Blaming Hitler, Stalin, Sadam, Bin Laden, or the Catholic Church is useless. Let us look at ourselves. We did not care. We did not act. So let it be. We deserve it.

	A	B	C	D	E	F	G	H	I	J	K	L
1												
2												
3									6	6	6	
4										6	6	
5										6	6	
6												
7												
8		6					6					6
9		6				6	6	6	6			
10		6		6				6	6			
11			6						6	6		
12												6
13										6		
14										6		
15												
16												
17												

Fig. 226-a The number 666.

If man is the beast, what is the connection between the number 9 and the number of the beast-666? In this quadrant, the word *MSO* (666) is near the word *ISh* that means "MAN." Without the Kabalah, it would be impossible to relate the number 9 to 666. In the Kabalah, to facilitate early resolutions of problem solving, we reduce the multiple digits to a single digit by adding all the numbers until only one number remains. In the present case, if one adds all the three sixes, one will get the sum of 18, which when added again will sum up to 9. Thus 666 when added is equal to 9 is the number of "MAN," which affirms the saying in Revelation about the number of the beast being the number of man. Who then is the beast? It is MAN who has been responsible for the denudation of the forests, pollution of the seas and the atmosphere, the holocaust and the death of the human race. It is not the devil who has instigated the ruins and destruction of this world but Man. The devil is just the Tempter doing his assigned job, but man is the Sinner, the Doer who is supposed to have a free will and capable of surpassing the angels and become a god!

Maurice Cotterell cited Peter Lorie about another interesting interpretation of the number 666 wherein Lorie said that perhaps the number 666 may not have anything to do with evil for the number 6 is not considered evil in almost all non-Christian religions. Even in the esoteric tradition of the Jews called the Kabbalah, 6 is related to the perfection of numbers—the six days of creation and to the six hierarchies of angels and the planets.

> In the Hebrew Gematria the number 666 does not signify anything particularly evil, but means a MESSIAH—an individual who has a particularly divine message to relate . . . the word apocalypse actually means A PROPHETIC DISCLOSURE, A REVEALING OF THE TRUTH . . . . We might therefore consider the possibility that the apocalyptic animal numbered 666 might actually be human, and one who brings a revelation, A MESSIAH (who could be an anti-Christ, insofar as he would not preach the old word of God but a new word). Thus, our new messiah could be a GOOD messiah and still be an anti-Christ . . . . Of course he will "blaspheme" because he will be against conventional Christianity but still preach the word of God.[4]

This quotation is a very thought-provoking one that needs our attention. It touches many doctrines like the teaching that only the members of one's congregation can be saved. Whose doctrine is this? Is this not the doctrine of an Antichrist, for it espouses division or disunity and not unity or oneness? Did not Jesus tell us not to judge, but to love one another?

b) Events leading to the Apocalypse

There are supposed to be signs that foretell the coming apocalypse. Sometimes we refer to the Bible or Nostradamus to look for these signs. Some of these signs have already happened, but we were unaware of them like the following:

1. Year 2000 U.S. Presidential Election
2. 9-11-2001 Tragedy
3. Wars and Famines
4. Reelection of U.S. President G. Bush
5. Weather changes

1. Year 2000 U.S. Presidential Election

Many will be puzzled why the U.S. Presidential Election of 2000 is included in the events leading to the possible cataclysm of year 2006 that will be a prelude to the Apocalypse. Without the grid, it will be difficult to connect the election to the coming cataclysm. Thus, the election passed by with the people unaware of the important connection it has with the possible global conflict in the year 2006 and the 2012 cataclysm. The importance of the result of the election escaped us, for we did not know if Mr. Bush would win, there would be great dangers in this world. The name of Bush in the grid was surrounded by ominous words relating to danger. Events after his election confirmed the truth of the dangers.

Friends asked me who would win in the election. I told them that based on the grid, it would be Bush. I told them about the dangers surrounding the name of Bush. Even the integrity of the election would be raised because the word *Cheat* appeared in the grid below the name of Bush. Thus during the initial period of President Bush's incumbency, he was confronted with the problem about the

supposed cheating in the presidential election. However, it was his destiny to become president of the United States.

		A	B	C	D	E	F	G	H	I	J	K	L
1						U	Sh	B					
2													
3						Ch	A	T		V			
4						E	Ch	A					
5													B
6			Sh										
7		B											
8			U										
9													
10									O				
11							E	R					
12					G								
13													

Fig. 227 The names of Bush and Gore and the word *Cheat.*

The basis for my saying that Bush would win in the election was the appearance of his name three times in the grid despite there being only three letter Bs in the grid while the letters composing the name Gore, though they could be permutated to form the name, were not in ELS or lumped together in a small quadrant as shown in figure 227. There was only one example of Gore's name while President Bush had three examples, one with ELS. The first example of President Bush's name could be found at G-1, E-1, and F-1; and by permutation, the name Bush is formed. The second example is found at L-5, I-3 and F-1 with ELS of twenty-six letters. The third example is in the quadrant composed of A-7, B-8, and B-6.

Thus based on the grid, Bush would win in the election; however, the incumbency of President Bush is wrought with dangers. The China problem will always be there for him. But what is disturbing is that during his presidency, the possibility of a war or a nuclear incident is present. His name is surrounded by the words *Nuke, Biochem,* and *Attak.* Dangers surround him. Events after his election confirmed these dangers like the 9-11 tragedy and the Iraq war.

There are only three Bs in the grid, yet the name of President Bush is always near the word *NUKE* as if to imply that Bush will be figuring prominently with the question about nuclear weapons or even the possibility of a nuclear incident. The occurrence of a nuclear holocaust can cause untold hardships, immense

destructions, and collapse of the world economies. We hope that this could be prevented. What the United States is doing now by applying more security precautions and fighting terrorism anywhere in the world are steps on the right direction; however, this will also be the time when the United States will be misunderstood not only by its allies but also by many countries in the world more particularly the Muslim countries.

	A	B	C	D	E	F	G	H	I	J	K	L
1					U	Sh	B					
2						T	K	A				
3						A	T	A	V			
4												
5											O	B
6		Sh									I	
7	B									Ch	E	M
8			U	K	E							
9	N	U										
10				N	U	E						
11			N	U	K							
12			N	U								
13												

Fig. 228 Dangers surrounding Bush.

Although it is a welcomed event that Russia has become a part of the NATO and an ally of the United States, the prophecy about the United States and Russia becoming allies to fight China in the future is materializing. Even the present religious conflicts betweens the Jews and the Muslims, the Hindus and the Muslims, the Catholics and the Protestants are coming into place. Even the conflict in Iraq is being turned into a religious conflict between the Christians and the Muslims. The incumbency of President Bush is faced with much conflict. Let us hope for the best.

2. 9-11-2001

The date 9-11-2001 was a very important one for it was the start of the dangerous journed of President Bush's incumbency. It was the date when the United States was shaken by an ignominious suicidal attack on the Trade Center Tower in New York that resulted in the death of thousands of innocent people.

The terrorist attack resulted not only in the destruction of the twin towers and the airplanes used in the attack but the fall of global business. The effect on the world economy was so massive that all countries were affected. Is it possible to find this incident in the grid? To satisfy my curiosity, I searched the grid for the possible clues. Here is my finding:

As there was already so much sorrow and pain because of the terrorist attack, my first impulse was not to search anymore if the painful event was in the grid. But there was this pestering thought that was haunting me as to whether said event could have been prevented, so this section of the September 11, 2001, attack.

	A	B	C	D	E	F	G	H	I	J	K	L
	A	B	C	D	E	F	G	H	I	J	K	L
1			E	N	U	Sh	B					
2			M	Y	I	T	K					
3			E	Y	Ch	A	T					
4			U	T	E	Ch	A					
5				9		5						
6				1	1							
7					9							
8										5		7
9		6		1		7						
10							5	7	6	1		
11												
12												
13						6						
14												
15												
16												
17						1						

Fig. 229 Overview

There is a quadrant shown in figure 229 consisting only of twenty squares composed of columns C-D-E-F-G and rows 1-2-3-4 that are very intriguing as they contain letters that by permutation can provide information as to the tragic event that happened on September 11, 2001. Details about the suicidal attack like the names of the people and places involved are contained in the quadrant. It is uncanny that even the exact date of the occurrence was shown in the grid. Figure 229 shows an overview of the quadrant.

Figure 229-a shows some of the people involved in the tragic event.

BUSH = President of the United States
CHENEY = Vice President of the United States

	A	B	C	D	E	F	G	H	I	J	K	L
1			E	N	U	Sh	B					
2			M	Y		T						
3			E		Ch	A	T					
4					E		A					
5												

Fig. 229-a Bush and Usama.

USAMA = head of the Al Keda terrorist group
ATTA = pilot of one of the planes that slammed one of the Twin Towers
ENEMY = the terrorists

	A	B	C	D	E	F	G	H	I	J	K	L
1					N	U	Sh					
2					Y		T	K				
3							A	T				
4						E		A				
5												

Fig. 229-b Details about the 9-11-2001.

Figure 229-b shows the details about the event on September 11, 2001, the place of the occurrence, the buildings involved, and the planes used in the attack.

NY = New York City
UA = United Airlines
AA = American Airlines
TT = Double *T* referring to the Twin Towers
SHAKE = the towers were shaken by the impact of the airplanes
slamming

Is the actual occurrence of this tragic event mentioned in the grid? If we will search for the date 9-11-2001, we will never find the date. However if we will look for the Hebrew date equivalent to 9-11-2001, we will be surprised that said date has been mentioned thrice in the grid. This is another uncanny occurrence. As we scan the grid, there was something unbelievable that came out of the grid. There at the center of the grid was the date of the incident, 9-11-5761. What has the date 9-11-5761 to do with the date 9-11-2001? Well, the Hebrew year 5761 means the year 2001. Thus 9-11-5761 means September 11, 2001. By substituting the letters with their corresponding numbers, we arrive at this conclusion. The letter *Tz* with a numeral value of 90 or 9 has been used only thrice in the grid, yet two of these letters are strategically positioned near the Hebrew year. The date 9-11 is equivalent to the letters *Tz* (9), *A* (1), and *I* (1) while the year 5761 is equivalent to the letters *N*, *O*, *V*, and *A*. The three examples of the date shown in figure 229-c are mind-boggling.

The month can be found at D-5 and E-7 while the day is at D-6 and E-6 while right at the center of the grid at column F going vertically down is the Hebrew year 5761 with each number having ELS of three letters between them and the other two examples of the Hebrew year.

Examples	Coordinates				ELS
1st	5 = F-5	7 = F-9	6 = F-13	1 = F-17	3 letters
2nd	5 = J-8	7 = L-8	6 = B-9	1 = D-9	1 letter
3nd	5 = G-10	7 = H-10	6 = I-10	1 = J-10	None

It is incredible that three examples can be found in a very small grid. What could be the mathematical ratio of finding such beautiful examples in ELS?

	A	B	C	D	E	F	G	H	I	J	K	L
1			E	N	U	Sh	B					
2			M	Y	I	T	K					
3			E	Y	Ch	A	T					
4			U	T	E	Ch	A					
5				9		5						
6				1	1							
7				9								
8										5		7
9		6		1		7						
10							5	7	6	1		
11												
12												
13						6						
14												
15												
16												
17						1						

Fig. 229-c 9-11-5761 or 9-11-2001

In the quadrant are also the following Hebrew words relevant to the occurrence. Their translations and meanings need no explanation.

AIB = enemies

ISh = man

NI = lament

KSh = knock, shake

AK = calamity

ASh = fire

BK = to weep

ChL = penetrate

	A	B	C	D	E	F	G	H	I	J	K	L
1					N		Sh	B				
2						I	K					
3					Ch	A						
4												

Fig. 229-d Hebrew words relevant to the event.

Also in the quadrant are the following Egyptian words relevant to the event whose translations and meanings are also obvious.

ANU = abode of the dead
TA = burn
TUT = evil beings
ATIU = evil beings

	A	B	C	D	E	F	G	H	I	J	K	L
1				N	U							
2					I	T						
3						A	T					
4							A					

Fig. 229-e Egyptian words relevant to the event.

It is eerie to find all these words lumped together in a small quadrant with the names of the people involved, the planes used, the target, the date. It tells the story of the September 11, 2001, suicidal attack on the Trade Center Tower in New York, which resulted not only in the destruction of the Trade Center but the death of more than three thousand innocent people whose only fault were being there to earn a living. The Trade Center has become the abode of the dead. The terrorists were able to penetrate the security measures employed by the United States. The impact of the planes hitting the towers shook and knocked out the towers. There was so much sorrow and weeping. The incident not only caused the death of people but also the death of relationships and businesses. Many have become widows and orphans. Businesses fell. Many have been devastated physically, emotionally, and financially. The heinous attack did not only affect the United States but the whole world.

3. Wars, Conflicts, and Famines

Luke[5] said,

> Wars and insurrections. These things are bound to happen first, but the end does not follow immediately . . . . Nation will rise against nation and kingdom against kingdom.

These verses are very apt to the situations prevailing in the world today. There is the U.S.-Iraq war, the Israel-Palestine conflict, the Czechen-Russia conflict, the ethnic and racial wars in the African countries, and the Catholics and Protestants conflict in Ireland. There is so much disorder and chaos in the world today. As stated in the Bible, these events would happen, but the end will still follow; thus, these occurrences are just a prelude to the future events that might happen in the years 2006 and 2012.

4. Reelection of U.S. President Bush

I tried very hard to have this book published before the 2004 U.S. presidential election to inform the people about some possible consequences with the reelection of President Bush. But it would seem that the right time for the publication of this book is after the reelection of Bush. As stated previously, the incumbency of the president is surrounded with dangers; thus, his reelection would mean the dangers would persist. We have discussed these dangers with some people who are also in on the study of occult matters.

Like in figure 227 where the names of Bush and Gore were shown, figure 230 shows the names of Bush and Kerry with the name of Kerry written as Kere. With three examples and the name of Bush properly spelled, the only conclusion was that President Bush would be reelected.

	A	B	C	D	E	F	G	H	I	J	K	L
1					U	sh	B					
2												
3			E						v			
4		K										
5		R	E									B
6		Sh										
7	B		R	E								
8			U	K	E							
9												
10												

Fig. 230 The names of Bush and Kere (Kerry).

Fig. 230-a also shows why Bush will be reelected. The Hebrew year 5766 that is year 2006 goes with the name of President Bush. It means that by the

year 2006, Mr. Bush will still be in the White House; however, figures 231 to 233 show that he might be involved in a global conflict.

The reelection of Bush and the victory of the Republican Party in Congress would seem to confirm the destiny of President Bush to lead the United States in a global conflict in the year 2006. President Bush now feels that he has the mandate of the people to pursue his goals against terrorism aggressively and implement the preemption doctrine that he espoused. With the majority of Congress behind him, there will be fewer obstacles to President Bush's programs.

	A	B	C	D	E	F	G	H	I	J	K	L
1						Sh						
2												
3									6V			
4										6		
5											7	B
6		Sh										5
7	B											
8		U6										
9		6										
10		7										
11		5										
12												

Fig. 230-a The name of Bush with the date 5766.

There is a possibility for President Bush to be aggressive and act unilaterally thereby earning the animosity not only of his allies but the Muslim world. President Bush may or may not lead us to another global conflict. This book might just be a reminder to be cautious. It is debatable as to whether a global conflict is good for the world. We know the consequences: the hardships, chaos, and rehabilitations that follow. But this might be the only way for us to learn, a shock treatment to awaken us from our stupidities. Will a new global conflict teach us a lesson?

5. Weather Changes

The year 2004 has reported many changes in the weather condition in the world that can culminate in a precessional reversal that is discussed in the chapter on "End Times."

Luke[6] said,

> There will be great earthquakes, plagues and famines in various places—and in the sky fearful omens and great signs.

All these events are supposed to be a prelude to the cataclysm that will happen in the "End Times," which is supposed to happen on or before the year 2012. Presently, these events are occurring now. There is flood in Texas, fires in California, tornadoes in the Midwest and consecutive hurricanes in Florida, earthquakes in Japan, famines in some countries in Africa. Volcanoes are beginning to erupt. Four thousand miles of glaciers have melted and disappeared due to global warming. Since 1970, four hundred thousand miles of glacier have melted thereby endangering the wildlife in the arctic continent. Chicago experienced the coldest summer since a century ago. An earthquake of 9 magnitude occurred last December 26, 2004, striking twelve countries in Asia and Africa, creating a gigantic tsunami that killed more than 150,000 people, injured more than 500,000 people, and rendered homeless more than five million people. Due to the great destruction, disease and famine now face the survivors. Even the heavens are showing great signs. Due to the solar flares in the sun, the aurora borealis or the northern lights that are generally seen in the Northern Hemisphere are now seen in eleven states of the United States. There will be bigger and more catastrophic disasters in the future culminating in the year 2012. These geographical and weather changes are warnings to us, but they seem not to bother us. Maybe there is really a need for shock treatment for us to awaken from our lethargy.

c) The year 2006

The grid prominently mentions the Hebrew year 5766 or the year 2006 and in fact six examples are given in the grid of the Hebrew year 5766 that is equivalent to year 2006 as shown in figure 231. What is so important about the year 2006?

No. of examples		Coordinates			ELS
1st example	5 = L-6	7 = K-5	6 = J-4	6 = I-3	12 letters
2nd example	5 = B-11	7 = B-10	6 = B-9	6 = B-8	11 letters

Going vertically upward, the letters are on top of one another without ELS.

3rd example	5 = D-8	7 = L-8	6 = H-9	6 = D-10	7 letters
4th example	5 = J-10	7 = J-11	6 = I-11	6 = I-10	none

Going clockwise around a perfect square, the numbers are side by side without ELS.

5th example	5 = K-12	7 = J-11	6 = I-10	6 = I-9	12 letters
6th example	5 = J-16	7 = J-15	6 = J-14	6 = J-13	11 letters

Going vertically upward, the numbers are on top of one another without ELS.

Mr Drosnin[7] found one example of the year in the Bible. He said that the Hebrew year 5766 relates to a possible great earthquake and a nuclear holocaust. The six examples shown in figure 231 with different ELS in a code consisting of only 198 letters compared to the Bible's 304,805 letters is very disturbing, especially if these examples are surrounded by letters/words relating to *Nuke*, a word that was unknown during the time of Jesus.

	A	B	C	D	E	F	G	H	I	J	K	L
2												
3									6			
4										6		
5											7	
6												5
7												
8		6		5-								7-
9		6						6-				
10		7		6-					6	5		
11		5							6	7		
12											5	
13										6		
14										6		
15										7		
16										5		
17												

Fig. 231 Hebrew year 5766 or year 2006.

In figure 231-a are the examples of the year 5776, which are surrounded by the letters connected to NUKE, or NUCLEAR and BIOCHEM.

	A	B	C	D	E	F	G	H	I	J	K	L
1												
2												
3									6			
4										6		
5											O7	B
6											I	5
7				E						Ch	E	M
8		N6	K	E5								7
9	N	U6						6-				
10		7	N	U6	E				6	E5		
11		N5	U	K				R	6	7	L	
12		N	U						A	Ch	N5	
13										U6		
14										6		
15										7		
16										5		
17												

Fig. 231-a The date 5766 with the word *Nuke*.

There are three quadrants shown in figure 231-a, namely: (a) First quadrant composed of columns I to L and rows 3 to 7; (b) Second quadrant composed of columns A to E and rows 7 to 12; and lastly (c) Third quadrant composed of columns H to K and rows 9 to 16. Based on the three quadrants, a nuclear war or incident would seem to be inevitable on year 2006. I hope the world leaders will heed this warning to prevent the destruction of the world.

Starting with the first quadrant shown in figure 232, it shows an unbelievable grouping of words that collectively imply the same effect: chaos, destructions, sufferings, and pains.

Across the quadrant is the name BVSH in small letters, implying that Bush has a connection with the letters/words contained in the quadrant.

	A	B	C	D	E	F	G	H	I	J	K	L
1						sh			Sh	M	A	
2									D	A	Sh	
3									V	O	M	
4									A	S	S	
5									K	M	O	B
6												

Fig. 232 Overview

Hebrew Words:

ADMA = Earth   DM = Blood
MA = Nation, earth   AK = Calamity
SM = Drug, poison   MS = Sufferings: found at K-3-4 and J-5-4

	A	B	C	D	E	F	G	H	I	J	K	L
1										M	A	
2									D	A		
3											M	
4									A	S	S	
5									K	M		
6												

Fig. 232-a Sufferings and pains.

ShO = Destruction; found at K-2 and J-3   ASh = Fire
MSh = Sex   ShD = Demon, devil

In figure 232-b is the Hebrew word *ShD* that means "DEVIL" or "DEMON." Even the English word *MAD* is in the quadrant. What is uncanny is that besides these words are the names of SADAM and OSAMA with the name of BVSH crossing their names and the quadrant shown in figure 232-c. Who is being referred to in this quadrant as Devil or Mad? Even the numbers 666 are in this quadrant as shown in figure 232-c.

		A	B	C	D	E	F	G	H	I	J	K	L
1										Sh	M	A	
2										D	A	Sh	
3											O	M	
4													
5													
6													

Fig. 232-b Destruction, Fire

It is intriguing that in a small quadrant can be found words that relate to SADAM. OSAMA, BVSH, ShD (Demons), SM (drugs), MSh (sex), AK (calamity). ASh (fires) and DM (blood) that can bring ShO (destruction) and MS (sufferings) to a MA (nation) that is happening now.

Drug addiction has become a world problem that has created much miseries, sufferings, and pains to families and communities all over the world. Maybe it is time for us to think and ponder about the destiny of man. Let us save our race and be a ten. This quadrant is a wake-up call for the world. This small quadrant can be compared to a computer diskette that contains much information.

		A	B	C	D	E	F	G	H	I	J	K	L
1							Sh						
2										D	A		
3										V		M	
4										A	S	S	
5												O	B
6													

Fig. 232-c Mad: Sadam, Osama, and Bush.

Figure 232-d shows the possible year and months when those matters discussed will possibly happen. There are four AVs mentioned and written horizontally, diagonally, and vertically at the end of the year 5766. It is obvious that the word *AV*, which means the months from July to August will be involved. Another month mentioned is MAY. If something will happen on year 2006, the possibility is that it will happen during those months mention.

	A	B	C	D	E	F	G	H	I	J	K	L
1												
2								A		A.		
3								A	V6			
4								Y	A	6		
5								A			7	
6								M				5
7												

Fig. 232-d Year and months

The possibility of the use of biochemical and high technological machines are imminent as shown in figure 232-e. What was feared to happen in 2003 because of the Iraq war could happen in 2006.

Who are the possible personalities involved? The quadrant mentions BVSH, CHENEY, SADAM, OSAMA BIN LADEN and AL KEDA, CHINA, and MOSKOV are also mentioned here. Will they be involved?

	A	B	C	D	E	F	G	H	I	J	K	L
4												
5									K	M	O	B
6									K	A	I	N
7									E	Ch	E	M
8								T				
9												

Fig. 232-e Words about Biochem, Moab, Techno, and Machine.

The grid would seem to say that Osama Bin Laden and Sadam Hussein will still be alive by 2006 and will be again the possible enemies of the United States who will be led again by President Bush who would be reelected as president of the United States.

	A	B	C	D	E	F	G	H	I	J	K	L
1												
2									D	A		
3									V6		M	
4									A	S6		E
5									K	M	O7	B
6									K	A		N5
7								L	E	Ch	E	M
8												
9												

Fig. 232-f Are Sadam and Osama still alive in the year 2006?

Although Sadam has already been captured and maybe executed, his loyal faction in Iraq would still be a big factor in the coming conflict. It would seem that presently a peaceful and unified Iraq would be difficult to achieve. If Sadam will be executed for his crimes, it will be difficult to predict what the effect will be to the Iraqis and the Arab world.

Figure 232-g shows the Hebrew year 5766 crossing the names of Bush, Osama, and Sadam as if to say that these personalities are still the ones to be reckoned in that year. However, there is a disturbing word that crosses the names of Bush and Sadam, the Hebrew word *ASN* that means "sudden death." A sudden death can be caused by a heart attack, an accident, or an assassination. If this is so, who will then die suddenly? Maybe this is a warning to President Bush to be careful. "Sudden death" can also mean "sudden downfall" of a regime or administration.

	A	B	C	D	E	F	G	H	I	J	K	L
1						sh						
2									D	A		
3									v6		M	
4									A	S6		
5										M	O7	B
6										A		5
7												
8												
9												

Fig. 232-g Bush, Sadam, Osama, and the word *ASN*.

Here we are faced again with another quadrant containing the same messages of destructions and ruins. I have broken down this quadrant into several illustrations for convenience and easy reference as shown in figure 233 broken down as figures 233-a to 233-f.

	A	B	C	D	E	F	G	H	I	J	K	L
5												
6	A	Sh	M	A	I	Y						
7	B	A	R	E	Tz	E						
8	H	U	K	E	Y	N						
9	N	U	H	A	Y	O						
10	L	O	N	U	E	T						
11	Y	N	U	K	A	Sh	E					
12	Ch	N	U	G	A	M						

Fig. 233 Overview

Hebrew words:

Ash = Fire
AK = Calamity
BH = To be broken, confused
BSh = Troubled mind, to be ashamed
MR = Bitterness, violent
MSh = Sex
HK = To go
HU = Power

NUR = Fiery
RSh = Poverty

BU = Sex
BA = To go
RA = Evil
ARETZ = earth

	A	B	C	D	E	F	G	H	I	J	K	L
5		R										
6	A	Sh	M	A	I							
7	B	A	R	E	Tz							
8	H	U	K	E								
9												
10												

Fig. 233-a Hebrew words

English Words and Names

NUKE	ARM	RUN	BARE
SHAKE	BUSH	GUN	

		A	B	C	D	E	F	G	H	I	J	K	L
5													
6			Sh	M	A								
7		B	A	R	E								
8			U	K	E								
9		N	U										
10				N	U	E							
11			N	U	K								
12			N	U	G								

Fig. 233-b English words: Nuke, Arm, Gu.

International bodies, countries, states, cities that can possibly be involved:

U.S. (Bush)	UK	UE		KOREA (North and South)	UN
IRAK	IRAN	KASHMIR	YEMEN		NEU YORK

Who will be involved in the conflict? The grid says that Bush, China, Irak, Iran, the Arabs, N. Korea, UK, UE, and the UN will be involved. The contention will be about nuclear weapons. Actually this conflict has already started in 2003 with the war in Irak that began because of the fear by the United States of Irak's weapons of mass destructions. There is also the conflict with North Korea about its nuclear program and possibly Iran.

		A	B	C	D	E	F	G	H	I	J	K	L
5													
6		A	Sh		A	I							
7		B	A	R	E								
8			U	K	E								
9		N											
10			O		U	E							
11				U	K								
12		Ch		U									

Fig. 233-c Bush, Irak, Arab, N. Korea, China, UE, and UK.

Figure 233-d shows the year 2003. However, it would seem that this conflict with Irak will go over 5766 or 2006 that might end up in a nuclear incident. There is a profound implication here with the mention of the year 2006. It would mean that Bush would be reelected as U.S. president. His reelection, however, may mean a possible nuclear incident 2006, for that year has been mentioned in the grid five times with the word *Nuke* always nearby. Furthermore, even the Bible code says that the year 2006 will be the year of the nuclear holocaust. In 2006, there will still be the continuing confrontation between Bush and the loyalists of Sadam and Osama.

	A	B	C	D	E	F	G	H	I	J	K	L
5												
6			3		A	I						
7				R	E							
8			6	K	E							
9		5										
10			7		U	E						
11				6	K							
12				5	3							

Fig. 233-d Year 5763: N. Korea, Irak, and UK.

Figure 233-e besides showing the Hebrew year 5763, uncannily mentions the Hebrew year 5766 that is equivalent to the year 2006. We have already shown that the date September 11, 2001, was clearly written in the grid and which resulted in a tragedy. What can this mean? Can it mean a more tragic and catastrophic event?

Figure 233-e shows the possible month that the incident can happen. The month mentioned here is also AV, but this time written three times as AU, which can mean the same as both have the numeral value of seven. It is intriguing that both AV/AU have been mentioned three times.

Again, the grid mentions President Bush with the word *NUKE* written several times near his name. To find the English words *nuke, arm, run, bare,* and *shake* in a Hebrew grid is earth shaking more especially if they are together with the Hebrew words Ash (fire), Nur (fiery), Ak (calamity), and Mr (violence).

	A	B	C	D	E	F	G	H	I	J	K	L
6												
7		A										
8		6U										
9	5	6		A								
10		7		U								
11		5	6									
12			U	3								
13			A									
14												

Fig. 233-e Month and Year

They all convey the same things about fire, conflagration, and chaos. It can only mean that there will be a nuclear war that will cause so much devastation, violence, and shaking, which can make the earth barren causing man to run and go. It also talks about evil, troubled mind, and power, which are the tools that can drive a demented leader to start a nuclear war that will bring devastations, violence, and poverty to this world.

	A	B	C	D	E	F	G	H	I	J	K	L
5												
6		Sh										
7	B			E								
8		U	K	E								
9	N	U										
10			N	U	E							
11		N	U	K								
12		N	U									

Fig. 233-f Bush with the word *Nuke*.

Thus, the possibility of a nuclear attack or nuclear incident including use of chemical weapon is also very imminent. Again BUSH and CHENEY are mentioned, but SADAM is missing and OSAMA is still mentioned. The word

ARAB is, however, stated that could mean a wider conflict due to the involvement of other Muslim countries in the conflict. The city of New York (NY) is mentioned here together with CHINA; however, RUSSIA is missing.

	A	B	C	D	E	F	G	H	I	J	K	L
5												
6		A	Sh	A								
7		B	A	R								
8			U									
9		N										
10												
11		Y	N									
12		Ch	N									
13												

Fig. 234 Bush, Cheney, NY, China, and Arab.

Figure 235 shows the third quadrant containing the examples of the Hebrew year 5766. In the quadrant, we will actually see three examples of the year 5766. Based on the letters surrounding the three examples the following words by permutation can be formed, namely: NUC(H)LEAR, RUSSO, MOSCHOV, U.S., LA, NY, IRAN, IRACH, and CHINA.

	A	B	C	D	E	F	G	H	I	J	K	L
7												
8							U	T	E		L	
9							M	U6	S	L	A	
10							H	O	6V	5E	Th	
11							E	R	6S	7O	L	A
12							A		A	Ch	5N	U
13								Y	N	6U	V	I
14								Y	N	6U		
15									Y	7O		
16									Y	5N		
17												

Fig. 235 Dates and Places involved in 2006.

Again the month AU/AV is mentioned and the zodiac sign LEO, which refers to July is also mentioned. Now we are talking not only of chemical and high technology but also nuclear and neutron weapons that can cause much destruction in the world and can affect the polarities of earth. No wonder in this quadrant the word *SUN* is mentioned in different languages, namely, the Greek *OM*, the Egyptian *HER* and *ON*, the Roman *SOL*, the Jewish *CHO*, and the Filipino word *ARAO*. This possible conflict might affect the orbit of the EARTH, thus affecting the radiation coming from the SUN. We can apply the discussion on the "END TIME" with respect to this figure 235.

Now we are aware why the two U.S. presidential elections are very important for the future of the world. President Bush may or may not lead us into another global conflict, but whatever happens, whether it is painful or not is always for the evolution of mankind. And we hope this time we will learn our lessons. Our ancient ancestors: the Sumerians, Egyptians, the Semites, the Aryans, the Chinese, the Mayans, the Incas, and the Indians did not write about the different worlds and ages for nothing.

	A	B	C	D	E	F	G	H	I	J	K	L
7												
8							U	T	E		L	
9							M	U6	S	L	A	
10							H	O	6V	5E	Th	
11							E	R	6S	7O	L	A
12							A		A	Ch	5N	U
13								Y	N	6U	V	I
14								Y	N	6U		
15								Y	7O			
16								Y	5N			
17												

Fig. 236 The sun in different languages.

The grid has already shown its accuracy in the two U.S. presidential elections, 9-11-2001 incident, Irak crisis, foiled coup d' état and the presidential election in the Philippines. Is this not a time for us to consider the future and change our ways? If not, then maybe it is time to prepare for the worst, and that is the year 2012. The Egyptians and the Mayans said that would be the "END TIMES."

d) End Times

Of all the quadrants conveying present and possible future events, this quadrant is the scariest and horrifying of them all, for it talks about the possible "End Time" due to the probable cataclysm and catastrophes that might happen.

The Hebrew words *YTzA, ITzA, KTzA,* and *KETz* all mean "END" while the word *HAYOM* or *YOM* means "DAY." If these words are put together, the phrase "END OF DAY" in the English language is formed.

As the words "END TIME" or "END OF DAYS" in the Hebrew, the Egyptian and the English languages can be found in the grid as stated in the chapter on Apocalypse, then this subject matter must therefore be discussed.

	A	B	C	D	E	F	G	H	I	J	K	L
1												
2	Y				I							
3												
4												
5				Tz								
6									K			
7					Tz							
8	H			E								
9			H	A	Y	O	M					
10												
11				K								
12				A					A			
13												
14												

Fig. 237 End Time in Hebrew.

Although the previous quadrants are already depressing and disturbing, the present quadrant speaks of more horrible and terrible events. This is a very comprehensive quadrant that talks about diverse matters.

It speaks about evil, ungodliness, uncleanliness, 666, perversion, and greed that can be the beginning and the end of the world. There is a possibility of a religious conflict between the Christians, the Muslims, and the Jews with the Antichrist emerging to lead a global conflict, which will be fought with nuclear bombs, missiles, and chemicals. The United States, Russia, China, and the EU would

also be possibly involved in this global conflict. It would seem that because of these negative acts and vibrations there would be earthquakes, volcanic eruptions, upheaval of the seas, divisions of the mountains, and even tilting of the earth causing melting of the North and South poles; thus bringing another global flood and the return to the Stone Age. The 1957-1958 International Geophysical Year's data showed that thirteen thousand years ago the oceans all over the world rose two hundred feet. No wonder that this quadrant says that men are terrified and there will be much sorrow, pains and devastations, men will move out, run and seek protection. These words were never used in the other quadrants. Another terrifying scenario is the possible return of cannibalism as the survivors after the Noachian flood was said to have resorted to because of the scarcity of food.

The Sun

This quadrant talks about the sun in different ancient languages SOL, OM, ON, HER, CHEMOSH, SHEMESH, ARAO, and CHO, which means "Heavenly Sun," as if to emphasize the importance of the sun and so that the readers will not overlook the message being conveyed. What that message is, I am at a loss. It seems that something will happen to the sun. In our solar system, the most important planet is the sun, for it does not only give us light but supports our very existence like the air we breathe. If something bad will happen to the sun, then it could be the end of the human race. We hope that it is a miracle concerning the sun that will occur as prophesied in the Bible and in Marian apparitions and not a catastrophe.

Figure 238 shows the Egyptian, Sumerian, Latin, Greek, and Hebrew words relating to the sun.

Hebrew words:

ChO = the Heavenly Sun   AR = the light of the Sun

Egyptian words:

SU = sunlight   HER = ancient name of the sun
HERU = the sun   RA = sun god
AMENTU = the sun god

Sumerian words

CHEMOSH = the sun   SHEMESH = the sun
UTU = sun god

	A	B	C	D	E	F	G	H	I	J	K	L
1												
2												
3										O	M	
4						Ch						
5		R			O	N				M	O	
6	A			A								N
7		A	R									M
8				E		N		T				O
9	N		H			O	M	U				Ch
10		O	N					H	O			
11		N					E	R	S	O	L	
12							A	N	A	Ch	N	
13										U		
14									N			
15										O	N	
16					A					N		
17					A	R	A					

Fig. 238 The sun in different languages.

Greek words:

    OM = the sun   ON = the sun

Latin word:

    SOL = the sun

Philippine word:

    ARAU/ARAO = means sun

The Sunspots

There are supposed to be signs that will warn us about the coming cataclysm. One of these is the change in our weather conditions. In the United States, Chicago had the coldest summer since a century ago. There were floods in Texas and fires in California and neighboring states. There are supposed to be signs also in the sky. Recently there was a sunspot that resulted in an aurora borealis seen in Texas. One of the signs that we are supposed to look for is the activity in the surface of

the sun called the sunspots that affects the earth's magnetic field. The sun creates sunspots due to the intense magnetic field it generates, which is twenty thousand times more powerful than earth's magnetic field. When there are more sunspots, the climate is warmer while when there are no sunspots, the climate is colder. The sunspots have a cycle of eleven years. At the start of the cycle, the sunspots appear at the sun's poles, then travel to the equator of the sun and return to the poles at the end of the cycle. The movement of the sunspots across the equator takes twenty-six days while the movement at the poles takes thirty-seven days. At the start of the cycle, the magnetic polarity of the sunspots reverses creating tremendous nuclear explosion equivalent to one hundred billion exploding hydrogen bombs. The Egyptians and the Mayans knew about the cycle and the movements of the sunspots. How they learned these movements when only stat satellites in orbit can see the polar field is a wonder. This knowledge enabled the Egyptians and the Mayans to predict the pending catastrophes in the world.

According to Patrick Geryl and Gino Ratinckx,[1] over the last two million years, earth had encountered ten long and forty short periods of ice ages. The average time of an ice age is around eighty thousand to one hundred thousand years. In the last 330,000 years, Europe has known three warmer periods followed by colder periods lasting for one hundred thousand years. Ten thousand years ago, the warmer period started up to the present. They also said that a gigantic reversal of the sun magnetic field would badly affect the magnetic field of the earth by overcharging it. When this happens, the earth's magnetic field reverses, and the earth will spin in the other direction.

The Zodiac

The sun, planets, and the stars have become very important to the Mayans and the Egyptians because of their sad experiences in the past; thus they kept very detailed records about the positions and movements of the stars and the constellations. Based on their keen observations, they were able to predict the cataclysms and catastrophes that would happen on earth. The zodiac, which are the twelve-star constellations enveloping earth became very important to them. They gave these constellations names and are now known as

> Sagittarius, Capricorn, Aquarius, Pisces. Aries, Taurus, Cancer, Leo, Virgo, Gemini, Libra, and Scorpio

The ancients termed the stay of the sun in each constellation as AGE; thus when the sun is in Leo, it is called the Age of Leo. It is fascinating to see the words *Yuga* and *Age* appearing in the form of a cross in the grid as if it is representing the axis of the world.

	A	B	C	D	E	F	G	H	I	J	K	L
7				E								
8												
9												
10												
11												
12			U	G	A							
13				Y								
14												
15												
16												
17				A								

Fig. 239 The words *Yuga* and *Age*.

Presently, the astronomers and the scientists calculate a zodiacal cycle as 25,920 years for the twelve signs. However, according to Patrick Geryl and Gino Ratinkcx,[2] the ancients knew that the constellations were different in sizes, and they used different periods for an age in each constellation although the result was also 25,920 years.

	A	B	C	D	E	F	G	H	I	J	K	L
1										4		
2												
3												
4												
5												
6												
7												
8											30	
9												
10												
11												
12												
13												
14												
15												2
16						30						4
17												

Fig. 240 Durations of Aries, Taurus, Capricorn, and Sagittarius.

The zodiacal cycle of 25,920 years for the twelve signs is divided into the following:

Leo and Virgo = 2,592 years
Aries, Taurus, Capricorn, and Sagittarius = 2,304 years
Pisces and Aquarius = 2,016 years
Scorpio, Libra, Cancer, and Gemini = 1,872 years

There are three examples of the duration of Pisces and Aquarius, namely:

Number of examples		Coordinates		ELS
1st example	20 = I-5	1 = I-4	6 = I-3	None
2nd example	20 = I 5	1 = I-7	6 = I-9	1 letter
3rd example	20 = I-6	1 = I-8	6 = I-10	1 letter

	A	B	C	D	E	F	G	H	I	J	K	L
1												
2												
3									6			
4									1			
5									20			
6									20			
7									1-			
8									1			
9									6-			
10									6			
11												
12												

Fig. 241 Duration of Pisces and Aquarius = 2,016 years

All the different periods for the constellations are in the grid except the periods for Leo and Virgo of 2592. This period might be missing to affirm the findings of Geryl and Ratinkcx[3] that the complete precessional cycle of 25,920 years is not culminated, for upon reaching 25,776 years, the cycle reverses and directions change with the east becoming the west. This reversal is the basis of the legends and myths about the destructions of civilizations in the world. Based on Egyptian and Mayan writings, this reversal happened on February 21, 21,312 BCand July 27, 9792 BC when Atlantis was supposed to have been destroyed.

According to Mr. Geryl and Ratinkcx, on December 21, 2012, the stars would be in the same positions as they were when the cataclysms happened; thus, there would be a repeat of the cataclysm. Their findings are based on an astronomical computer program.

	A	B	C	D	E	F	G	H	I	J	K	L
7												
8			-2									
9				1.								8
10		-7						7.				
11				2.								
12	-8											
13												-1
14												
15												

Fig. 242 Scorpio, Libra, Cancer, and Gemini = 1,872 years

Due to the importance of the prediction, I searched for the numbers 25,776 as the numbers 25,920 could not be found. I was surprised to find the complete numbers in the center of the grid as if to emphasize its importance. The numbers have ELS of five spaces. The grid would seem to confirm the theory of Geryl and Ratinkcx that the true precession reversal occurs after 25,776 years and not 25,920 years that do not appear in the grid.

	A	B	C	D	E	F	G	H	I	J	K	L
7												
8												
9								6				
10		7						7				
11		5						2				
12												
13												

Fig. 243 The polar reversal happens every 25,776 years.

This discovery encouraged me more to look for the past precession reversals of 21,312 BC and 9,792 BC. Again, it was surprising to find the date 21,312 BC in the grid, but the year 9,792 BC is missing.

The year 21,312 BC is in the middle of the grid with the numbers side by side without ELS and can be read forward and backward. Its location in the center of the grid without ELS would seem to emphasize that it really happened and could have been the most destructive precession reversal and has to be remembered. The nonappearance of the date 9792 BC in the grid does not mean that it did not happen, but that the 21,312 BC is the more important and to be wary about in the year AD 2012. What happened in 21,312 BC can happen again in AD 2012.

	A	B	C	D	E	F	G	H	I	J	K	L
4												
5		2										
6	1	3										
7		1	2									
8												
9												
10												
11					2	1	3	1	2			
12												
13												

Fig. 244 The polar reversal in 21,312 BC.

Precession Reversal

As discussed previously, the sun passes through all the signs of the zodiac and stays in each sign for a period of time. Presently, the sun goes counterclockwise from Sagittarius to Capricorn to Aquarius. When it turns and goes clockwise from Aquarius to Capricorn to Sagittarius, a precession reversal has occurred. Why is the precession reversal very important to us? What happens when it occurs? In all the alleged catastrophes, there is a gigantic reversal of the sun's magnetic field creating super sun flares that will escape the sun. The energy released by one gigantic sun flare is equivalent to one hundred billion exploding hydrogen bombs. Trillion of particles will reach the earth's poles and burn them. There will be movement of the earth crust. Due to the continuous stream of electromagnetism, the earth's magnetic field will be short-circuited and will crash. Without the magnetic protection, the entire atmosphere will be bombarded by the electromagnetic particles everywhere, for there is no magnetic field to direct the incoming particles to the poles. There will be a precessional reversal. Earth will spin the other way. The zodiac is now going the other way based on

earth's rotation. Due to this reversal, unknown electrical forces will be generated everywhere, destroying all electrical equipment, computers, and appliances.

Polar Shifts

The poles will shift, creating strong magnetic fields that will induce currents that can destroy all electronics. This will be a technological disaster. The precession displacement of the earth's crust and magnetic reversals could cause the annihilation of life in this planet. Due to the reversed spin of the earth, everything moves even the North and South poles exchanges positions, the North becomes the South and vice versa. According to Prof. Charles Hapgood,[4] he had evidence to prove that the North Pole had moved to three different places in recent times. By radiocarbon dating, it could be shown that the North Pole was at the Hudson Bay fifty thousand years ago. It is not only the poles that will move but also the earth's crust, triggering the eruptions of all volcanoes, active or dormant. Mountains will disintegrate and new ones will rise. Islands will sink, and new ones will appear. Gigantic tidal waves reaching up to kilometers high caused by the crust movement of the earth and its reversed rotation plus the melting of the polar ice will cover the highest mountains. Climate will change, and the sun will not be seen. All nuclear matters will be destroyed, polluting air and water with radiation. There will be total darkness because of the dust and the volcanic ashes. Life will almost be extinct except for a few survivors. Once the sky clears up, there will be a new earth and a new heaven for the poles and the continents have new locations. This is the basis of the ancient legends about what happened to the sun.

Egyptian and Mayan writings narrated these catastrophes more particularly the latest translation of the Egyptian Book of the Dead by Albert Slosman. It tells about the flight of the royal family of Isis, Nepthys, Horus, and Seth to Egypt before Atlantis (Aha Men Ptah) sank under the sea. It is told that in 10,000 BC, 208 years before the cataclysm, the royal family was warned that on July 27, 9792, BC a cataclysm would occur similar to the February 21, 21312 BC cataclysm due to the same positioning of the stars and the constellations. The new translation mentioned dates and positions of the stars and constellations at the stated time. The new translation seems credible as Geryl and Ratincykx were able to confirm the veracity of the dates and positions of the planets Venus and the sun and the constellations Orion and the Pleiades at the time of the supposed catastrophes by the use of a computerized astronomical program that goes back 100,000 BC. They say that the first cataclysm occurred in 29,808 BC with the first polar reversal. East became west. In 21,312 BC the earth turned seventy-two degrees in the zodiac in half an hour. However, there was no polar reversal. In 9,792 the second polar reversal occurred. The fourth is supposed to happen on December 22, 2012. It happened before, it will happen again. History repeats itself.

Yugas/Ages

Ancient legends all over the world talk about ages or suns. The Mayas counted their ages by the names of the catastrophes that happened when something happened to the orbit of the earth or the rotation of the sun. Thus when there was much flooding, it was called the water sun; and when there were plenty of earthquakes, it was called the earthquake sun. Four suns or ages have already elapsed, the water sun, the earthquake sun, the hurricane sun, and the fire sun. Each sun or age is equivalent to 5,200 years. Five suns are equal to 26,000 years, the equinoctial precession. The present sun is supposed to end on four Ahua eight Kan Kin that means December 23, 2012, preceded by eight years of increasing numbers of bigger and more disastrous calamities. The Mayans are correct in foretelling that the year 2004, which is eight years from 2012, will be full of strange disasters culminating on December 21-22, 2012. Last December 26, 2004, a 9-magnitude earthquake created a widespread tsunami in Southwest Asia killing more than 160,000 people. There will be more cataclysms in the years to come with a possible nuclear incident in 2006.

The Hindu Yuga cycle is equivalent to the zodiacal precession cycle of 2,200 years that if multiplied by the twelve signs of the zodiac is also equivalent to 26,000 years. The modern computation is 25,920 years for the precessional cycle. Geryl and Ratincykx however believe that the actual precessional cycle now is 25,776 years.

Ancient Accounts of Cataclysm

From the Sumerian myth "Erra and Ishum 1" dated 800 BC, the god Marduk said to Ishum:

> A long time ago, when I was angry and rose up from my dwelling and arranged for the Flood;

> I rose up from my dwelling, and the control of heaven and earth was undone.

> The very heavens I made to tremble, the positions of the stars of heaven changed, and I did not return them to their place.[5]

How long ago was the god Marduk referring to? Was it around 10,000 BC? Was it the time when the earth changed its orbit?

The Egyptians have their own version of the changing of the position of the sun. Herodotus was told by the Egyptian priests that the sun had twice risen where it now sets and twice set where it had risen. These could have been the

events on February 21, 21312, BC and July 27, 9792, BC. The year 21,312 BC must have been a very important as it is written in the middle of the grid and can be read back and forth.

In Breasted's *Ancient Records of Egypt* 111, section 18,[6] it was said that Horakhte (Horus), the sun god rose from the west and set in the east.

In other Egyptian documents like the Papyrus Anastasi 1V, Magical Papyrus Harris, and Papyrus Ipuwer, it was said that the Earth was turned upside down resulting in the reversal of the seasons. This event seems to be captured in the painting in the ceiling of the tomb of Senmut, architect to the Egyptian queen Hatshepsut, where the night sky was shown with the constellations and the zodiac in complete reverse order along the Eastern ceilings with time disorientation and the sun failing to rise.[7]

The Buddhists in its sacred book the Visuddi Magga[8] spoke about seven suns or ages that like the Mayas involved catastrophes related to the elements of fire, water, or wind.

The aborigines of North Borneo still believe that the sky was originally low, and that six suns have already shone in the sky before the present sun.

The sacred book of the Muslims, Sura LV of the Koran[9] speaks of the time when there was a Lord of two easts, and of two wests.

The Jewish sacred book, the Talmud stated that seven days before the deluge God changed the order of things with the sun rising in the west and setting in the east. Again this could have a reference to the Egyptian and Mayan writings about the cataclysms. It was also said in another rabbinical source that in the time of Moses, there was confusion in the course of the heavenly bodies.

In the book *Beyond Prophesies and Predictions* Mr. M. Timms[10] said that there was a story in the Finnish epic poem Kalavela saying that there was a time when earth was enveloped by "dreaded shades," and the sun was sometimes out of its orbit. It was also narrated that the sun and the moon were stolen from the sky, and after a period of darkness, two new luminaries came out. The author also talked about the creation myth of the Hopi whereby twin beings were stationed at the North and South poles to keep the earth in orbit, but that after the end of the three worlds, the twins were told to leave and the "world was plunged into chaos" and "rolled over twice," after which a new world was born."

It is intriguing that ancient writings and records of different civilizations located in different parts of the world spoke about the same changing pattern with respect to the course of the Sun. These events must have happened. They could not just have been a myth. These occurrences could be the reason why despite vast distances between them, the ancient civilizations of the world were able to synchronize their calendars from the "360 days" to "365 days."

In the earlier creation myths of the Hebrews, it was related:

In the beginning God created numerous worlds, destroying one after the other as they failed to satisfy Him. All were inhabited by man, a thousand generations of whom He cut off, leaving no record of them.[11]

It is intriguing that this creation myth was not included in Genesis. New studies would seem to confirm that there are older civilizations than what the Bible stated. The story relates to other ancient stories about Yugas, Suns, and Ages related by other civilizations.

Meteors and Hailstorms

The Old Testament[12] narrated that at the command of Joshua, the sun and the moon stood still for an extra day and that Israel's enemies, the Amorites, were killed when great hailstones fell from heaven.

This quadrant also talks about hailstones, meteorites, tektites, comet, axis, and rotation of the earth that Mr. M. Timms[13] describes in his book. He said that scientists have confirmed that every time there was a geomagnetic reversal it was often accompanied by rains of meteorites and tektites that due to its volume slowed down the rotation of the earth and might have affected the orbit of the earth. During the last magnetic polarity reversal, it was learned that at least a quarter of a billion tons of these fragments covered almost a tenth of the earth's surface. He further said,

Accounts of great cataclysms on the Earth almost always appear to have been accompanied by meteor showers and heavy hailstones. This has become generally accepted that major extinctions, like the disappearance of the dinosaurs, correspond to impact of large extraterrestrial bodies on the Earth.

According to ancient writings and the Bible, these catastrophes more particularly involving the sun have happened, will these events happened again like what Isaiah said in the Old Testament.

So, the Lord empties the land and lays it waste; / He turns it upside down scattering its inhabitants.[14]

The earth will burst asunder, / the earth will be shaken apart, / The earth will be convulsed. / The earth will reel like a drunkard / and it will sway like a hut;[15]

The heavens shall be rolled up like a scroll.[16]

Jesus also prophesied in the New Testament about the "last days":

> Immediately after the tribulation of those days ... the sun and the moon will be darkened ... The star shall fall from heaven, and the powers of the heaven shall be shaken.[17]

> And there fell upon men a great hail out of heaven every stone about the weight of a talent.[18]

A talent weights about seventy-five pounds and for sure many will die if the hailstones will hit them.

Despite these worldwide stories by ancient people about the precessional reversal, most of us still believe them as myths. Scientific evidences have shown the movement of the poles, yet we still cannot believe it. However, the recent earthquake and tsunami in southwest Asia have confounded us, for they have moved the big island of Sumatra one hundred yards and the Maldive Islands 120 yards from their original positions. The Strait of Moluccas near Sumatra which was four thousand feet deep is now to shallow for the big ships to navigate. Even the rotation of the earth was affected. The earth has tilted an extra inch.

What Does the Grid Say?

Can we find words in the grid related to what have just been discussed? Yes! The Hebrew and English words shown in figure 245 carry ominous warnings about nuclear war, missile attacks, conflagrations that can affect the heavens and the earth and possible religious conflict that will lead to the "END TIMES."

	A	B	C	D	E	F	G	H	I	J	K	L
5												
6							I	M	K	A	I	N
7							T	L	E	Ch	E	M
8							U	T	E	N	L	O
9							M	U	S	L	A	Ch
10							H	O	V	E	Th	E
11							E	R	S	O	L	A
12							A	N	A	Ch	N	U

Fig. 245 Overview

For convenience and easy reference, figure 246 shows the Hebrew words whose letters are side by side without ELS.

Hebrew Words:

TIL = Missile   ASN = Ruin, destruction
ML = Cut, divide   LM = Protect
AK = Calamity   TM = Unclean
RA = Evil   HM = Greedy

	A	B	C	D	E	F	G	H	I	J	K	L
5												
6							I.	M.	K.	A.		
7							T.	L.		Ch		
8								T.			L	
9							M.				A.	
10							H.		V		Th	
11								R.	S.		L.	
12							A.	N.	A.	Ch		

Fig. 246 Hebrew words.

413

ChTh = terrified   ChL = profane, unholy
ATh = Beginning and the End   HR = Mountain
AN = Pain, sorrow   NUR = fiery   NAR = fiery
MET = death   HU = power   MS = sufferings

By permutation the following Egyptian words can be formed:

HERU = judgment time
MEH = to be submerged
NHR = storm
TUT = evil being

	A	B	C	D	E	F	G	H	I	J	K	L
6												
7							T					
8							U	T				
9							M	U				
10							H	O				
11							E	R				
12								N				

Fig. 247 Egyptian words.

By permutation, we get the following English words:

LASER   ARSON   SEA   TILT
MOVE OVER   HEAVEN   MELT
MOVE OUT   SEEK   LOSS
RAN   ROUT   MEN

Countries and international body that can possibly be involved:

MOSCHV/MOSCOW   CHINA
U.S.   LA   UN   EU   ROME

The words are very obvious in their meanings, are we still bereft of understanding? With scenarios like these, are we still not going to change? Are we not going to stop our insanity? We are supposed to be intelligent beings. Yet why cannot we stop ourselves from destroying our race? Do we really deserve to be saved or maybe we really deserve judgment.

	A	B	C	D	E	F	G	H	I	J	K	L
4												
5												
6							I	M	K	A	I	
7							T	L	E	Ch	E	
8							U	T	E	N	L	
9							M	U	S	L	A	
10							H	O	V	E	Th	
11							E	R	S	O	L	
12							A	N	A	Ch	N	

Fig. 248 English words.

	A	B	C	D	E	F	G	H	I	J	K	L
1										4		
2												
3												
4										6		
5												
6			4									
7										8		
8								4				
9		6										
10								6				
11												
12	8									8		
13												

Fig. 249 Duration of 864 years to pass twelve degrees of the zodiac.

Geryl and Ratinkcx[19] said that there are certain numbers that are very important to the ancient people like the numbers 25,776, 1872 (Fig. 242), 864 (Fig. 249), 432 (Fig. 250), 144, 72, and 36 besides the numbers 12, 24, and 60. Looking over the numbers, they are still important to us, for they relate to occurrences in this world. But what is fascinating is to how the ancients arrive at fantastic astronomical numbers, calculations, and records without the use of calculators, computers, and other highly technological equipment. I searched the grid and found those numbers in beautiful ELS.

	A	B	C	D	E	F	G	H	I	J	K	L
4												
5									2			
6												
7								3				
8			2								3	
9							4					
10												
11				2								
12												
13												
14		3										
15												
16												4
17												

Fig. 250   The number 432 representing 432000 and 4.32 million.

f) Judgment Time

It is the belief among Christians that after the second coming of the Messiah, which will be preceded by calamities and destructions, judgment will be meted out by the Messiah and the good will be separated from the bad. The Bible said:

> And before him shall be gathered all nations; and he shall separate them one from another, as a shepherd divideth his sheep from the goats.
>
> And he shall set the sheep on his right hand, but the goats on the left.[20]

This quadrant is different from the other quadrants in that it talks about spiritual chastisement due to the sins and omissions of men. Figure 251 shows the overview of the quadrant that has been broken down into several illustrations for easy reference.

	A	B	C	D	E	F	G	H	I	J	K	L
10	L	O	N	U	E	T						
11	Y	N	U	K	A	Sh						
12	Ch	N	U	G	A	M						
13	L	H	A	Y	A	V						
14	A	L	T	I	V	I						
15	Y	D	E	Y	N	I	S					
16	I	I	M	H	A	L						
17	I	N	H	A	R	A						

Fig. 251 Overview

There is only one letter *G* in the grid, but the word *GAY* clearly manifests. Even the English words *SIN* and *HELL* are clearly spelled out. This would seem improbable to come out from a Hebrew grid. Does it mean that presently this subject about GAY will be a powerful issue or force in the world? Remember, several years ago, TV programs and movies about the supernatural and UFOs were taboo. But today, they are accepted. Are we now being introduced to this new mode of morality to test our reaction? Nothing exists in this world without a reason. Is this an introduction to other universal laws or future existence prevailing in other solar systems? The Bible is very clear about this issue, but can there be a higher law that transcends this issue like LOVE that does not distinguish genders to express it?

Another intriguing thing is that the two words *SIN* and *HELL* are near the Hebrew words *MET, GY, AL DIN,* and *HARA,* which mean "DEATH," "VALLEY OF DEATH," "HIGH JUSTICE" or "DIVINE JUSTICE," and "EVIL."

	A	B	C	D	E	F	G	H	I	J	K	L
10												
11												
12				G								
13	L		A	Y	A							
14		L										
15			E		N	I	S					
16				H								
17												

Fig. 251-a Gay, Sin, and Hell

By permutation, the words *DEATH* and *DIE* can be formed, and they are besides the Hebrew word *MET*, which means "DEATH." The Latin word *HADES* and the Egyptian words *ANU* and *DUAT*, which mean "ABODE of the DEAD" are grouped together including the words *DEVIL* and the phrase "IH EL DIN" which means "LORD GOD OF JUSTICE."

	A	B	C	D	E	F	G	H	I	J	K	L
10												
11												
12				G								
13				Y								
14	A	L	T									
15		D	E									
16		I	M									
17		N	H	A	R	A						

Fig. 251-b Hebrew words.

Even the other words mentioned in this quadrant relate to fire and burning like the Egyptians words *NULCH, NUKH, TA,* the English words *NUKE* and *HELL* and the Hebrew word *NAR.*

	A	B	C	D	E	F	G	H	I	J	K	L
10					E							
11		N	U	K								
12		N	U	G								
13	L		A	Y	A							
14	A	L	T									
15		D	E		N	I	S					
16		I	M	H	A							
17		N	H	A	R	A						

Fig. 251-c Words about Sin, Gay, Fire, and Hell.

It would seem that a message is being conveyed that because of so much evil in this world caused by ungodliness, wretchedness, perversion, immorality,

and sins, there will be great pains, sorrows, blood, lamentations, destructions, and death in this world. We have never learned from the experiences in the past. Hitler, Lenin, Stalin, and Sadam, the holocaust and Hiroshima would seem not to be enough lessons that what is needed is the Antichrist.

For the believers, it would seem that up there is a divine justice and a hell whatever its meaning is to an individual to compensate for the wrongs, omissions, and sins committed in this world.

Some events mentioned here have already happened like the lahars in the Philippines where people have to run for survival, the ongoing Iraq and United States conflict, the Israel and Palestine bombings. These scary scenarios are mentioned in this quadrant. Maybe by a proper understanding of the Lord's Prayer, these events can be averted and changed into a more positive and fruitful events. The appendix on the "Harnessing the Power of the Lord's Prayer" will show the way to avert the impending cataclysm. The word *GAHAL*, which means "REDEMPTION" is contained in this grid. It can only mean that there is still hope for redemption of the human race. As the word *AMEN* is in the quadrant then, "SO BE IT."

	A	B	C	D	E	F	G	H	I	J	K	L
10					E							
11		N	U	K								
12		N	U									
13	L											
14		L										
15			E									
16				H								
17												

Fig. 251-d Hell and Nuke.

After that discussion, let us locate the Hebrew, Egyptian, and English words in the concerned quadrant.

Figure 251-e shows the Hebrew words.

HT = Perversion   ChL = profane, unholy   LHT = burn
GY = Valley of the Death GAHAL = redemption/redeem
NAR = Fiery   NA = Pain, sorrow

	A	B	C	D	E	F	G	H	I	J	K	L
10												
11												
12	Ch			G								
13		L	H	A	Y							
14		A	L	T								
15												
16												
17												

Fig. 251-e

RA = Evil
HI = Lamentation
DM = Blood

Valley of Death and Redemption.

NI = Lament
DL = Wretched
MET = Death

	A	B	C	D	E	F	G	H	I	J	K	L
10												
11												
12												
13												
14	A	L	T									
15			D	E		N						
16			I	M		A						
17			N	H	A	R	A					

Fig. 251-f Death and End Time.

MA = Specie, nation
AL DIN = Divine Justice
IH EL DIN = Lord God of Justice

ADMA = Earth
HARA = Evil

The Egyptian words are shown in figure 251-g.

NENTI = End of Time
TA = Burn
HERU = judgment time

DUAT = Abode of the Dead
NULCH = to be burnt
NUKH = to be burnt

	A	B	C	D	E	F	G	H	I	J	K	L
10												
11		N	U	K								
12	Ch	N	U									
13		L	H	A								
14				T	I							
15		D	E		N							
16				H								
17					R							

Fig. 251-g Egyptian words.

English Words:

NUKE   GUN   HELL   SIN   GAY   DIE
DEATH   DEVIL   EVIL   AIDS   HARM
HATE   LAHAR   RAN   HALT

	A	B	C	D	E	F	G	H	I	J	K	L
7												
8												
9												
10					E							
11		N	U	K								
12	Ch	N	U	G								
13		L	H	A	Y							
14		L	T	I	V							
15		D	E		N	I	S					
16		I	M	H	A	L						
17				A	R							

Fig. 251-h English words.

Countries and international bodies possibly involved:

INDIA   CHINA   UK   IRAN   UN
MANILA   VIETNAM   MALAYSIA   TAIUAN

	A	B	C	D	E	F	G	H	I	J	K	L
10												
11			U	K								
12	Ch	N	U	G								
13			A		A							
14	A	L	T	I	V							
15		D	E	Y	N	I	S					
16	I	I	M		A	L						
17			N		A	R	A					

Fig. 251-i Countries involved

If we are not bothered by these warnings and still continue with our wayward ways, maybe it is really time for judgment for it has never been the will of our Father that we kill one another and destroy our world.

Positive Effects of End Times

According to Jewish tradition, the earth before the flood was almost level with plenty of valleys, meadows, and hills. There were few mountains, full of trees and vegetations. The light of the sun struck Earth at the center of the equator, thus giving equal light to both sides of the equator. There was perpetual spring. As both sides of the equator received equal energy from the sun, all living matters on earth, the minerals, the vegetables, the animals, and the humans were healthy, strong, and lived longer. There were giants who according to some traditions reached up to sixty feet in height. Thus lions, tigers, and cheetahs were just fleas to them. They could roam the earth from one end to another. Excluding Enoch, the average age according to the Bible was 912 years. The women gave birth after a few days of pregnancy with the babies able to walk after birth like horses. Women gave birth to quadruplet or quintuplets. Ancient Sumerian documents said that the Annunakis gave birth after nine days of pregnancy.

During the supposed End Time, Isaiah (40:1-4) said that the ravines would be raised up, the mountains and hills would be lowered, and the rocky places would become meadows. This will happen due to the movements and clashing of the tectonic plates forming new land mass, continents, seas, and oceans. A new earth will emerge that will be level and fertile like before the flood. There will be a polar shift with the North Pole exchanging position with the South Pole, creating a new magnetic energy and atmosphere. The zodiac will be orbiting in a reverse direction; instead of going from Sagittarius to Capricorn, it will now be Capricorn to Sagittarius. Due to the movement of the tectonic plates and the polar shift, the earth will tilt and like before the flood, the rays of the sun will

strike the Earth at the center of the equator creating perpetual spring. As the Earth will be receiving equal energy, all living matters will become healthier and stronger and live longer. The Earth will have shorter orbit like before when the 360 days calendar was used. There would be peace for hundreds of years, for there are fewer people who are separated by long distance without means of modern transportation. There will be no boundaries for nations ceased to exist. There will be no wars between nations. There will be no more missiles, warplanes, and warships. Hospitals and drugs will cease to exist with people relying on herbal or alternative healings. There will be no toxic foods to cause obesity and other ailments. We will go back to the land and be attuned with Earth and be strong. For a modern man accustomed to easy habits, cars, planes, electronic gadgets, and appliances, this will be a difficult experience. However, this will be the fulfillment of the promised Age of Peace and Love for the survivors have finally learned to exist in harmony not only with others but with Earth.

PART VII

FURTHER EVIDENCE OF A CODE

Another compelling evidence of a code in the Lord's Prayer is the number count involved in the construction of the prayer. It will be very difficult to show another ancient prayer that can resemble the Lord's Prayer in its numerical construction. Only a Kabalist and an expert in numbers could have made this kind of prayer. It is not an ordinary prayer. It is out of this world.

Chapter IX

GEMATRIA/ISOPSEPHY

By numbers the world has been created, so is the Bible written mathematically with hidden numeral valuations, the nonperception of which will leave one ignorant of the esoteric teachings of the Bible. Thus, the Old Testament was written in Hebrew and the New Testament in Greek, for they were the only two languages since ancient times with numeral correspondences for every letter of the alphabet. As numbers are universal in nature and can be understood by all, the Hebrew and the Greek languages are said to be the languages of the God. It is believed that behind the literal words of the Bible is a code that once unlocked would reveal the hidden spiritual meanings of the words.

Kabalists[1] say that the Hebrew Scriptures can be interpreted in four ways, namely,

a) Literal Interpretation (Pshat)
b) Allegorical (Remez)
c) Sermonic (Daush)
d) Secret (Sod)

In this chapter, the method of interpretation that will be used will be the secret or sod method by way of gematria or numbers.

Presently, the science of giving numeral value to a letter, word, verse, or phrase to decipher or reveal hidden meanings or future events is called numerology. To the Hebrews, it is called gematria[2] while to the Greeks, it is known as isopsephy.[3] As each letter has a corresponding numeral value, the word, verse, or phrase formed out of the letters would have also corresponding values. There seem to be interconnection and kinship between letters, words, and phrases having the same numeral values like the words EL and ABBA, which both relate to God. Since they are both equal numerically, they can be interchanged as shown by the following illustration that shows the similarity of the numeral values of the words:

EL = E (1) + L (3) = EL (4)   ABA = A (1) + B (2) + A (1) = ABA (4)
EL (GOD) = 4   ABA (FATHER) = 4   EL = ABA   GOD = FATHER

Words that are equal numerically can be interchanged. Thus, it can be said that EL is GOD and GOD is our FATHER. By this method of gematria, it can be shown the relationship between certain letters, words, or verses to one another. In gematria, that is being used in the cited example the letter *E* has the equivalent value of A or 1. In numerology, *E* has the numeral value of 5.

Whenever we talk about God, we always refer to God as "ONE" or "ALEPH." As God is the origin of everything, we represent God as the first of the alphabet—ALEPH—that has also a numeral correspondence of 1 being the first number of a count and the origin of numbers. Since God is always first, then God is ALEPH and number 1. Thus, God is "One."

Another good example of gematria is the word *HOLY* or *HOLINESS*. Why is it that whenever we use the word *HOLY*, we are always referring to GOD and not to man no matter how saintly? What is in the word *HOLY* that makes us think of GOD? Why are the words *GOD*, *HOLY*, and *ONE* synonymous with one another? By gematria, the Hebrew word *QADASh*, which means "HOLINESS" has a numeral value of 1; thus, HOLINESS and GOD both being ONE are related and interchangeable. Only by gematria can we connect the words mathematically and logically. Based on this assumption, can we relate the Lord's Prayer with the first verse of Genesis and ultimately to God through gematria?

It must be noted that the Hebrew words can be written in two ways. One is called full when every letter, consonant, and vowel of a word is written like in the word *SHEKINAH*. The other way is called defective when a word is written without the vowel(s) like *ShKNH*.

In the Tanak,[4] the Hebrew Bible, the first verse of Genesis is written in its defective form as:

BRASHIT   BRA   ALHIM   AT   H—SHMYM   VATH   H—ARTZ
2-2-1-3-1-4   2-2-1   1-3-5-1-4   1-4   5-3-4-1-4   6-1-4   5-1-2-9

I placed underneath the letters their corresponding numerals that are reduced to their single digits to simplify addition. The sum of the numbers is 82, and when added the result will be 10, which when reduced to a single digit by taking out the 0, it becomes 1. Since the Lord's Prayer is written in full, then I will give every letter its corresponding number.

Since the first verse of Genesis is equivalent to number 1, it therefore relates to God. Will the Lord's Prayer or its verses also sum up to number 1 and therefore relate to God? To find out the answer we will use the different methods of

numerology like modern numerology, Aiq Beker of the Hebrew gematria, and the Greek method called isopsephy.

All the letters as written will be given their corresponding values. By the use of the three methods, will the letters or verses of the Lord's Prayer add up to 1 to show its uniqueness and rarity? Is it truly a prayer to God and without equal in the world? If the Lord's Prayer will pass this test in numerology, then truly this is a remarkable prayer. For only a Kabalist or one not of this world will make a prayer that is based on numerology, gematria, or isopsephy. If the Lord's Prayer will also pass the more difficult Hebrew method of Aiq Beker, then this prayer has no equal in this world. It must have come from outside this world. To pass also the Greek method of isopsephy will already be an impossibility unless this prayer is from a divine source? What prayer can pass three methods—modern numerology, Greek isopsephy, and Hebrew gematria—with three different valuations yet getting the same answer of ONE or GOD? Only the Lord's Prayer passes that test! If it is so then there is no prayer that can equal the Lord's Prayer in the way it was esoterically and exoterically prepared. Since this is only a semblance of the original, what could possibly be the nature of the original version? It is said that the first set of the Ten Commandments was destroyed and replaced by another set of commandments, for the people were not prepared to accept the first set. Could this also be the reason why the original version of the Lord's Prayer in Hebrew is missing? If a semblance of the original could create this kind of book, how much more the original?

a) The Number of the Lord's Prayer

Is the Lord's Prayer really a prayer not from this world? Is there really a secret number code in it? Let us see.

In the square Hebrew script the letter K in $KADASH$ is always written as a Q hence the written word is $QADASH$, but for pronunciation purpose it is spoken of as "KADASH." In this case, I used the letter Q instead of the letter K. The letters will be given the corresponding numeral values based on the combination of Aiq Beker and modern numerology shown in table 6 where the letter E is given the numeral equivalent of number 5.

9	8	7	6	5	4	3	2	1
T	F	Z	V/U	H/E	D	G	B/C	A/I
Ts Tz	P	O	O/S W/X	N	M T/Th	L	K R	J/Y Q

Table 7

For convenience, we have reduced the sum of each word into a single digit. The computation is on the right side of the verses.

Avenu Sh'ba Sh'maiyim	$5 + 5 + 5 = 6$
Yit Qadash Shemeycha	$6 + 9 + 2 = 8$
Tavo Malkutecha	$8 + 6 = 5$
Y' asseh Retzoncha	$6 + 8 = 5$
K'mo Ba-Sh'maiyim	$3 + 8 = 2$
Kain B'Aretz	$9 + 1 = 1$
Et Lechem Hukeynu	$9 + 6 + 3 = 9$
Ten-Lonu Ha-yom	$5 + 2 + 8 = 6$
U'slach Lonu Et Hovetheynu	$5 + 2 + 9 + 7 = 5$
K'Asher Solachnu Gam	$3 + 7 + 8 = 9$
Anachnu L' Ha Yaveynu	$7 + 9 + 7 = 5$
Vi-al Tivi-Aynu	$2 + 3 + 4 = 9$
Li-y 'Dey NisaYon	$5 + 1 + 7 = 4$
Ki Im Hal-Tzeynu	$3 + 5 + 8 = 7$
Min Hara[5]	$1 + 9 = 1$

$$82 = 10 = 1$$

It is unbelievable that the sum total of the Lord's Prayer is also the sum total of the first verse of Genesis, which is 82. They both sum up to 1. Is this coincidence or plain luck? I do not think so. This was a deliberate act by someone whose intelligence is beyond us. With a total of 1, it can be said that not only the letters or the words or verses relate to God but also mathematically, the prayer speaks about the ONE GOD. Even if the making of the Lord's Prayer is done deliberately to sum up to 1, still it will be a difficult prayer to conceive. How much more if this prayer will also pass the Hebrew and Greek methods of numerology? What will be our conclusion?

Now let us go to the more difficult method of Aiq Beker where a letter can be given two interpretations or two numerical valuations. In Aiq Beker, the letters are given the following corresponding numbers:

TET	Ch	Z	V/U/O	H	D	G	B	A/E
9	8	7	6	5	4	3	2	1
Ts	P	Aa/O	S	N	M	L	K	J/I/Y
90	80	70	60	50	40	30	20	10
Tz	P/Ph	N	M	K	T/Th	Sh	R	Q
900	800	700	600	500	400	300	200	100

Table 8

A little explanation is needed with respect to the form of the Hebrew letters when they are written in Latin characters or in the square Hebrew characters and in their pronunciation. When the letters are written in Hebrew characters, there is no problem as to what is the intention of the writer. But when the letter is written in a Latin character, there is a problem as to what is the intent of the writer. An example is the letter *T*. When it is written in its Latin character, it cannot be distinguished as to whether it is a Teth or a Tau unless you are an expert in the Hebrew language. However, if the letter *T* is written in the square Hebrew character, either as Tau (ת) or Teth (ט), even if one is not a Hebrew expert, one will know what number to assign to the letter. Another example is the letter *K*, which is written as a *Q* in the square Hebrew form and which for pronunciation purpose is written as "K." Thus, instead of the letter *K* with a value of 20, I use the letter *Q* with a value of 100; hence the word *KADASH* becomes *QADASH* with a value of 100 or 1. Also in the Latin character, the letter *VAU* can be written as "V", "U", "W" or "O" for pronunciation purpose. However in the square Hebrew script, if it is written as "ו", then one will not make a mistake of writing the letter as AYIN that is sometimes written also as an O. As I am not an expert in the Hebrew language, it is a great help for me if the letter is in the square Hebrew script and not in the Roman form, for I will know the number correspondence of the letter, for the letter *VAU* in Hebrew has the number 6 as its correspondence while the letter AYIN has the number 70 as its correspondence. Although in the word *Avenu* the letter *V* is written as VAU, however in the Hebrew script, it is written as "ב" or a "BETH"; hence it can be given the numeral correspondence of 2. Further, the letter ALEPH is sometimes written as an "E" for pronunciation purposes; however in the square Hebrew form, it is always written as "א" or "ALEPH" hence there is no problem in the giving of the number correspondences for the letter *A* is always given the number 1 as its correspondence number while the letter *E* is given the number 5 as its number correspondence in numerology. Thus, if the letters in the code will be written in the script form of the Hebrew and will be given the values as stated in Aiq Beker with the word *Kadash* written as "Qadash" with the letter *O* as "Ayin" with a value of 70 and the use of the final *N* with a value of 700, and the letter *E* having a value of 1 as it is written as "Aleph" or *A* and with the letter *U* having a value of 6, then the sum of the letters of the Code will be "12,007" or reduced to a single digit is equal to "One". As the Lord's Prayer is written in its full form—I gave every letter its corresponding number.

I placed the results of the computation of each set of verses on the right side and reduced to its single digit.

Avenu Sh'ba Sh'maiyim	
Yitqadash Shemeycha	
Tavo Malkutecha	
Y'asseh Retzoncha	3,502 = 10 = 1
K'mo Ba-Sh'maiyim Kain B'Aretz	
Et Lechem Hukeynu Ten-	6,751 = 19 = 1
Lonu Ha-yom U'slach	7,138 = 19 = 1
Lonu Et Hovetheynu	
K'Asher Solachnu Gam	
Anachnu L'Ha Yaveynu	9,271 = 19 = 1
Vi-al Tivi-Aynu	9,811 = 19 = 1
Li-y 'Dey NisaYon	
Ki Im Hal-Tzeynu Min	11,800 = 10 = 1
Hara[6]	12,007 = 10 = 1

Based on the preceding, it will be noted that the verse beginning with the word *Avenu* (Our Father) to the word *Retzoncha* (Will), which means "Our Father who art in heaven. Holy be your Name. Your kingdom come. Your will" has a total numeral value of 3,502, which if reduced to a single digit is equivalent to 1. Thus, this verse of the Lord's Prayer can be said to relate to the first verse of Genesis and to God since it has the numeral value of 1. Just as the word *QADASH* or *HOLY* has the numeral value of 1, then the said word is also related to the verses quoted. The words *SHMAIYIM* (HEAVEN) and *SHEMEYCHA* (NAME) have also numeral values of 1. Thus, HOLY relates to GOD and to NAME. Thus, GOD is HOLY, and HOLY is His NAME, and He is in HEAVEN. Here we can see the interconnection and interrelation of the different words with one another. This is the beauty of the Kabalah and gematria, which the method of ELS can not equal.

The whole prayer has a numeral value of 12,007 or reduced to a single digit—it is equal to 1. Whether modern or ancient, it has never changed. It is still about the ONE, the GOD of all. This is one prayer that we can say mathematically refers to GOD. I do not think that there is a prayer as long as the Lord's Prayer that has an equivalent mathematical equation. Presently, one may be able to conceive a prayer with such mathematical pattern, but can it be as simple and as beautiful as the Lord's Prayer? As if it is not enough that the total verses will equal to 1, it could be gleaned that there are seven verses in the Lord's Prayer that are equal to 1. Thus, these seven verses can all be said to refer to God as they all have the numeral sum of 1. Even the number of verses relating to number 1 alludes to God as the number 7 refers to spirituality and therefore to God. If the numeral value of the whole Lord's Prayer is 1 and it has seven verses equal to 1, can this be a coincidence and not a deliberate act? By numerology which is a modern method

unknown to the author of the code and by gematria, the author has shown that the Lord's Prayer is not an ordinary prayer compiled from different sources like the Talmud or Osirian prayers but truly a universal prayer that is being prayed maybe not only on earth but all over the universe; thus it is a prayer to a Father not only of the Christians, the Jews, the Muslims, the Hindus, the Buddhists, or the earthlings but by all creations. After this discovery, I am now convinced that the model of the Lord's Prayer used in this book is fairly accurate or similar to the Lord's Prayer in Hebrew that is missing.

After looking over the mathematical composition of the Hebrew version, let us now turn our attention to the Greek version of the Lord's Prayer to see if the verses also equal to 1. It has been alleged that the Greek started the science of gematria or isopsephy, so my interest in finding out if the Greek version has a mathematical computation. The difficulty in deciphering the Greek version of the Lord's Prayer is that the different authors on the book about the Greek New Testament were not uniform in their translation of the original Greek text of the Lord's Prayer. Sometimes one author writes just the Latin form of the letter *O*, which means "Omicron" with a numeral correspondence of 70 when what was in the original text was "Omega," which is also an *O* but with a numeral correspondence of 800. There are other problem areas like the letter *H*, which is sometimes written as an E and the letter EE. However, despite these difficulties, I was very much surprised to find the Greek version shown here with ten verses equal to number 1 while the Hebrew version has only seven verses equal to 1. Remember that the number 10 is a very sacred number, for it is the number of the Creator, the Alpha (1) and Omega (0), the Beginning (1) and the End (0). Thus, one can see the emphasis made when the verses equivalent to 1 are made to sum up to 10 verses. A message is being conveyed to the effect that the Lord's Prayer is heaven-sent and not just an ordinary prayer made by man but an entity we call Jesus, Horus, Krishna, Quetzalcotl, or the ONE. It is overwhelming that the Greek and Hebrew version both total to 1 with different letters and valuation. This is a mathematical wonder that could have been done only by a superintelligent being. It can be said that the Lord's Prayer whether in Hebrew or in Greek is truly a gift from heaven. This is a prayer beyond equal, for the source is beyond equal too.

Pater Hmoon O EN	
Toiw Ouranoiw	2,602 = 10 = 1
Agiasth H Too	3,934 = 19 = 1
To Onoma Sou El The Too	
H Basileia Sou	7,291 = 10 = 1
Genhth H Too To	
Thelhma Sou Oow En	10,468 = 19 = 1

Ouranoo Kai Epi Ghw	
Ton Arton Hmoon Ton	
Epiousion Dow Hmin	
Shmeron Kai A Few	16,390 = 19 = 1
Hmin	16,498 = 28 = 1
Ta Ofeilhmata Hmoon Oow	19,468 = 28 = 1
Kai Hmeiw	
Afhkamen Toiw	
Ofeiletaiw Hmoon Kai	
MH Eisenegkhw	
Hmaw Eiw Peirasmon	23,896 = 28 = 1
Allla Rusai Hmaw	24,265 = 19 = 1
Apo Tou Ponhrou[7]	25,614 = 18 = 9
Ponhrow	25,570 = 19 = 1

The word *Ponhrou*[8] as written in the text ends with the letter *U*, however on page 1,620 of the same book on the glossary of words the word ends with a *W*—Ponhrow. Although phonetically the words *Ponhrou* and *Ponhrow* sound the same; however, mathematically they are not equal as the letter *U* has a value of 400 while *W* has a value of 6. Mathematically therefore, these letters will give different valuations to the words. If the word is spelled as "Ponhrow," then the total of the verses will be 1. With ten verses equaling 1 and the total verses of the prayer equaling 1, will we be still in doubt as to whether this prayer is a code?

The results of the three methods of decoding are so overwhelming that it is difficult to describe. What ancient and modern prayer can equal to uniqueness of this prayer that can pass the three methods of decoding by numbers? It is safe to say that this prayer has no equal in the world, esoterically and exoterically?

In the book *Original Code in the Bible* by author Del Washburn[9] opined that the verses in the Bible have a mathematical ratio. With this in mind, I tried to find out if there is a common denominator in the verses of the Lord's Prayer. As written, the verses are not divisible by any number except by one or itself to produce a whole number without a fraction. However, if the letters will be written in its square Hebrew script and given the corresponding numbers, then the Lord's Prayer is divisible only by 3 but not by 6, 9, or 12, etc. Also, I discovered that if the verses are rearranged and some of the letters of the Hebrew alphabet are used in their final forms like the letter *N* being used in its final form; then we can discover a common denominator which in this case is the number 3. The verses are shown in their reduced sum for convenience. It will be observed that the reduced digits are divisible by the common denominator three. As this is a code one has to find out if the letters are being used in their final forms with their corresponding values or not. Even the letter in the middle of a word like

the letter M can be given the value of a final letter if that is the intention of the author. Hence, one has to truly analyze and study the code.

In the following example, the letter E is substituted by the letter A and therefore has the numeral value of 1. The letter V in AVENU, which is written as a "B" in square Hebrew script is given the numeral value of 2.

Verses	Corresponding Numerals
Avenu Sh'ba Sh'maiyim	$60 + 303 + 411 = 774$
	Divisor = / 3 = 258
Yit Kadash Shemeycha	$420 + 326 + 361 = 1107$
	/3 = 369
Tavo Malkutecha	$413 + 507 = 920$
Y'asseh Retzoncha	$137 + 356 = 493$
	$920 + 493 = 1413$
	/3 = 471
K'mo Ba-Sh'maiyim	$66 + 3 + 411 = 480$
	/3 = 160
Kain B'Aretz	$81 + 294 = 375$
	/3 = 125
Et Lechem Hukeynu	$401 + 80 + 98 = 579$
	/3 = 193
Ten-Lonu Ha-yom	$543 + 62 = 605$
U'slach Lonu Et Hovetheynu	$105 + 92 + 401 + 485 = 1083$
	/3 = 361
K'Asher Solachnu Gam Anachnu	$522 + 161 + 44 + 116 = 843$
	/3 = 281
L'Ha Yaveynu	$36 + 84 = 120$
	/3 = 40
Vi-al Tivi-Aynu	$47 + 493 = 540$
	/3 = 180
Li-y 'Dey Nisayon	$50 + 15 + 187 = 252$
	/3 = 84
Ki Im Hal-Tzeynu	$30 + 50 + 193 = 273$
	/ = 91
Min Hara[10]	$100 + 207 = 307$

$$10,164 / 3 = 3,388$$

If we change the numeral value of O from 6 to 70 as AYIN, then the total is 9,327, which is still divisible by 3.

The Greek version of the Lord's Prayer if it ends with a *U* as discussed previously will have a total of 25,614, which is also divisible by 3.

This will further attest to the intricacy and depth of the making and composition of the Lord's Prayer that an ordinary human could not have conceived. For both the Hebrew and Greek version with different letters and number correspondences to have the same sum total of 1 and divisible both by 3 is unbelievable.

I know this is not the end of this book, for I have stirred up a hornet's nest. But what is important is a step has been taken to awaken the little gods in us.

Chapter X

A SECOND LOOK AT THE GRID

After the apocalyptic messages, let us now look over the grid again as a whole and see if there are other hidden messages we can uncover.

Presently, there is supposed to be an ongoing debate as to the use of the word *Father* in the Lord's Prayer as being sexist and not inclusive as it excluded the Mother. Actually, this is true if we will use the English language. One cannot interpret the word *Father* as "Father-Mother." However, there is no problem and debate in the ancient Hebrew language used by Jesus in addressing the Father as ABBA. Kabalistically, the letter *A* usually represents God or God the Father or Masculine Energy while the letter *B* represents a Container, Daughter, Feminine Energy or Mother. As the holy name IHVH represents (I) Father, (H) Mother, (V) Son, and (H) Daughter so is the word *ABBA*, which means (A) Father, (B) Mother, (B) Daughter, and (A) Son. Thus, in these two holy names the masculine and feminine energies and the four elements are represented. These holy names show the equality of the sexes. They also have profound meanings. A good Father should manifest the tenderness of a Mother, and a good Mother should have the sternness of a Father to have a well-rounded child. The English word *Father* does not contain the feminine energy of *B* while the English word *Mother* does not contain the masculine energy of *A*; thus, the complete separation of the masculine and feminine energies. Maybe it is time to use the word *ABBA*.

As all alphabets start with an *A* and all counts begin with 1, then the Lord's Prayer also starts with the letter *A* for all creations originate from *A*, the Father whose name is ABBA or ABA. Just as the Lord's Prayer begins with an *A*, it also ends with an *A* like ABA. Even HARA or evil ends with an *A*, for everything will go back to its source, the Creator, the Father. God never created anything evil for everything was created for a reason for without evil, duality will not exist. There will be no free will. Evil is just a concept of man. Evil as known by man came with creation, for how can there be duality if everything is good? For creation to manifest, the opposite must exist. The beauty of this world is that spirit and matter are together or good and evil can be together. One has a choice.

The Lord's Prayer also begins with the letter *A* and not with the letter *B* as in the Torah because Jesus has already revealed *A* (God) to the people while during the time of Moses God was still unrevealed to the Jews.

Another reason why the Lord's Prayer begins with the letter *A* and ends with the letter *A* is the name of the Father is ABBA and the name of the Mother is AMA, which both begin and end with the letter *A* as the Father/Mother is the beginning and end of everything. Why are ABBA and AMA one? The reason is that both names have the numerical value of six (6) and therefore interchangeable as they are one.

	A	B	C	D	E	F	G	H	I	J	K	L
1	A	V	E	N	U	Sh	B	A	Sh	M	A	I
2	Y	I	M	Y	I	T	K	A	D	A	Sh	Sh
3	E	M	E	Y	Ch	A	T	A	V	O	M	A
4	L	K	U	T	E	Ch	A	Y	A	S	S	E
5	H	R	E	Tz	O	N	Ch	A	K	M	O	B
6	A	Sh	M	A	I	Y	I	M	K	A	I	N
7	B	A	R	E	Tz	E	T	L	E	Ch	E	M
8	H	U	K	E	Y	N	U	T	E	N	L	O
9	N	U	H	A	Y	O	M	U	S	L	A	Ch
10	L	O	N	U	E	T	H	O	V	E	Th	E
11	Y	N	U	K	A	Sh	E	R	S	O	L	A
12	Ch	N	U	G	A	M	A	N	A	Ch	N	U
13	L	H	A	Y	A	V	E	Y	N	U	V	I
14	A	L	T	I	V	I	A	Y	N	U	L	I
15	Y	D	E	Y	N	I	S	A	Y	O	N	K
16	I	I	M	H	A	L	Tz	E	Y	N	U	M
17	I	N	H	A	R	A						

Fig. 252 The Grid.

Again, the letter "Aleph" is written in the Latin form *A* thirty (30) times to remind us that every day of the month we should be with our Father. The number 30 can also be reduced to 3 to remind us of the Trinity.

The second letter of the code is actually the letter *B* of the Hebrew alphabet but is written in the form of "V" for pronunciation purposes and to signify the "Son" whom the Holy Spirit said, "This is my beloved Son in whom I am well pleased."[1] The letter *V* (the Son) is between the letter *A* (the Father) and the letters *EM* (the Mother) for the Son is the link between the Father and the Mother, the result of the union of the masculine and feminine energies. The letter *V* is a

conjunction in the Hebrew language and the second letter of the code to signify that it links *A* (God) with the rest of the letters or creation.

If the letter *V* will be taken in the context that it is the second letter of the Hebrew alphabet and is written down as *B*, then it signifies that the Lord's Prayer is a blessing to man as the Torah is a blessing to the Jews, for it begins with the letter *B*, which is the initial letter of the word *BERACHAH*, which means "BLESSINGS." The Lord's Prayer is a blessing given by Jesus to man. The letter *B* also represents the feminine entity, the Mother thus the name ABA has a *B* for *A* the Father and *B* the Mother are always conjoined and are one.

The third word is *E* connected to the letter *M* forming the word *EM* that signifies the Mother, the origin of life, the Holy Spirit. The first three letters of the code allude to the Holy Trinity—the Father, the Son, and the Mother or the Holy Spirit. The third person of the Trinity as stated here is not the sexless, neutral entity portrayed by the church as "IT." It is the Trinity shown in other religions of the world—the Father, the Son, and the Mother—not a neutral entity represented by a dove that is actually a feminine symbol.

If we take the letter *E* as is, numerically it is equivalent to number five (5), the number of the Mother as the symbol of justice. Hence, God's justice will be imposed in this world "What you sow, you shall reap."

The letter *E* is also the beginning of the holy name EL, the merciful Father. If we take the letter *E* as an *A*, then it means that *A* the Father and *B* the Mother as AB are conjoined as one God.

Under the letters *A*, *V*, and *E* is the letter *I*. If we will arrange the letters to form the word *IAVE*, this is the pronunciation suggested by some Greek Kabalists to the unpronunciable name of God "IHVH." There is another formation of the same letters in row 13 of the grid.

It is said that truth will set us free. Thus, the word *EMET* meaning "TRUTH" is twice written in proximity to the word *AVE* to emphasize the truth. It is said that EMET binds all opposites for Ameth, or Emet starts with an *A*, which is the first letter of the Hebrew alphabet and ends with a *T*, which is the last letter of the Hebrew alphabet. The beginning and the end, extreme opposites like the Father and the Mother are bound in the word *Ameth/Emet*. And the truth is AVEMET or the Father and the Mother are one, always conjoined with one another for existence to continue. For if creation or birth stops, then there will only be destruction or death. The Father and the Mother are one as EL is in ELHA and ELHA in EL. Where EL is I am. Where I am EL is. Without the Mother, this world will not exist. EM or AM is the Mother of the living from whom life came into being.

The three succeeding letters *N*, *U*, and *Sh* all refer to the Son. The letter *NUN* symbolizes the "Fish" by which Jesus is known, the Fisher of Men. *U* or *V* is the letter in the holy name IHVH, which refers to the Son, the result of

the union of *I*, the Father and *H*, the Mother. The letter *SH* is the fire of God that is attributed to the Son or Jesus that is the reason why the name of Jesus is IHShVH or YEHOSHUAH.

The letters *B* and *A* still refer to the Father/Mother, but this time the letter *B* is ahead of *A* for the next four letters relate to the four elements, which are ruled by the Mother.

The letters *Sh*, *M*, *A*, and *I* refer to the elements of FIRE, WATER, EARTH, and AIR, which are the basic elements for the existence of life in this world. Alternatively, the letter *SH* refers to the Daughter, Shekinah or to the Son, for he is the "Shin" or fire of the Father, while the letter *M* refers to "Matronit" the Mother or Mary, the mother of Jesus. And lastly, the letter *A* refers to the names of the Father and Mother ABA and AMA while the letter *I* refers to Iesus, the Son of the Father and to Yod the "Power."

The letters *Y*, *I*, *M*, *Y*, and *I* mean that powers in whatever forms whether *Y* or *I* on the right or left of *M*, the Mother should be balanced and not be used to oppress or suppress others.

The letter *T* refers to the Torah, and like Jesus let us learn the Torah, for it is a blessing. And that is the reason why it is mentioned seven (7) times in the code, for it teaches spirituality, which should not be practiced only on the Sabbath but seven times a week. As King David said in Psalm 119, "Seven times a day, I have praised you."[2]

The word *KADASH* means "HOLY," which should be our aim for the Father is holy.

The name AEShHU, a variant of Yeshu is at the center of the grid, for Jesus is the center of our existence. The name AEShHU is resting on AMA and AVE, for the Mother and the Father have glorified the Son AEShHU as the Son has glorified the Mother and the Father.

"Chi" meaning life has been repeatedly written three times without ELS to emphasize that man should look at "life" tridimensionally: (a) as he lives "life" physically, (b) as he aims for "life" spiritually, and (c) as he dies for "life" in the name of God.

The word *TZ* refers to righteousness that should be part of our lives.

The word *Devil* starts with the letter *D*, which is in the middle of the word *KADASH* meaning "HOLY" for without the Devil or Temptation, one cannot become holy. Temptation is needed for man to evolve. *D* can also mean "Devotion," which is needed to overcome temptation. The letter *D* is written in the grid two (2) times because the number 2 symbolizes conflict and controversy, which we should avoid.

The letter *K* is the beginning of the word *Kadash* meaning "Holy." It has been written seven times to emphasize the spiritual message being conveyed. "As the Father is Holy, shall we be Holy."

Seven times have the word *ChN*, which means "Immaculate," been written to emphasize that holiness is our spiritual goal.

The letter *CH*, which is the initial letter of Christos meaning the Anointed or the Messiach has been written seven (7) times to emphasize the spirituality required by the Messiah.

The letter *T* the symbol of the cross in Hebrew has been written seven times for us to remember that we should carry the cross of love like Jesus.

The letter *R*, which is the initial letter of the word *REDEEMER* is written four (4) times to show that Christ will not only redeem one corner of the world or the Christians, but the four corners of the world or the whole humanity. Resh in Hebrew means the "Heaven," which is our home.

The letter *M* which is the initial letter of the names MATRONIT, MIRIAM, or MARY is written twelve (12) times to show that the Mother is not only the mother of the twelve (12) tribes of Israel but of all humanity. The letter *M* also refers to the MESSIAH, the Redeemer of the World.

The letter *H* which is the initial letter of HEAVEN or HOLY is written seven times to show the seven words and the seven heavens described by the Talmud and for us to become holy. *H* can also refer to "HELL."

Before I was hoping that the letters of the code will fill up all the rows of the grid, however the seventeneth row has six (6) vacant spots after the word *HARA*, which means "EVIL or DARKNESS," and then I realized that this is the world of duality and after HARA or DARKNESS, there is LIGHT; thus, the six vacant spots which can also mean the six days of creation and on the seventh day, God rested.

CHAPTER XI

AUTHOR OF THE LORD'S PRAYER

Now we come to the point when we have to ascertain as to whether somebody really prepared this code, or is this just a fantasy. If indeed there is a code in the Lord's Prayer, who is the very erudite author of this code? Based on what we have read and seen in the illustrations, it would seem remote that the code was just a coincidence, and it was not intended by the author. One way or another, the name of the author must appear in this code like an artist who signs his painting. Figure 253 shows the name LUKE written diagonally and which in the Hebrew alphabet would seem improbable to appear as the name LUKE is in English.

	A	B	C	D	E	F	G	H	I	J	K	L
5												
6			M									
7			R	E								
8			K									
9		U										
10	L											
11												
12												

Fig. 253 Luke and Mark

According to Biblical scholars, the Gospel of Luke is based on the Gospel of Mark considered the earliest Gospel. If we will find the name of Mark in this code, it will be amazing. To find it very close to Luke's name will be intriguing. To find it sharing a common letter with Luke's name will be fantastic. Further, it would imply two things: (a) confirmation that Luke

based his account on the Gospel of Mark and (b) Luke was a very honest man who acknowledged the source of his Gospel. The letters *MRK* vertically rest on the name of LUKE, which is written diagonally. Both names share the letter *K*. The proximity of the names and the use of even a common letter for the names will show that this is not a coincidence. If therefore Luke is the author of this code, then he is a Kabalist and a Baal Shem Tov, a master of the holy names of God.

I was very sure that Luke was the author of this code until those matters about Egypt, Sumer, and the other ancient civilizations came up; and doubt crept into my mind as to the real author of the code, for the secrets unraveled in said matters pointed to a person whose knowledge and wisdom transcended human capabilities, and this could only be Jesus, the real author of this code. This might be the reason why Cayce in his readings about the Sphinx and the Pyramids always refer to Jesus, for Cayce saw in his visions about Jesus secret knowledge of the Sphinx and the Pyramids. This referral to Jesus by Cayce has always been a mystery, and maybe this code can lend a hand in solving that mystery.

Maybe the names of Mark and Luke are in the grid because they were supposed to be the Evangelists who wrote down the Gospels. And here another question surfaced. If Mark's Gospel was the earliest account of Jesus, why was there no mention of the Lord's Prayer in said Gospel? Does it mean that Mark did not know about the prayer or nobody has told him about it? Could the Lord's Prayer just be an addition to the account of Luke and Matthew? If Luke and Matthew's Gospels are based on Mark's account, where did they get the Lord's Prayer? Who caused the inclusion of the Lord's Prayer in the Gospels? Even Paul in all his writings never mentioned the Lord's Prayer and he was even quoted in Roman 8:26[3] to have said that the early Christians did not even know how to pray. It was even alleged that Luke and Paul were companions during that time. Luke could not have just copied his version of the Lord's Prayer from Matthew, for they were very different in format and style. Where did the Lord's Prayer come from? Even the Gospel of St. John never mentioned the Lord's Prayer, but actually quoted another prayer said by Jesus for the apostles. It would be unthinkable that Mark, John, and Paul would not write about the Lord's Prayer if they knew that Jesus taught this prayer to the apostles more particularly John, the Beloved Apostle. There are some Hebrew prayers to God as a Father, but they are very different in format. Who then is the author of the Lord's Prayer? Furthermore, there are evidences to show that the Gospels were written not by the purported disciples but people who were there to protect the interest of the church and that these supposed

gospels were nonexistent during the first two hundred years AD hence the conflicting versions of the gospels.

Another very controversial finding related to the authorship of the Lord's Prayer is the conclusion made by many Bible scholars that Jesus was only a myth and never actually existed. Many well-researched books like *The Jesus Mysteries* by T. Frank and P. Gandy and the book *The Christ Conspiracy* by Acharya S have presented arguments and evidences questioning the historical existence of Jesus, which are very difficult to refute. If it is true that Jesus is only a myth and did not actually exist, who placed the Lord's Prayer in Luke's and Matthew's accounts? Who is then the author of the Lord's Prayer and the code? Even John and Paul as earlier mentioned did not know the Lord's Prayer. Even the Gnostics did not write nor mention the Lord's Prayer in all their writings. We will end up in a position similar to the question about who built the pyramids.

It is intriguing to find two quadrants whose letters when permutated form the same phrase but in two different languages—Hebrew and English. Figure 254 shows the quadrant composed of A-7-8, B-6, C-6-7-8, and D-6. From the letters, the following Hebrew words can be permutated:

ShMA = Listen   ShM = Name   MKHBR = Author

	A	B	C	D	E	F	G	H	I	J	K	L
4												
5												
6		Sh	M	A								
7	B		R									
8	H		K									
9												

Fig. 254 ShMA ShM Mkhbr

These words can be formed into a phrase "ShMA ShM MKHBR" meaning "Listen: The Name of the Author."

	A	B	C	D	E	F	G	H	I	J	K	L
4			U	T								
5	H	R	E		O							
6			M	A								
7		A		E								
8												
9	N											

Fig. 255 Name/Author

Figure 255 shows the quadrant composed of A-5-9, B-5-7, C-4-5-6, D-6-7, and E-5 whose letters can be permutated to form the English words *NAME* and *AUTHOR*.

The other quadrant composed of F-9-12, G-10-11-12, and H-9-10-11-12 shown in figure 256 contains also letters that can be permutated to form the words *NAME* and *AUTHOR*.

	A	B	C	D	E	F	G	H	I	J	K	L
8												
9						T		U				
10							H	O				
11							E	R				
12						M	A	N				

Fig. 256 Name/Author

Figure 257 shows the Hebrew words *ShMA ShM MKHBR*, which means "Listen: the Name of the Author."

.	A	B	C	D	E	F	G	H	I	J	K	L
7												
8												
9												
10							H					
11				K		Sh		R				
12						M	A					
13						V						

Fig. 257 Shma Shm Mkhvr

The figures 254 to 257 would seem to imply that the name of the author of the Lord's Prayer is in the grid. However, looking over the grid, there are many names of ancient saviors mentioned. I divided these names into two groups. The first group contains the names of ancient saviors that are within the two quadrants and would seem to have a connection to the author of the code. The other group contains the names of other ancient saviors but outside the two quadrants.

a) Presence of Ancient Saviors

During our search for the name of Jesus in the grid, we encountered many names of ancient saviors that puzzled me. Although, we found many names of Jesus even in different languages, yet there still persisted the feeling to look deeper into the authorship of the Lord's Prayer due to the cluster of names surrounding the words found in the center of the grid. These names were not ordinary names, for they were the names of ancient saviors who had come into this world thousands or hundreds of years before Jesus. Why does the grid enumerate their names is the big question. Could it be that these ancient saviors were connected to the author of the Lord's Prayer?

There are four ancient saviors whose many similarities with Jesus have raised questions about the existence of Jesus. They existed thousands of years before Jesus, yet they have so many similarities with Jesus that it would seem that the story of Jesus was just a compilation of their different stories into one. These ancient saviors were Horus, Krishna, Mithra, and Zoraoster.

Let us discuss the name HORUS as a start. The similarities between Horus and Jesus have been discussed in the chapter "Why Egypt is in the Grid?"

At the left side of figure 258 is a beautiful pattern composed of C-9, D-8, C-7, and B-8 forming the word *HERU*, the ancient name of Horus. Another example is found in the quadrant composed of A-5, C-5, B-5, and C-4 forming again the word *HERU*. The last example is found in the quadrant composed of G-10, H-10, H-11, H-9, and I-9 or I-11 forming the word *HORUS*.

	A	B	C	D	E	F	G	H	I	J	K	L
3												
4			U									
5	H	R	E									
6												
7			R									
8		U		E								
9			H					U	S			
10							H	O				
11							E	R	S			
12												

Fig. 258 Horus or Heru

HERU/HORUS = the Son of Osiris and Isis who was also called IUSA
who preceded Jesus by thousands of year.

It is uncanny that Horus was also called IUSA, which is a variant of ISSA or ISHUA. If Jesus is a myth that is supposed to be based on the story of Horus, then could Horus be the author of the code? As I am a Catholic, I was hoping that Jesus would be the author of the Lord's Prayer, but it seemed that evidences at hand showed that the author of the code was more ancient than the person called Jesus. If, however, we believe that Jesus existed, could it be possible that Jesus actually taught a code in the guise of a prayer only to a few apostles, for it is said that Jesus taught the apostles differently according to their spiritual evolutions? The vast reservoir of knowledge revealed by the code is mind-boggling and could not have been conceived by any ordinary mortal. Maybe if the whole grid is permutated and decoded, greater things maybe revealed. Be that as it may, whether Jesus existed or not, what is important is the legacy left behind—the Lord's Prayer that teaches us to love one another. The Lord's Prayer is not just a prayer for the Christians but for all, for it was never said "Father of the Christians but our Father, the Father of all."

Another story that is unsettling to the Christians is the five thousand years old story of the Hindu Savior KRISHNA/CHRISNA/CHRISNU known also as JESEUS who preceded Jesus by thousands of years. His story is said to be the basis of the Jesus myth and from whose name the word *Christ* supposedly emanated.

	1	2	3	4	5	6	7	8	9	10	11	12
4												
5												
6		Sh										
7		A-	R-									
8		U-	K-									
9	N-											
10												
11								R-	S-			
12								N-	A-	Ch		
13									N-	U-		
14												

Fig. 259 Krishna

It is alleged that the Gospel of Marcion was based on the story of Krishna that Apollonius brought from his journey to India. It was for this reason that the Gospel of Marcion did not contain anything Jewish and was neutral about the origin of Jesus. The similarities between Jesus and Khrisna were so many that the Hindus rejected the offer of conversion by the Christian missionaries. For the Hindus, it was just a case of just changing the name of the savior. Even the infancy stories of Jesus were based on the child Khrisna. Thus they were not included in the New Testament. In the book *The World's Sixteen Crucified Saviors* by Kinsey Graves gave 346 similarities between Krishna and Jesus. With that many similarities between Krishna and Jesus, it is no wonder that scholars conclude that the story of Jesus is the old story of Krishna. Some of the similarities between KRISHNA or JESEUS and JESUS according to Acharya S. are the following:

1. Chrisna was born of a virgin on December 25.
2. His father was a carpenter who went to pay his tax when he was born.
3. A star in the east signaled the birth of Krishna, attended by angels and shepherd, at which time he was presented with spices.
4. The heavenly hosts danced and sang at his birth.
5. A tyrant who ordered the slaughter of thousand of infants persecuted Krishna.

6. A woman whom he healed anointed Krishna on the head with oil.

7. He is depicted as having his foot on the head of the serpent.

8. He worked miracles and wonders, raising the dead and healing lepers, the deaf, and the blind.

9. Krishna used parables to teach the people about charity and love, and he "lived poor and he loved the poor."

10. He castigated the clergy, charging them with "ambition and hypocrisy. Tradition says he fell victim to their vengeance."

11. Krishna's beloved disciple was Arjuna or Ar-jouan (John).

12. He was transfigured in front of his disciples.

13. He gave his disciples the ability to work miracles.

14. His path was "strewn with branches."

15. In some traditions he died on a tree or was crucified between two thieves.

16. Krishna was killed around the age of thirty, and the sun darkened at his death.

17. He rose from the dead and ascended to heaven "in the sight of all men."

18. He was depicted on a cross with nail holes in his feet, as well as having a heart emblem on his clothing.

19. Krishna is the "lion of the tribe of Saki."

20. He was called the Shepherd God and considered the Redeemer, Firstborn, Sin-Bearer, Liberator, and Universal Word.

21. He was deemed the Son of God and our Lord and Saviour, who came to earth to die for man's salvation.

22. He was the second person of the Trinity.

23. His disciples purportedly bestowed upon him the title Jezeus, or Jeseus meaning "pure essence."

24. Krishna is to return to judge the dead, riding on a white horse, and to do battle with the Prince of Evil, who will desolate the earth.

It is said that the Phoenicians brought the story of Krishna to Europe around 800 BCE. It was reintroduced by Alexander the Great, and about AD 38-40, Apolonius of Tyana carried a copy of the Krishna story and translated it into Samaritan with changes in the story according to his philosophy. After he died, Marcion, another Samaritan found the story and copied it and made changes according to his understanding. In AD 130 while in Rome, he translated it to Greek and Latin that became the basis of his Gospel of the Lord, which in turn became the basis of Mark and Luke Gospels. From this sequence emerged the story of Jesus.

Another compelling story that is very similar to the story of Jesus is that of Mithra.

MITHRA = He is a very ancient god known in Persia and India predating Jesus by thousands of years. During the early Christian era, Mithraism was the most popular and widely spread pagan religion. The Christians took advantage of the similarities between Jesus and Mithra in converting people to Christianity.

1. Mithra was born of a virgin on December 25 in a cave, and shepherds bearing gifts attended his birth.
2. He was considered a great traveling teacher and master.
3. He had twelve companions or disciples.
4. Mithra's followers were promised immortality.
5. He performed miracles.
6. As the Great Bull of the Sun, Mithra sacrificed himself for world peace.

	A	B	C	D	E	F	G	H	I	J	K	L
3												
4				T								
5	H	R										
6	A		M	A								
7		A	R									
8								T				
9							M					
10							H					
11								R				
12							A		A			
13												
14			T	I								
15												
16			M	H	A							
17					R							

Fig. 260 Mithra, Mitra, or Mtra

7. He was buried in a tomb and after three days rose again.
8. His resurrection was celebrated every year.

9. He was called the Good Shepherd and identified with both the Lamb and the Lion.
10. He was considered the Way, the Truth, and the Light and the Logos, Redeemer, Saviour, and Messiah.
11. His sacred day was Sunday, the Lord's Day, hundreds of years before the appearance of Christ.
12. Mithra had his principal festival on what was later to become Easter.
13. His religion had a Eucharist or Lord's Supper at which Mithra said, "He who shall not eat of my body nor drink of my blood so that he may be one with me and I with him, shall not be saved."
14. "His annual sacrifice is the Passover of the Magi, a symbolical atonement or pledge of moral and physical regeneration."

In figure 261 is the name S(Z)ARATHUSTRA/S(Z)OROASTER, founder of the Persian religion, which is alleged to be ten thousand years old. By permutation, the name can be found. It starts with the letter Z at D-5, E-5, B-5, C-4, D-6, A-6, D-4, E-4, and C-7. The similarities between Zoroaster and Jesus are discussed in the chapter on "Sumer and Egypt."

	A	B	C	D	E	F	G	H	I	J	K	L
3												
4			U	T	E							
5		R		Tz	O							
6		Sh		A								
7			R									
8												

Fig. 261 Zoroaster

The saying of John the Baptist that after him would come one who would baptize with fire, and the Holy Spirit came directly from the teaching of Zoroaster. Most of the Christian doctrines like heaven and hell, baptism by fire, Messiah, last judgment, good and evil, angels and demons, paradise, apocalypse, prophesy, Armageddon, and the defeat of Satan came from Zoroaster.

HESUS = Another ancient savior who existed before the time of Jesus and was worshipped by the Celtics and the Gaelics around 834 BC. The Filipinos call Jesus as Hesus.

	A	B	C	D	E	F	G	H	I	J	K	L
8												
9								U	S			
10							H					
11							E		S			
12												

Fig. 262 Hesus

HERMES = Egyptian and Greek god born of the virgin Maia and called the Logos because he was the Messenger or Logos of the heavenly Father Zeus. It is said that Hermes was actually Thoth, the Egyptian god of wisdom.

	A	B	C	D	E	F	G	H	I	J	K	L
7												
8												
9												
10							H					
11							E	R	S			
12						M						
13												

Fig. 263 Hermes

MOSES = the Israelite Patriarch who brought the Hebrews out of Egypt and instilled in them the monotheistic idea of a one God.

	A	B	C	D	E	F	G	H	I	J	K	L
O												
9							M		S			
10							O					
11							E		S			
12												
13												

Fig. 264 Moses

AEShHU = the unknown entity whose mysterious name appears in a beautiful pattern in the middle of the grid.

	A	B	C	D	E	F	G	H	I	J	K	L
8												
9				A				U				
10					E		H					
11						Sh						
12						M						
13												
14												

Fig. 265 Aeshhu

b) Names of Other Ancient Saviors

Other names of ancient saviors in the grid with similarities to Jesus are as follows:

GAUTAMA (BUDDHA) = Another Savior of the ancient world who predated Jesus by five hundred years. Most of the Christian tenets like brotherhood of men, the virtue of charity, and turning the other cheek are basic Buddhism tenets. A number of Jesus's parables were taken from Buddhism most specially the parable of the prodigal son. Again, the similarities of Jesus and Buddha are astonishing.

1. Buddha was born of the virgin Maya and a Star of Announcement; wise men and angels singing heavenly song attended his birth.
2. At his birth, he was pronounced ruler of the world and presented with "costly jewels and precious substances."
3. A king "who was advised to destroy the child, as he was liable to overthrow him" threatened to kill him.
4. Buddha was of royal lineage.
5. He crushed a serpent's head (as was traditionally said of Jesus) and was tempted by Mara, the Evil One, when fasting.
6. He performed miracles and wonders, healed the sick, fed five hundred men from a "small basket of cakes," and walked on water.
7. Buddha abolished idolatry was a "sower of the word" and preached "the establishment of a kingdom of righteousness."
8. His followers were obliged to take vows of poverty and to renounce the world.

9. He was transfigured on a mount when it was said that his face "shone as the brightness of the sun and moon."
10. Buddha ascended bodily to Nirvana or "heaven."
11. He was called Lord, Master, the Light of the World, God of Gods, Father of the World, Almighty and All-knowing Ruler, Redeemer of All, Holy One, Author of Happiness, Possessor of All, the Omnipotent, the Supreme Being, and the Eternal One.

		1	2	3	4	5	6	7	8	9	10	11	12
10													
11													
12			U	G	A	M							
13			A		A								
14			T										
15													
16													
17													

Fig. 266 Gautama

As we go over the similarities of Jesus with the other saviors, we cannot help but feel how the stories were knitted into one. Still there are other stories of other saviors that have to be told.

		A	B	C	D	E	F	G	H	I	J	K	L
4													
5									A				
6								I					
7								T					
8									T				
9										S			
10													
11													

Fig. 267 Attis

ATTIS = another ancient savior who predated Jesus by centuries. He was born on December 25 of the Virgin Nana and was crucified on a Black Friday and killed for the salvation of mankind. He descended to the underworld and on the third

day that was March 25 he was resurrected like Jesus and declared Most High God. He was born the Divine Son and was called also the Only Begotten Son and Saviour. His worshippers ate his body as bread.

SALIVAHANA = the Hindu Saviour known as the Divine Child born of a virgin and the son of a carpenter, whose name means "Cross-borne (Salvation).

ISA/ISSA = the Arabian Saviour who was born of the Virgin Mary and was considered the Divine Word by the Nazarenes around 400 BCE or four hundred years before Jesus. He lived in the western Arabian region of Hijaz where also existed the places known as Galilee, Bethsaida, and Nazareth. The town of Nazareth mentioned in the Bible did not exist in the supposed time of Jesus. There are many examples of the name Isa shown in the previous discussion about the names of Jesus.

	A	B	C	D	E	F	G	H	I	J	K	L
12												
13					A							
14					V							
15					N	I	S	A				
16					A	L						
17												

Fig. 268 Salivahana and Isa

c) Why Are the Names of Ancient Saviors in the Code?

The names of the ancient saviors mentioned could be found in one of the quadrants that contain the words *ShMA ShM MKHBR* or "NAME/ AUTHOR."

What is the meaning of the ancient names of these revered saviors being together with the English words *NAME/AUTHOR* and the Hebrew words *SHM MKHBR*, which means "Name of the Author." What does it imply? It would seem that the Egyptian God Heru/Horus or the Persian and Indian god Mithra or the Hindu God Krishna or the Iranian prophet Zoroaster and Moses have a connection with the author of the Lord's Prayer. Why do the names of these ancient gods be mentioned in a Hebrew grid? Is this not blasphemy, names of other gods? What is their connection to the Christian Jesus? Plenty! For this relates to the allegations in the book *The Christ Conspiracy* by Acharya S that the

story of Jesus is just a myth and based on the Egyptian story of Horus explained in section "Why is Egypt in the Grid?." Another ancient saviour whose similarity with Jesus was like Horus was Zoroaster whose teachings became the basis of most of the Christian doctrines like heaven and hell, baptism by fire, Messiah, last judgment, good and evil, angels and demons, paradise, apocalypse, prophesy, Armageddon, the defeat of Satan. The saying of John the Baptist that after him would come one who would baptize with fire, and the Holy Spirit came directly from the teaching of Zoroaster.

It is obvious that the stories of Horus, Krishna, Mithra, and Zoroaster were thousands of years; yet like in India and Mexico, the missionaries and the early Christian fathers reasoned out that the devil was very clever that the story of Jesus was concocted before the birth of Jesus to confuse the faithful.

With the similarities between Jesus, Horus, Krishna, Mithra, and Zoroaster, the pestering question still haunts me as to why the names of ancient saviors are around the words "Name of the Author." What is the connection of Jesus to these ancient saviors? Is this the way to show that the story of Jesus is based on these ancient saviors?

After reading the similarities between the ancient saviors, one is at a loss as to who is the real author of the Lord's Prayer, for there is now the tendency to believe that the story of Jesus is based on the ancient saviors. If Jesus is a myth, then who is the author? I never thought that it would come to this point that all along I did not know the author of the Lord's Prayer or the code. I was very sure it was Jesus. Now there is doubt. However, as to whether the story of Jesus is a myth or based on the stories of Horus, Krishna, or Zoroaster, what is important is the teaching left behind "to love one another."

With the similarities of the stories of ancient saviors, it is difficult not to wonder if there really was just one original story about a savior who in the passing of the centuries became known in different names. There is even a question now if Jesus really existed. For many it would be hard to accept Jesus as a myth, but does it really matter whether Jesus was a myth or he was Krishna or Horus or Zoroaster or Mithra or Buddha? If it matters to us, then maybe we are missing the point. The names of the ancient saviors are in the grid to remind us that their spiritual teachings are more important than their personalities. If Krishna or Buddha was the one who told us to love one another, are we not going to follow?

PART VIII

CONCLUSION

It is only now that the code has been revealed, for there is still time for man to save himself from extinction as man has done to other species in this world. The Apocalypse may or may not happen, but the way man treats his fellow men and this planet, the end might not be too far. The Lord's Prayer is a way to save humanity.

Chapter XII

THE HEART

As can be gleaned from the Lord's Prayer, the heart is very important not only in the physical existence of a person, but in his spiritual life, for it is where the kingdom of God is, where love grows. Thus, the Egyptians had a ritual called the weighing of the heart to ascertain who is worthy to be with Osiris. This reminds us of the beautiful Sermon on the Mount when Jesus said,

Blessed is the Pure of Heart, for he will see God.[1]

Based on the sermons given by Jesus, it is only the pure of heart that can see God. The others will be given different rewards.

This is also the reason why Jesus said,

The kingdom of God is within you.[2]

As God is love, then His kingdom is love. As the heart is the seat of love then the kingdom of God is within us. And where love is, God is there. If God is not in our hearts, then we will never find God anywhere.

Sai Baba, a holy man from India referred to the heart of God as like butter that melts at the warmth of man's love.

With this in mind, I look for the Hebrew word for heart, which is *LEB* but which is usually written as LEV. As expected, the word *LEV* is in the middle of the grid to show its importance. In the Kabalah, the heart is in the third Sephera Binah, which is the Supernal Mother. It is just a reminder that LOVE is feminine in nature, hence its tenderness. This is the message of the Father to us to love one another; and His begotten sons Mohammed, Jesus, Buddha, Confucius, Zoroaster, and Krishna tenderly conveyed that message to us by saying love one another and forgive one another.

The teachings of the Sons of God are all the same LOVE. It is not the name of our religion that will save us, but our personal relationship with our God whatever His name is.

> Men will know my disciples by the love that they have for one another.

> A new commandment I leave you: Love one another as I have loved you.

With that, let us now look for the word *LEB* or *LEV* in the grid.

> The first example LEV has ELS of thirty-eight letters between the encoded letters *L* at H-7, *E* at E-4, and *V* at B-1, which seems to emphasize that spirituality starts with the heart and ends with God.

> The second example LEB has ELS of twenty-two letters between the desired letters *L* at J-8, *E* at K-7, and *B* at L-5.

> The third example has ELS of three letters between the encoded letters *L* at A-10, *E* at E-10, and *V* at I-10. The example starts on A-10 for God is the Alpha and Omega and God is first. It is in the middle of the grid for God must be the center of our lives.

> The fourth example has ELS of sixty-eight letters between the encoded letters *L* at A-13, *E* at D-7, and *B* at G-1.

> The fifth example of LEV is found in the quadrant composed of J-9-10 and I-10. By permutation, the word is formed. The word *LOVE* is also found in this quadrant.

The Hebrew word *AHAB* and the Filipino word *MAHAL* both mean the English word *love*.

	A	B	C	D	E	F	G	H	I	J	K	L
1		V	E				B	A				
2								A				
3							T	A				
4					E							
5												B
6	A											
7	B	A		E			L				E	
8	H											
9										L		
10	L				E				V	E		
11										O		
12												
13	L											
14												
15												
16				M	H	A	L					
17					A							

Fig. 269 The Heart

The heart is very important to the Egyptians not only physically but spiritually for only the pure of heart can see Osiris. Thus they have the following words for the heart:

AB = Heart

TA-AB = Pure Heart

AAB = Great Heart

AM AB = What is in the heart?

AAAB = Great Heart

AA = wash the Heart

TAT-AB = Heart's desires

	A	B	C	D	E	F	G	H	I	J	K	L
1		V	E				B	A				
2								A				
3							T	A				
4					E							
5												B
6	A											
7	B	A		E				L			E	
8	H											
9										L		
10	L				E				V	E		

Fig. 270 Leb, Lev, or Heart

AMI AB = He who is in the heart.
URT AB = He whose heart is still

	A	B	C	D	E	F	G	H	J	K	L	M
1							B	A		M		I
2						T		A				
3						A	T	A				A
4			U	T								
5		R										B
6	A		M		I							
7	B	A										
8												

Fig. 271 He who is in the heart.

CHAPTER XIII

WHY ME?

After trying to resolve the authorship of this code comes the question "What made me write this book?" Why did I decipher the Lord's Prayer when I am not even a theologian or a biblical scholar? I do not even speak or understand the Hebrew language. Thus, my research would be suspect for my lack of qualifications. Yet how come that nobody bothered to search for a code in the Lord's Prayer? Why me?

I encountered many obstacles in writing this book like a bugging computer, and in the whole office, it was only my computer that was hit by the Chernobyl virus that wiped out my draft of this book. After writing another draft, I got hospitalized, and when I requested my secretary to print the new draft, the diskette was completely blank. It would seem that somebody does not want it to be printed.

There were other instances that really boggled the mind. When I started writing the book, I only knew the basic in computer but not how to italicize, emphasize, or change the style of the letters or the format; thus it was surprising to turn on the computer and find the format or style of some of the letters changed or selected phrases or names of God italicized. Usually, my paragraphs were indented, the headings were in the center and not italicized as I did not know how; thus it was surprising to find out the change in the format of every chapter. As edited by this unseen hand, I was intending to leave the revision as it was, but according to some requirements in manuscript writing, I should not do it. So I followed the rules.

	A	B	C	D	E	F	G	H	I	J	K	L
1												
2												
3												
4										S		
5								K	M			
6							M	K	A	I		
7							L	E	Ch	E	M	
8										L		
9												
10												

Fig. 272 MKS

I did not know the reason why I was chosen to write this book until I saw what was written in the grid, the initials of my name. Figure 272 shows the letters *M*, *K*, and *S* written diagonally in ELS of ten (10) letters interval. In gematria the letter *K* is interchangeable with the letter *C*, for both have the same numerical value of two (2); thus MKS can become MCS, which are the initials of my name. Another uncanny thing is that the letter interval or ELS is ten (10), the name of our group. Even my nickname MIKE is written in Hebrew MKA, sharing the letter *M* with MKS and side by side with my initials MKS. Now I knew why I wrote this book and started deciphering the code. It was written in the stars (code).

To clinch the matter, my son Miggy told me to look for the words *one tenth* or similar-sounding words; and if I would find them, then it would really be a confirmation as to why I should write the book, for we have a group called the 1/10th involved in spiritual healing. I was surprised to find the name of our group printed many times in the grid as "One Ten." It would seem that even from the start when the group was formed the name to be used was already prepared.

	A	B	C	D	E	F	G	H	I	J	K	L
1												
2						T-						
3												
4				T	E							
5					O	N						
6												N
7				E-		E	-T		E		E	
8				-E		N		T	E	N		O
9	-N					O						
10					e	T.		O		E.		
11		N.					E			O		
12		n-						N			N,	
13						E,						
14			T,									
15												
16												
17												

Fig. 273 One Ten

Another amazing discovery is that the name and the complete birth date of the person who narrated the mental travel to the Pyramids and the Sphinx are contained in a quadrant of just only nine (9) letters.

Chapter XIV

AMEN—SO BE IT!

This portion should have been under the chapter on the holy names of God, but because of its meaning and its use as the proper ending of any prayer or petition, I decided to place this holy name at this portion. The holy name of God AMN or AMEN means "So Be It," and in Egyptian means "hidden." It is also one of the holiest names of the Egyptian god AMENRA, which means "He who is hidden." Another name of RA, AMENOA means "He whose name is hidden."

AMN is a very powerful name as it is equivalent to the two holy names of God—IHVH with a numeral value of 26 and ADNY with a valuation of 65 or a total of 99 or 1. AMN with the numeral correspondences of 1, 40, and 50 has also the numeral value of 1; hence, they are interchangeable. Thus, AMN is equal to AYDHNVYH or YAHDVNHY. Also by permutation, AMN can become MNA, which means "the bread from heaven."

AMEN can also be written down as AM. EN., which means "Mother-God."

Figure 274 shows two examples of the holy name in different ELS.

The first example of the name AMN is written vertically in ELS of two (2) letters starting with the letter *A* on J-2, the letter *M* on J-5, and the letter *N* at J-8.

The second example of AMN is written horizontally on D-6, H-6, and L-6 with ELS of three (3) letters between the encoded letters.

	A	B	C	D	E	F	G	H	I	J	K	L
1												
2										A		
3												
4												
5										M		
6				A				M				N
7												
8										N		
9												
10												

Fig. 274 Examples 1 and 2.

The third example of AMN with an ELS of nine letters between the desired letters *A* on B-7, *M* on L-7, and *N* on J-8.

The fourth example has an ELS of sixty-three letters between the letters *A* on L-10, *M* on H-6, and *N* on D-1.

The fifth example is AMN written with ELS of six letters between the letters *A* on H-15, *M* on C-16 and J-16.

	A	B	C	D	E	F	G	H	I	J	K	L
1				N								
2												
3												
4												
5												
6								M				
7		A										M
8								N				
9												
10												
11												A
12												
13												
14												
15								A				
16			M							N		
17												

Fig. 275 Examples 3, 4, and 5.

The sixth example is the beautiful design in the quadrant composed of E-11-12-13, F-12, G-11-13, and H-12.

The seventh example is *IMN*, the Egyptian word for AMN.

	A	B	C	D	E	F	G	H	I	J	K	L
10												
11					A		E					
12					A	M		N				
13					A		E					
14												
15					N							
16			M									
17	I											

Fig. 276 Examples 6 and 7.

The examples with the minimum skip intervals of two, three, six, and nine letters clearly show that this holy name AMEN was deliberately placed in this grid by the author of the Lord's Prayer code.

History has taught us bitter lessons about the effects of greed and ambition that have produced people like Hitler, Lenin, Stalin, and Sadam. Yet we have never learned. We are still obsessed and possessed by these unbridled passions. When will we stop our insanities? Nobody knows.

This is the only prayer that is coded as shown in the chapter in Gematria/Isopsephy and further sums up to number 1—GOD. The discovery of this code composed of only 198 letters but which brings us to a period of time from the ancient people, nations, and civilizations of the ancient world to the present and even a peek into the future could only confirm that a God or a superhuman being whether his name was Jesus, Horus, Krishna, Quetzalcoatl, or Attis has made this code.

The codes in the Bible and in the Lord's Prayer are being revealed now because God loves us very much. We have to be reminded of our follies and stupidities. Whatever the prophecies and apocalyptic messages are in the Bible code or the code, the solution is also in the codes. It is up to us as to what we want of this world and of ourselves. We can be like little gods or beasts, but whatever our decisions will be, so be it (AMEN).

PART IX

MISCELLANEOUS

APPENDIX A

HARNESSING THE POWER OF THE PRAYER

After reading this book and trying to fathom its validity, are we just satisfied with the additional knowledge we have imbibed, or is there still something missing? Do we fully understand the prayer despite this additional input? Can we perform the miracles the apostles did after understanding the prayer? Do we have full knowledge and understanding of the prayer to empower us to perform miracles as Jesus promised "greater than this you can do?" How do we harness the power of the Lord's Prayer so we can perform the miracles the apostles did?

First of all we have to know and understand the Lord's Prayer. Very few know that the Lord's Prayer is a source of powerful energy—love. Every letter is energy. Every word is energy, and the whole prayer itself is a field of energy. Through this prayer, we can connect with the source of energy, God. This is the reason why Jesus taught this prayer. There is so much negativity in the world, and only through the energy of Love can it be overcome.

For some people, it is difficult to talk about energy especially when we consider people as energy or holograms. How can we be energy or holograms when we see one another and can even touch each other? Can we touch a hologram? Just consider 3D movies, dreams, and hypnotic trances, they seem real, yet they are just illusions. In our dreams, we experience everything as real. But when we wake up, we realize they are only dreams. What if God is dreaming and we are part of that dream? When God wakes up, where will we be?

God is Energy. As everything created came from Energy, then everything in this world is energy. Our thoughts, deeds, bodies, are all energy. As we are all energy, we are connected with one another. We are interwoven and interlocking like an energy field. Since planet Earth is also energy, then we are connected with Earth. When we harbor negative energy, we affect the energy field and also affect others and Earth. Earth is already blanketed by too much negative energy. It cannot take anymore additional negative energy. If we will not change

our negative vibrations, then something will happen as had happened before when earth will protect itself by releasing the energy within through earthquakes, tsunami, and volcanic eruptions. There will be massive landmass movement. The North Pole will become the South Pole and vice versa. How do we prevent this? Earth changes cannot be stopped, but the polar reversal can be if more people will use the love energy. One way to connect and use the love energy is through the Lord's Prayer.

Before we examine the meaning of the Lord's Prayer, let us first define the meaning of the word *prayer* as understood in Jesus time. Jesus spoke Aramaic and not English. The translation from one language to another has oftentimes caused mistranslation. As the Lord's Prayer was said originally in Aramaic, we will examine the meaning of the word *prayer* in Aramaic. The word prayer in Aramaic is "slotha," which means "to set a trap." Thus, prayer in Aramaic means "to set the mind like a trap to catch the thoughts of God." One way of setting a trap is to still the mind so it can focus or attune with the vibration of God. God is a spirit or energy that is all around us. We try to tune in or beam in on this pervading energy instead of focusing on other forms of vibrations like anger, hate, envy, and jealousy. This is also the reason why another meaning of "prayer" is "to focus or to tune in." We should therefore prepare and adjust our minds to receive the transmission from God who is constantly sending, beaming, and signaling to us. We should be able to tune in on this transmission. God is the transmitter, and we are the receiver. We should be on the same frequency. We have the capability as God gave us his spirit to be like Him.

Prayer is not telling God what to do. He knows what He is doing. He runs the universe in perfect order. He does not need to be reminded everyday of our needs and those of our relatives and friends. This is the reason why in Matthew 6:7-8, it is said, "And when you pray, do not repeat your words like the pagans, for they think that because of much talking they will be heard. Do not be like them, for the Father knows what you need, before you ask Him." Our prayers cannot change God, for He is the unchangeable. He cannot be more loving as He was before, now, and in the future. He needs not add or subtract as He is perfect. The purpose of prayer is for us to listen and change and not God listening to us and change. As I was inputting the words, a story came into my mind as follows:

> A young boy was praying to God asking for many things. Then he heard a voice saying, "Focus on your school and finish your studies, and you will get your wish." The young boy answered, "I prayed to you because you are God and nothing is impossible to you." "Yes, I am God and nothing is impossible to Me," replied the voice, "but I am telling you what you need to do to have your way." "But I need these now and

not after my studies," answered the impatient boy. Then the voice said, "You said I am God, yet you are telling me what to do and to follow you. Are you my god?" The answer silenced the boy, and he felt sorry. Does this story sound familiar?

Another word that needs clarification is the word *God*. Our religious upbringing has taught us about a personal God who gets angry, jealous, and cares only for those who believe in Him as Jesus, Yaweh, Allah, Buddha, or Krishna. For the Aramaic-speaking people, God was known as Alaha that meant "Essence, Substance, Energy or Spirit." As God is an energy or a spirit, then God is everywhere, and anybody can connect to this energy if one knows how. And this explains why Jesus said pray in my name or Beshemi.

Beshemi or in my name has been misunderstood by many for centuries. Many thought that by just mentioning the name Jesus, miracles can happen or their petitions will be answered. Beshemi in Aramaic means "according to my technique, my way, method, approach, or my understanding." Thus, Jesus taught the apostles to pray in the manner that he prayed. One does not fly an airplane by saying, "In the name of my flying instructor, let us fly." One operates an airplane according to the technique or method taught by the instructor and not by his name. This is the most difficult part for Jesus is a very loving, sincere, and honest person. It is with those traits that the prayer should be understood and said.

Presently, there is supposed to be an ongoing debate as to the use of the word *Father* in the Lord's Prayer as being sexist and not inclusive as it excluded the Mother. Actually, this is true if we will use the English language. One cannot interpret the word *Father* as Father-Mother. However, there is no problem and debate in the ancient Hebrew language used by Jesus in addressing the Father as ABBA and written as Avenu meaning "Our Father" in the prayer. Kabalistically, the letter *A* usually represents God or God the Father or Masculine Energy while the letter *B* represents a Container, Daughter, Feminine Energy or Mother. As the holy name IHVH represents (I) Father, (H) Mother, (V) Son, and (H) Daughter, so is the word *ABBA* which means (A) Father, (B) Mother, (B) Daughter, and (A) Son." Thus, in these two holy names the masculine and feminine energies and the four elements are represented. These holy names show the equality of the sexes. They also have profound meanings. A good Father should manifest the tenderness of a Mother, and a good Mother should have the sternness of a Father to have a well-rounded child. The English word *Father* does not contain the feminine energy of *B* while the English word *Mother* does not contain the masculine energy of *A* thus, the complete separation of the masculine and feminine energies in the English words. Maybe, it is time to use the word *ABBA*. Further, the word *ABBA* has a numeral value of 6 while the word *AMA* meaning "Mother" has also a numeral value of 6, which means they are equal.

There is another Hebrew term in the Kabalah that means the continuous union of the Father and Mother—AIMA—the name of the Mother in the third heaven. For me, I would prefer the term *AMAINA*, which means "Father-Mother" in Filipino.

Even the prayer as conveyed to us in the Bible through Matthew and Luke has different forms and style. The Lord's Prayer that we pray today is a composite of both. Although billions of people know the Lord's Prayer, 99 percent or more however do not understand it; thus, we are unaware that the Lord's Prayer is a love story. It is a story about a Father whose name is Love, whose kingdom is Love, and whose will is to love one another. He loved us so much He asked His beloved Son to descend and redeem us. His Son knew the pains, humiliation, and death He would suffer in this world, but still He obeyed His Father out of respect and love. And we, the people in return crucified that Son. Yet despite our ungratefulness, the Father could still love us, forgive us, and protect us. What a sad story of an unrequited love.

Jesus supposedly told this story which we named as the Lord's Prayer. Unfortunately, we do not appreciate the story that is why we do not understand it. And for this reason, the promises of Jesus remain unfulfilled.

Jesus said,

> Anything I do, you can do, much greater than this you can do for I will go to the Father for You.

Jesus performed many miracles—the dead came back to life, the lame was able to walk, and the deaf was able to hear; yet how come that His disciples now—the priests, nuns, pastors, ministers, evangelists, and the preachers cannot perform the miracles that He has promised? What is wrong?

Again, Jesus said,

> Knock and it shall be opened unto you.

Yet the door remains unopened despite the billions of people not only knocking but banging and ramming that door.

Jesus still added,

> Ask and it shall be given unto you.

Billions of people are not only praying but pleading and imploring God for the solutions of their problems, yet the petitions remain unanswered. Many are sick, unemployed, poor, starving, and beset with problems. Why? Because they pray the Lord's Prayer with their minds and not with their hearts. Our Father is

the God of Love, and love can only be found in the heart and not in the mind. If God is the God of Mind, then only the geniuses, the educated, the literates, and the intellectuals will know God. But because God is in the heart and everybody is capable of loving, God can be found in babies, idiots, morons, innocents, uneducated, and the illiterates.

Open our hearts that we will understand God. It is not the mind but the hearts that truly appreciate the beauty of nature, the setting of the sun, the chirping of the birds, the dance of the flowers, the swaying of the trees, and the language of the animals.

This is the reason why Jesus said,

> The kingdom of God is within you.

This is really true for the kingdom of God is Love and love is in the heart, not in the mind. If we cannot find God in our hearts, we can never find God anywhere. Open up our hearts that we will feel God and experience God. How can we feel God if there is so much hate and vindictiveness in our hearts? How can we touch Him when there is a wall of indifference around us? How can we smell God when there is garbage of depression around us?

Jesus taught us the Prayer of the Heart so that our hearts can have direct communication with God's heart. This is what is called the Twin Hearts, the hearts of men and the heart of God.

> Blessed is the pure of Heart for he will see God.

It is not the rich nor the poor, nor the beautiful nor the ugly, nor the conqueror or the conquered that will see God, but only the pure of heart.

As Sai Baba, a holy man from India said:

> The Heart of God is like butter that melts at the warmth of man's love.

Jesus told us to address the Father as Abba, a term of endearment in Hebrew like Papa, Mama, or in Filipino Itay or Inay to show the special relationship between a loving Father and an obedient child. He told us to pray.

> Our Father who art in heaven
> "Avenu Sh'ba Sh'maiyim"

Jesus told us to begin the Prayer of the Heart by saying "Our Father who art in Heaven" to instill in us that there is only one God who is a Father to all of

us. He is a loving, understanding, and forgiving Father who knows the number of hairs in our heads and would forgive us seventy times seven and knows our needs. We call Him Our Father because we are supposed to be one family; we are brothers and sisters, children of only One Father. We are supposed to love one another and care for each other as one family. Thus we should not harm, hurt, destroy, or kill each other.

Holy be Thy Name
Yit Kadash Shemeycha

As we are one family, let us keep holy the name of our Father. It is not just by worshipping in the church or temple that we keep holy the name of God, but by the words that come out from our mouths. Religiosity is different from spirituality. Religiosity is obeying church or sect laws like going to church, confession, or communion, tithing, etc. Spirituality is obeying God's law—"love one another." There are many who go to church but do not know how to love. There are those who go to confession and communion but do not know how to forgive. In the Philippines, the elders usually tell the younger generations, "We have only one name, do not destroy it." We dishonor the name of Our Father when we cheat, steal, lie, and slander others. Let us not desecrate that name by our immoral and illegal acts, nor shall we kill in His name, for it is His wish that we love one another. The greatest form of worship and honoring our Father is by loving one another.

Thy kingdom come
"Tavo Malkutecha"

Once we keep holy His Name, we easily become part of His kingdom of love where one treats another with justice, mercy, fairness and understanding. We can only be heirs to His kingdom if we empty our hearts of our hurts, pains, disappointments, anger, and hate so that Love can have a place in our hearts and we will be part of the kingdom.

Thy will be done on earth as it is in heaven

Y'asseh Retzoncha K'mo
Ba-Sh'maiyim Kain B'Aretz

If we become part of the kingdom, it is easier to fulfill the will of our Father to love one another. It is not His will that we cheat on our spouses, abuse our children, exploit others, and denude our forests and destroy our marine life.

476

Cheating on our spouses create emotional and financial problems. Abuse of our children produces trauma and future problems to our children, exploitation of our workers incites unrest and strikes and denudations of our forests result in floods and draught. It is His will that we love not only one another but also our home, planet Earth.

Give us this day, our daily bread
"Et Lechem Hukeynu Ten-Lonu Ha-yom"

A simple phrase, yet we do not understand. Remember we only ask for our daily bread not a supply for a thousand years. Yet we keep on hoarding and accumulating wealth and riches and more often at the expense of others. Yet why are we still poor physically, emotionally, and spiritually? The reason is we do not trust the Father. We do not believe in Him. We believe more in our fears. For this reason our Lord said, "Do not be afraid for what you will eat, what you will drink, what you will wear, does not the Father in heaven know your needs? Our Father is a generous giver. He gave us air to breathe, water to drink, fruits of the earth to eat, and a soul to be like Him. As our Father is a giver, then let us be a giver, not a taker. Let us be contented with what we have. It is not wrong to be rich, but let us share our surplus with others that we will be "Father like Son," a Giver. Trust our Father and do our works, and we will be blessed. If we obey His commandments, we become His heirs, and we will be entitled to all His blessings and prosperity.

Forgive us our sins, as we forgive those who sinned against us
"U'slach Lonu Et Hovetheynu
K'Asher Solachnu Gam Anachnu"

As we become givers, it is easier also to give our love and understanding for others. We will be able to forgive. Forgiveness is easier said than done. Ask those who have just gone to confession and received communion. "Have you forgiven your philandering husband? Have you forgiven your brother or sister who has defrauded you of your inheritance? Have you forgiven your best friend, your business associate, or your neighbor whom you trusted very much who still cheated you? No, yet we tell God forgive us for we have forgiven. Remember what our Lord said, "Unless we forgive, our Father in heaven will not forgive us." If our Father will not forgive us, then we are disinherited and would not enjoy His blessings. We will become poor physically, emotionally and spiritually. Hate, resentment, and anger in our hearts produce stress and tension resulting into sickness like cancer and diabetes. Once we become physically sick, we become moody and cranky, and then we will blame everybody, even God for our illnesses

and misfortunes. Forgiveness creates peace, serenity, and good health. Once we have controlled our emotion, then we will be strong against temptation.

Lead us not into temptation but deliver us from evil.

"L' Ha Yaveynu Vi-al Tivi-Aynu Li-y 'Dey Nisayon
Ki Im Hal-Tzeynu Min Hara"

It is ironic that man loves temptation and seeks evil. He buys lewd magazines, pornographic DVDs, VCDs, tapes, and diskettes and even keeps them in the house, yet he says deliver us from evil.

Temptation will always be with us, for temptation is necessary for us to evolve spiritually. Even Jesus was tempted to show His love for our Father. How can we truly say we love our Father if there is no one to tempt us to cheat, lie, steal? We need our Father to be strong from all the evils and temptations around us. Our Father will always be there to help us. If our Father is with us, what is there to be afraid of?

We want to be one with our Father. We seek the Father of Love, but how can we when we have the God of hate in our hearts? We want to see the Father of Truth, but how can we when we are all lies? Our Lord said, "Anything I do, you can do, much more than this you can do for I will go to the Father for you." The dead came back to life, the deaf was able to hear, and the blind was able to see. Yet how come that most of the disciples now can not do what our Lord promised? Because they forgot what our Lord said, "Men will know my disciples by the love that they have for one another." Not because one is a priest he knows how to love, not because one is a nun she knows how to forgive. The Lord's Prayer is a prayer of love and forgiveness. If we cannot be a brother to our brethren, if we cannot follow the will of God to love one another, if we cannot obey the commandment of God to forgive, then we have no right to say the Lord's Prayer. But if we can pray the Lord's Prayer with love and forgiveness in our heart, "ask and it shall be given unto you, knock and it shall be opened to you. Anything I do, you can do much more than this you can do for I will go to the Father for you."

The door to God is the Door of Love, and no key can open that door except the Key of Love.

Secret of the Lord's Prayer

The Lord's Prayer is a prayer of love. Understand it, pray it sincerely and honestly with love and forgiveness, and the miracles will be there. The Lord's Prayer is an energy prayer that vibrates with the energy of love. If one is truly

loving and caring, one will be able to connect with the love energy of Christ, and anything is possible when Love is the healer.

The Lord's Prayer creates positive emotion or vibration. Jesus taught this prayer because of the overwhelming negative vibrations around. There are so much religious biases, killings, racism, hatred, anger, abuses, and exploitation that the Son of Love has to come down and sow love. "Man will know my disciples by the love that they have for one another."

Cause and Effect

Another way of looking at the Lord's Prayer is the doctrine of cause and effect. It is said for every cause there is an effect, for every action there is a reaction. In the Lord's Prayer, it can be noticed that the first half is about the cause and the second half is about the effect. The first half consists of the following actions:

1. Believe in a God who is our Father. Trust Him. Just do our work.
2. Keep holy His name by not committing illegal or immoral acts.
3. Be a part of the kingdom where there is sharing and caring.
4. Do His will by loving and forgiving.

If we will create the cause the following will be the effects:

1. God will give us our daily bread. We don't have to worry.
2. God will forgive us.
3. He will not let us fall.
4. He will deliver us from evil.

Family Relations

Begin at home. Let us review our relations with our parents? All of us have fathers and mothers, but do we know one another? Do we communicate with our parents? To whom do we relate more often, with our father or mother? Why? If our relationship with our parents can be graded from 1 to 10, how will we grade our relationship? Why did we rate it that way? Do your parents know what you want? Do you have privacy in the house? Do your parents or relatives abuse you physically, emotionally, mentally, or sexually? If so, have you confided the abuse to anyone? If not, why? What house rules do you violate more often? Why? Are you happy in your home? If not, why? Is there favoritism in your home? Are your parents both working? Do you go out with your parents for outings, seeing movies, or eating outside? Do you consider your family poor or middle-class? Do

you buy signature clothes? Do you have meat in the table? Do you regret being borne in that family?

As we reviewed our relationship with our parents, so let us also look at our relationships with our spouse or relatives. Let us ask similar questions and come up with honest answers. Only after we have resolved our relationships with them can we truly pray the Lord's Prayer. "Therefore, if thou art offering thy gift at the altar, and there remember that thy brother has anything against thee, leave thy gift before the altar and go first to be reconciled to thy brother, and then come and offer thy gift."

APPENDIX B

POSSIBLE PHILIPPINE EVENTS

As I come from the Philippines, I am very much concerned to know the future of the country. Looking over the grid, I found some disturbing findings that made me write this portion. I sent this article to some friends in the Philippines last January 2003 to warn the present president of the Philippines, Gloria Macapagal Arroyo also known as GMA about the coming problems. She was destined to become president as her appellation could be found several times in the grid like that of President Bush. From the grid one could see her ascendance to the top. It was her fate.

	A	B	C	D	E	F	G	H	I	J	K	L
1												
2												
3								A.				
4												
5												
6										A-		
7												M.
8												
9							M-					
10												
11					A							
12				G-	A	M						
13					A							
14												
15												
16												
17												

Fig. 1 The name GMA.

The first example of the appellation GMA has ELS of thirty-two letters between the letters *G* at H-12, *M* at G-9, and *A* at J-6.

The second example of GMA has ELS of fifty-one letters between the letters *G* at H-12, *M* at L-7, and *A* at H-3.

The third example is found in the quadrant composed of D-12, E-11-12-13, and F-12. By permutation or repositioning of the letters, one can form the name.

As the presidency was handed down to President GMA through a bloodless revolution by the unseating of the then incumbent president, there had been intense animosities between the political parties. There were rumors about possible harm and assassination of the president. But it is said that these threats come with the position. However, the grid would seem to confirm these threats, which reminded me of what the author of Bible code 1 and 11, Mr. Michael Drosnin did. When Mr. Drosnin saw in the code table of Bible code 1, the phrase "assassin will assassinate" crossed the name of Prime Minister Yitzhak Rabin of Israel; he sent a letter on September 1, 1994, to Mr. Rabin warning him of the possible assassination try and the probable date. On November 4, 1995, Mr. Rabin was assassinated. He did not heed the warning. The case of Mr. Rabin is based on only one finding; however, in the present case there are several examples.

When I was still in the Philippines, I and some gifted friends discussed this possible event and the probable weapon to be used. I was surprised by what appeared in the grid. The details were unbelievable. The words in different languages appeared yet pointing to the same results.

Figure 2 shows the instrument that would be used in the assassination—a gun. The word *GUN* is mentioned twice and sharing the letter *G* with the president's appellation, GMA.

	A	B	C	D	E	F	G	H	I	J	K	L
1												
2												
3								A.				
4												
5												
6										A		N-
7												M.
8												
9							M	U-				
10												
11					A							
12		N-	U-	G-	A	M						
13					A							
14												
15												
16												
17												

Fig. 2 Weapon to be used: a gun.

The first example of the word *GUN* has ELS of thirty-one letters between the letters *G* at D-12, *U* at H-9, and *N* at L-6. The word *GUN* runs diagonally upward alongside and between the two appellations GMA.

The second example starts also in D-12 and sharing the letter *G* with the word GMA, and going in reverse direction, the letters are side by side without ELS.

With the word *GUN* intimately connected with the initials GMA, what does it imply? Does it mean that her presidency will always be at the barrel of a gun? Will there be a possible assassination try on President GMA? When will this possibly happen? What will be the outcome? What is ominous in the grid? Is the figure of a fallen cross composed by the words *GUN* and *GMA*. It is the sign of a fallen leader. Is it a fall caused by actual assassination or ouster through the barrel of a gun or a coup d'état? Or could it also mean the fall of materialism so that spirituality will be free? Will there be a cleansing in the Philippine government and its people?

In 2003, there will be many domestic and international factors that will really rock the administration of President GMA due to their economic impact to the Philippines. The irony of it is that no matter what she does, many are still complaining. These maybe the contributing factors why the year 2003 will be risky for President GMA. The year 2003 is indicated three times in the grid and would seem to be the possible time frame of the event. This message is so uncanny for it is very vivid and clear. This is a warning to the Philippine president to take care. This message was given ahead of time to prepare and for the event to be possibly averted. I hope the assassination plan will not happen although this will destroy the credibility of the prediction. But what is a false prediction compared to a life lost.

In the quadrant composed of A-9, B-10, C-11, and D-12 are the letters *N*, *O*, *U* and *G* going diagonally downward with ELS of twelve letters. By the Hebrew method of gematria that is the basis of modern numerology, the letters can be converted into single digit numerals with the following correspondences:

	A	B	C	D	E	F	G	H	I	J	K	L
1												
2												
3								A.	6			
4									6			
5											7	
6		3								A		N-
7								3				M.
8		6					6			7		
9	5	6				7	M	U-	6			
10		7			5			7				
11		5	6		A		5					
12		5N	U	3G	A	M						
13					A							
14												
15												
16												
17												

Fig. 3 The years 5763, 5766, and 5767.

What is so important about these numbers? Well, these numbers 5763 relate to the Hebrew calendar year 5763 that corresponds to the modern year 2003. Again, the year was mentioned starting in B-12 and going vertically upward with ELS of one letter between the encoded letters at B-10, B-8, and B-6. This time the letters replaced by the numbers are as follows:

$$N = 5 \qquad O = 7 \qquad U = 6 \qquad Sh = 3$$

As if the two examples are not enough, a third example was given starting at E-10, F-9, G-8, and H-7. It goes diagonally upward with ELS of ten letters. The letters are *E, O, U,* and *L.* Again, in their numeral correspondences, they become 5, 7, 6, and 3 or the Hebrew year 5763 or the modern year 2003.

If one will notice, the first example points to the word GMA even sharing the letter *G* while the second example shares the letter *N* with the word *GUN* and the third example running alongside the appellation GMA.

The way things are, it would seem that that the event is inevitable and something terrible would happen before the year 2004, which is the presidential election in the Philippines, which political analysts say might be a very bloody election.

Figure 4 gives additional information as to what might happen in the year 2003. At the start of the first example of the Hebrew year 5763 are three Filipino words that are interrelated and would have been impossible to appear in a Hebrew grid. The mathematical ratio of these interrelated words appearing together in the grid is amazing. The Filipino words are found in the quadrant composed of H-7 to H-10 and V-1 to V-5.

BUHAY = means "LIFE"
HUKAY = digging or a hole on the ground for burial purpose
LUHA = means "TEARS"

	A	B	C	D	E	F	G	H	I	J	K	L
6												
7	B											
8	H	U	K									
9		U	H	A	Y							
10	L											
11												

Fig. 4 Filipino words

It would seem that a life would be taken and a burial plot has to be prepared. Would there be a shedding of tears in 2003? This can happen if the president

is assassinated. The possibility of death is further enhanced by the unbelievable grouping together of four words all referring to death. These words are at the start and the end of the two examples of the Hebrew year 5763.

	A	B	C	D	E	F	G	H	I	J	K	L
5												
6		3										
7	B							3				
8	H	6U	K				6					
9	5	U	H	A	Y	7						
10	L	7			5	T						
11			6				E					
12		5		3G	A	M						
13		H	A	Y	A							
14			T									
15		D	E									
16		I	M									
17												

Fig. 5 Words related to death.

In the quadrant composed of F-12, G-11, and F-10 is the Hebrew word *MET* which means "DEATH." It shares the letter *M* with the word *GMA*. Again, the word *MET* is found in C-16-15-14 going vertically upward without ELS. As if to emphasize the meaning of the word, two English words *DIE* and *DEATH* with the letter *D* at B-15 are alongside and even sharing the letters *E* and *T* with the word *MET*. And as if this emphasis is not enough, the Hindu and Tibetan name of the god of death YAMA with the letter *Y* at D-13 has been mentioned twice and even sharing letters with MET and GMA. What can we say? This is mind-boggling. The mathematical probability of all these words being lumped together and even sharing letters is unbelievable.

	A	B	C	D	E	F	G	H	I	J	K	L
5												
6	A	Sh	M									
7	B	A-	R					3				
8	H-	6U	K-			6						
9	5N		H	A	Y	7						
10		7			5							
11				6	K	A	Sh					
12		5	U	3G								
13		H										
14	A											
15												
16												
17												

Fig. 6 Possible problems.

At the end of the first example and the beginning of the third examples near the letter *G* are the words in Filipino without ELS—*KASh* meaning "money on hand" and *KUHA* meaning "take" or "get." Also at the end of the second example are letters that by permutation would also form the words *KASh* and *KUHA*. What is meant by these words? Will there be a resurgence of kidnapping for ransom, big bank robberies, or graft and corruption? Further at the end of the second example are the words *ARM*, *ABU*, *NUR*, *HUK*, and *RAM*. This is mind-boggling especially for Filipinos who know the meaning of the words cited. It means problems for the president. If we will include the following Hebrew words, then it will be devastating.

RA = means Evil	AK = calamity	ASh = fire
BK = lamentation	MR = violence	RSh = poverty

These are the words at the end of the second example, 2003. If the Filipinos will not shape up, any Philippine president will have a difficult time. I pity whoever will be president in 2004 for all the difficulties and problems will still be going up and peaking in the year 2006.

With the year indicated, could the time frame of the possible event like the month be also known? The grid has given the approximate time.

On top of the third example of the Hebrew year 5763 running alongside the appellation GMA and near the number 3 are the words *MAY* and *AV*, which could mean the months of the year. The Hebrew word *AV* covers the months of July to August. Again in the first example of the Hebrew year 5763, which points to the word *GMA* are found the words MAY and AV. Could it be that this event would happen between the months of May to August 2003? Now that we have the possible months and year, what are supposed to happen?

	A	B	C	D	E	F	G	H	I	J	K	L
1												
2								A		A		
3								A	V6			
4								Y	A	6		
5							Ch	A			7	
6							I	M				5
7		B					3					M
8		H	U6	K			6			7		
9		5	U6	H	A	Y	7		6			
10		L	7		5	T		7				
11			5	6	A		E5					
12			N	U	3G	A	M					
13		L	H	A	Y	A	V					
14			L	T		V		A				
15			D	E	Y							
16			I	M		A						
17					A							

Fig. 7 Possibilities

There is something mysterious in the grid. In the beginning of the first example of the Hebrew year 5763, the Filipino word *BUHAY* which means "LIFE" is found while at the end of the year; the Hindu and Tibetan word *YAMA*, which means "GOD OF DEATH" is located. While in the third example, the Hindu and Tibetan word *YAMA* is at the start of the Hebrew year 5763, and at the end of the Hebrew year is the Hebrew word *CHI* which means "LIFE." All these words in Filipino, Hebrew, Hindu, Tibetan, and English all refer to life and death. The first example could mean that a possible sad event might happen in the Philippines. This is only a possibility and a warning for the concerned person

to be careful. If this happens then the Philippines will terribly suffer politically and economically that can lead to its financial collapse or death. Death here can mean the downfall of a person or the country being represented by the person. The third example offers HOPE for in this example DEATH came first then LIFE. DEATH can mean not physical death, but the death of materialism or material desires so that spirituality can blossom. If a president of a nation will forget graft and corruption, nepotism and self-interest and work for love of God and country, then there will be LIFE for that president and for the nation for GOD will always be there! There are other information in the grid that could only be given to the person concerned.

Fate and destiny are two different matters. Fate can be altered, but destiny cannot be stopped. It is the fate of a person to become president, but it is his destiny not to rule forever, for he is destined to die.

God acts in a mysterious way. Why was this information given ahead of time? What is the purpose? Is this only a warning? Is this fate or destiny? In the case of Prime Minister Yitzhak Rabin of Israel, he was assassinated. If President GMA heeds the warning and take precaution, would she be saved? If this is fate, then this early warning is a way of averting what will happen, but if it is her destiny, then no one can stop it except God.

	A	B	C	D	E	F	G	H	I	J	K	L
1												
2												
3					P			a	6	7	4	
4			6	4	5E	P				6	6	5
5			E		7O		P			4	7	
6										A		5
7							4	3		P	E	M
8						5	6	4		7		O
9							7	4	6	6		P
10				6	5	4	5	7	6	E	4	E
11					A		5			O		
12				G	A	m				P		
13					A							
14												

Fig. 8 GMA, Poe, and the Hebrew years 5764 (2004) and 5766 (2006).

I sent a copy of this part of the book to the Philippines last January 2003. I do not know if it reached the president. As prophesied, a failed mutiny took place

last July 27, 2003, and the possible assassination of GMA was thwarted according to reports. It was reported that GMA was warned about the possible coup d'état. Although the year 2003 will be dangerous year for GMA, I think she will survive it and even run for reelection. The Hebrew years 5766 (2006) and 5767 (2007) are running along her name. Her decision not to run for the presidency will be changed. The dark horse in the coming election is Fernando Poe whose name is hidden under the name ChOE. As stated previously, the letter *CH* has the numeral value of 8 and is interchangeable with the letter *P* whose numeral value is also 8. Thus ChOE can become POE. By temurah the name can be formed as shown in figure 8. The name is mentioned many times in the grid that means Poe is more popular than President GMA, but the Hebrew years 5764 (2004) and 5766 (2006) are far from his name while the name of GMA is crossing the years. Thus it is questionable if Mr. Poe can translate his popularity in the coming election although it is a tight contest. Many things can happen in an election. The vice presidency can be a foregone conclusion. I furnished a copy of this section to the Philippine Consulate in Chicago three months before the 2004 Philippine presidential election. I just do not know if it reached the president.

		A	B	C	D	E	F	G	H	I	J	K	L
1													
2											A		
3									A.	6	7		
4											6	S6	5
5											7		
6											A		N-
7													M.
8			6								7		
9		5	6					M	U-	6			
10			7					5	7	6			
11			5			A		5					
12			N-	U-	G-	A	M						
13						A							
14													
15													
16													
17													

Fig. 9 GMA and the Hebrew years 5766 and 5767

Looking over what I have written in 2002, it would seem that the problems shown in figures 5, 6, and 7 would continue to persist and even worsen. President GMA will face the same problems she faced in 2003, 2004, and 2005 and much worse for there is the continuing global problems and the addition of the Hebrew word *ASN* at J-2, K-4, and L-6, which means "sudden death." It is alongside the Hebrew years 5766 and 5767 and between the initials of GMA as shown in figure 9. "Sudden Death" can mean physical death by assassination, accident, or sickness; or it can mean death or downfall of her administration by her removal from office by legal or illegal means. As this is an advanced warning, there is a possibility of the event being prevented. However, if President GMA will not take care, she might end up at the losing end. This is also the reason why I do not believe that any plot against the president this 2005 will be successful as this is not the "Ides of March." What is intriguing is that the administration of President Arroyo parallels that of President Bush as shown by previous figures about President Bush. It can be said that both presidents will face the same problems. I hope they will overcome the problems.

Appendix C

WHO IS SENATOR BARACK H. OBAMA?

One of the most interesting revelations in the grid is the appearance of the complete name of Senator Barack H. Obama. He is the only person, past, present, and possibly future whose complete name appeared in the grid, Barak H. Obama. It puzzles me why his full name appeared together with the Hebrew years 5766 and 5768, which are equivalent to the modern years 2006 and 2008. I can understand if he is prophesied to be become president of the United States like President Bush whose surname appeared three times in the grid. The question is what is the future for him that his name has to be fully mentioned in the grid? Is he the modern savior or the Antichrist?

With the Hebrew version of the Lord's Prayer and the right grid, I used the anagram method where one repositions letters in the anagram to search for the hidden message. If one will look at figure 1, one will find some Hebrew letters of the Lord's Prayer. I only took that section of the grid that contains the complete name. The anagram in this case contains only a minimum of three columns, namely, A, B, and C and three horizontal rows, namely, 6, 7, and 8—if one will use the letter U instead of the letter O for the surname as the letters can be interchanged, for they are numerically equal and are almost phonetically the same in sound. After repositioning the letters, the name appears, Barak H. Ubama. To have a full name in a small anagram consisting only of nine spaces is truly incredible. If one wants to use the letter O, row 10 just has to be included.

	A	B	C	D	E	F	G	H	I	J	K	L
6	A		M									
7	B	A	R									
8	H	U	K									
9												
10			O									
11												
12												
13												
14												

Fig. 1 The name: Barak H. Obama

After finding the name, I look for the Hebrew years connected to the name. I increased the number of rows from number 6 to number 11, which is still a small anagram.

By gematria or numerology where every letter has a corresponding number, the numbers 5766 and 5788 appeared as shown in figure 2. These are the Hebrew years which correspond to the modern years 2006 and 2008. By the ELS method where one looks for equidistant sequencing of letters or numbers to produce a pattern, the Hebrew years are discovered. The numbers 5, 7, 6, and 6 are lined up vertically one after the other, pointing to the name. In 5766 or 2006, Mr. Obama easily won a senate seat. The other numbers, namely, 5, 7, 6, and 8 start from the middle initial H with an interval of two spaces between the numbers and going in the right direction. In year 5768 or 2008 is the U.S. presidential election. Will Senator Obama win if he runs?

	A	B	C	D	E	F	G	H	I	J	K	L
6	A		M									
7	B	A	R									
8	H5	6	K									
9		U6	H5			7			6			8
10		7										
11		5										
12												
13												
14												

Fig. 2 Hebrew Years 5766 and 5768 = Years 2006 and 2008.

The letters *C* and *K* are numerically and phonetically the same in Hebrew thus the name Barack and Barak are the same. The ancient Hebrew language does not contain the letter *W* thus by numerology the letter *U* can replace the letter *W*. Thus, the initials UH can mean WH, which can be the "White House" with the direction pointing to year 2008. There are so many mind-boggling coincidences, one can only wonder.

Many of the revelations contained in the book have already been fulfilled; thus I am not afraid to include in the book my observation about Senator Obama.

The name of Hillary Clinton does not appear in the grid; thus there is doubt as to her capability to win.

GLOSSARY OF HEBREW WORDS

A

A—From
AAA—Ahih Ashr Ahih, name of the Father
AB—Father, Zodiacal month Leo, fruits
ABA—Father
ABD—Lost, Ruined
ABL—Second son of Adam and Eve
ACh—Brother
AChAD—Unity
AChTh—One
AD—Vapor, Mist
ADAM—First Man, Husband of Eve
ADMA—Earth
AG—Initials of Elohim Gibor, God name for the fifth Sephera God of Power, swear
ADNI HA-ARETZ, God name for the tenth Sephera
AEQ BEKER—Another method of Gematria
AHA—Name of Venus
AHEBAH—Love
AI—Island, first and tenth Sepheroth
AIMA—Father, Mother
AIN/AYN—Nothingness, Infinity
AIN SOPH—Infinity
AIN SPOH AUR—Infinite Light
AK—Certainly, Calamity
AL—God, Power
AM—Mother, Source, Origin
AMA—Name of God the Mother
AMK—Thy Mother
AMEN—A name of God

AMET—Truth
AMSh—Air, Water, and Fire
AN—Pain, Sorrow, ancient name of Heliopolis
ANA—I beseech
ANI—I
AO—Circular lights descending through the ten Sepheroth
AOB—Familiar spirits
AOTZR—Treasures
AR—Light of the Sun
ARETZ—Earth, world
ARV—Means lion
AS—Rim, Initial of Ain Soph, Infinity, without end, to conceive
ASAH—To make
ASh—Fire, heat
AShH—Woman
AShKR—Gifts, offerings
AShM—Air, Fire, Water
AShMA—Name
AShER—That
ASN—Ruin, Destruction
AT—Diviner
ATE—Thou
ATEM—You
ATh—Essence, sign
ATz—Hasten, hurry, initials for Alhim Tzabaoth, God's name for the eight
    Sephera
AV—Desire, will
AVE—Father
AYA—A name of God

B

BA—To go
BAR—Son
BARA—To create
BATh—Daughter
BET—Daughter
BH—To be broken, confused
BI—Dwell within, in me
BINAH—Understanding

BK—To weep, lament
BN—Son
BO—To seek, request, pray
BSh—Initial of Beth Shemesh, House of the Sun, troubled mind, to be ashamed
BS—To trample, step, pile up
BT—Swell, burst forth, shine
BTOh—Trusted
BU—To come in, enter into, sexual union

C

Ch/ChETh—Life
ChAY—Living
CHESED—Mercy
ChI—Vinegar, penetrate
ChL—Profane, Unholy, Wall, Rampart
ChM—Ancient name of Egypt, hot sun
ChN—Without sin, Immaculate
ChO—High, Heavenly Sun
ChOL—Profane, Unholy
ChS—God spare him, forbearance
ChT—Dig, Hollow, Failure, Sin, Wretched
ChTh—Terrified, broken, fear
ChV—Bosom
CHYL—Wealth

D

DA—To know
DAL—Wretched
DBA—Riches, Power
DH—Go slowly, to walk
DI—Something hanging, Weak, Feeble
DL—Feeble, Weak, wretched
DM—Blood, Life
DIN—Justice
DO—Knowledge, Knowing
DSh—Entrance, Door
DT—Upper Chamber
DV—Love, Friendship
DY—Plenty

E

EL—Compassionate God
ELOHA—Name of God
ELU—These are
EM—Mother
EMET—Truth
EN—Son
ETh—Time, Season
ETz—Tree

G

GAHAL—Redeem
GAL—Redeemer, redeem, heap
GALH—Redemption
GBA—Gather, Collect
GEMATRIA—Substitution of letters with the same numeral values
GK—Thy altar
GR—Dwelling
GU—Among
GY—Valley of Death

H

HA—Mother
HARA—Evil
HAY—Life
HCh—Last and first letter of Chih, life force
HE—Pray to Him to refrain from sin and reconcile with your enemies
HK—To go
HI—Lamentation
HL—To shine, Praise God
HM—Excited, Greedy, Envious
HN—Behold, Enjoyment
HO—Search for, Sexual contact
HOD—Splendor, eight Sephera
HOKMAH—Wisdom
HON—Riches

HR—Pyramid, Mountain
HS—Salvation, to be silent
HSh—Relief, Salvation, I pray
HT—Perversion, Coition
HUA—Avenging Angel
HV—Mother and Son
HU—God, Power

I

IAV—Initials for Ihvh Eloah Vau Daat, God name for the sixth Sephera
IHVH—Highest name of the Hebrew God
IK—To be firm, stand upright
IL—Bring forth, Beget, Child
IM—Ocean, Lake
IN—Awaken, Dove, Wine
IO—Shovel, Hail
IS—Foundation, Support
ISh—Ancient of Days, Elder, Man
ITz—Go forth, bring forth, initials for IHVH Tzabaoth, God name for the
    seventh Sephera

K

KABALAH—Esoteric tradition of the Jews
KAIN—First son of Adam and Eve
KBSh—Lamb
KCh—Strength, power
KETHER—Crown, First Sepheroth
KI—Whole, Totality, One
KL—Altogether, One, All
KM—How many, much, long
KMT—Another ancient name of Egypt, which refers to the silt deposited by the
    Nile during its inundation, making the land looks black. The other variants
    of the name are KM and ChEM.
KN—Base, Stand, Position in life, Honest
KR—Lamb, Meadow
KS—Throne
KSh—Knock, Strike, Shake

L

LCh—Green, moist
LEB—Heart
LEKACH—Doctrine
LM—Protect
LN—To rest, nighttime
LO—Throat, tongue, language
LR—Below, beneath
LS—Cheek, jaw
LTh—That which clings to a person, fate
LTz—Bad company, Scorn

M

MA—Earth, nation, specie
MAG—Magus
MALKUTH—Kingdom, tenth Sepheroth
MRA/MARA—The Sea, root word for the name Mary
MEM—Water
MEN—Portion
MET—Death
MH—Which, what
MI—Who, which
MIN—Specie, nation
ML—To cut, divide
MN—Manna, portion, receding
MO—Womb, belly
MOL—To lie
MOREH—Teacher of Righteousness
MR—Bitterness, violent, speak, hasten Lord
MS—Suffering, consumed with the desire
MSh—Intercourse, sex, worldly affairs, search for
MSO/MSU—666, the number of the beast
MTz—press, suckle

N

NA—Please pray to NA in time of trouble and perturbation, pain, sorrow
NAR—Fiery
NETzACh—Victory, Seventh Sepheroth

NI—Lament
NILE—The river Nile in Egypt
NO—Thebes, shaking, motion
NR—Lamp, candle, light, prosperity
NS—Something lifted up, warning sign
NTz—Hawk, flower, blossom
NUN—Pray to Nun for safe journey and success, symbol of the Fish
NUR—Fiery, fire

O

OI—Ruins
OR—Awake, denude
OTh—Accumulation of wealth, number 24
OSh—Ursa Major, to do, work, prepare
OTz—Tree of Life

R

RA—The Jews made the God of Egypt, Evil
RAB—Many, weighty
RASh—Inheritance
RAShAH—Inherit
REShIT—In the beginning
RSh—Poverty, crushed, Power
RU—Abundance
RUACh—Spirit, wind

S

SACh—Initials for Sadai Al Chai, God Name for the ninth Sephera
ShALM—Peace
ShALOV AOT—Equidistant Letter Sequence
SEMIPHORAS—Names of God
SETh—First spiritual son of Adam
Sh—Fire
ShD—Demon, devil
ShEKINAH—God the Daughter
ShI—Soft
ShiLH—Messiah
ShLOH—Messiah

ShM—Name
ShMA—Hear, Listen
ShMI—My name
ShMO—His name
SM—Drug, poison
SMK—Circle, serpent biting its tail
SO—Company, council
SOD—Secret
SOTER—Messiah
SR—Low spirited, courage has left
ST—Transgressed
STz—Picture of images

T

TAU—Symbol for the cross, last letter of the Hebrew alphabet
TI—Potter, clay
TIL—Missile
TIPhERETh—Beauty, sixth Sepheroth
TL—Lamb, cover, veil
TM—Unclean, to defile, whore, perfect
TN—Basket
TO—Idol, to go astray
TSh—To hide, protect, to be hidden
TTz—Pretense, concealment
TzION—signs
TzI—Slip, dryness

V

VI—Hand, initials for Son and Father
VIA—Way
VCh—Last, outmost
VL—Child, number 36
VM—Initials for Rose of Heaven
VN—Weak, meek
VO—Addition, increase
VR—Rose, heart
VS—Stain, color

Y

YA—Shovel
YAH—God of Wisdom, Name of God in the second Sepheroth
YAVE—One of the suggested pronunciation of the unpronounceable name of God
YATzAR—To form
YEShUA—Hebrew name of Jesus, which means "He shall save."
YHVH—The highest name of the Hebrew God
YHShUH—Kabalistic name of Jesus
YESOD—Foundation, ninth Sepheroth
YEYA—Name of God
YH—Name of God in the second Sepheroth
YOM—Day
YONAH—Dove
YOTzAI—Begotten
YShU—Variant of Yeshua
YShUH—Variant of Yeshua

The Hebrew words contained in this brief glossary are compiled from the following sources:

1. *The Key of It All-Book I* by D. A. Hulsey
2. *The Ancient Qabalistic Writings* by D. J. Conway
3. *777 and Other Qabalistic Writings* by A. Crowley
4. *The Bahir* by A. Kaplan
5. *The Golden Dawn* by I. Regardie
6. *The Alef-Beit* by Rabbi Y. Ginsburgh
7. *The Book of the Sacred Magic of Abra-Melin* by. S. L. Macgregor-Mather
8. *A Comprehensive Dictionary of the Gods* by A. S. Baumgartner
9. *Cracking the Bible Code* by J. Satinover
10. *The Englishman's Hebrew Concordance of the Old Testament* by George V. Wigram
11. *Webster's New World Hebrew Dictionary* by Hayim Baltsam
12. *The Wisdom of the Zohar* by Isaiah Tishby

I did not choose the holy names that will be in italics. They just appeared. What is intriguing is that only chosen holy names were italicized.

Glossary of Egyptian Words

A

AA—Great One; the name is written several times in the grid
AA—Wash the heart, sin against god, boat
AAAB—Great heart
AAAUR—Incarnation of the spirits that praise the sun
AAB—Offerings, presents
AAB—Great heart
AAHU—Moon god, the name is found in several quadrants
AAI—Three divine beings connected with RA
AAIT—Divine old men
AAKU—Deified human beings
AAKU—God of light and splendor
AAKU—Group of gods
AANU—Adoration
AAR—Serpent
AARAT—Snake goddess
AARTI—Two snake goddesses, Isis and Nepthys
AARTU—Living serpent
AARU—Portion of the abode of the blessed world
AAT—Kingdom of Osiris
AAT—Great one; the word is written several times in the grid
AAT—Two ancient goddesses, Isis and Nepthys
AATA—Priest
AATEB—Flood, rainstorm
AATI—Two kingdoms of Osiris
AATI—Two ancient goddesses, Isis and Nepthys
AAU—To praise
AAU—Portion of the abode of the blessed
AB—Heart, to purify, altar
ABA—Heart-soul, entrance

ABARU—Open the mouth

ABATA—Opener of the earth

ABIT—The insect that brings the dead to the Hall of Osiris

ABSHE—Monster crocodile that eats hearts of lost souls

ABT—Eastern region of Egypt

ABTA—Monster serpent that guards the underworld

ABTI—Doubly holy

ABTU—Maternal and paternal ancestors

ABTU—City god of Abydos

ABTU—Maternal and paternal ancestors

ABU—The island of Elephantine

AB UR—A title of Osiris

AKB—Flood

AKB/AKBA—Celestial Nile, which refers to the Milky Way and the Orion Constellation

AKABIO—Divine beings

AKAU—Name of a god

AKHAB—To give to drink

AKHEN—Guardian serpent of the underworld

AH—Moon god, the name is written many times in the grid

AHAT—Means palace, ancient goddesses identified with Hathor, her form is the cow or a woman

AHIT—Goddess who supplied the dead with food

AHTI—Another name of Osiris

AHU—God connected with offering

AKER—Ancient of the earth gods

AKERIU—A group of earth gods appearing as serpents

AKERU—Ancestor gods of Re

AKHAB—To give

AKHU—Shining Ones, Star people

AKIT—Chamber

AMA—Priest

AM AB—What is in the heart?

AMAM—Monster beast that eats the hearts of sinners

AMENOA—He whose name is hidden

AMENT—Hidden place, to hide

AMENT—Another name of Osiris, abode of the departed souls

AMENTIU—Goddess of Amenti

AM HEH—Eater of Eternity

AMI—Dweller in Ausek; chamber

AMI AB—He who is in the heart

AMI—MU—He who is in the water
AMN/AMEN—Great Father
AMSI—God of generation
AMT—Chamber
AMU—Divine beings
AMU/AAMU—Gods of fire
AMUI TA—Those on earth
AN—Name of a god
ANAT—Lady of Heaven
ANHUR—God of war
ANI—Treasurer of offerings
ANKH—The symbol of life associated with Egypt. It is a cross with the sun
    on top of it.
ANT—Solar boat
ANTIU—Four beings with four serpent heads each
ANTU—Pure offerings
ANU—Abode of the dead; gifts offerings
ANU—Gifts, offerings
ANU—Another name for Heliopolis or On
ANUKIS—A goddess
AOB—Hebrew word for "familiar spirits"
ARAU—Name of a god
ARI—Guardians
ARU KHUT—Beings of light, guardians
AS/AST—Another ancient name for ISIS, the Great Mother
ASAR—Ancient name of Osiris, the husband of Isis and the father of Horus
ASAR NEB HEH—Osiris, Gold of Eternity
ASBIO—Fiery spirits
ASEB—Fire god
ASHAR—Name of a god
ASHEM—Forms in which gods appear before men
ASHER—Name of an ancient city in Egypt.
ASHER—Name of a god
ASHU—Name of a god
AST MATI—Where the law is administered
AT—Hall, palace
ATEM/TEM—God of Night
ATEN—God of the solar disk
ATER—Canal, stream
ATI—Ancient name of Lower Egypt
ATIU—Evil beings

ATON—One God
ATTU—God connected with offering
ATU—Food offerings
ATUM—The Creator
AU—Offerings
AUA—God of the extended arms; the name is contained in several
    quadrants
AUHER—Bearer of the sky
AUI—Gods
AUKERU—Gods of the Heliopolitan
AUSU—Scale, balance
AUUR—Pregnant goddess

B

BA—Soul
BAH—To be flooded; flood
BAI—Divine soul
BAIU—Divine souls
BATA—A shepherd god
BEKA—Tomorrow
BES—God of the Dwarfs; enter
BESI—A god of the underworld
BSh—Means "House of the Sun" or more figuratively "The Land of the Sun" of
    which Egypt is known due to its burning sun and scorching desert.

C

ChEOCh—In the Egyptian desert, stands one of the most beautiful pyramids
    in the world called Cheop. In this illustration, the word *ChEOCh* appears.
    One may say that there is no pyramid in Egypt called Cheoch for the
    greatest pyramid in Egypt is called Cheop. This is correct, but by the
    method of Gematria, the letter *Ch* and the letter *P* can be interchanged
    for they have the same numerical value of 8; hence Cheoch can become
    Cheop. The Pyramid was also called in ancient times as EAKU or
    YAKU.[11]

E

EL—Means "stars"

H

HA—The hieroglyphic symbol of the western desert. It is intriguing that the word *HA* appeared eight times on the western part of the Grid, the eastern part of the Grid being where the words *SOL, OM, ON,* and *CHO*, which all mean "SUN" are placed.

HAH—God of Infinity

HAI—Light

HAU—Time, period

HEBT—Flood

HEFEM—One hundred thousand

HEH—Million

HEH EN SEP—Millions of times

HEKA—God of magic;

HEMI—A guardian of the underworld

HENHENU—Flood

HER—Ancient name of the sun

HERU—Judgment day

HO—Means search

HORUS / HERU—The son of Isis and the third person of the Egyptian Trinity

HR—Means pyramid

HU—God of Food; ancient name of the Sphinx

HUL—Ancient name of the Sphinx

I

INNU—Another ancient name of Heliopolis and the Sphinx

ITUM/ATUM—The Creator; the name is found on the sixth horizontal row and seventh vertical row and reading vertically downward, the letters are side by side without ELS

ITY—God of music

IUSAS/IVSAS—Goddess with a scepter in the right hand and an ankh in the left

K

KA—Spirit

KA—Divine Bull; the word is written several times in the grid

KADASh—Goddess of Love

KAS—Chamber

KAU—Food

KA TESHER—Red Bull

KHA—One thousand
KHAT—Physical body
KHEMEM—Eight
KHEMT—Thrice, third
KHU—Spirit soul

M

MAA—Egyptian word for "Lion"
MAA—The Mother, Wife of Thoth, Daughter of Ra
MAAT—The Mother
MAB—Thirty
MAKHA—Pair of scales
MASHERU—Evening
MAU—Another Egyptian word for lions; the word is written several times in the grid
MAW—Today
MEH—To be submerged; cubit
MEHEN—Serpent goddess
MEHIT—Goddess of the world; flood
MENU—Chamber
MESU NEBU—The human race, all children
MER—Also the name of the Pyramid in ancient time
METES—A guardian of the underworld
MIN—God of Fertility
MSH—Means guardians
MUT—World Mother, Giver of Life, Queen of Heaven, Wife of Amen—Ra
MUT—Weights
MUT NETCHET—Mother of God

N

NAU—Serpent with seven heads
NEB—Late times
NEB AB—Lord of hearts, Lord of offerings
NEB HEH—Lord of Eternity
NEB KAU—Lord of food
NEHEH—Forever
NEHES—Another divine companion of RA
NEITH—War goddess
NEHIT—Eternity without beginning or end

NEMENT—Forty

NENNUI—Beginning

NENTI—End of time

NER—Name of the Herd god

NERI—Mighty one

NET/NIT—Mother of the Gods, Great Goddess

NETCHEM—God of love

NETER—The general name for God

NETERU—Common name for the gods

NHR—Storm

NI—God with two bird's heads

NILE—Which in biblical Hebrew is called YR or YEOR. Geologists believe that millions of years ago, an ocean covered a portion of Egypt that was cited by Herodotus in his book *The Histories* as the Triton Sea. When the waters receded, islands were formed and the huge ancestral Nile appeared. The *National Geographic Magazine*[7] wrote that 5.5 million years ago, the Mediterranean Sea was dry and the ancient Nile emptied to the dry seabed. Around 800,000 BC, the Nile delta expanded. According to Stephen S. Mehler,[8] the ancient Nile still existed between 60,000 to 20,000 BC and the scientists and the geologists called the primodial river UR NIL.

NM—Dwarfs, to live again

NO—Another ancient name of Thebes

NUB HEH—Eternal Gold, Osiris

NU—Great Mother; season, time, hour

NUN—Goddesses of the Ocean; the name is written several times in the grid.

NUT—Large collection of water; night sky

NUT—Life Giver, Mother of Gods and of all living symbolized by a cow

O

ON—Ancient names of Heliopolis and the Sphinx

R

RA/RE—Sun God; the name is written twelve times in the grid as if to imply that RA or the SUN travels through the twelve signs of the Zodiac yearly.

RAU—Divine companion of RA

REM—A god symbolizing the tears of Ra

REN—Name of the dead

RENENET—Goddess of good fortune

RUTY—God with a lion face, a guardian

S

SA—God of Knowledge; the name is written several times in the grid

SAA—Shepherd, a title of Osiris

SAH—Refers to the constellation of ORION, the constellation of Osiris; mummy

SAHU—Spiritual body

SAN—Means "stars"

SAS—Six

SATI—Two divine daughters, Isis and Nepthys

SATIS—Goddess who spreads the water of the Nile over the land

SEB—Husband of Nut, God of Earth

SEK—To decay

SEKHMET/SEKMET—Lion-headed goddess, the Powerful

SER—Osiris

SHAI—The goddess of destiny

SHAT EA SHAU—Known as the book of the Pylons that deals with Osiris and Tuat, the underworld

SHAY—Male guardian angel

SHAYT—Female guardian angel

SHE—Chamber of embalmment of Osiris

SHETA—Hidden, mystery

SHETA HER—Hidden face

SHETAIT—Hidden place

SHHU—Lord of the Sky and Air, Brother of Tefnut, separated heaven and earth

SIA—God of knowledge

SMEH—To be submerged

SMEHIT—Flood

SU—Sunlight

T

TA—To pass away

TA—Means "Hot," which is another reference to the Land of the Sun.

TA AB—Pure land

TAAB—Pure Heart

TAITI—Osiris

TAIU—Land, world

TAMERU—Ancient name of Upper and Lower Egypt

TA MEH—The Delta

TATA—To give
TAT AB—Heart's desire
TATAU—Gift
TA-UR—Great land
T—CHATCHAT—Council of gods
T-CHAUI—Two snake goddesses, Isis and Nepthys
T-CHERTI—Two snake goddesses, Isis and Nepthys
TEMAR—Ancient name of Osiris
TENI—A city near Abydos
TESHER—The desert or Red Land
TESHERT—Crown of Lower Egypt
TESUR—Another name of Osiris
TH—Gifts
TUAT—Other world
TURA—To purify
TUT—Evils beings, evil

U

UA—One, path
UAHTU—Mummify
UAR—Passage
UASH—watch UASH—To worship
UAST—Ancient name of Thebes
UAT—Path
UATCHIT—Two fire goddesses, Isis and Nepthys
UATCH UR—Ancient name of the Mediterranean Sea
UAU—Waterway
UHEN—To decay
UHEM—A second time
UI—Dual
UKHA—Night, darkness
UNES—Metropolis of Lower Egypt
UNNU—Another name for the ancient city, Hermopolis, the city of Thoth
UNNUT—Goddess of the hour, a moment, an hour
UR HEKAU—Deity powerful in magic
URMA—High priest
URSH—Watchers
URT—Palace, flood
URT AB—He whose heart is still, a title of Osiris
URTI—Two ancient goddesses, Isis and Nepthys

USHAU—Night
UT—Abode of Anubis
UTAU—Class of divine beings
UTEN—Bring offerings
UTET—Begetter, name of Osiris
UTHES—To lift up
UTIT—Chamber
UTU—Embalmment

Y

YOHR—Storm

Glossary of
Sumerian Words

A

A—Water
AB—Cow
AKKAD/AKAD—Part of the Kingdom of Sumer
AIA—Wife of the sun god
AMARU—Deluge; the letters are in the form of a boat
AN—The highest god of Sumer who is considered the Father; the Moon god; heaven
ANSHAR—Refers to the planet Saturn
ANU—The planet Uranus; the Father—God of Sumer
APSU—The "Sun"
ARALI—Place of the Neters of the Shining Lodes
ARU—Conceive
ASAR—Another name of Marduk
ASHERA—Mother goddess
ASHUR—Another ancient city of Sumer
ATRA-HASIS—Ancient text dated around 1,700 BC describing the Sumerian gods called the Annunakis and the Igigis and describing how the gods constructed canals, waterways, channels, and the Tigris and Euphrates rivers.
A.(T)ZU—Means water physician

B

BARU—Seers
BA-U—Wife of Nin-Urta

D

DILMUN—Ancient place considered a paradise whose location is unknown

E

EA—Second son of An, the god of wisdom who saved mankind from the flood

EAKU—Ancient name for the Pyramid Cheop. The name sounds very Sumerian as it is a combination of two Sumerian words EA, the name of the Sumerian water god EA who had authority over Magan (Egypt) and E. KUR meaning "House of Mountain," an ancient Sumerian term for the Pyramids. Although the word EA.KU can mean "The land of EA," it is also possible that the complete name for the Great Pyramid was not EAKU but EAKUR, which means "The Mountain House of EA" or the "Pyramid of EA." Whether the name is EA.KU or EAKUR, it shows the link between Sumer and Egypt. However, there will be a serious implication for it means that the Great Pyramid is older than the age being attributed to it now; that the Pyramid was constructed in an earlier period beyond the recorded time of the Egyptian.

EAMU—Meaning the "waters of EA" or "abode of the divine beings"

EANU—Ancient name of Heliopolis; it can mean the "Abode of Anu" the God the Father of the Sumerians) or AN (Sumerian term for Heaven or Anu).

EBIH—The Kur (mountain) that the goddess Innana fought

E. DIN—Home of the Righteous Ones, which became the basis of the Christians' "Garden of Eden."

E.KUR—House like a Mountain, the name given by the Sumerians to the pyramid.

EN—Lord

ENLL/ENLIL—Eldest son of An, lord of the airspace; he destroyed the earth with flood

ENU—Change, replace

G

GAGA—Refers to the planet Pluto

H

HA—Fish

HAKATHA—Ancient text from Babylon containing about one hundred pages of instructions on how to build a flying machine and admonitions about responsible flying respectively.

HAY—Rain

I

IA. (T)ZU—Oil physician
ISIN—Another ancient city of Sumer

K

KA—Month
KALAH—Another city of Sumer
KEBAHNU—The Ark
KI—The planet Earth, ancient name of Sumer
KINGU—The planet Moon
KISHAR—Is the planet Jupiter in Sumerian

L

LAGASH—One of the first five cities in Sumer
LAHAMU—The planet Venus
LAHMU—The planet Mars

M

MAH—High
MAR—Son
MARDUK—The name of the chief god of the Babylonians whose name was
    given to the twelve planet
MARUKA—Other name of Marduk
ME—Divine force
MUMMU—Means the planet Mercury
MUL—Star

N

NAG—Drink
NANNA—Moon god
NIN—Lady
NINEVEH—A city of Sumer
NINLL—Wife of Enlil
NIN-TI—Lady of Life, title of Ninhursag
NI-SI—Mankind; the word is underneath "Amaru"

R

REHOBOTH—Another city of Sumer
RESEN—A city between Nineveh and Kalah

S

SAR/SAROI—One year of the Annunakis, which is equivalent to 3,600 years of earthly time. Thus, one year for these advanced beings would be equivalent to 3,600 earthly years.
SHE—Barley
SHINAR/SINAR—Name given by the Bible to Sumer
SHU—Means "seven"
SHUMU—Seven shining ones
SIN—the Sumerian or Mesopotamian moon god An
SUMER/SHUMER—An ancient civilization reputed to be older tan Egypt or India; The Feats and Exploits of Ninurta—ancient story about the battle between Ninurta, son of Enlil, and the Kur. When the Kur was defeated, a calamity occurred. The primeval water that Kur held in cheek rose to the surface preventing the fresh water from irrigating the farms. So Ninurta, put up heaps of stones over the dead Kur like a wall to hold the water and as a result the waters of the lower region could not rise up to the surface anymore. The waters that had flooded the land, Ninurta collected and channeled to the Tigris River. This story connected the Kur to water. Another version of the story is called the Ninurta Myth Lugal E written around 2150 BC.

T

TI—The Sumerian word for life
TUTU—Another name of Marduk
UR—The city where Abraham came from
UTU—The Sun god

Y

YABU—Ancient name for the Egyptian town Kherara, which actually was EABU that means the "Land of EA," the Sumerian water god. EABU is a combination of the Sumerian word *EA* and the Khemetian word *BU* meaning "place or land." Actually, EA and YA are phonetically and numerically the same. EA, the Sumerian god of wisdom, also became YA, the Semitic god of wisdom.
YAM—The sea
YNANNA/INANNA—Daughter of Anu; the source of the goddess cult

BIBLIOGRAPHY

Part I The Search

Chapter 1 The Lord's Prayer

1. Magic in Theory and Practice by Aleister Crowley
2. Mathew 13, 10-10 'The Holy Bible by Good Council Publishers 1966
3. Ibid 13:13
4. Historical Jesus by John Dominic Crossan p. 294
5. Matthew 6:9 The Holy Bible by Good Council Publishers 1966
6. Luke 11 The Holy Bible by Good Council Publishers 1966
7. Who Wrote the Gospels? By Rondel Mccraw Helms p. 6
8. Tempest and Exodus by Ralf Ellis p. 31
9. Isaiah 6:16-17 p. 625 The Holy Bible by Good Council Publishers 1966
10. Ibid 64:8-9
11. Readers Digest Book "The Bible through All the Ages"
12. Sacred Book of the Jews by Harry Garsh p. 34-35
13. World Study Greek English New Testament by Paul R. McReynolds
14. The Jesus Mysteries by T. Freke and P. Gandy p. 360
15. Jovial (June 27) "Hebrew is the Language of Matthew by Joe
16. Who Wrote the Gospels? P. 42 by Rondel Mccraw Helms
17. The Secret Teachings of Jesus by Marvin W, Meyer containing the Nag Hammadi Scroll "The Secret Book of James" Chapter 1, 2-3
18. Words of Power: Sacred Sound of East and West p. 225 by Brian and Easter Crowley
19. Internet: a) Targum Franz Delitsch
             b) Version given by the Convent of Pater Noster
             c) Version from the database called the Scripture of the World

Part II Discovery of the Code

Chapter 2 The Grid

1. Bible Code 2 by Michael Drosnin p. 242
2. Proverbs 25, 2 The Holy Bible, King James Version by Camex International
3. Gospel of Truth" cited in "The Nag Hammadi Library" by James M. Robinson p. 40:
4. The Greek Kabalah by Kieren Barry
5. The Mystery of Numbers by Anne Marie Schimmel p. 34 Oxford University Press 1993
6. The Cylinder of Gudea cited in the book "The Harp that Once" by Thorkild Jakobsen p. 412

Chapter 3 Methods of Decoding

1. Encyclopedia of Mystical and Paranormal Experiences by R.E. Guiley
2. The Bible Code 2 by Michael Drosnin
3. His Name is Jesus by Yakov Rambel p. 49
4. The Mysterious Bible Code by Grant R. Jeffrey p. 27
5. The Bible Code 2 by Michael Drosnin

The Old Testament is a Code

1. Gospel of John 1:1 King James Version and the Good Council Version
2. Ibid 14:10 The Holy Bible by The Good Council Publishers 1966
3. The Kabbalah Unveiled by S.L.M. Mather p. 8
4. Gospel of John 10:30 The Holy Bible by The Good Council Publishers 1966
5. The Mysterious Bible Code by Grant Jeffreys

Part III The Findings

Chapter 4 The New Testament

1. Matthew 5:44, The Holy Bible by the Good Council Publishers 1966
2. Ibid 5:38
3. Luke 23:34 The Holy Bible by the Good Council Publishers 1966
4. The Mysterious Bible Code by Grant Jeffreys
5. The Lost Years of Jesus by Elizabeth C. Prophet
6. The Christ Conspiracy, The Greatest Story Ever Sold by Acharya S.

The Mysterious Names

1. Gospel of John 17:26 The Holy Bible by the Good Council Publishers 1966
2. The Lost Years of Jesus by Elizabeth C. Prophet
3. The Christ Conspiracy by Acharya S
4. The Sirius Connection by Murry Hope p. 92
5. The Bible Code by Michael Drosnin p. 247
6. Revelations 3:12 The Holy Bible by the Good Council Publishers 1966

Symbols

1. Gospel of John 1:29 The Holy Bible by the Good Council Publishers 1966
2. Mathew 4:18-19 The Holy Bible by the Good Council Publishers 1966
3. Kabbalah by C. Ponce page 172
4. Mythology by C. Scott Littleman p. 348
5. Karunungan ng Diyos by M. Sabino
6. The Christ Conspiracy by Acharya S

Christian Doctrines

1. Gospel of St. John Chapter 6:35 The Holy Bible by The Good Council Publishers 1966
2. Ibid 7:12
3. Ibid 14:5-7
4. Ibid 4:16
5. John 7:16 King James Version
6. Luke 1:34-35 The Holy Bible by the Good Council Publishers 1966
7. John 1:14 The Holy Bible by the Good Council Publishers 1966
8. Ibid 5:16

Mary, the Mother of Jesus

1. Luke 1:28 The Holy Bible by the Good Council Publishers 1966
2. The Gospel of the Hebrews
3. John 19:27
4. Ibid 19:26
5. Ibid 16:7

Mara Magdala

6. Gospel of Mary cited in the Nag Hamadi Library by James M. Robinson p. 473
7. Ibid p. 473
8. The Gospel of Philip cited in the Nag Hamadi Library by James M. Robinson p. 135
9. The Christ Conspiracy by Acharya S.

Authenticity of the Gospels

1. Christ Conspiracy by Acharya S citing Bronson Keeler, author of "A Short History of the Bible"
2. "The Book Your Church Doesn't Want You to Read" by John Remsberg quoted in "The Christ Conspiracy" by Acharya S.
3. Christ Conspiracy by Acharya S.
4. The Woman's Encyclopedia of Myths and Secrets by Barbara Walker

Existence of the Gospels

1. The Christ Conspiracy, the Greatest Story Ever Sold by Acharya S p. 24
2. Ibid p. 37, Luke 9:22
3. The Christ Conspiracy by Acharya S p. 38-39
4. Ibid

Chapter 5 The Old Testament

Genesis Creation Story

1. Genesis 1:26-27
2. Ibid 2:7
3. Ibid 2:21-22

Interplay of Words

4. Isaiah 43:7
5. Sefer Yetzirah by Aryeh Kaplan p. 43
6. Earth Chronicles by Zecharias Sitchin
7. Genesis 1:26

Companion of God in Creation

8. Ibid 1:26-27
9. Wisdom 9, 9
10. Proverbs 8:27-30
11. Ibid 3, 19
12. Ibid 1:36
13. Wisdom 9:4

Sumerian Creation Story

14. Myths of Cattle and Grain cited in Sumerian Mythology by S.N. Kramer p. xx
15. Divine Encounter by Z. Sitchin p. 117
16. Atra Hasis, Myths from Mesopotemia by Stephanie Dalley, Oxford U. Press 1998
17. The Earth Chronicles by Zecharias Sitchin
18. Divine Encounters by Z. Sitchin p. 8
19. Genesis, 11:1
20. Sumerian Mythology by Samuel N. Kramer p. x Greenwood Press Publications Westport Connecticut 1961
21. Genesis 10:25
22. Ibid 11:8
23. Ancient Near Eastern Texts relating to the Old Testament by James B. Pritchard, Princeton U. Press, 1950; Lamentation on the Destruction of Ur
24. Sumerian Mythology by Samuel N. Kramer p. 157 U. of Pennsylvania 1972
25. Encyclopedia Britannica p. 929 Vol. 5 Encyclopedia Britannica Inc. p. 1980
26. Sumerian Mythology by Samuel N. Kramer p. x Greenwood Press Publications Westport Connecticut 1961
27. Divine Encounters by Z. Sitchin p. 28

Time and Numbers

28. Psalm 90 verse 4
29. Encyclopedia of Mystical Places by Robert Ingpen and Philip Wilkenson, p. 83
30. Ramayana by Ramesh Menon p. xv, North Point Press NY 2001
31. Myths from Mesopotemia by Stephanie Dalley, Oxford U. Press, 1998

The Calendar

32. The Sirius Mystery by Robert Temple p. 44
33. The Sirius Connection by Murry Hope p. 19, 116-117
34. Who's Who in Egyptian Mythology by Anthony S. Mercante, Metro Books 2002
35. Manetho by W.G. Woddell p. 99 Harvard U. Press, 1990
36. Genesis 4:26 Tanak, Baal Haturim Chumash Vol. 1 Bereishis by Rabbi Avie Gold, Mesorah Publications LTD. 1999
37. Mysteries of the Creation by Rabbi Dovid Brown p. 89 Targum Press Inc. 1997
38. The Orion Prophecy by Patrick Geryl and Gino Ratincykx

Dating Methods

39. The Genesis Race by Will Hart p. 189 Bear & Co. Rochester Vermont 2003

Origin of Man

1. Past Worlds, Atlas of Archeology by Harper Collins p. 54
2. Genesis 6:3
3. Divine Encounters by Z. Sitchin p. 43
4. Psalms 90 verse 10
5. Matt. 19:6

DNA

6. The Cosmic Code by Z. Sitchin p. 149
7. Ibid. p. 115

E. Din

1. Genesis 2:8
2. Myths of Cattle and Grain quoted by Z. Sitchin in the Divine Encounter p. 17
3. Genesis 2-10
4. Ibid 11-14
5. Divine Encounter by Z. Sitchin p. 22
6. Isaiah 20:13

Amphibious Ancestors

7. The Sirius Mystery by Robert Temple, Chapter 9 "A Fable"
8. Ibid p. 279
9. Ibid
10. Sumerian Mythology by Samuel N. Kramer p. 70

Deluge

1. Genesis 6, 19-21

Different Deluge Stories

2. Myths from Mesopotemia by Stephanie Dally, p. 110
3. Ibid p. 112
4. The Ancient World to A.D. 300, Epic of Gilgamesh p. 12 by Paul J. Alexander
5. Flood Myth by Alan Dandes p. 36-37 U. of California Press 1988.
6. Babyloniaca by Berossus
7. Epic of Gilgamesh
8. Divine Encounters by Z. Sitchin p. 94
9. Before the Flood by Ian Wilson p. 5

Abraham

1. Koran 21'53
2. Ibid 21'63
3. Genesis 12-1

King and Pharaoh

4. Ibid 14-14
5. Ibid 15-18
6. Ibid 20:12
7. Jesus, The Last Pharaoh by Ralf Ellis

Part IV Revelations

Chapter 6 The Secret Doctrines

1. Matt. 10, 11 and 13

2. Ibid. 13, 34

3. Ibid 7:6

4 "The Secret Teachings of Jesus" Chapter 1:2-42 by Marvin W. Meyer, one of the scrolls found in Nag Hammadi called "The Secret Book of James" written approximately in the 2nd century A.D.

5. The Secret Book of John 1:68

The World of Unity

6. Ibid

The World of Duality

7. Ephesians 1:21 and in Collosians 1:15

8. The Jesus Mysteries by T. Freke and P. Gandy p. 196

The Tree of Life

9. Exodus 3:14

10. Sefer Yetzirah by A. Kaplan p. 12

Law of Opposites

11. Jeremiah 44, 17-17

12. Jeremiah 8:18

13. Judges 3:7; 6:25-26, 30; 1 Kings 16:33; 18, 19

14. 2 Kings 21:7; 2 Chronicles 17:6,

15. Judges 2, 13; 10, 6; 1 Samuel 31, 10; 1 Kings 11, 5, 33; 2 Kings 22. 13

16. Judges 3, 31; 5:6

17. Jeremiah XLIV. 15-19; Hebrew Myths by Graves

The Father

18. John 17:26

19. Ibid

The Mother

20 Evangelium of the Hebrew

Apocrypal Writings

Existence of the Mother

21. Sirach 33:15

Dove as a Symbol of the Mother

22. Matt. 3:11-17
23. Matt. 13:13
24. Secret Book, Nag Hamadi Library by J. Robison
25. Gospel of the Hebrew, The Non-Canonical Gospel Texts, The Other Gospels by Ron Cameron p. 25
26. Gospel of Thomas
27. Theorem of Occult Magick vol. 3 p. 71
28. Ibid p. 72

Who created the World?

Mary, the Christian symbol of the Mother

29. Luke 1:28
30. Matt. 11:11

Origin of Mary

31. (Mary in the New Testament p. 244)
32. Karunungan ng Diyos by M. Sabino
33. Matt. 12, 48-49
34. Ibid 12:50
35. Luke 1:38
36. (Lord's Prayer)
37. August 25, 1997 issue of Newsweek p. 53

Semiphoras (Names of God)

38. 6th and 7th Books of Moses
39. John 17, 6:
40. Exodus 3:14

41. Number 6:22-27
42. Leviticus 16:30-34
43. Karunungan ng Diyos by Sabino
44. Matthew 8:3
45. Karunungan ng Diyos by M. Sabino
46. Ibid

The Speech of Babies

47. Matt. 11:25 Gideon International, The Holy Bible 1982 Edition
48. Matt. 11:25 The New American Bible
49. Matt. 11:25 Good News Bible by Phil. Bible Society 1982 Edition
50. Psalms 8:3
51. Wisdom 10:1
52. Matt. 11:25 Gideon International, The holy Bible 1982 Edition
53. Psalm 8:3

Part V The Lord's Prayer and the Ancient Civilizations

Chapter VII Ancient Civilizations

1. The Sirius Mystery p. 54 by Robert Temple
2. The Orion Prophecy p. 170 by Geryl Patrick and Gino Ratinckx
3. The Hakatha of Babylon quoted in the book "The Anti-Gravity Handbook" by D. Hatcher Childress

A. The Land of Egypt

1. The Land of Osiris by Stephen S. Muehler p. 40
2. Ancient Eastern Text by James B. Pritchard
3. The Sirius Mystery by Robert Temple p. 96, 111, 135
4. The Land of Osiris by Stephen S. Muehler p. 39
5. The Sirius Mystery by Robert Temple p. 19
6. The Land of Osiris by Stephen S, Mehler p. 140)
7. The Imperiled Nile Delta by Peter Theroux, National Geographic Magazine vol. 191
8. The Land of Osiris by Stephen S. Mehler p. 133
9. The Dead Sea Scroll p. 297 by Martin Abeggdr Jr. Peter Flint and Enger Ulrich, Harper San Francisco 1999
10. Section 5, Business Chicago Tribune June 29, 2003
11. Tempest and Exodus by Ralf Ellis p. 16

12. The Sirius Connection by Murry Hope p. 6
13. Ibid p. 7
14. Manetho W. G. Waddell Harvard University Press 1940
15. The Sirius Connection by Murry Hope p. 6
16. The Sirius Connection by Murry Hope p. 17-18
17. Koran 20:56, quoted by Ralph Ellis in Tempests and Exodus
18. Tempests and Exodus by Ralph Ellis p. 71

Egyptian Religion

1. The Tutankhamun Prophesies by M. Cotterell p. 40
   Angels and Other Spirits
2. The Great Book of Magical Art, Hindu Magic and Indian Occultism by L. W. de Lawrence

Book of the Dead

3. Book of the Dead by Sir. E.A. Wallis Budge
4. The Orion Prophecies by Patrick Geryl and Gino Ratincyxk

Weighing of the Heart

5. Matt. 5:8 Holy Bible by Good Council Publishers 1996
6. Luke 9:49-50 Holy Bible by Good Council Publishers 1996
7. Ancient Mystic Rites by C. W. Leadbeater p. 20

Hidden Records

8. The Orion Prophecies by Geryl Patrick and Gino Ratincyxk
9. Keeper of Genesis p. 92
10. Fingerprints of God p. 442 by R. Bauval and G. Hancock

The Pyramids

1. Exodus 20:24-26 The Holy Bible King James Version
2. The Sacred Marriage Rite p. 37 by Samuel N. Kramer
3. The Sirius Mystery p. 31 by Robert Temple
4. The Cylinder of Gudea quoted in the book "The Harp that Once" Thorkild Jacobsen, Ninurta Myth Lugal E
5. The Sirius Mystery by Robert Temple p. 139
6. Tempest and Exodus by Ralf Ellis p. 16

7. Ibid p. 166
8. The Sirius Connection by Murry Hope p. 31
9. Ibid. p. 31
10. The Harp that Once. P. 386 by Thorkild Jacobsen
11. Manetho by W.G. Waddell p. 55-57
12. Joshua 22:26, 28 34 The Holy Bible King James Version
13. cited by Ralph Ellis in his book "Tempest and Exodus" p. 40
14. Gospel of the Egyptians, Nag Hamadi Library by James Robinson
15. Isaiah 19:21 Holy Bible James Version
16. Ibid 19-24
17. Ibid 19:25
18. Ibid 19:18
19. Ibid 19:19, 20
20. Jeremiah 32:18, 20 Holy Bible King James Version
21. author of the book "The Land of Osiris"
22. Isaiah 2:2 Holy Bible King James Version
23. Ibid
24. Ibid 2:3
25. Tempest and Exodus by Ralf Ellis p. 166-7
26. The Orion Prophecy by Geryl Patrick and Gino Ratincyxk p. 96-98
27. author of the book "Tempest and Exodus" p. 167
28. Exodus 19:12 Holy Bible King James Version
29. Ibid 19:23-24
30. Ibid. 19:18

The Sphinx

1. Stairways of the Gods p 32 by Zecharias Sitchin
2. Keeper of Genesis by R. Bauval and G. Hancock p. 10
3. Fingerprints of the Gods by G. Hancock p. 443-446,
4. Ibid
5. author of "The Sirus Mystery"
6. The Orion Prophecy by Patrick Geryl and Gino Ratincyxk

Why Egypt is in the Grid

1. the book "Christ Conspiracy" by Acharya S p. 115
2. Ibid.
3. Tempest and Exodus by Ralf Ellis p. 78
4. Gen. 14:14 Holy Bible King James Version
5. Ibid. 20:12

6. Manetho by W.G. Waddell
7. Genesis 47:10 Holy Bible King James Version
8. Ibid. 50:7
9. Ibid. 50:11
10. Admonition of Ipuwer cited by Ralf Ellis in the book Tempest and Exodus p. 40; Ancient Near Eastern Texts Relating to the Old Testament by James B. Pritchard, p. 441, Princeton U. Press 1950
11. Exodus 6:3, Holy Bible King James Version
12. Koran 21:56 cited by Ralf Ellis in Tempest and Exodus p. 66
13. Koran 6:78 Tempests and Exodus p. 7 by Ralf Ellis
14. Isaiah 19:2 Holy Bible King James Version
15. Prophecies of Nefertiti" quoted by Ralph Ellis, author of "Tempest and Exodus" p. 36; The Prophecy of Nefer Rohu cited by J. B. Pritchard in Ancient Near Eastern Texts
16. Isaiah in 19:17 Holy Bible King James Version
17. Tempest and Exodus p. 42, 59, 67 by Ralf Ellis. Josephus AA p. 249-50
18. Isaiah said in 19:18-19: Holy Bible King James Version
19. Tempest and Exodus p. 235 by Ralf Ellis
20. Isaiah 11:11 Holy Bible King James Version
21. Ibid. 11:15
22. The Dead Sea Scroll p. 289 by Martin Abeggdr Jr. Peter Flint and Enger Ulrich, Harper, San Francisco 1999
23. Isaiah in 19:5-6 Holy Bible King James Version
24. Dead Sea Scroll p 297 by Martin Abeggdr. Jr., Peter Flint and Enger Ulrich
25. Ancient Near Eastern Texts Relating to the Old Testament by James B. Pritchard p. 145 Princeton University Press 1950

B. Sumer

1. Genesis 10:10 Holy 'Bible King James Version
2. Ibid 13.9
3. Ibid. 13:11-12
4. Author of the book "12th Planet"
5. The Earth Chronicles by Z. Sitchin
6. The Sumerians by C. Leonard Wolley, W.W. Norton & Co. New York-London 1965
7. The Sirius Mystery by Robert Temple p. 97
8. The Land of Osiris by Stephen Mehler p. 23-58
9. The Sacred Marriage Rite p. 167

10. Enki and Nin-Hursag—Affairs of the Water gods, Sumerian Mythology S. N. Kramer p. 58.
11. Enki and World Order, History Begins at Sumer by S. N> Kramer p. 94, Double Day Anchor Books 1959
12. Epic of Gilgamesh (The Sacred Marriage Rite p. 40), The Sirius Mystery by Robert Temple p. 120
13. Enki and World Order, History Begins at Sumer by S.N. Kramer
14. quoted by S.N Kramer in Sumerian Mythology p. 42
15. History Begins at Sumer p. 228-230 by S.N. Kramer
16. Ibid
17. Ibid
18. The Land of Osiris p. 114 by Stephen Mehler
19. Ibid. 79
20. Ibid p. 68
21. Tempest and Exodus by Ralf Ellis p. 26, 158
22. The Orion Prophecy by Geryl Patrick and Gino Ratinckyx 151; The Sirius Mystery by Robert Temple p. 18
23. The Sirius Connection p. 10 by Murry Hope

Builders of the Pyramids

24. The Feats and Exploits of Ninurta
25. The Harp that Once by Thorkild Jacobsen p. 249-252 Yale U. Press 1987
26. Ibid p. 403
27. The Sacred Marriage Rite. 37
28. Ibid p. 403
29. Ibid 407
30. The Harp that Once by Thorkild Jacobsen
31. Ibid
32. Ibid
33. The Harp that Once by Thorkild Jacobsen p. 270 Yale University Press 1987
34. Ibid
35. Sumerian Mythology p. 55 by S.N. Kramer
36. Ibid
37. Myths of Cattle and Grains, Sumerian Mythology p. xx by S.N. Kramer
38. p. 9 of Myths from Mesopotemia by Stephanie Dalley
39. The Babylonian Story of the Flood, Epic of Atra-Hasis by W.W. Lambert and A. R. Millar p. 14
40. The Harp that Once by Thorkild Jacobsen

41. Enki and Ninhursag p. 39
42. The Sirius Mystery by Robert Temple
43. Ibid. p. 138
44. Manetho by W.G. Waddell
45. Tempest and Exodus p. 180 by Ralf Ellis
46. Ibid p. 19
47. Ibid p. 180
48. Ibid p. 16
49. Ibid p. 16
50. Ibid p. 208
51. Tempest and Exodus by Ralph Ellis page. 208
52. p. 78 "Land of Osiris by Stephen S. Mehler.
53. Genesis 10-6 Holy Bible King James Version
54. Isaiah 19:24: Holy Bible King James Version
55. Christ Conspiracy by Acharya S.

C. China

1. Past Worlds, Atlas of Archaeology Harper Collins p. 60
2. The Sirius Mystery by Robert Temple p. 292
3. Mythology, The Illustrated Anthology of World Myths and Story Telling by Gen. Editor C. Scott Littleton Duncan Baird Publishers London 2002
4. The Genesis Races by Will Hart p. 89-90 Bear & Co. Rochester Vermont 2003
5. Ibid. p. 91
6. Ibid p. 90
7. Ibid p. 94-95
8. Ibid p. 94

Part VI Apocalypse

Chapter 8 Prophecies

1. Matthew 24:25 Holy Bible King James Version
2. Bible Code 11 by Michael Drosnin
3. Revelation 13, 18 Holy Bible King James Version
4. "The Tutankhamun Prophecies", by Maurice Cotterell, page 152, the author cited Peter Lorie, author of the book "Revelation"
5. Luke 21:9-11, The New American Bible by P.J. Kenedy 7 Sons, New York 1970

6. Ibid. 21:11
7. Bible Code 11 by Michael Drosnin

End Time

1. authors of the book, "The Orion Prophecy" p. 187
2. Ibid p. 85
3. Ibid p. 81
4. in his book "The Path of Pole" cited in (The Orion Prophecy p. 37),
5. Erra and Ishum 1, Myths of Mesopetemia, p. 290 by Stephanie Dalley
6. Ancient Records of Egypt 111 Sec. 18 by James H. Breasted
7. Prophecies and Predictions by M. Timms
8. The Visuddi Magga cited by M. Timms in "Prophecies and Predictions
9. Sura LV of the Koran
10. Prophecies and Predictions by M. Timms, p. 82-83
11. (Hebrew Myths by Graves p. 45)
12. Joshua 10, 11-13)
13. author of Prophecies and Predictions p. 78-80
14. Isaiah 24, 1
15. Ibid 24, 19-20
16. Ibid 35, 4
17. Matt. 24-29
18. Ibid. p 78-80
19. The Orion Prophecies by Geryl Patrick and Gino Ratincyxk

Judgment Time

20. Matthew 25:32 Holy Bible King James Version

Part VII Further Evidence of a Code

Chapter 9 Gemetria

1. Baal Haturim Chumash Bereishis. The Art Scroll Series by Menorah Publications LTD 1999
2. Ibid
3. The Greek Kabalah by Kieren Barry
4. Baal Haturim Chumash Bereishis The Art Scroll Series
5. The Words of Power: Sacred Sound of East and West p. 225 by Brian and Easter Crowley

6. Ibid
7. World Study Greek English New Testament by Paul R. McReynolds
8. Ibid
9. Original Code in the Bible by Del Washburn
10. The Lord's Prayer

Chapter 10 Second Look at the Grid

1. Matt. 3:17
2. Psalm 19:164

Chapter 11 Author of the Code

1. The Christ Conspiracy by Acharya S.
2. Ibid

Chapter 12 Heart

1. Matt. 5:8
2. John 13:35
3. Ibid 13:34

BIBLIOGRAPHY

Fingerprints of the Gods by Graham Hancock Crown 1995

The Orion Mystery by Robert Bauval William Heinemann Ltd. London 1994

The Gods of the Egyptians by E.A. Wallis Vols. 1 & 2 Dover Publications New York 1969

Egyptian Magic by E.A. Wallis Routledge & Kegan Paul London 1979

Amulets and Talismans by E.A. Wallis Collier Books, Toronto 1979

The Book of the Dead by E.A. Wallis Kegan Paul/Trench, Trubner & Co. London 1901

Practical Egyptian Magic by Murry Hope Aquarian Press Wellingborough, 1984

The Lion People by Murry Hope Thoth Publications, Bognor Regis 1988

The Sirius Connection by Murry Hope Elements Book Inc. 1997

Zohar: The Book of Splendor by Gershom Scholem Schocken Books Inc. 1949

The Bahir by Aryeh Kaplan Samuel Weiser Inc. 1979

Sefer Yetzirah The Book of Creation by Aryeh Kaplan Samuel Wesier Inc. 1990

Word Study Greek-English New Testament Paul R. McReynolds Tyndale House Publishers Inc. 1998

Mahzor for Rosh Hashanah & Yom Kippur by Rabbi Jules Harlow Rabbinical Assembly 1972

The Pleiadian Agenda by Barbara Hand Clow Bear & Co, Publishing 1995

The 12th Planet by Zecharia Sitchin Santa Fe: Bear & Co. 1991

The Wars of God and Men by Zecharia Sitchin Santa Fe: Bear & Co. 1992

The Christ Conspiracy The Graatest Sstory Ever Sold by Acharya S. Adventures Unlimited Press 1999

Isis Unveiled by Helena Blavatsky Theosophical University Press 1988

The Secret Doctrine by Helena Blavatsky Theosophical University Press 1988

The Gods of Eden by William Bramley Dahlin Family Press 1990

The Children of Mu. By James Churchward BE Books 1988

The Lost Continent of Mu by James Chuchward BE Books 1991

The Secret Books of the Egyptian Gnostics by Jean Doresse Inner Traditions International 1986

The Aquarian Gospel of Jesus the Christ by Levi Dowling
The Apocrypha by Edgar Goodspeed Vintage 1989
The Egyptian Book of the Dead by Gerald Massey Health Research
The Missing Books of the Bible Halo 1996
The Gnostic Gospels by Elaine Pagels Vintage 1989
The Forgotten Books of Eden by Rutherford Platt Crown 1981
The Lost Realms by Zecharia Sitchin Avon 1990
When Time Began Zecharia Sitchin Avon 1993
When God was a Woman by Merlin Stone Dorset 1976
The Dead Sea Scrolls by Gezsa Vermes Penguin 1987
Kabalah by Charles Ponce The Theosopical Publishing House 1986
The Kabbalah Unveiled by S.L.M. Mathers Weiser 1968
The Cipher of Genesis by Carlo Suares Shambala 1971
Major Trends in Jewish Mysticism by Gershom Scholem Schocken 1969